Les Sauvages Américains

Note:
genre determines / treatment of
Time, space, place,
character - etc.

What are genres
or "forms"
or "patterns" of
Children's lit?
see p 82

How do these resemble or
repeat adult lit?
travel narrative / novel
explorers wielded great
authority — p 83
journal or diary p 85
descriptive reports

Les Sauvages Américains

Representations of
Native Americans in French
and English Colonial Literature

GORDON M. SAYRE

THE UNIVERSITY OF
NORTH CAROLINA PRESS
Chapel Hill and London

© 1997 The University of North Carolina Press
All rights reserved
Manufactured in the United States of America

The paper in this book meets the guidelines for permanence and
durability of the Committee on Production Guidelines for
Book Longevity of the Council on Library Resources.

Library of Congress Cataloging-in-Publication Data
Sayre, Gordon Mitchell, 1964–.
Les sauvages américains: representations of Native Americans in
French and English colonial literature / Gordon M. Sayre.
       p.   cm.
Includes bibliographical references and index.
ISBN 0-8078-2346-5 (cloth: alk. paper).—
ISBN 0-8078-4652-X (pbk.: alk. paper)
   1. American literature—Colonial period, ca. 1600–1775—
History and criticism.   2. Indians of North America—Historiography.
3. Indians of North America in literature.   4. French-Canadian
literature—History and criticism.   5. French-American literature—
History and criticism.   6. Canadian literature—History and criticism.
7. Colonies in literature.   I. Title.
PS173.I6S29   1997
810.9'3520397'09032—dc21   96-36993
CIP

01   00   99   98   97   5   4   3   2   1

Contents

Illustrations

Preface

Names

In Genesis 2:19, God delegates to Adam the task of naming the animals, and Adam names them not as the animals call one another, but simply as he sees fit: "And out of the ground the Lord God formed every beast of the field, and every fowl of the air; and brought them unto Adam to see what he would call them: and whatsoever Adam called every living creature, that was the name thereof." Early European travelers to America frequently imagined that they were visiting ancient or biblical times, and a race of people descended from the Hebrews or Scythians. In effect, they exercised the same power as Adam to name the groups they encountered, for these names have acquired an irrevocable referentiality in Western languages and culture, even if many are absurd accidents. "America" was coined by adding a feminine ending to the first name of Amerigo Vespucci (or Americ Vespuce, as his name is rendered in French) despite the fact that he was just one of many explorers who journeyed across the Atlantic shortly after Christopher Columbus. The "Indians" have been so called ever since Columbus and other explorers thought they had landed in the East Indies.

In the narratives of exploration the power of language and reference seems obvious. The ethnocentrism of Adam and of European explorers imposes names on unfamiliar people and places, refuses to recognize the Others' names for themselves, and forces them into the history and geography of the known or "Old World." The monopoly on printed discourse held by the Europeans then enforces this act of dispossession by spreading it in print to all European and colonial markets. However, it is not always so simple. As Harold Jantz and others have argued,

"America" appears to have origins in both European and native New World names.[1] Moreover, consider this story:

> Ils lui dirent le lendemain que quand les hommes seroient arrivez ils le remercieroient. Ainsi se nomment tous les Sauvages entr'eux, appellans les François François, & les peuples de l'Europe du nom de leur nation. Ils se persuadent qu'il n'y a qu'eux dans tout le monde qui soient de veritables hommes, & le plus grand éloge qu'ils puissent faire d'un François dont ils reconnoissent la valeur est lors qu'ils disent tu es un homme, & quand ils veulent lui rémoigner qu'ils le méprisent, ils lui disent qu'il n'est pas un homme.

> [On the next day they told him that when "the men" arrived they would render him thanks; it is thus that all the savages are designated among themselves, while they call the French "French," and the (other) people from Europe by the names of their respective nations. They are persuaded that in all the world they are the only real men; and the greatest praise that they can bestow on a Frenchman whose worth they recognize is when they say to him, "Thou art a man." When they wish to show that they have contempt for him, they tell him that he is not a man.][2]

In this report on names, attributed to the French fur trader and Indian agent Nicolas Perrot (the "him" of the first line) by the colonial historian Bacqueville de La Potherie, we are informed that the Indians' names for Others are equally ethnocentric as the Europeans'. The suggestion is that every culture claims for itself the universal name (the "unmarked term" in the jargon of some social scientists, by which more specific names, including "woman," are "marked"), which signifies not membership in a social group but the essence of humanness. To call oneself "a man" is mundanely obvious and yet implies one's superiority to others who bear labels signifying a specific ethnic identity rather than simple humanness. If we can generalize from observations of this naming strategy in two very different cultures, ethnocentrism and prejudice against the Other would paradoxically be itself a universal principle. However, we know this anecdote only from Bacqueville de La Potherie, who was not present, and we are not given a transliteration of the word as it was spoken to Perrot in the Miami tribe's language that day around 1690.

This report of a strategy of ethnocentric differentiation common to both Europeans and Amerindians is available only in translation. If we did read the Miami word, the apparently simple lesson would again be confused, for the recognition and universality of the term "homme/ (hu)man" would be destroyed if it were given in the Miami language. We would be forced to consider who these Miami were, how distinct their language was from other bands' dialects, and whether their identity as "Miami" should be defined linguistically, geographically, or ethnologically. These are all difficult questions, answerable only through a discourse of historical anthropology which is itself implicated in ethnocentric abuses of language and power. But even without answering these questions, we can still learn a great deal from Perrot and Bacqueville de La Potherie's anecdote—that colonial explorers and fur traders recorded interactions with Indians and brought to print voices that are conscious of the problems of cultural identity and communication, including the vital issue of the continuum between universal humanism and ethnic specificity, and even aware of the ironies contained in such problems.

In our era of decolonization, many peoples have struggled to regain the power of naming themselves. The process has been formalized on the scale of the nation-state but remains contentious for people who, through subjugation, extinction, or diaspora, have no nation. Because aboriginal North America was home to so many small, autonomous societies, identifying and separating (which amounts to the same thing as naming) each one or groups thereof is extremely difficult. "At least sixty-eight mutually unintelligible tongues" were spoken among the eastern North American woodlands tribes who are the topic of this book,[3] and these groups constantly moved, assimilated, and split apart from one another, even before European contact. Any name such as Algonquin or Miami does not have a fixed referent but appeals to geography, linguistics, or history to constitute a group of a size located somewhere between the universality of "human" and the specificity of each dialect's version of that word. Many complex contingencies are bound up

with the history of Europeans' names for American Indians. To take one
example: the names Wyandot and Huron refer to the same original
cultural group, with its homeland in southern Ontario between Lake
Huron and Lake Simcoe, but have come to have different referents as
determined by interactions with French and English colonists. Although the people's own name had been recorded (as "Houandate") by
Gabriel Sagard, who in the 1620s became one of the first Europeans to
live among them, the name Huron had already been coined by the
French, alluding to the practice of shaving the head except for a few small
tufts or "straight locks, like the bristles of a wild boar . . . as this is what
hure signifies in French" (*JR* 38:249). The Hurons, starting with Samuel
de Champlain in the 1610s, were allies of the French, enemies of the
Iroquois, the object of the Jesuits' most intense missionary efforts, and
the most common tribal affiliation for French portrayals of the Noble
Savage. But the idea of a single Huron nation or confederacy became
problematic after about 1650, when wars with the Iroquois and diseases
introduced by the French scattered the tribe's members as refugees all
around the Great Lakes. "Wyandots [was] an older name for the Hurons
that had gone largely unused for generations" until it was revived by a
group who left the French trading post and refuge at Detroit about 1740
and allied with the British.[4] Thereafter, bands living in Ohio were called
Wyandots, and those at the refugee settlement of Lorette near Quebec
and elsewhere in Canada remained Hurons, but in practice the name
depended more on the identity of the namer than of the named. Georges
Sioui, raised in Village-des-Hurons in Quebec, prefers the older name
"Wendats" for his people and uses it as the title of his 1994 "auto-
ethnography" of the culture. However, he further distinguishes between
Wendats, the name of descendants of inhabitants of Wendaké, the region
in today's Ontario more commonly called Huronia, and Wyandots, the
name for "Wendats, Tionontatés, Attiwandaronks et Ériés qui migrèrent
vers l'ouest, après la destruction de leurs pays au milieu du XVIIième
siècle" (15) [. . . who migrated toward the west, after the destruction of
their lands in the mid-seventeenth century (my translation)]. Francis
Parkman, writing histories from the Anglo-American point of view,
preferred the term Wyandots for all the bands, whether allied with the

French or the English in the Seven Years' War. French historians rarely use Wyandot at all. In James Fenimore Cooper's fiction, Hurons is the name for a tribe whose members are foes of the Anglo-Iroquois alliance in the Seven Years' War and are the worst of the Ignoble Savages, in pointed contrast with the French impression of the people and the name.

Not only are names for groups of Indians in colonial America problematic and contentious, but names for places as well. It is ironic that Indian place names are so common in North America and so commonly misapplied, whereas local awareness of their signification is so limited. European colonists frequently used Indian names as a compromise between settlers from different backgrounds or between competing authorities. The Mormon settlers wanted to give their state a name rich in religious meaning, "Deseret," but to gain admittance to the United States, they were forced to, as well as renounce polygamy, agree to the local native name Utah. The French priest and explorer Louis Hennepin named the Great Lakes Orleans, Condé, Conti, Dauphin, and Frontenac, which would never have caught on with the English colonials. The Mississippi was called both the Saint-Louis and the Fleuve Colbert, in spite of the fact (or perhaps because) the king and his powerful finance minister opposed its exploration and settlement in the 1670s. The names of the Sauk chief Black Hawk and the Seminole Osccola, celebrated at the time of their defeat, were given to several towns and counties in the United States, often far from these tribes' homelands. Today, indigenous names are again being politicized, and some long-familiar names are being superseded by new titles of self-identification, such as Diné to replace Navajo.

There is no one set of accurate, politically sensitive, widely recognized names for American Indian groups. When discussing a group encountered by a certain travel writer, I will use the name used by that writer. Many of these names were not the ones used by the peoples to refer to themselves, and some have origins more absurd than "Indians," but most of them are still used today, and in many cases it is difficult to correct a misnomer because the identity of the native group and its possible descendants is uncertain. I have chosen this approach because I wish to preserve the colonial authors' perceptions, representations, or prejudices. For instance, Cadwallader Colden calls the Algonquins "Adirondacks," and this is a peculiarity of his text that may have some explanation or significance worth preserving, although I cannot explain it. Two further difficulties are the inconsistent spelling of many names by seventeenth- and eighteenth-century writers and the varying translations or transliterations of the names from French into English. One can easily guess that the Algoumequins are Algonquins, that the Renards are the Fox (a direct translation from French), that the Canzés are the Kansas, and the Ayouez the Iowas (though not all historians would agree on these), but who could guess that the Seneca and Mohawk tribes of the Iroquois Confederacy were called the Tsonnontuan or Sonontouaronons and Ganiegueronons or Agniez by seventeenth-century French colonists? The reader can come to appreciate the difficulty of communication between the European colonists and the nations they encountered by reading with his or her ear to identify likely correspondences, keeping in mind that such a pair of names may not refer to precisely the same people, places, or times. Indeed, the vagaries of names and their spellings are one possible way that the voices of individual, frequently nonliterate Indians and colonists can be made to speak again from out of the past. As Gerald Vizenor has written in discussing the names for his tribe, variously known as Chippewa, Ojibway, Anishinaabe, or by many other spellings of these three, "variations in transcription are common, showing the differences in regional pronunciation of tribal words as well as the distance between the oral tradition and written languages. The oral tradition has no lexicon, of course; speakers must remember what is heard and repeated. Written languages must impose what appears to be standard pronunciation" (16).

My title promises an examination of the depiction of *les sauvages américains*. This name is also difficult. First, it refers to a collective body of people defined only as and after they were united by a common experience of displacement, death, and discrimination. A resident of the Hochelaga valley in 1534 had no name for the ethnicity of all the people who lived on his side of the great ocean into which the Hochelaga (St. Lawrence River) flowed, no identity to contrast with the people on the other side, some of whom were soon to sail upriver. Second, the word

naming   "*sauvage*"
                            Indios

sauvage has an unfortunate cognate in English. In French, the adjective *sauvage* means wild as opposed to domesticated, which also gives an idea of its meaning as a noun. There was no French word *indien* until much later. Indian, or wild person, would be the best translation into English of *sauvage* in the French works discussed in this book, yet the connotations of each of these two are quite different in English. English works of the colonial period, and the translations of the French colonial texts, frequently used the term "savages" rather than "Indians" (or the potentially ironic Jacobean spelling "salvages" used by John Smith and William Strachey). In English, the meaning of the word is more distant from its root in the Latin word for forest, yet through this it refers back to the European legend of the Wild Man or unsocialized forest dweller who verges on being a beast.[5] In Dutch, according to Adriaen Van der Donck, "The original natives of the country . . . although they are composed of different tribes, and speak different tongues, all pass by the appellation of wild men [Dutch *Wilden*]" (73). Conversely, Spanish writers opted for *indios* starting with Columbus. Another possible translation might be "primitive," which connotes much the same in English as *sauvage* does in French, but it creates similar problems of anachronism and sensitivity. The time, some twenty-five years ago, when Stanley Diamond could embrace the term primitive as describing a resistant tradition in Western culture now seems to be behind us. In what follows, I use *sauvage* in italics, as a term imported from the French language and from the texts of New France.

I wish to call attention to the ethnocentric power inherent in naming, and to the tension between the universal and the particular, Man and Miami, in the selection of names, in order to ask the reader to expect controversy and confusion in the names applied to American Indians, and to read different names not as more or less accurate or culturally sensitive, but as representing different theories that Euramericans had and have about the origin and status of the natives of America, theories and codes of representation that are the topic of this book. The origins of the names Indian and Savage are short lessons in the cultural history of colonial America, and another part of this history is that some have always objected to the prevailing names and have proposed new ones. A few French writers sensed the prejudice in the word *sauvage* even if they continued to use it. Marc Lescarbot, writing in 1609, included the disclaimer, "De sorte que si nous les appellons communement sauvages, c'est par un mot abusif, & qu'ilz ne meritent pas, n'étans rien moins que cela, ainsi qu'ils se verifiera par le discours de cette histoire" (1:230) [So that if we commonly call them Savages, the word is abusive and unmerited, for they are anything but that, as will be proved in the course of this history (1:32–33)]. Le Page du Pratz also objected to *sauvages*, using instead *naturels*, a term occasionally used by early-seventeenth-century English colonists.

French colonial writers also did not use the word *tribu* or tribe but instead referred to confederacies or bands as *nations*. Nations, as a term for a plurality of independent groups, avoids the anachronistic generalization of *les sauvages américains*, and the resonance of its political meaning in an era of resurgent nationalism is an irony worth evoking. This word also has an interesting origin and connotation. It comes from Latin, where it meant "tribe" or "birth," and in translations of the Old Testament it was used to refer to the heathen peoples as distinct from the Israelites. Deuteronomy 4:27, "And the Lord shall scatter you among the nations," is a verse that contributed to New England Puritans' typological fears of the Indians. Distinct from both Savages and Indians, nations alludes to the theory that the Native Americans were cultural Others within the history recounted by classical authors and in the Bible. As gentiles they might be analogous to, or even descended from, liminal, nomadic peoples such as the Scythians described by Herodotus. This theory employed what in Chapter 3 I define as the trope of substitution, in opposition to the trope of negation used to deny the Indians' status as humans. "Nations shared a common language, culture, and ethnic identity, but the various villages of a nation did not necessarily share a common homeland," writes Richard White, who uses the term to describe the refugee natives of the Great Lakes region such as the Hurons, because "the conventional units of discourse about the Indians —tribes with their distinct territories and their chiefs—are misleading" (16–17).

In Canada today, the term "First Nations" is the rough equivalent to

First Nations = Native americans [handwritten annotation]

Native Americans in the United States. It is understandable that Canadians would wish to avoid using the same name for natives of their land that they apply to the nationals of the United States. Moreover, "Native Americans" was used during and after the American Revolution to refer to the Anglo-American colonists in opposition to the English colonial government and to immigrants from places other than England, so its current usage as a nonracist term for Indians is ironic. That the two neighboring countries use different terms to refer to the peoples native to both sides of the border suggests the intellectual isolation of Canada and the United States from one another's history, an argument I develop in Chapters 1 and 2.

The contrast between different names, their etymologies and connotations, should therefore be viewed as a microcode of the historical and rhetorical phenomena explored in the chapters that follow. At the opposite end of the spectrum from the universalizing "man" and the generalizing Native Americans, or *sauvages américains*, lies the specificity of a name applied to a nation by an individual explorer, such as the Baron de Lahontan's Essenapes, a specificity so great that it may exist only in that writer's imagination, as we will see in the discussion of Lahontan in Chapter 1. The paradox of writing the history of peoples who, lacking the technique of writing, were believed to be without history or literature is examined in Chapter 4. Chapter 5 considers the possibility that the techniques of ethnography developed to name, classify, and rhetorically preserve the original forms of primitive human cultures might also be applied to an advanced animal culture, the beaver.

N. Scott Momaday devotes much of his autobiographical memoir, *The Names*, to reflections on the difficulty of naming one's identity amid the many cultures of one's upbringing, and the importance to American Indian cultures of customs in which a person receives new names. Confronting this plurality of names can force a Westerner, who takes for granted the singularity, permanence, and legality of his or her name, who accepts as natural the complex process by which a signature represents a subject in a bureaucratic state, to be jolted out of these institutions of subjectivity. For this reason I will not apologize for a confabulation of different terms, for switching from Indian to Amerindian to

sauvage to nations. And what is true for personal names is equally valid
for places. The discourse of ethnography, as well as the 1990s version of
the Noble Savage trope, includes the notion that native cultures are
static and traditional, characterized by a strong and ancient attachment
to a homeland. This is true only by contrast with the perceived rootless-
ness and constant movement of modern Western culture. Amerindian
life was dynamic and mobile both before and after European contact.
The Sioux did not live on the plains of the Dakotas but in the forests of
Minnesota when Hennepin encountered them; the Tuscarora moved
from the Carolinas to become the Sixth Nation of the Iroquois and settle
near Niagara Falls; the Sauk of Black Hawk once lived with other Algonquians in the St. Lawrence valley and encountered early French
explorers there; the Natchez migrated to the Mississippi delta from
Mexico, where they had been paying tribute to the Aztecs.

Citations and Translations

This book is a broad study of how Indians have been represented
in literature in two languages across more than two hundred years and
the eastern third of the continent of North America. At the end there is a
bibliography of more than two hundred sources. The methods of citation and translation and the choice of texts require some explanation.

It is a key part of my argument that French texts deserve better
attention from scholars of colonial North America, and that all colonial
texts, written in French, Spanish, German, Dutch, Swedish, or another
language, must be read with attention to the context in which they were
created and published. Therefore I have quoted French primary texts in
the original and provided English translations immediately following
the quotations. I have used, as often as possible, translations that appeared shortly after the publication of the French original. In the eighteenth century literary ties across the channel were strong and new
works were quickly and routinely translated, be they novels or travel
narratives. In the case of texts that have not been translated or were
translated in abridged form, such as those by Antoine Le Page du Pratz

and Claude Lebeau, I have provided my own translations. For recent scholarship written in French, I have quoted a published translation or, when none exists, quoted the original and given my translation.

As the care to quote in the original indicates, I have treated the texts of colonial exploration and cultural encounter as literature. As with literary works, the style and rhetoric of each author and the historical context at the time of publication are important. I have not done research to try to demonstrate the popularity or sales figures and thereby the influence of the books of Lahontan, John Smith, or Louis Hennepin, but I work from the assumption that they were read by nearly as many people as read what is today the canonical literature of that period. Documents that were not originally intended for publication, such as letters from colonial officials and proceedings of treaty negotiations, have been for the most part excluded, though as much from an economy of research effort as from methodological principle. Nonetheless, a few works that were not prepared by their authors for publication and that appeared only centuries later, such as the *Voyages* of Pierre-Esprit Radisson, are too important to exclude.

As part of the attempt to convey the impact and flavor that texts had at the time of their publication, I have preserved the original spelling and punctuation found in these books to the degree that my access to old editions and facsimiles has made it possible. Readers of French should be aware that in seventeenth- and eighteenth-century French, far fewer accents were printed than is the custom today, and spelling was not standardized. The only editing I have done in quotations is in changing the letters of archaic typography—*v* to *u* and vice versa, *i* to *j*, the long *s* which resembles *f* back to *s*—and replacing the omitted *n* indicated by a tilde on the preceding vowel. I have also rendered many words in italics in regular type, for both French and English printers often used italics for all proper nouns or simply for variety and attractiveness on the page.

In an effort to limit the number of notes and provide references as efficiently as possible, I have used page citations in parentheses following quotations from the most important primary sources and their translations. See the note preceding the Works Cited for an explanation of specific editions and pagination methods.

Acknowledgments

This book was written in the relatively short span of six years, inspired by the excitement of vicarious exploration in the wilderness of North America and a love for old books and obscure titles. More mundanely, the project began as a dissertation in the Program in Comparative Literature at the State University of New York at Buffalo. I want to thank the members of my committee there, Dennis Tedlock, Roland LeHuenen, and Neil Schmitz, as well as the faculty in Comparative Literature. My research and writing in the literature of New France began in France while I was working as an instructor at the Institut Charles V, Université Paris VII. I am grateful to the Department of Romance Languages at Buffalo, which sent me to Paris on their exchange program, and to the Bibliothèque Ste. Geneviève, where I did most of the early research. I send special thanks to *bibliothèquaire* François Dupressoir.

Many thanks also to Richard Stein and Molly Westling and my other colleagues at the University of Oregon English Department who have done so much to encourage and enable this work.

My research and writing has been aided by a fellowship from the Canadian Studies Grant Program of the Canadian Embassy to the United States and by a New Faculty Award from the University of Oregon.

Parts of the book have already appeared in print or have benefited from a public forum at conferences and colloquia. A version of Chapter 5 appeared in the *Canadian Review of Comparative Literature/Revue Canadienne de Littérature Comparée* 22:3–4 (September–December 1995). A version of the part of Chapter 4 about tattooing was published in *Proceedings of the Nineteenth Meeting of the French Colonial Historical Society/Actes*

du Dix-neuvième Colloque de la Société d'Histoire Coloniale Française, which
met in Providence, Rhode Island, in May 1993. My thanks to both for
permitting me to reprint this material, and to Janet Whateley for her
helpful commentary in the latter volume. I would like to thank Roland
Greene and the Program in Comparative Literature at the University of
Oregon, as well as the Mesa Verde research group there, for inviting me
to share other excerpts with them.

Many colleagues, friends, and family have read, critiqued, and ad-
vised me in my writing. Bridget Keegan and Nathan Sayre helped with
proofreading and advice. Bruce Greenfield read the manuscript with
insight and encouragement, and UNC Press editor Sian Hunter White
was an enormous help through the revision process. Cornelius Jaenen
kindly served as outside reader for the dissertation. Robert Sayre was a
great help for his faith and love and for his knowledge in all fields of
American literature. I hope I may be as good a professor as he, but not
exactly the same. Finally, my love and the dedication of this work goes to
a fellow Ph.D. and lover of reading, Marsha Ginsberg.

Les Sauvages Américains

CHAPTER I

Colonial American Literature across Languages and Disciplines

The Library a wilderness of books. Looking over books on Canada written within the last three hundred years, could see how one had been built upon another, each author consulting and referring to his predecessors . . .

I saw that while we are clearing the forest in our westward progress, we are accumulating a forest of books in our rear, as wild and un-explored as any of nature's primitive wilderness. The volumes of the Fifteenth, Sixteenth, and Seventeenth Centuries, which lie so near on the shelf, are rarely opened, are effectually forgotten and not implied by our literature and newspapers.

(Thoreau, *Journal*, March 16, 1852, 3:352–53)

Thoreau often wished to create the impression that he spent more time in the woods than in the library, and perhaps it is because the opposite was true that he characterizes these obscure works as a forest, a surrogate wilderness. Indeed, reading narratives of exploration is fas-cinating for the hiker or paddler, the lover of wilderness who would like to have seen Niagara Falls or Detroit in its pristine state, or to have met Indians in their villages nearby. The library can be a place for vicarious adventure across a landscape, such as Niagara, now so urbanized that it is hardly recognizable as the place described by Louis Hennepin, the Baron de Lahontan, or Pierre François-Xavier de Charlevoix. Seeking such a re-creation of wilderness America, Thoreau read extensively in this "forest of books" written by French explorers in Canada, or New France, from Jacques Cartier in 1535 to the conclusion of the Seven Years' War in 1763. In his "Indian Books" and "Canadian Notebooks and Record of Surveys," which have still never been printed, he took notes and copied passages from many of the early French colonial texts, including those of Cartier, Roberval, Champlain, Lahontan, Bacqueville de La Potherie, and the *Jesuit Relations*.[1] In *Cape Cod*, which was published just after his death, Thoreau referred to the narratives of Lescarbot, Champlain, and many other explorers of several nations in a brief but thorough history of European exploration of the cape and the coast to the north of it. Thoreau pointed out that "the Englishman's history of *New* England commences, only when it ceases to be, *New* France" (1011, Thoreau's italics), and that "The English were very backward to explore and settle the continent which they had stumbled upon. The French preceded them both in their attempts to colonize the continent of North America (Carolina and Florida, 1562–64), and in their first permanent settlement (Port Royal, 1605)" (1012).

Unfortunately, the books Thoreau read in his researches are rarely read today by scholars of American literature or even of Thoreau. Historians continue to read these texts, draw facts from them about Indians and colonists' lives, and cite the names of the explorers and missionaries who wrote them, but rarely do they explain what these books look like and how they work as texts. Instead, a cut-and-paste method has become common, in which discrete historical or ethnographic facts about colonial exploration or about the American Indians are lifted out of the context in which eyewitness observers presented them. These accounts of exploration and of encounters with the American Indians deserve to be read as narrative literature, in the same spirit in which I believe Thoreau read them, and in which so many read Thoreau's travel and nature writing today.

The image of New France was formed for nineteenth-century readers in the United States, not by Thoreau, who did so much research but never wrote a history, but by Francis Parkman, one of the most popular American historians of a time when history had a much larger popular audience than it does today. Parkman's seven-part *France and England in North America* (1865–92), with its emphasis on heroic explorers and national destinies, placed him alongside George Bancroft and William Prescott as founders of the nineteenth-century American colonial self-image. Parkman read the French sources, admired their authors, and recognized that the French colonists journeyed farther into the continent sooner and knew more Indian nations better than did the English colonists. In a provocative generalization, he wrote, "Spanish civilization crushed the Indian, English civilization scorned and neglected him, French civilization embraced and cherished him."[2] Parkman did not intend this to be praise for the French colonials, however. A Whiggish anglocentrism pervades his massive history of colonial North America. The French sympathy for the Indians entangles them in a common destiny with the stereotype of the Vanishing Indian: "Could the French have maintained their ground, the ruin of the Indian tribes might long have been postponed; but the victory of Quebec [i.e., the British conquest of Quebec] was the signal of their swift decline. Thenceforth they were destined to melt and vanish before the advancing waves of Anglo-American power, which now rolled westward unchecked and unopposed."[3] This jingoism was not Parkman's alone. Thoreau, writing of his travels through Quebec in 1850, expressed the same idea: "The impression made on me was, that the French Canadians were even sharing the fate of the Indians, or at least gradually disappearing in what is called the Saxon current."[4] Yet from the seventeenth to nineteenth century and down to today, French Canada has continued to thrive. Although it is disputable whether the French really were kinder to the Indians, there is little doubt that French colonists' writings include more lengthy and subtle representations of the American Indians than can be found in the English colonial texts. To perceive how patterns for written descriptions of the Indians evolved in the seventeenth and eighteenth centuries, and to understand how European colonists learned from and set themselves apart from the Indians they encountered in the northeastern forests, one must read the French narratives. The literature of New England and Virginia is not sufficient to explain the image of the American Indian in North American literature and culture.

American (or, more accurately, U.S.) literary history generally ignores French, Spanish, and Dutch colonial American literature, even when these texts tell the history of regions that are now part of the United States. The sermons, promotional tracts, and historical narratives of New England and Virginia are deemed to be important for the development of the literature of the nineteenth century, whereas the writings of New France are neglected, although Thoreau knew them well and Parkman did much to popularize them. The hegemony of New England in American letters, which began in the mid-nineteenth century when Boston publishing houses established a canon of American literature centered around the "big six" New England authors—Ralph Waldo Emerson, Nathaniel Hawthorne, Henry Wadsworth Longfellow, James Russell Lowell, Oliver Wendell Holmes, and John Greenleaf Whittier—and continued with the canonization of Thoreau and Herman Melville after the turn of the century, endures in the twentieth-century preoccupation with Puritan literature and sensibility as the foundation of the American self or mind in the works of Perry Miller and Sacvan Bercovitch. Virginia has since World War II received much less attention from U.S. literary scholars than New England, and New France hardly any at all.[5] Mainstream U.S. history is almost as narrow-minded. In a review of popular history textbooks, James Axtell has commented that "the French suffer more misunderstandings and errors than do either Indians or Spaniards" and has documented many errors in these school texts.[6] U.S. literature has reinforced the separation between colonial legacies and between languages by shunning Canada and French colonial literature.

North of the United States, of course, a quite different historical and critical tradition exists. Canadian scholars are forced to familiarize themselves with the French material if they are to study the history of their nation and of the First Nations in Canada. The work of anthropologist Bruce Trigger, historians Cornelius Jaenen and Olive Patricia Dickason, literary scholars Maurice Roelens and Réal Ouellet, and art historian François-Marc Gagnon accommodate both French and English sources regardless of the language in which they write their findings. Canadians have also done invaluable translations and exhaustive editing of the major French travel and missionary narratives, notably as part of the Champlain Society publications and more recently in the series Bibliothèque du Nouveau Monde from the University Press of Quebec. The literature of New France is hardly inaccessible; it is only an intellectual nationalism that maintains the division between United States and Canada, Anglophone and Francophone. Because my goal is to arouse interest in French colonial American literature among students and scholars of American literature in the United States, I will draw many comparisons between the representations of Native Americans by French colonists with those by the English and suggest influences the French texts had on the subsequent history and culture of North America generally, not Canada or Quebec alone. As I was raised and educated in the United States, I am sure that my work reflects some of its nationalism and myopia, and I cannot pretend to put my analysis equally in the context of contemporary Canadian and U.S. self-images.

French and English Colonial Topographies

The topographic and economic patterns of French and English colonization in the American Northeast differed greatly, and an understanding of these differences explains many of the contrasts in the French and English representations of America and its natives. For example, the lesser emphasis that the English colonists placed on exploration resulted in fewer texts combining exploration and ethnography, and the greater potential for agriculture meant more attention to the plants and landforms of the mid-Atlantic coast. Differences between the shape of New England and New France can be explained in terms of national instinct (as Parkman hinted), political organization of the colonies, economics, geography, or even climate. I will suggest in the next chapter that the influence of the local Indian leaders on the early explorers John Smith and Samuel de Champlain had a decisive impact on the history and attitudes of Jamestown and Quebec. Seeking a single master explanation is fruitless, for the contrast is overdetermined and manifests itself on many registers, in the literature as well as in the geography of the colonies. Thus it will be figured by a series of spatial metaphors in the third chapter; line versus space, travel itinerary versus landscape description or map, network versus surface, river versus forest.

English colonies on the Atlantic coast, especially in New England, maintained an insular and defensive relation to the New World and its inhabitants. They established beachheads and spread inland slowly as the Indians were driven out and land was appropriated and cultivated by colonists. In the 1600s English explorers and Puritan colonists actually believed that New England was an island.[7] New England benefited enormously from being able to occupy agricultural land cleared or maintained by the Indians and then left vacant by the death of a majority of their population from epidemics of disease in the early seventeenth century. The Puritans' memory of persecution and their strong emphasis on social cohesion and control, and the Virginians' memory of violent confrontation with native nations during and after the 1622 "massacre," served to create a vision of a colony as a fort, with high walls blocking out the dangers and temptations of the wilderness. Virginia's population was less concentrated than New England's, dispersed among tobacco plantations along the James River, but officials feared that this posed a security risk.[8] In the mid-1640s Governor William Berkeley circumscribed his colony with forts built on the "fall line" connecting the first major falls on each river flowing into Chesapeake Bay.[9] During the same period the Plymouth colony resisted the founding of new towns and churches at Wessagusset and at Nauset in favor of maintaining the unanimity of a single congregation.[10] The fear of Indian attacks was used to keep the colonies centralized. Even at the end of the 1600s, when Cotton Mather published the captivity narrative of Hannah Swarton, he reported her belief that "God delivered us into their [the Indians'] hands to punish us for our sins. . . . I had left the public worship and ordinances of God where I formerly lived (*viz.* at Beverley) to remove to the north part of Casco Bay where there was no church."[11]

The psychology and topography of the French colony looked very different, although there were some circumstantial similarities to the English colonies. New France began at roughly the same time and proclaimed the same goals as the colony of Virginia: imperial expansion, religious conversion, and economic exploitation. Under the leadership of Samuel de Champlain, a heroic figure comparable in many aspects to John Smith (a comparison I will develop in the next chapter), the French established settlements at Port Royal (on the Nova Scotian shore of the Bay of Fundy) and Quebec. Settlement based on agriculture proved unattractive, however, compared with the huge profits obtainable in the fur trade. The Indians had developed long-distance trading networks before European contact, and those around the Gulf of St. Lawrence had engaged in trade with seasonal Portuguese, Breton, and West England fishermen for at least a quarter century before French settlers arrived. The customs of trade were therefore well established before Champlain, and he immediately traveled inland to seek new markets. Fur trading and alliances were facilitated by *truchements*, boys left with the Indians to learn their language and serve as interpreters to later explorers. French fur traders or *coureurs de bois* were often renegades from the colony's authorities but soon became its breadwinners and leading explorers. These men learned native languages, customs, and travel routes. They traded for pelts, hired native guides, made alliances, and traveled ever farther in search of more furs. They were responsible for the wealth of accurate observations of the Amerindians by French writers because they forged the contacts, even if they did not write many of the narratives, and they set the pattern whereby knowledge of Indian cultures and customs was considered essential to the success of the colony. For successful trade and for security New France depended on good relations with the Indians, for it was small and easily severed from its root at the mouth of the St. Lawrence.

The trade and travels of French colonists made a colony not in the form of an expanding island but of a network of outposts along the shores of the Great Lakes that extended across a huge area but occupied little land and supported only a small population.[12] On a map of North

American colonies in 1700, the French would appear to have held an
enormous advantage in the race for imperial control, although the population and military power of New France was actually less. In the 1620s
Virginia was already home to 2,000 settlers, whereas Quebec was an
outpost of 60 year-round residents. By the 1650s New England had
nearly 30,000 European residents, ten times as many as Virginia or New
France. In 1700 the French population in the St. Lawrence valley was
still less than 20,000. Yet in the first half of the eighteenth century,
while the English colonies were considering possible expansion beyond
the Allegheny Mountains, French posts lined the Mississippi River, all
five Great Lakes, and reached up toward Lake Winnipeg, and French
explorers were on the Great Plains from the Arkansas River to Saskat-
chewan. Accordingly, French colonial writings throughout the seventeenth century emphasized exploration and trade over settlement. Official ecclesiastical and settlement histories after the manner of William
Bradford's *Of Plymouth Plantation* and Edward Johnson's *Wonder Working
Providence*, designed to forge quickly a sense of permanence, community
identity, and religious unanimity, do exist for seventeenth-century Canada, such as the efforts by Gabriel Sagard, François du Creux, and Chrestien LeClercq, but they are less significant in the literature than the
narratives of voyages to the Mississippi, to Hudson Bay, to Lake Superior
and Minnesota. The New England colonial writings of the first half of
the seventeenth century that offer the best descriptions of Indian lifeways, Thomas Morton's, William Wood's, and Roger Williams's, were
not written by explorers and do not include narratives of the authors'
travels. In the texts of New France before 1650, such as Lescarbot's,
Sagard's, and Champlain's, the juxtaposition of exploration narrative
and ethnographic description is the prevalent form, a form that I will
analyze in this study.

English colonists and officials did not immediately understand the
reasons for the French success in exploring and amassing territory. But
by the 1720s the wealthy and influential Virginian William Byrd II, in
his *History of the Dividing Line*, suggested one explanation in the context
of describing his difficulties traveling overland through the foothills of
the Appalachians:

... so long as Woodsmen continue to range on Horse-back, we shall be Strangers to our own Country, and few or no valuable Discoveries will ever be made.

The FRENCH COURIERS [*sic*] de Bois, who have run from one End of the Continent to the other, have performed it all on foot, or else in all probability must have continued as ignorant as we are.

Our Country has now been inhabited more than 130 years by the English, and still we hardly know any thing of the Appallachian Mountains, that are no where above 250 miles from the sea. Whereas the French, who are later comers, have rang'd from Quebec Southward as far as the Mouth of the Mississippi. (260)

Without any jingoistic calls for taking back England's share, Byrd recognized the vast extent of French exploration. He was no doubt right in placing part of the blame for Virginia's close frontiers on the horse, commenting, ". . . my Dear Countrymen have so great a passion for riding, that they will often walk two miles to catch a Horse, in Order to ride One" (258), but he was wrong to ascribe French superiority to travel on foot, just as he was wrong to claim that the French were "later comers" to America. The French facility of travel was due to an Indian invention, the birchbark canoe, which (unlike today's recreational canoe), commonly was built thirty feet long to carry as many as fourteen men or more than a ton of pelts or merchandise. The Baron de Lahontan pointed out the important features of such canoes:

ils pesent si peu que deux hommes les portent à leur aise sur l'épaule, chacun par un bout. Cette seule facilité me fait juger qu'il n'y a point de meilleure voiture au monde pour naviguer dans les Rivieres du Canada qui sont remplies de Cascades, de Cataractes & de courans. Car on y est obligé ou de les transporter par terre le long de ces passages, ou de les trainer dans l'eau le long du rivage. (1:36)

[they are so light, that two Men carry 'em upon their shoulders with ease. This conveniency of lightness and easie carriage, renders 'em very serviceable in the Rivers of Canada, which are full of Cataracts, Waterfalls, and Currents: For in these Rivers we are oblig'd either to transport 'em over-land where such obstructions happen, or else to tow 'em along. (1:27–28)]

The English explorer Martin Pring was amazed that "though it carried nine men standing upright, yet it weighed not at the most above sixtie pounds . . . a thing almost incredible in regard of the largnesse and capacitie thereof."[13] Though most others including Lahontan disagreed, William Wood reported that the Indians' skills in the craft extended to open-water travel, that in canoes "wherein an English man can scarce sit without a fearfull tottering, they will venture to Sea, when an English Shallope dare not beare a knot of sayle; scudding over the overgrowne waves as fast as a winde-driven ship, being driven by their padles" (102). The birchbark canoe was ideally suited to travel on the Canadian shield, and French fur traders and explorers paddled the same routes and plodded the same portages with the same boats that the Indians had used for centuries.[14] South of the Great Lakes, where the suitable birch trees did not grow, bark canoes were inferior, making long-distance river travel more difficult. Along the southern coasts the natives built instead pirogues hollowed out of huge logs, which, like the boat built by Robinson Crusoe's tedious labor, weighed far too much to carry.

Byrd's own purpose in his *History* was also symptomatic of the slow pace of English exploration relative to the French. The English, profiting more from fields than furs, and divided by conflicting claims between various companies and charters, such as the border Byrd was establishing between Virginia and Carolina, placed more importance on surveying boundary lines than on exploring the land. Later in the eighteenth century Thomas Jefferson's "Plan for Western Government" draws lines across unfamiliar land with no regard for the rivers and mountains that will affect settlement and to which government should be adapted. It is as if once the land was symbolically possessed through such a survey, actual settlement could wait.[15] And the work of such a survey, the work that Byrd performed in driving a straight line across the land, effectively discouraged exploration because it was a far more difficult manner of travel than following the path of least resistance, a river. Byrd's crew was forced to cross and recross the same rivers, to burrow straight through the Great Dismal Swamp, efforts that would explain why they went away with an impression of exploratory travel as wearisome and pointless. Byrd's *History of the Dividing Line* can be read as a travel narrative turned to parody by taking the principle of a linear journey to a hyperrational extreme, though Byrd's own parodic intent lay in making fun of the North Carolinians.

During the seventeenth century there was one report written by a Virginia explorer who made a long voyage inland and wrote of the Indians he encountered there. John Lederer, a native of Germany, wrote a brief account in Latin that was translated and published by the secretary of Maryland, William Talbot, in 1672. It is distinctive for its exceptional similarities to the exploration-ethnography texts of New France. In the second and longest of three expeditions during 1669 and 1670, Lederer traveled west toward Virginia's Blue Ridge Mountains with a group led by one Major Harris. Harris refused to follow the directions of local Indians, and instead the party "shaped their course by the Compass due West, and therefore it fell out with us, as it does with those Land-Crabs, that crawling backwards in a direct line, avoid not the Trees that stand in their way, but climbing over their very tops, come down again on the other side, and so after a days labor gain not above two foot of ground" (20). Frustrated with this straight-line route, Lederer abandoned the party and, accompanied only by a Susquehannock Indian guide, skirted the mountains as he moved toward the southwest, arriving at last at a large lake called Ushery. Here he encountered the strange customs of the Oustack, whose women fought in wars, and the Oenock, who sold their labor as porters; he also heard that men with beards, whom he presumed to be Spaniards, lived two and a half days' journey farther on. Lake Ushery does not comport with the area along the Catawba River where Lederer appears to have turned back, but it does correspond with Gerhard Mercator's 1606 map of Virginia and Florida and with contemporary surmises about large bodies of water to the west. John Smith, too, had placed a lake in the country of the Massawomecks (Iroquois) on the very edge of his map of Virginia of 1612, although it may have been the Great Lakes that Champlain had also heard of. Alexander Whitaker had written in 1613 that "a great ridge of high hils doe runne along the maine land, not farre from whom the Indians report a great Sea doth runne, which we commonly call a South Sea, but in respect of our habitation is a West Sea" (38). This secondhand knowl-

edge of the Great Lakes easily became confounded with the dreams
Europeans cherished of finding an easy passage to the "South Sea," the
Pacific Ocean, and Lederer might have sought to report what the maps
showed as the most credible proof that he had traveled so far.

In spite of these clues suggesting that he wrote of what he saw on
maps or heard from Indians as well as what he saw with his own eyes,
Lederer's journey and text are remarkable in the English colonial literature during the one hundred years between John Smith and John Lawson. In many respects his narrative resembles French colonial works of
the late seventeenth century, particularly those of Hennepin and Lahontan.[16] Lederer traveled alone or only with native guides. As he traveled
farther away from the white settlements, he described unusual Indian
customs that strain, without quite breaking, historical credulity. He
appears to have adjusted the report of his discoveries to match contemporary geographic expectations and desires. Finally, he synthesized his
experiences into short descriptive chapters on subjects such as "Conjec-
tures of the Land beyond the Apalatæan Mountains," "Touching Trade
with Indians," and "Of the Manners and Customs of the Indians inhabit-
ing the Western parts of Carolina and Virginia." These issues of independence, fabulist creativity, and descriptive synthesis will be key aspects of my analysis of exploration literature in Chapter 3. But whereas
Hennepin's and Lahontan's discoveries were celebrated and quickly
drawn into new maps, Lederer's efforts and reports were not appreciated
in Virginia. According to Talbot's preface, Lederer "met nothing but
Affronts and Reproaches" (5) and "he was not safe in Virginia from the
outrage of the People, drawn into a perswasion, that the Public Levy of
that year, went all to the expence of his Vagaries" (6). He did, however,
open up the trade route to the Cherokees that became important to
English traders in the eighteenth century.

Lederer's and Byrd's narratives indicate that westward exploration
from Virginia in the seventeenth century was rare, poorly planned, and
not strongly supported by colonial authorities. In New England, Puritan fear of the wilderness and anxiety about decentralization ensured
that exploration efforts in that century were even more limited. Part of
the difficulty, compounding the absence of good birchbark for canoes,

was due to the accident that English colonies did not take hold at the mouths of the rivers that afforded the easiest passage into the interior of America. The English along the mid-Atlantic seaboard missed the Delaware, which was later colonized by the Swedes, and the Hudson, which, although it took its name from an Englishman in 1608, was colonized by the Dutch, who made up much of Henry Hudson's crew. Again on a smaller scale within New England, the English colonists were forced away from the best river trade routes. English explorers of the Penobscot and Kennebec drainages between 1605 and 1611—Ferdinando Gorges, John Smith, George Popham, and Humphrey Gilbert—all drew hostile reactions from the native Abenaki because they kidnapped individuals and refused to engage in ceremonial trading reciprocity. The French under de Mons, Poutrincourt, and Champlain also alienated the Abenaki by allying with their enemies, the Micmac of today's Nova Scotia, but their greater familiarity and cooperation with native trading customs secured better relations than the English had. Pushed east of the Connecticut River by the Dutch and south of the Kennebec by unpleasant memories of the Abenaki, Thomas Dermer in 1620 wrote back to England that the best site for a future colony would be Patuxet on Cape Cod, the hometown of his captive and interpreter, Squanto. Another reason for this choice was the devastating virgin soil epidemic that had taken the lives of 75 to 90 percent of the native population of this region, leaving fertile, cleared land unoccupied.[17] The Pilgrims ended up accepting Dermer's advice, renamed Patuxet Plymouth,[18] and so began the Puritan pattern of agricultural, seaboard settlements.

In Virginia, the Chesapeake region resembled Cape Cod insofar as it encouraged dependence on the sea rather than on the interior forests. It was too far from the homes of thick-furred beavers to make the pelt trade lucrative, and without birchbark canoes, transportation was too difficult. Captain John Smith and his men sailed their own boats as far as the first falls on each river, where, unable to portage, "we returned to the fals, leaving a mariner in pawn with the Indians for a guide of theirs. Hee that they honoured for King followed us by the river. That afternoone we trifled in looking upon the Rockes and river (further he would not goe) so there we erected a crosse" (1:31) and turned back downriver.

Later the line connecting the falls on the James, Potomac, and Pamunkey became Governor Berkeley's "Fall Line" frontier. Still today the
wide tidal York and James Rivers take on Indian names upstream of the
falls and forks: Mattaponi, Pamunkey, and Appomatox.

The problem was not only the lack of a portable boat. Smith's guide
would not proceed because this was the limit of the Powhatans' territory,
and the guide feared either an enemy attack or a trade and military
alliance of these enemies with the English against the Powhatans. The
Powhatans could be generous with their food only if they could resell the
knives, beads, and other commodities they obtained from the English to
inland nations for a higher price. This strategy depended on preventing
the English traders from themselves contacting the interior peoples, and
in Powhatan's realm the English had encountered the most powerful
band of Indians on the coast.[19] Preserving monopolies was therefore not
the concern of Europeans alone, and in fact the Indians appear to have
been more successful at it. In the *Map of Virginia* Smith deplored the
traitorous conduct of Dutchmen in Jamestown who traded for extra food
without his sanction. Powhatan's people succeeded in breaking the English trade restrictions while maintaining their own and in confining
Smith's expeditions to a small area on the eastern side of Chesapeake Bay.
The only success Smith had at breaking the monopoly came when he
traded with some Massawomeks (Iroquois) at the head of the Chesapeake
for their shields and then awed the Tockwoghs by claiming that he had
taken these things by force (2:171).

So long as the English colonists remained confined to small regions
and short stretches of navigable river, exploration and its narratives did
not flourish, and ethnological knowledge of Indian nations in remote
areas was of little concern. For the beaver trade, Dutch and English
traders continued through the seventeenth century to rely on Indian
middlemen to bring the pelts down to the colony. Their major innovation in this trade was wampum. Dutch colonists, who called it "zewant,"
obtained it cheaply from the Pequots on Long Island Sound and bought
pelts with it from the Iroquois around Albany or Beverwijk.[20] Although
the officials of New France sometimes wished to keep the trade near
Montreal, French *coureurs de bois*, usually accompanied by Indian guides,

took their goods westward to Michilimackinac and other posts on the Great Lakes and returned with canoes laden with pelts.[21] The Indians were reluctant to bring their pelts to Montreal because they feared attack by Iroquois along the way or exploitation at the trade fair when they arrived.[22] The loosely allied Algonquian groups of the Great Lakes region, known at the time as the *pays d'en haut* (Upper Canada, "the land up high" or upstream), could not hold the French within a small region as the Powhatans held the English at Jamestown. They aimed only to prevent trade with the Sioux to the west. For the French, exploration meant an expansion of trade, and knowledge of Algonquian and Iroquoian customs was instrumental to success at trade and at evangelization. Several missionaries undertook exploration and wrote about it: Claude Allouez went to the western end of Lake Superior in the 1660s, Louis Joliet and Jacques Marquette descended the Mississippi to the Arkansas River in 1673, and Louis Hennepin paddled up the Mississippi to the site of today's Twin Cities in 1680. Secular adventurers also capitalized on the interest in such narratives not only among traders and officials but also among an armchair audience in Europe. Exploration and ethnographic texts sold well. The expeditions of La Salle down the Mississippi and in search of its mouth spawned a series of narratives, by Hennepin, fellow Recollet Zenobe Membré, Henri de Tonti, La Salle's son Jean Cavelier, and Henri Joutel, each of whom sought to correct or add to the previous books and build on Hennepin's success with his initial 1683 volume. Lahontan's *Nouveaux voyages* saw eighteen editions in three languages between 1703 and 1750. Publishers put together compilations such as J.-F. Bernard's eight-volume *Receuil des voyages au nord* (1715–17) and five-volume *Relations de la Louisiane* (1720).

English and French colonies did share the goal of converting the heathen to their respective kinds of Christianity. But behind a common declaration of intent, missionary strategies in New England and New France were very different, and the English effort was much more modest. "English colonists actually produced the smallest number of missionary personnel, allocated less financial support for their work, and exhibited greater indifference toward missions than other Europeans," admit the editors of writings by John Eliot, the leading Puritan missionary in New England.[23] New England colonists occasionally reproached one another for these shortcomings, interpreting them as a failure in the battle against Catholicism. Cotton Mather's narrative of Hannah Swarton's captivity reports: "My Indian mistress was one that had been bred by the English at Black Point and now married to a Canada Indian and turned papist. And she would say that had the English been as careful to instruct her in our religion as the French were to instruct her in theirs, she might have been of our religion."[24]

One reason for the weak missionary effort was the decentralized structure of the Protestant and especially the Puritan clergy, who depended on their individual congregations for support. Puritan missionaries often had wives and families, whereas the Catholics, of course, did not. Additionally, there were in the seventeenth century no Protestant orders that recruited missionaries and raised funds in Europe for missions in the remotest parts of America, as did the Jesuits, Recollets, and Ursuline nuns for New France. The dissenting New England Protestants could not raise funds for missionary work from members of the established Church of England, and the various short-lived English missionary societies formed in the seventeenth century had little success.[25] Nonetheless, Puritan New England took the goal more seriously than did Cavalier Virginia. In Virginia's search for investment, missionary work was only a secondary concern behind the promise of profits or was folded into a general conviction that God was favoring the English plantation, and English imperial goals required expansion.[26]

The topographic patterns of missions reproduced in many respects the contrast between English and French settlements. Recollet Gabriel Sagard journeyed hundreds of miles from Quebec to Huronia in the early 1620s; he published his narrative and an ethnography of the Hurons in *Le grand voyage du pays des Hurons* (1632). The Jesuits Paul Le Jeune and Jean de Brébeuf, among several others, went to Huronia in the mid-1630s and wrote from there some of the earliest and most interesting installments of the *Jesuit Relations*. Le Jeune had also previously written of his experience among the Montagnais north of Quebec. The Jesuits' method of living in the natives' villages, often as guests in

parallel
indeed
emerge *check*
Hookin for
Puritan
P   sources.
from adult culture

specific lodges, entailed a degree of cultural submersion that no Puritan ministers would undertake. The Jesuits followed the tribes in their periodic transplantings within a region that had no permanent French outpost. Francis Jennings has compared attitudes of Jesuit and Puritan missionaries and admitted: "Such contrasts explain why the *Jesuit Relations* are today an invaluable mine of ethnological information in spite of bias and cant. There is nothing comparable in Protestant literature until we reach the reports of the Moravian missionaries in the mid-eighteenth century."[27] Moravian John Heckewelder's *An Account of the History, Manners, and Customs of the Indian Nations Who Once Inhabited Pennsylvania and the Neighboring States* (1819) is indeed the first ethnography by an Anglo-American missionary comparable in scale and detail to Gabriel Sagard's and to the *Jesuit Relations* from nearly two centuries earlier.

Daniel Gookin wrote the best ethnography by a Puritan missionary, *Historical Collections of the Indians in New England,* in the 1680s, but it was not published until 1792. In it, he described the first effort of his mentor, the leading Puritan missionary John Eliot, in 1646 in these words: "The first place he began to preach at, was Nonantum, near Watertown mill, upon the south side of the Charles river, about four or five miles from his own house" (28). When Gookin proposes an expedition to preach among a distant tribe, the Maquas or Mohawk, it is no more distant from Boston than the Hudson River, and he suggests sending a party of "not less than forty to fifty English men" (19) with horses (like Byrd's party) to carry their "furniture" or tools and supplies. Roger Williams had a greater commitment to sharing and learning about Indian life than Gookin or Eliot, but after rejecting ties to all established English churches and being exiled to Rhode Island by the Massachusetts and Plymouth colonies, he did not work to convert or assimilate the Narragansetts into any sect or church. Williams would have appreciated the resolve of the French Jesuits, for he wrote that he had "a constant zealous desire to dive into the Indian language" and "a painful Patient spirit to lodge with them, in their filthy smoke holes . . . to gain their tongue."[28]

The design for Indian conversion in New England became not a lonely missionary in the wilderness but the "praying town," where con-

verted or sympathetic Indians were isolated from their heathen compatriots and forced to give up hunting for a more intensive agricultural subsistence. The praying towns, thirteen of which were founded by 1674, failed because the colonists segregated them and refused to believe that even a converted Indian was trustworthy (as exemplified by the string of accusations in Mary Rowlandson's "Nineteenth Remove" of her captivity narrative). Eliot and Gookin were only itinerant preachers, and both admitted that it was impossible to recruit enough English teachers, much less ordained ministers, to have one in each praying town. The praying towns became as isolated as the English imagined their own settlements to be and might be figured as small lakes of assimilation within the island of "civility" within a sea of "savagery." The most successful settlement of praying Indians in New England was itself an island, the one established by Thomas Mayhew on Martha's Vineyard. The mainland praying towns were surveyed and circumscribed; as Gookin wrote, "the general court of Massachusetts hath bounded, stated, and settled, several townships and plantations of lands unto these praying Indians." By relocating converted and refugee Indians the French colonists developed settlements similar to the praying towns, such as Loretteville near Quebec, yet the French Catholic missionaries' emphasis on remote mission work continued into the eighteenth century in the Illinois country and Mississippi valley, and French colonists were more willing than the New Englanders to accept converts as allies, even spouses.

Colonial Narrative Genres

Having looked briefly at the shape and intent of the colonies of New France, New England, and Virginia, and at some of the many factors that account for the contrasts between them, let us consider the writing produced in each. Again, there is a sharp contrast between the French and the English patterns; perhaps the best proof is the absence of any scholarly survey or formulation of genres that accounts for both. The generic taxonomies that scholars have proposed are so different that they

clearly pertain to different traditions occupying the same time and adjoining spaces.

Even within the literature of New France, easy classifications are lacking. Geoffroy Atkinson, who along with his mentor, Gilbert Chinard,
was in the early twentieth century the leading American scholar of
French *récits de voyage* proposed the narratives of the colonial officer or
trader and of the missionary or *homme sensible* (he cited Lescarbot as an
example of the latter class) as the two basic types of travel or exploration
narrative. These two groups were often at odds over policies in Canada,
and their goals appear to have been in opposition. One is charged with
converting wilderness to empire, the other with converting heathen to
Christian. One deals with money and possessions, the other with people,
beliefs, and representations. Atkinson called the first type strictly utilitarian, "Il ne voit rien ou presque rien de remarquable à l'étranger" [He
sees nothing or almost nothing of interest in foreign lands (my translation)],[29] while including under the second rubric the more readable and
engaging narratives. But the argument is circular—Atkinson's judgments determine the contents of his categories. Some soldiers or officers,
such as Champlain and Joutel, are among the best observers of Amerindian societies. On the other hand, some Jesuits and Recollets participated in officially sponsored explorations, such as Marquette on the
Wisconsin and Mississippi Rivers and Hennepin and Membré accompanying La Salle. And one must also think of an unnamed third category,
the *coureurs de bois*. For it was these men who traveled most and knew
native languages and customs best. Because some were illiterate and few
of those who were literate wrote of their experiences, their contribution
to the literature of the colony was limited. The writings of the fur traders
Pierre-Esprit Radisson, Nicolas Perrot, and, later during the English
rule in Canada, Samuel Hearne and David Thompson should be studied
carefully because they are so rare, and because inevitably the trappers'
interests ran counter to the missionaries', the officials', and the Indians'.[30] It is a great loss that the journal of Joliet, who with Marquette
was the first Frenchman to paddle on the Mississippi, was lost when his
canoe capsized a few days before returning to Montreal.

One can also try to divide the corpus into genres according to the activities of the writer, instead of by his position in society. "Discoverers, Explorers, Settlers" is the trio proposed by Wayne Franklin in his book by that title about English colonization of the mid-Atlantic coast, to which I have already referred for its analysis of geometrical settlement schemes projected on the American landscape. Yet Franklin defines these three genres of colonial narrative rhetorically, not historically. The distinction between the three rests not in whether the traveler is the first to visit a certain region, or even if he stays to settle, but in the degree to which the writer imagines the plans for colonization as already implicit in the land he describes. The utopian schemes of the English surveys were influenced by the potential uses of the land, agricultural potential that was often lacking in Canada. But Franklin does not critique them ecologically or historically, he analyzes them as dreams or schemes. Similar stages of colonization and narrative are proposed in a recent study by Pierre Berthiaume entitled *L'Aventure Américaine au XVIIIe Siècle* and divided into four sections: "Journaux de navigation," "Rapports et récits d'exploration," "Relations de voyages," and "Lettres des missionaires" [Journals of Navigation, Reports and Narratives of Exploration, Travel Narratives, and Missionary Letters (my translation)]. This is a false evolution; all four existed in 1600, as well as 1800, and differ largely in the degree to which they were edited for the reading public. The ship's log, for one, was rarely intended for public consumption.

A few of the most interesting narratives of New France have been published in dry tomes of colonial documents; several fine narratives were buried in the French colonial archives until published by Pierre Margry in his six-volume collection (1879–88), and Deliette's memoir of the Illinois country first appeared in 1934 in *Illinois Historical Collections*, volume 23. The recognition of these texts as literary creations is inhibited by their apparent status as official reports between colonial authorities, as Berthiaume's and Atkinson's genres suggest. The *Jesuit Relations* are likewise official reports of the missionary effort and are published in an imposing set of seventy-three volumes without separate titles or authors. New England Puritan texts avoid this stigma because, as a dissenting religious community in exile, their writings were never official reports, and because dry official or personal texts have been accepted into the canon of New England Puritan literature. William Bradford's accounts of complex negotiations with the "adventurers" (investors) in London make up a large part of another seventeenth-century New England literary classic, *Of Plymouth Plantation*, and John Winthrop's journal was published as *The History of New England*. The personal, the political, the religious, and the literary are nearly interchangeable in the lives and writings of these Puritan patriarchs.

Accordingly, in Richard Slotkin's list of Anglo-American colonial genres, it is the purpose of writing that determines the genre, not the motive or position of the author. He identifies four: narratives of travel and exploration, tracts promoting or opposing colonization or describing the founding of colonies, captivity narratives and narratives of Indian war, and finally sermons (which often addressed the issues of the other three in a strict formulaic structure).[31] The missionary narrative is notably absent. The Boston elite, such as Cotton Mather, John Eliot, and William Bradford, wrote in all of these genres, and the same tropes are found in all of them. Foremost among these were scriptural motifs, above all the twin images of the flight of the chosen Israelites out of Egypt and their captivity in Babylon. Puritan writers subsumed the American landscape and inhabitants under the antithetical themes of Canaan, a promised land to which the chosen people had fled out of the Egypt of England and to which God gave them title over the objections of native Canaanites, and Babylon, a hell on earth where the faithful were tested by temptation and sin.

It was the captivity narrative, Slotkin argues, that most powerfully evoked the myths that informed later American literature. The captivity plot incorporated both the Canaan and Babylon themes—"The ordeal is at once threatful of pain and evil and promising of ultimate salvation" (94–95)—and enacted the Puritans' relation to both the land and the Indians. It is therefore one of the strongest features of the contrast between French and English colonial American literature that the captivity narrative genre does not exist in French. The tales of the martyrdom of Isaac Jogues and Jean de Brébeuf and the captivity of Pierre Millet achieved some renown, but there was no published account of a French lay colonist, male or female, being captured, surviving removal,

torture, or assimilation, and then returning to civilization. The exception would be Radisson, who was captured by the Iroquois in 1651 and
escaped to continue an amazing career as a trader, guide, and mercenary
for both the French and English colonies until the 1680s. However, his
exploration narratives were not published until 1885, and then entirely
in English, and therefore cannot be said to represent a French colonial
captivity genre.

There are several possible explanations for this surprising absence of
the captivity genre from French colonial American literature. Perhaps
the most obvious relates to religious ideology. For French Catholics,
suffering for one's faith led naturally to death, as it did for Christ and for
martyred saints, and not to deliverance. The *Jesuit Relations* are full of the
"private" reflections of young missionaries who resolutely endured the
sufferings of life among the Hurons or other nations while wishing
masochistically for a martyr's fate such as Brébeuf and Jogues found. In
the *Relation of 1647* the death of Jogues is analyzed:

> C'est la pensée de plusieurs hommes doctes, & cette pensée est plus
> que raisonnable que celuy-là est vrayement martyr devant Dieu, qui
> rend tesmoignage au Ciel & à la terre, qu'il fait plus d'estat de la Foy &
> de la publication de l'Evangile que de sa propre vie, la perdant dans les
> dangers où il se jette pour Jesus Christ, avec connoissance, protestant
> devant sa face, qu'il veust mourir pour le faire connoistre, cette mort
> est la mort d'un martyr devant les Anges. C'est dans cette veuë que le
> Pere à rendu son ame à Jesus Christ. (31:118–21)

> [It is the thought of several learned men, and this idea is more than
> reasonable, that he is truly a martyr before God, who renders witness
> to Heaven and earth that he values the Faith and the publication of the
> Gospel more highly that his own life,—losing it in the dangers into
> which, with full consciousness, he casts himself for Jesus Christ, and
> protesting before his face that he wished to die in order to make him
> known. This death is the death of a martyr before the Angels. It was
> with this in view that the Father yielded up his soul to Jesus Christ.]

Jogues went among the Iroquois willingly; in fact, he escaped from
captivity and torture and wrote of his experience, only to return to the

"Captivity" always burdened with religious and moral significance

mission, where he was finally killed in 1646. His death offered no threat, but instead glory for New France. The situation was quite different for the New England captive who was violently abducted from the bosom of church and family and whose fate was tied to that of the whole colony. For the Puritans, the temptation figured by Indian freedoms was a threat to every individual and, through each, to the colony itself. Just as the Protestant individual read and interpreted the Bible within a sacred community, he or she faced the evils of the wilderness as a representative of that community. The pious attitude of self-abasement appropriate to the female Puritan was entirely different from Jogues'. She subordinated the value of her own life to that of her family and community and wished to be redeemed because it might typologically figure the redemption of the community. The Jesuit interpreted his fate by a very different typology. In martyrdom, he individually was lifted out of worldly suffering through an apotheosis for which the savior's own crucifixion was the best metaphor (see Chapter 6 below). The greater mortification of the Jesuit's body accentuates his individual importance, and his sacrifice is on behalf of the sinners, the Indians, rather than the saints, the other colonists.

Another reason lies in the very notion of captivity. Secular explorers such as Champlain, Radisson, or Joutel (and the more humble soldiers and *donnés* or lay servants to the missionaries) accepted the privations and temptations of Indian life almost without comment as a consequence of coming to America. "Captivity" for these men was not burdened with religious and moral significance. Champlain spent the winter of 1615–16 with the Hurons because, following his participation in the siege of an Iroquoian stockade at Oneida, the winter freeze began and his allies were unable to escort him back to Quebec. He considered himself a guest rather than a captive, and the privations he suffered were of practical, not religious, significance. When Radisson was captured by the Iroquois, he wrote, "I dreamed that night that I was with the Jesuits at Quebec drinking beere, which gave me hopes to be free sometimes" (30). Mary Rowlandson certainly did not draw strength from such profane imaginings!

Many French colonists lived among the Indians unwillingly but still did not call themselves captives. The earliest of these individuals were the *truchements*, of whom Etienne Brulé is the most famous, sent to live among the Indians to learn their language and serve as interpreters for French explorers. Henry Spelman and Thomas Savage were placed in the same role by the first Jamestown colonists. However, whereas the French more often followed the Amerindian practice of exchanging and adopting children to cement an alliance between two nations, the English more often kidnapped Indians in the hope that they could learn English and then promote their captors' interests among their tribe. Later the *truchements* ceased to be the only interpreters as Indian traders learned the French language and the *coureurs de bois* assimilated Indian ways, often marrying into tribal alliances. Although the colonial officials feared these cultural defectors for the dangerous examples of independence and racial mixture they offered to other colonists, the pattern of their departure and return never formed a popular myth. Furthermore, in New England the phenomenon of captivity rode the popularity of published captivity narratives until it exceeded actual events. Many captives were quickly passed from their Indian captors to the French and endured the "torture" of papism, not savagism.[32] Several other Anglo-Americans, including John Gyles and Mary Jemison, were adopted into Indian families and assimilated their ways yet nonetheless were labeled "captives" when their narratives were published.

Amid this confusion of exploration and promotional narratives, captivity and war narratives, sermons and settlement histories, I wish to propose a genre categorization based on the point of view of the author and his or her descriptions of the Indians. The two genres I find most salient are the *récit de voyage* and the *mœurs des sauvages*, exploration narratives and ethnographic descriptions, or simply writing about the land and the act of moving through it, and writing about the inhabitants of the land. Each genre, whether written by soldiers, explorers, traders, or missionaries, English or French, whether closer to 1600 or 1763, stands out as a cohesive body of work because its rhetorical codes are so strong. Both genres are also extremely flexible and enduring. The *mœurs des sauvages* could be written in just a few pages as part of a description of a colony (as Adriaen Van der Donck and Daniel Denton did for New Netherlands and Alexander Whitaker for Virginia), or it could run to two quarto volumes like Joseph-François Lafitau's. Nineteenth-century travelers such as Edwin James, John Dunn Hunter, and even Herman Melville in *Typee*, continued to produce "manners and customs of the Indians," and readers continued to expect them, until finally anthropology professionalized the production of ethnographies of the cultural Other. Exploration narrative, for its part, belongs to a tradition from Marco Polo to Columbus to contemporary accounts of arctic exploration and single-handed sailors' circumnavigations of the world.

Although exploration narratives and ethnographic descriptions were frequently written and published independently, this study will focus on the published texts by men who spent time in America and wrote both a description of the *sauvages* and a narration of travel in frontier regions. The genre distinction does not separate some texts from others but cuts through the middle of them. The explorer-ethnographers used this form, I will argue, because each genre legitimates the other through a series of complementary relationships. The author of such a text can, for instance, both convey the knowledge he has learned from the Indians about America and deploy European knowledge to control this representation of the foreign culture. The rhetoric of exploration narrative individuates the writer and invests great value in his accuracy and authenticity, and the rhetoric of ethnography applies this credibility to the representation of another culture.

The French colonial writers, whether missionaries, explorers, or fur traders, excelled at ethnography, producing texts that are rich in information about early Native American cultures. English colonists, notably Roger Williams and John Lawson, also produced a few fine ethnographies, but they did not realize the full potential and popularity of the genre until after the Seven Years' War, in a few books examined in the Epilogue below. Scholars of New England Puritan and Virginian American literature have accordingly given little attention to ethnography. Therefore, it is not surprising that within the United States in the twentieth century it has been ethnohistorians, in attempting to write histories of colonial America from the Amerindians' point of view, who have made the best use of the French colonial literature. Combining archeology, contemporary accounts of exploration and settlement, and

oral history, ethnohistory in the last forty years has begun to propose a
new Euramerican-Amerindian history—one of evolving and interacting
societies, each with its own contexts and problems. Much research in
ethnohistory has been motivated by native peoples' efforts to document
their history in support of tribal land claims. Works by James Axtell,
Francis Jennings, Richard White, Neal Salisbury, and Bruce Trigger, to
name only a few, draw on both French and English sources to explain the
dynamics of cultural contact in North America, particularly New England, and also show the biases and elisions in traditional histories.[33]
Still, ethnohistory looks to the texts for historical information rather
than analyzing them as literary works and routinely gleans facts from
works that also include fantastic fictions. Historians also often cite only
English translations of French texts and documents without acknowl-
edging the limitations of selective or abridged translations. It is, of
course, not the language of colonists that matters to historians so much
as the events to which the language refers, and therefore historians rarely
present the sources in their full literary or rhetorical complexity. In
addition, ethnohistories and general colonial histories usually take a
regional focus, whether that of an Indian nation or confederacy, a European colony, or that colony's metropole.[34]

Histories tend to supercede their sources; as Thoreau puts it, scholarly
progress, like westward progress or imperialism, buries or leaves behind
what it has consumed and expelled. Exploration and ethnography texts
have not continued to receive the praises Thoreau gave them, but instead they have often in the last quarter century been dismissed as
ethnocentric and inaccurate, as second-rate history and third-rate literature, even by those who depend on them as sources. To cite one example,
Helen Rountree, in the opening paragraph of *Pocahontas's People*, the
second of a two-volume ethnohistory of the native peoples of Virginia,
dismisses the value of ethnography by John Smith, William Strachey,
and others:

> The English colonists at Jamestown left a few moderately comprehen-
> sive descriptions of this way of life [that of the Powhatan Indians],
> though not nearly so comprehensive as an anthropologist would wish.

The English writers lived in an era before the advent of any of the social sciences. Full and objective descriptions of alien cultures were not even conceived of back then. The colonists were also male, with all that that meant in early Jacobean England, and they came to Virginia not to observe Indians but to explore the territory and to make their fortunes. The descriptions of Indian lifeways are therefore spotty and essentially incidental to the records they left about their colonizing enterprise. (3)

Presumably, if the early-seventeenth-century Jamestown colonists had written an ethnography that met today's standards for anthropological research, Rountree's book would not be necessary. Yet to argue that today's social sciences can, at a four-hundred-year remove, create "objective descriptions of alien cultures," that the early ethnographies were written with an "incidental" rather than a "comprehensive" motive, and that one must be a professional ethnologist to write a good ethnography merely restates the idea that the social sciences as such did not exist when Jamestown was founded; it does not prove that the colonists' accounts are untrustworthy. After all, Rountree's two studies rely overwhelmingly on the colonists' writings to construct a portrait of Powhatan culture in the seventeenth century and before. In *Pocahontas's People* there are hundreds of footnotes to John Smith's writings alone.

Our conviction of the extreme cultural difference between Europeans and Indians at the time of initial contact has affected too strongly our reading of the accounts of that contact. We are justly skeptical of any description of indigenous peoples that smacks of the preconceptions and prejudices of Europeans. Columbus's coining the term "Indians" is one of the most obvious and best known of these misconceptions of the explorers. Yet our own conception of the Native Americans' "true" culture has to come from somewhere, and most of it comes from the writings of these same explorers and missionaries whose prejudices we wish to overcome. Oral history cannot be ignored, even for supposedly extinct tribes such as the Pequot, but it is not always available. Archeological evidence rarely provides a solution to the problem of ethnocentric representations, because for many regions in North America it is very limited. In fact, some of the cultures that archeologists have learned most about, such as the Anasazi of the desert Southwest and the mound builders of the Midwest woodlands, had already changed unrecognizably by the time Europeans reached these areas and met the subsequent inhabitants and therefore are not represented in explorers' ethnographies.

Both ethnohistorians and literary scholars get caught on the horns of a hermeneutic dilemma when they approach the representations of American Indian cultures in the early colonial era. Some try to see early America and the colonial "invaders" as natives did, whereas others look for the features of Indians that were important for the European colonists and their cultures and literatures. Shifting back and forth between these perspectives leaves one in an epistemological impasse, and although the dilemma has been confronted by many writers, it has not been formulated in terms common to all sides in the debate.[35] On the one hand lies an emphasis on the profound epistemological, psychological, and social differences of the cultural Other—in this case, American Indian cultures, separately and generally, from the Europeans. Taken to its extreme, this view holds that neither early explorers nor more recent anthropologists can fully understand the cultural Other, see as natives see and think as natives think, and that therefore all ethnographies are compromised by ethnocentrism. This extreme position has been articulated by recent theorists in literature and anthropology, and one effect has been to encourage readers to search for more "authentic" Native American voices in oral literature and in the few written texts in English by Indians before 1800.[36] In practice, however, anthropology, ethnohistory, and interpretation of Native American literature all stop short of this extreme insofar as they promise a better understanding of the Indians' cultures than conventional histories have provided and rely on indirect sources as well as the texts and artifacts produced by native peoples. Studies such as Rountree's generally fit the old data of what I will call exploration-ethnography texts (such as John Smith's) into new and presumably more accurate paradigms.

The opposite horn of the dilemma is not a naive acceptance of colonial ethnographies as objective descriptions, but a sense of human culture as an organic whole, of certain features, such as mythic archetypes, as operating in all cultures, and of the categories of the colonists' regard for the American Indians, such as the Noble and Ignoble Savage, as more than mere ethnocentrism. Studies by Anthony Pagden, Lewis Hanke. and Anthony Grafton emphasize the ways in which Renaissance and earlier European cultural stereotypes such as the Wild Man or Noble Savage or the philosophy of Aristotle were adapted to the New World natives.[37] Also in this spirit, Slotkin and Pearce examined the influence of Native American cultures on Anglo-American literature and the tendency for the self-proclaimed civilized Anglo-American culture to adopt the behavior of the Savages even as it defined itself in opposition to them. Karen Ordahl Kupperman's fine study, *Settling with the Indians*, asserts that in the early seventeenth century European technology was not in fact superior to the Native Americans' tools and weapons, that belief in supernatural forces was common in both cultures, and that in spite of the evident cultural chauvinism of the English, historians should not conclude that they "rejected Indian culture out of hand" (46, 106).

A reader who samples studies of colonial America from different disciplines faces a dilemma, for some scholars condemn the shortsightedness of contemporary witnesses while using their information to build more accurate conceptions of an Indian now made visible from afar; others examine the representations in terms of the Europeans representing rather than the native people represented. This dilemma between assimilative and Other-ing approaches, this Manichean attitude toward the ethnographic literature of American exploration, can be averted. Most scholarship, after all, does not adhere to one or the other extreme. Yet the attitude persists that even European explorers and missionaries who lived in American Indian communities for extended periods of time wore blinders that obscured their understanding of these cultures, and that this understanding is nevertheless somehow now available to the "enlightened" reader.

The solution lies in a more holistic approach to the sources, one that is both rhetorical and historicist. We must use the methodology that ethnohistory has used so well; sifting, comparing, and judging the texts of colonial authors along with other sources to find the facts that are most likely to be true and the opinions that are held by a consensus of eyewitness observers. Then we must also take into account the lives of these colonial writers and the shape of the texts that they wrote. Conventional European attitudes toward the Indian in the seventeenth century were not born out of a European collective unconscious, which feared hairy forest dwellers and dreamed of the innocence of primitive life; they were formed by books about the Indians, and therefore by the experiences of the authors, and the strategies for writing marketable texts about America. In Chapter 3 and beyond, I will analyze two major modes of publications about colonial America: the "New Voyages to North America" genre, and the "Manners and Customs of the Indians of North America" which frequently was published along with it. These are not simply ethnocentric constructs, but influential rhetorical traditions. The ethnological details contained in these texts cannot simply be lifted out of obsolete structures like the Noble Savage and laid down in more recent conceptions of, for example, matrilineal, nonstate, hunter-gatherer communities of northern Algonquians. Seventeenth- and eighteenth-century theories about the American Indians, such as their possible ancestors among the peoples of the biblical or classical world, are interesting not simply as curiosities of intellectual history, but as theories that affected an explorer's interactions with the Indians and the things that he learned from them and felt to be of value for his own life and for his society. These explorers' writings, in turn, had a profound effect on the attitudes of the settlers who followed them and the European literature that absorbed them.

Who are these explorer-ethnographers, so fascinating for Thoreau and so little known in the twentieth century? It is difficult to both define and analyze a genre of texts that are unfamiliar, as the literature of New France is to students of (Anglo-) American literature. Bacqueville de La Potherie, Samuel de Champlain, Pierre de Charlevoix, Louis Hennepin, Chrestien LeClercq, Nicolas Perrot, Gabriel Sagard, and the Baron de Lahontan all wrote between 1608 and 1751 texts that included a narrative of their journey to the Canadian frontier and a description of the manners and customs of the Indians, with each section organized in characteristic ways.[38] Among English colonial writers, John Smith, John Lederer, William Byrd, John Lawson, and John Bartram all published during this period texts that meet the same criteria. And there were many others, such as Robert Beverley, William Wood, and John Josselyn, who wrote books describing the land, flora and fauna, and native inhabitants, but not including a narrative of exploration.

The Baron de Lahontan as Explorer and Ethnographer

I hope to demonstrate the possibilities for a more holistic reading of the colonial writings about the Indians, and the special importance of texts that combine exploration narrative with ethnographic description, through a case study of Louis-Armand de Lom d'Arce, Baron de Lahontan. A rebellious, anticlerical deist, a soldier forced out of Canada by the hostility of his commanding officer, then forced into exile from France by his incendiary publication, Lahontan had idiosyncratic beliefs unusual among colonial explorers and relatively easy to isolate from his "objective" representations of the Indians. (To satisfy skeptics, the objective representations might better be called the ones that agree with others' accounts.) However, the deism and primitivism that he is often accused of imposing on the Amerindians, of placing in the mouth of the Huron character Adario in the philosophical dialogue that forms the third part of his text, were in fact learned from the Indians as much as imposed on them. Canada and its natives were Lahontan's Harvard College and his Yale, to crib Ishmael. Through an examination of the form of his text, and of the accounts of Indians and colonists that responded to concerns of his own, one can see what he learned. His text both analyzes Indian life for insights into European culture and imposes European categories on Indian culture.

The *Nouveaux voyages de M. Le Baron de Lahontan, dans l'Amérique Septentrionale* . . . of 1703 contains virtually all the modes of colonial American secular writing: exploration narrative, historical accounts of Indian wars, natural history, description of the geography and economy of the colony, promotion and criticism of its potential, ethnography or *mœurs des sauvages*, and a glossary of a native language. Finally, the last part of the text, a satiric dialogue between Lahontan and a Huron interlocutor named Adario, is a unique innovation in colonial writing, one that anticipates major texts of the French Enlightenment. To understand

Lahontan and to evaluate his representations of Indians, one must be acquainted not only with each of these genres, but also with Lahontan himself and how he was transformed by what he saw and learned from the Indians. *Nouveaux voyages* shows how Lahontan changed from a Frenchman to an American colonist, from a loyal member of a colonial army to an AWOL, from one who hoped to inherit a valuable estate in France to one disgusted with French society and its hierarchies, and from a Frenchman fighting against the English in King William's war to an exile in England providing the English with intelligence about Canada.

Lahontan's ethnographic "fieldwork" encompassed the two winters he spent hunting with groups of Algonquin Indians. No doubt he also learned much from native clients of fur traders at Fort St. Joseph (later Detroit), where he was in command for a time in 1687–88, and from allies who participated in military expeditions with him, such as Governor La Barre's aborted attack in 1684 and Governor Denonville's attack on the Seneca in 1687. Yet these hunting expeditions were an experience that Lahontan clearly treasured. They legitimate his descriptions of Canadian animals in letter 11 and in the *Mémoires*, descriptions that thereby carry the authority of the natives' knowledge as well as his own. Hunting was also the occasion for learning woodcrafts, for which Lahontan admired the Indians: "ils connoissent mieux la piste des hommes ou des bêtes sur l'herbe & sur les feuilles, que les Européens ne le pourroient connoître sur la nége ou sur le sable moüillé. . . . c'est une vérité dont je ne sçaurois douter après en avoir été tant de fois le témoin" (2:177–78) [they can trace the Footsteps of Men and Beasts upon Grass and Leaves, better than the Europeans can upon Snow or wet Sand. . . . This I have seen so often with my own Eyes, that there's no room left for the least doubt upon the matter (2:74)]. Observing and following a trail becomes a skill not only of hunting, but also of travel narrative. Lahontan tracks down truth with a skill learned from the Indians, and, as he insists, this skill supports his claims to have produced accurate written representations.

Hunting is a popular and populist pastime in America today, and in American literature there are many famous stories, William Faulkner's "The Bear" foremost among them, that portray hunting as the occasion for a rite of passage, a lesson to a naive protagonist from the wisdom of nature, of Indians, or of elder relations. Yet when seventeenth-century colonists observed the skill and importance of hunting among woodlands Indians, their reaction was quite different. Hunting in Europe was reserved for the nobility and pursued on lands where poaching was severely punished. As the "Lahontan" character states in the *Dialogues*, the laws of Europe, "défendent aux Païsans de tuer ni liévres ni perdrix. . . . Ces gens-là ont recû de leurs Seigneurs les terres dont ils joüissent, & ceux-ci se sont réservé la chasse, comme leurs Maitres" (3:44) [prohibit the Peasants to kill Hares or Partridges. . . . The Boors Farm the Grounds of their Landlords, who reserve to themselves the Priviledge of Hunting, as being Masters (2:131)]. To see primitives in America hunting where and what they pleased created part of the irony of the Noble Savage, and the subversion of class restrictions occurs among the colonists as well. At the opening of the *Voyages*, Lahontan describes the life of settlers in the St. Lawrence valley as confounding the social categories of Europe:

> Les Païsans y vivent sans mentir plus commodément qu'une infinité de Gentilshommes en France. Quand je dis Païsans je me trompe, il faut dire habitans, car ce tître de Païsan n'est non plus receu ici qu'en Espagne, soit parce qu'ils ne payent ni sel ni taille, qu'ils ont la liberté de la chasse & de la pêche, ou qu'enfin leur vie aisée les met en parallele avec les Nobles. (1:10)

> [The Boors of those Manors live with more ease and conveniencey, than an infinity of the Gentlemen in France. I am out indeed in calling 'em Boors, for that name is as little known here as in Spain; whether it be that they pay not Taxes, and injoy the libety of Hunting and Fishing; or that the easiness of their Life, puts 'em upon a level with the Nobility. (1:7)]

The published translation omitted Lahontan's comment that instead of peasants or "Boors," one should say *habitants*, and still today Québecois embrace with pride the nickname *habitants* for themselves and for their hockey team.

Lahontan perceived that the skill of hunting was so important for the Indians that the status of a man depended on it, rather than on birth or wealth:

> parmi eux, il faut pour être homme avoir le talent de bien courir, chasser, pêcher, tirer un coup de fléche & de fusil, conduire un Canot, sçavoir faire la guerre, connoître les Forêts, vivre de peu, construire des Cabanes, couper des arbres, & sçavoir faire cent lieuës dans les Bois sans autre guide ni provision que son arc & ses fléches. (2:99)

> [among them the true Qualifications of a Man are, to run well, to hunt, to bend the Bow and manage the Fuzee, to work a Canoo, to understand War, to know forrests, to subsist upon little, to build Cottages, to fell Trees, and to be able to travel an hundred Leagues in a Wood without any Guide, or other Provision than his Bow and Arrows. (2:9)]

These practical skills are the foundation for an American egalitarianism that later became part of the ideology of the young United States; they are the skills represented in "meritography," which I will discuss in Chapter 4. In the *Mémoires*, this passage is used to support a harangue against absolutist government and the arts and sciences:

> Ils nous traitent d'esclaves, ils disent que . . . nous nous dégradons de nôtre condition, en nous réduisant à la servitude d'un seul homme qui peut tout . . . Ils prétendent que . . . toutes nos Sciences ne valent pas celle de sçavoir passer la vie dans une tranquillité parfaite; qu'un homme n'est homme chez nous qu'autant il est riche. (2:98–99)

> [They brand us for Slaves, and call us miserable Souls, whose Life is not worth having, alledging, That we degrade our selves in subjecting our selves to one Man who possesses the whole Power . . . That all our Siences are not so valuable as the Art of leading a peaceful calm Life; That a Man is not a Man with us any farther than Riches will make him. (2:8–9)]

Perhaps aware of the implausibility of Indians having such a comparative perspective, he prefaces this passage with the qualifier, "Ceux qui ont été en France" [Those who have been in France]. In the *Dialogues*, Adario has been to France and can speak this sort of critique directly. Thus Lahontan adopts a voice informed by both cultures, professing an authority and a status gained from practical experiences in the forests of America such as hunting, juxtaposed with a knowledge of France that he shares with his readers and with one of his companions in the forest.

Lahontan's authority as a writer and an expert on America and Native Americans was acquired during his tour of duty as a soldier in the colonial army, where he, of course, had only as much authority as befitted his rank. Only during his command at Fort St. Joseph and during his explorations in the West was he the leader of a group of other colonists. He writes at several points in the *Voyages* of how requests to return to France to settle legal problems surrounding his inheritance were denied by Governor Frontenac. But toward the end of his ten-year stint in New France, he came up with a plan for a series of forts along the Great Lakes to defend them from the Iroquois (and the English). Frontenac sent him to Paris to present this scheme to the minister for the colonies, the Comte de Pontchartrain. His knowledge of the Indians and of the Algonquian language, learned on his two winters hunting, therefore proved to be of some value within the colonial hierarchy: "par un hazard peu avantageux pour moi, je me suis aquis leur estime & leur amitié, & c'est à mon avis la seule raison qui a engagé Mr. de Frontenac de me choisir préférablement à tout autre" (1:241) [by an accident which do's not tend much to my advantage, I have purchas'd the Esteem and Friendship of these Savages, which in my opinion was the only reason that mov'd Mr. de Frontenac to single me out for this Service (1:183)]. Yet ironically, part of this knowledge is that in the Indian "army," unlike the French one, there is no centralized structure of command: "chaque Village a son grand Chef de guerre, qui pour sa valeur, sa capacité, & son experience, a été proclamé tel d'un consentement unanime. Cependant ce titre ne lui donne aucun pouvoir sur les Guerriers; ces sortes de gens ne connoissant point la surbordination Militaire non plus que la Civile" (2:178) [each Village hath its General or Great Head of the Warriors, who in consideration of his Valour, Capacity and Experience is proclaim'd such by an unanimous Consent. But after all, this Title invests him with no Power over the Warriors; for these People are Strangers to a Military as well as to a Civil Subordination (2:75)]. Many other sources support Lahontan's statement that no Indian warrior was obliged to fight in a campaign if he did not wish to. In the ceremony he describes for the raising of a fighting force, each warrior sends his eating dish to the "General's" cabin as a token of his participation. Lahontan's knowledge of these preparations for war is both accurate ethnography and a commentary on his own position and difficulties as an officer in the French colonial forces.

As he returns to Versailles to try to claim his inheritance, he complains of the "mepris qu'on fait de ceux qui n'ont d'autre recommandation que leur merite" (1:224) [contempt that those meet with, who have no other Recommendation than Merit" (1:170)]. In the twenty-fifth and last letter, he writes of how, having been assigned to a post as commander of the French fort at Placentia, Newfoundland, he got into a feud with the governor there, Jacques François de Brouillon, which threatened to end in a duel. Lahontan portrays himself as a martyr to a form of authority inferior to the Indians' independence. He recounts his attempt to reconcile with Brouillon: "je lui parlai plus d'un quart d'heure en termes plus soûmis que n'auroit fait un esclave. J'ai honte de vous en faire l'aveu, car je rougis moi-même toutes les fois que je pense à cette bassesse" (1:259–60) [I spoke to him for a quarter of an hour in the most submissive Terms, that any Slave could use. I am asham'd to make this Confession to you, for I blush to my self every time I think of so mean a submission (1:197)]. When Brouillon rejects his apology, he asserts that "si je l'eusse percé de mon épée, les Soldats & les Habitans auroient favorisé mon retraite chez les Anglois" (1:260) [if I should have run him through with my sword, the Soldiers and Inhabitants would have favour'd my escape to the English (1:197)], but that he knows that the justice of his cause will never win out, "par un détestable principe de Politique, l'inferieur a toûjours tort, quelque bonne raison qu'il puisse avoir" (1:262) [by a detestable principle of Politicks, an inferior Person is always judg'd to be in the wrong whatever reason he may have on his side (1:199)]. Finally, he is forced to flee on an English ship and begins his travels in exile around much of Western Europe outside his native France.

Lahontan's explorations and experience with the Indians transformed his life, and the very possibility of transforming oneself, of escaping the place to which one has been assigned by birth, by name, by rank or subordination, and taking on a new identity, was inspired in part by the Indians' practice of adopting prisoners of war: "Il faut remarquer que les

Sauvages de Canada n'échangent jamais leur prisonniers. Dès qu'ils sont liez, ils sont considérez comme morts de leur Parens, aussi bien que de toute leur propre Nation" (2:185–86) [You must take notice that the Savages of Canada never exchange their Prisoners. As soon as they are put in Chains, their Relations and the whole Nation to which they retain, look upon 'em as dead (2:81)]. Although he did not convey a detailed understanding of the customs of adoption and "requickening" (which I will discuss at some length in Chapter 6), Lahontan did consider the possibility of crossing the cultural divide himself. In the climactic words of Adario in the *Dialogues*, he implores: "Croi-moy, fais toy Huron. Car je voi la diférance de ma condition à la tienne. Je suis maitre de mon corps, je dispose de moy-même, je fais ce que je veux, je suis le premier & le dernier de ma Nation; je ne crains personne, & ne dépens uniquement que du grand Esprit" (3:37) [Take my advice, and turn Huron; for I see plainly a vast difference between thy Condition and mine. I am Master of my own Body, I have the absolute disposal of my self, I do what I please, I am the first and the last of my Nation, I fear no Man, and I depend only upon the Great Spirit (2:124)]. Although the promise of a new life in America has been offered to or cherished by many immigrants, it is usually associated with the egalitarian tabula rasa of the U.S. political ideology or with a maternal rebirth.[39] Lahontan and the other writers on adoption practices show that the ideology is in part derived from the Indians. It was not a mere escapist fantasy of noble primitivism, but an actual cultural reality for a few captives, traders, and adopted prisoners.

Lahontan was never a captive and did not live with the Indians for as long as some other explorer-ethnographers. Yet he was more successful than many at "playing Indian," at writing in the voice of an Indian character. He did so with considerable literary sophistication in the sensational and salacious satire of the third part of his book, *Dialogues curieux entre l'Auteur et un Sauvage de Bon Sens Qui a Voyagé* (Entitled in the translation, "A Conference or Dialogue between the Author and Adario, A Noted Man among the Savages, Containing A Circumstantial View of the Customs and Humours of That People"). Because of its resemblance to later texts like Diderot's, Lahontan is perhaps the best known of all the writers of New France to scholars of French literature. The *Dialogues* is a Lucianic satire expressing what Lahontan had learned from the Indians through two voices—"Lahontan" and Adario—that enact a confrontation between his new and old selves. "Lahontan" is largely a straw man, inept at defending Catholicism and the legal and social structures that Lahontan felt had treated him unjustly. Adario is a synthesis of Indian culture and European radical deism whose speeches denounce prostitution, inequitable taxation, and absolute monarchy as well as praising the Hurons' control of their passions and disdain for the temptations of wealth. Though purportedly based on a real Huron named Kondiaronk, Adario is not an "authentic" voice but a hybrid conceived to invert the assumptions of colonial savagism. At one particularly ironic moment "Lahontan" accuses Adario of ethnocentrism, of being biased in favor of his "savage" culture. As Réal Ouellet has written, "Les *Dialogues* n'étaient pas un hymne à la superiorité du monde sauvage sur la civilisation européenne mais un parodie de deux discours conforme, l'un sur la civilisation, l'autre sur la sauvagerie" (90) [The *Dialogues* was not a hymn to the superiority of the Indian world over European civilization but a parody of two conformist discourses, one of civilization, the other of savagism (my translation)]. As *Nouveaux voyages* and *Mémoires* are the parts of greater interest to historians, the obviously fictional *Dialogues* has been a challenge to the historical status of Lahontan's writings, and the contradictory assessments of it by those who read it from the perspectives of different fields are typical of the exploration-ethnography genre. Pierre Berthiaume writes that this portrait of "l'autre" [the Other] is a projection of the European self, that whether noble or not, Lahontan's *sauvage* "n'a guère à voir avec la réalité" (372) [has no basis in reality (my translation)]. Yet historians continue to refer to Lahontan's *Voyages* and *Mémoires* as factual sources.

It is useless to try to divide Lahontan's text into facts worthy of evidence in history or ethnohistory on the one hand, and fabulations or fictions such as the *Dialogues* on the other. Instead, it can be more profitable to read history through fantasy. Take the most tendentious part of his ethnography, the account of "Amours and Mariages" that claims of the Indians "ils n'ont jamais eu cette sorte de fureur aveugle que nous appellons amour" (2:131) [they are altogether strangers to that Blind Fury which we call Love (2:35)] and implies that their behavior with regard to sexuality and other matters follows the pure light of reason. Lahontan interprets native customs through the lens of the Enlightenment belief that strong passions such as love and jealousy were contrary to reason, and led to pointless strife and violence. The ideals of freedom that he absorbed during his sojourn among the Indians include a sexual freedom that is not libertine, but rational, expressed in terms that anticipate the revolutions some seventy-five years later: "veillant toûjours à se conserver la liberté de cœur, laquelle ils regardent comme le tresor le plus précieux qu'il y ait au Monde. D'où je conclus qu'ils ne sont pas tout à fait si Sauvages que nous. . . . Les filles . . . ils disent qu'elles sont Maîtresses de leurs corps, qu'elles sont libres de faire ce qu'elles veulent par le droit de liberté" (2:132) [they are very careful in preserving the Liberty and Freedom of their Heart, which they look upon as the most valuable Treasure upon Earth: From whence I conclude that they are not altogether so savage as we are. . . . A Young Woman, say they, is Master of her own body, and by her Natural Right of Liberty is free to do what she pleases (2:35)].

It is in the area of sexuality that Lahontan's descriptions of the Indians most often differ from those of other early ethnographers. The freedom of unmarried girls to choose their partners and to engage in premarital sex is generally supported by other observers, even as many stress the modest comportment of the native women. But the absolute fidelity Lahontan attributes to married couples is contradicted by Sagard and Lafitau, and implicitly by many others who write of the harsh punishment for adultery. Certainly different tribes had different customs, yet the *Mémoires* rarely specifies which tribe's customs are being described, and although the portrait of sexuality in this chapter resembles the account given by the Huron Adario in the *Dialogues*, Lahontan knew several Algonquian tribes better than the Hurons. As Richard White has warned of the ethnographic sources, "A few relatively straightforward descriptions of sexual relations exist, but sources are often openly polemical" (61, see also 65), and observers less ideologically laden than Lahontan also failed to perceive that marriage and the nuclear family unit were not the fundamental categories of an Indian woman's life as they were for Europeans.

We cannot dismiss Lahontan's account outright as biased or fabricated. Some sources, notably Lawson and Lamothe–Cadillac, are in substantial agreement with his portrait of what Europeans called a libertine sexuality; others are not. But we should examine how Lahontan drew on what he learned from the Indians to propose ideas about sexuality that prefigure those of radical Enlightenment philosophers. The agency he attributes to the young Indian women makes a provocative counterpoint with his account in the second letter of the *Voyages* of French girls brought to Quebec as wives for the colonists. These "filles de moyenne vertu . . . étoient pour ainsi dire entassées les unes sur les autres en trois differentes sales, où les époux choisissent leurs épouses de la maniére que le boucher va choisir les moutons" (1:11) [Cargoe of Women of an ordinary Reputation . . . were heap'd up (if I may so speak) one above another, in three different Apartments, where the Bridegrooms singled out their Brides, just as a Butcher do's an Ewe (1:8)]. The bridegrooms chose their brides according to rational considerations: "les plus grasses furent plûtôt enlevées que les autres, parce qu'on s'imaginoit qu'étant moins actives elles auroient plus de peine à quitter leur menage, & qu'elles resisteroient mieux au grand froid de l'hiver" (1:11–12) [the fattest went off best, upon the apprehension that these being less active, would keep truer to their Ingagements, and hold out better against the nipping cold of the Winter (1:8–9)]. This passage has enraged many Québecois historians against Lahontan.[40] Regardless of the true character of these transported women, they seem to be presented as an ironic reversal of the customs described in the *Mémoires* and by Adario in the *Dialogues*. Just as the French men choose their wives from a lineup, with an eye to practical physical characteristics, so too do the Huron women, according to Adario: "les filles qui voient de jeunes gens nuds, jugent à l'oeil de ce qui leur convient. . . . Ainsi, chacune peut hardiment juger qu'elle ne sera pas trompée en ce qu'elle attend d'un Mari" (3:93) [the young Women taking a view of the Naked parts, make their choise by the Eye . . . any Woman may be well assur'd what she has

[handwritten annotation: observation is always set in context of observer's culture]

to expect in a husband (2:174)]. He adds that the men are fortunate that women do not judge them based on a single measurement alone. As in Diderot's account of Tahiti in *Supplément au voyage de Bougainville*, Lahontan represents among the Hurons a rationalized sexuality where the body is exposed to the gaze of the opposite sex, and therefore the moral dissimulations of flattery, wealth, and coquettry are stripped away to expose the physical basis of sex and the natural imperatives of reproduction. Adario draws Lahontan's conclusion; that clothes and wealth are contrivances to conceal physical weakness, that in France, "ce n'est que par le vêtement qu'on fait état des gens. N'est-ce pas un grand avantage pour un François de pouvoir cacher quelque défaut de nature sous de beaux habits?" (3:92) [Since in your Country Men are valued according to their Dress, is it not a great advantage to be able to cover any Defect in Nature with a handsome Habit? (2:174)]. Certainly we cannot know by what criteria young Huron women chose their partners in the courtship ritual Lahontan calls *courir l'allumette*, and the ethnographic format does not provide for a discussion with an individual woman about her choice. But Lamothe-Cadillac and Lawson both describe the same practice, whereby the suitor carries a torch ("allumette" or match) to his beloved's cabin and the girl blows it out if she wishes him to stay by her side.[41] Given that cross-cultural observations are always set in the context of the observer's culture, the significance of Huron sexuality does not depend merely on classifying Lahontan's account as true or false.

The scandalous account of the Quebec brides and the implausible sophistication of Adario are two reasons why Lahontan's text has often been denounced by historians, particularly those wishing to protect an image of the New France that Lahontan attacks. Canadian historiography has received Lahontan variously, according to the desires of various historians. The question of the veracity of his account of a westward voyage on the "Rivière Longue" fits into a tradition of travel hoaxes analyzed in Chapter 3 below. Another example of the selective use of Lahontan's writings is the curious fate of the "harangue" delivered by the Onondaga orator known to the French as "La Grand Gueule" or "The Big Mouth" (presumably not an insult but an allusion to his eloquence), to Lahontan as "La Grangula," to Cadwallader Colden as "Garangula," and to the Iroquois as "Otreouti." Without summarizing all the events leading up to the September 5, 1684, meeting at which Lahontan was present, suffice it to say that Otreouti perceived that the French were negotiating from a position of weakness, and he strongly asserted Iroquoian sovereignty:

> Nous sommes nez libres, nous ne dépendons d'Onnontio non plus que de Corlar, il nous est permis d'aller où nous voulons, d'y conduire qui bon nous semble, d'acheter & vendre à qui il nous plaît. Si tes Alliez sont tes esclaves ou tes enfans, traite les comme les esclaves, ou comme des enfans, ôte leur la liberté de ne recevoir chez eux d'autres gens que les tiens. (1:53)

> [We are born Freemen, and have no dependance either upon the Onnontio or the Corlar. We have a power to go where we please, to conduct who we will to the places we resort to, and to buy and sell where we think fit. If your Allies are your Slaves or Children, you may e'en treat 'em as such, and rob 'em of the liberty of entertaining any other Nation but your own. (1:41)][42]

The speech was copied from the English translation of Lahontan by Cadwallader Colden for his *The History of the Five Indian Nations*. From there it found its way into anthologies of Native American oratory, and it is quoted and analyzed in histories of Iroquoian-English relations such as Daniel Richter's. Yet Lahontan's text of the "harangue" is totally different from that contained in the official text of the negotiations preserved in the French colonial archives, a discrepancy that another leading historian of the Iroquois, Francis Jennings, believes results from La Barre's effort to portray his expedition as more successful than it was.[43] Still more troubling is Lahontan's own ambiguous admission that his translation of the speech may not be exact. In a preface he writes:

> le Lecteur est prié de ne pas trouver mauvais que les pensées des Sauvages soient habillées à l'Européane; c'est la faute du Parent à qui j'écrivois, car ce bon homme ayant tourné en ridicule la Harangue métaphorique de la Grand-gula, il me pria de ne plus traduire à la letter un langage si rempli de fictions & d'hiperboles sauvages; c'est ce

qui fait que tous les raisonnements de ces Peuples paroistront icy selon
la diction & le stile des Euopéans. (not paginated in original; Ouellet,
794–95)

[I would not have the Reader to take it amiss, that the thoughts of the
Savages are set forth in an European Dress. The occasion of that choice
proceeded from the Relation I Corresponded with; for that honest
Gentleman ridiculed the Metaphorical Harangue of the Grangula;
and intreated me not to make a literal Translation of a Language that ✓
was so stuff'd with Fictions and Savage Hyperboles. 'Tis for this reason
that all the Discourses and Arguments of those Nations, are here
accomodated to the European Style and way of Speaking.]

In the French edition this preface appears at the beginning of the third
volume, the *Suite des Voyages*, which contains the *Dialogues*. In this position the disclaimer must be read as an explanation of why Adario speaks
with so much familiarity of French customs and philosophical issues,
and, coming long after Grangula's speech in the first volume, it does not
necessarily comment on its authenticity. But in the English translation
this preface comes at the beginning of the entire work and thus throws
doubt on the accuracy of a translation he may have altered in response to
his "Parent's" objections. The anthologies of Native American oratory
offer no such disclaimers; Otreouti is presented as speaking directly to
the reader, as if without an interpreter and without historical distance
and uncertainty.[44] In the histories of the Iroquois, the dialogue with La
Barre and the military situation enter into the scene, but the authenticity of the words is still assumed. We must acknowledge that problems of translation and authenticity are pervasive in this speech, not
only between Onondaga and French, but between French and English,
between European and American Indian values of oratory, and between
the imaginations of different readers. Lahontan claims that he had a
specific listener for Grangula, his purported relative in France who is the
addressee of the letters of *Nouveaux voyages*. Yet this relative may be a
rhetorical device. The metaphorical and hyperbolic style of the Grangula's eloquence, such as the references to the "Tree of Peace," the style
that many readers still expect and admire in Indian oratory, may already

have been refigured into metaphors familiar to European readers. Finding ethnological truth, or determining what is "authentically" Indian, may appear simple at first glance, but it is fraught with paradoxes and uncertainties, including the differences of rhetoric and metaphor in different languages. The voice of Grangula is at once Other and a projection of the self through the Other, for as a celebrated instance of Indian oratory, it fulfills Euroamerican ideals of a defiant chief, a cherished image that is in part a projection of desires for an independence and bravery not available in one's own society. Grangula may not be much more "authentic" than Adario.

It was not only Lahontan or other explorer-ethnographers who learned from and began to act like the *sauvages*, and it was not only egalitarian virtues that they learned. In his account of William Phips's 1690 attack on Quebec, Lahontan wrote of the French defenders: "Comme avec une si petite troupe il étoit impossible de se battre à découvert, il falut donc se resoudre de combattre à la maniére des Sauvages, c'est-à-dire dresser embuscade sur embuscade dans ce bois taillis. . . . Cette maniére de faire la guerre nous réüssit à merveilles" (1:214) [It being impossible for so small a Party to come to an open Battle with a numerous Enemy, they were forc'd to fight after the manner of the Savages, that is, to lay Ambuscadoes from place to place in the Copse. . . . This way of waging War prov'd wonderfully successful to us (1:163)]. As we shall see in Chapters 2 and 6, Lahontan may be wrong in calling these ambush tactics an Indian method, but the sense that learning and practicing Indian techniques were essential for victory not only in wars against the Indians, but also against other colonial armies, was an important one. Benjamin Church had already learned it and was soon to publish his writings on it (in 1716), but the lesson did not fully sink in among the Anglo-Americans until after the Seven Years' War. There was also a more insidious side to such cultural exchanges across the barrier dividing "savagism" from "civilization." Frontenac, the governor of New France, was said to have learned from the Iroquois the barbaric practice of torturing prisoners of war (although he could easily have learned it in Europe, where torture was used frequently). Lahontan quoted him answering his wife and the Jesuits' objections with the logic that "comme ces Barbares brûlent presque tous les François qui ont le malheur de tomber entre leurs mains, il falloit les traiter de la même maniére, puis que l'indulgence qu'on avoit eu pour eux jusqu'a present sembloit les autoriser de s'approcher de nos Plantations" (1:233–34) [since these Barbarians burnt almost all the French, who had the misfortune to fall into their Hands, they must be treated after the same manner, because the Indulgence which had hitherto been shown them, seem'd to authorize them to invade our Plantations (1:177)]. In New France, as in the English America analyzed by Pearce and Slotkin, the self-proclaimed forces of civilization felt no scruples about adopting the practices of savagery.

Although he spent less time among the Indians than many missionaries, Lahontan felt that his secular perspective made his work superior to those that Recollets and Jesuits had published in the seventeenth century. He attacked the previous accounts of the Indians in the first lines of his preface for "un défaut essentiel, c'est le manque de desinteressement & de sincerité" [an essential defect, that is the lack of disinterestedness and sincerity (my translation)]. Later he denounced the missionary writers specifically for poor ethnography: "ils se sont grossiérement trompez dans le recit qu'ils font des mœurs, des maniéres, &c. des Sauvages" (2:91) [they are widely mistaken in their Accounts of the Manners and Customs of the Savages" (2:2)]. But he noted that only his own experience enabled him to set right their false accounts: "Si je n'avois pas entendu la langue des Sauvages, j'aurois pû croire tout ce qu'on a écrit à leur égard" (2:92) [Had I been unacquainted with the Language of the Savages, I might have credited all that was said of them (2:3)]. Lahontan expresses the reasons why I have concentrated in this study on the writings of secular explorers rather than the fine ethnographies by missionaries. By looking out for his own interests rather than those of a religious order, Lahontan projects sincerity. Although for ethnological accuracy they are equal to Lahontan and the best secular observers, the *Jesuit Relations* are often written in the collective voice of a group of missionaries, each of whom had foresworn worldly ambitions in favor of the goal of converting the Indians. Therefore, like settlement histories such as Bradford's that claim the voice of a group of settlers, the

Jesuit Relations do not really fit the exploration-ethnography genre, which was written by individual explorers who often claimed to be independent of European religions, ideologies, and even nations.

To understand the texts of Lahontan and the other explorer-ethnographers, one needs to problematize what may seem to be commonsense distinctions between history and fiction, between anthropological facts and ethnocentric stereotypes, between the authentic voice of a Native American and the speech attributed to a fictional character. Lahontan did not simply record eyewitness observations of indigenous Indian cultures, nor did he impose colonial preconceptions on them; he learned from native cultures, taught others about them, and applied his knowledge toward a better understanding of French and colonial society. One must also understand how Lahontan manipulated the conventions of exploration narrative and of ethnography, such as the different value each genre placed on specific empirical observations.

The following chapters analyze other texts in the genre I call "exploration ethnographies" of colonial America and continue the examination of what these writers learned from Indians and what the lessons meant for their readers and for their successors in the colonies. Unlike anthropologists, I am not concerned with determining as accurately as possible the traditions and customs of these people. As Edward Said writes at the outset of his study *Orientalism* (a discourse that awaits a comparison with "savagism"), "The things to look at are style, figures of speech, setting, narrative devices, historical and social circumstances, not the correctness of the representation or its fidelity to some great original" (21). It is the patterns of European representations of the *sauvages* that are my topic, the codes of perception and expression in colonial writing about Native Americans. The explorer-ethnographers all spent substantial time living with American Indians. Their eyewitness accounts are the source for much of what we know or ever can know about many Indian cultures, at the same time that their peculiar ways of describing the Indians reveal many misunderstandings.

In trying to escape the dilemma between a methodology that aims to recapture the cultural perspective of Native Americans and one that works within the perspective of the colonists, I have also been forced to strike a balance on another issue: between the analysis of individual writers such as Lahontan and the analysis of representations of the Indians that can be studied only through the collation of many writers' texts. In the next chapter I compare the careers and the writings of leaders of early French and English settlements, John Smith and Samuel de Champlain. The third chapter addresses the rhetoric of the exploration-ethnography genre of which Smith and Champlain are two early practitioners. In the second half of the book I discuss the representations of Indian cultures and behavior by following some of the categories frequently used in the ethnographies, such as clothing and warfare. These chapters frequently resort to a cut-and-paste exploitation of sources, because the existence of an Indian custom, or of a colonial impression of that custom, can be demonstrated only by the accumulation of examples from several texts. Moreover, the number of eyewitness sources in any one region is often so limited, and the diversity of different tribes so great, that one is often forced to consider evidence that does not all derive from a single tribe or region within a brief span of time. In any case, the corroboration of several observers is not necessarily a technique for establishing ethnological fact, for frequently the descriptions of different nations by different writers are so similar that it seems likely that the later authors copied the earlier texts, and instances of direct copying are numerous. Rather than discard such plagiarized information as unreliable, one needs to consider why the writers felt the need to copy it. My goal is not to construct an accurate image of Indian dress or trading practices or adoption of prisoners, but to show how each of these ethnographic categories is problematized by the different ways that Indians and Europeans conceived of and separated the ideas of gifts and money, clothing and ornament, writing and pictures, punishment and compensation, and even of the empirical and received knowledge from which the ethnological information is derived.

Writing in English about French and English exploration narratives and accounts of the Indians, I intend to introduce specialists in American literature to some of the fascinating texts of colonial New France, and to help bridge the national and linguistic divide that exists in North American scholarship. If this project for a broader early North American literature succeeds, the field will be forced to redefine itself in light of the challenges the French texts will pose to existing conceptions. The study of Native American cultures at the time of colonial contact will be encouraged to consider the rhetorical and literary patterns followed by the writers who provide the documentary information.

CHAPTER 2

John Smith and Samuel de Champlain

Founding Fathers and Their Indian Relations

The careers of John Smith and Samuel de Champlain, popular "founding fathers" of the French and English colonies in North America, are so uncannily similar that they invite comparison, and such a comparison offers a good point of departure for an attempt to integrate the study of colonial American literature in the two languages. More than merely the leaders of initial seventeenth-century colonies in Virginia and Quebec, each man, through his extensive historical and promotional writing, succeeded in identifying his own fate with that of the colony to the point where the former nearly subsumes the latter. Despite the existence of many narratives by other colonists such as William Strachey, Edward Maria Wingfield, George Percy, and Henry Spelman,[1] Smith's narratives have become central to the history of the Virginia colony up to the 1622 "Massacre," "the slandered Smith becomes, in his own writings, the best synechdoche for slandered Virginia."[2] Or, as Wayne Franklin puts it, still more portentously, Smith "embodies in his own condition the ruin of a colonial ideal" (188). Champlain's story, which has fewer competing narrators for the history of his colony than does Smith, similarly becomes the story of Quebec up through the brief conquest by the English under David Kirke in 1629.

Due to the stature of these founding father figures, history and textuality meet and intertwine, and it becomes necessary to analyze not only the historical circumstances in which Smith and Champlain found themselves in America, but also the image that each man sought to create of himself through his writings and the spin that subsequent nationalist histories have given to them. Most important, I believe that both were strongly influenced by Indian leaders whom they faced in battles and power struggles, leaders who contributed to the ideas of authority that Smith and Champlain deployed in the colonies and in their writings, even as they in part misunderstood these native adversaries. Much as Lahontan learned from the natives about alternatives to French society and dramatized this education in the dialogue with Adario, Smith and Champlain learned from Indian leaders about how power could be maintained in America. And just as Adario is a projected representation of Lahontan's acquired "Indian" values, Smith and Champlain's foes are alter egos of the leaders who write about them. The first half of this chapter examines the two men's historical reputations, which have complicated the reception of their texts even more than Lahontan's. The second half turns to an analysis of episodes and illustrations from their books that reveal the impact of the Native American leaders, particularly Smith's great rival, Powhatan.

The French had attempted to settle at Quebec in the sixteenth century, and the English Roanoke colony of 1587 had mysteriously vanished in the area southeast of Jamestown. Samuel de Champlain and John Smith, therefore, have the mystique of founders because their colonies were the first of each nation that survived continuously to the present, but also because they published so much about their efforts. Smith published more writing about America than any previous Englishman; Champlain's collected works are comparable only to Lescarbot among French colonial writers of the early seventeenth century. Moreover, there are striking similarities in the form of the publications of Captain Smith and Captain Champlain (as he is called in the title of the 1620 edition of his third book). Smith published three accounts of Virginia, each longer than the previous one and incorporating more geographic, ethnographic, and historical material around his own explo- ✓ rations: *The True Relation of such occurences and accidents of noate as hath hapned in Virginia since the first planting of that Collony . . .* (1608), *A Map of Virginia* (1612), and *The Generall Historie of Virginia, New England, and the Summer Isles* (1624). *A Map*, as explained in its full title, is comprised of "A Description of the countrey, the Commodities, People, Government and Religion" and a second part, "The Proceedings of those Colonies, since their first departure from England, with the discourses, Orations, and relations of the Savages." Thus Smith conceived this book in the hybrid generic model so common in colonial literature—divided between a historical narrative and a description of land, flora, fauna, and native peoples. Yet only this one of all Smith's publications followed that form.

Champlain also published three increasingly lengthy travel narratives, and his works are also unusual for not explicitly dividing description from narrative. The first, *Des Sauvages, ou Voyage de Samuel Champlain, de Brouage, fait en la France nouvelle* (1603) [On the "Sauvages," or Voyage of Samuel Champlain, of Brouage, Made in the New France], is a brief, spare account of that same summer's trip to the St. Lawrence and includes a short ethnographic section. *Les Voyages du Sieur de Champlain Xaintongeois* (1613) [The Voyages of Mr. Champlain of Xaintonge] (these two titles include the names of Champlain's hometown and region in western France near La Rochelle) covers the establishment of the Port Royal colony on the Bay of Fundy and explorations of the New England coast in 1604–7, and then the founding of Quebec, battles with the Iroquois, and the establishment on a firm footing of the fur trade during the years 1608–11. In 1619 he published *Les Voyages et Descouvertures du Sieur de Champlain* [The Voyages and Discoveries of Mr. Champlain], narrating further adventures in the Great Lakes area, battles with the Hurons against the Iroquois, and the beginnings of missionary work among the Indians. Champlain's first three books are contiguous, not overlapping like Smith's. However, his final work, *Les Voyages de la Nouvelle France Occidentale* (1632) [The Voyages of Western

New France], resembles Smith's *Generall Historie* (as well as Lescarbot's and Sagard's histories) in that Champlain compiles accounts by earlier French voyagers to North America since Cartier, reprises his own previous accounts in condensed form, and continues the story of the colony down to the date of publication.

Both were men of well-to-do but not noble families who rose to positions of power through their colonial service. Both acquired training in war and seamanship before setting out for North America. Champlain fought against the Spanish in the 1590s, then commanded Spanish West Indian trade vessels around the turn of the century. Smith was shipwrecked in the Mediterranean, fought in Transylvania, was captured by the Turks, enslaved in Tartary, and escaped to travel overland across Russia and Europe back to England. Each man's account of his early adventures has been received with skepticism by historians. Champlain's *Brief discours des choses plus remarquables que Samuel de Champlain de Brouage a reconneues aux Indes occidentalles au voyage qu'il en a faict en icelles en l'année 1599 et en l'année 1601* [Brief discourse of the most remarkable things that Samuel de Champlain of Brouage encountered in the West Indies on a voyage that he made there in 1599 and 1601] is a fifty-page travel narrative and natural history illustrated with sixty-two of his drawings. It was not published until 1859, and twentieth-century scholars have questioned its veracity because the log of the Spanish fleet commander under whom Samuel served does not match Champlain's itinerary of the voyage.[3] Smith's autobiography, *The True Travels, Adventures, and Observations of Captaine John Smith, in Europe, Asia, Africa, and America, from Anno Domini 1593 to 1629* (1630), repeats again the story of his Jamestown exploits and adds to it an account of his eastern European adventures so amazing that many have doubted its accuracy. Finally, each man published a short navigational primer, Champlain's being included in his 1632 history and Smith's, *An Accidence or the Pathway to Experience: Necessary for All Young Seamen, or Those That Are Desirous to Goe to Sea* and its glossary, *A Sea Grammar, with the Plaine Exposition of Smiths Accidence for Young Sea-men, Enlarged*, published separately in 1626 and 1627.

Though best known for Quebec and Virginia, the paths of the two adventurers both passed through New England (or "Norumbega," as Champlain called it) in the early 1600s before the Pilgrims and Puritans arrived, and the two may even have stood on the same spot in Plymouth Harbor or "Port St. Louis"—Champlain in July 1605, Smith in August 1614.[4] The major difference between the two careers is that Champlain remained in command of his colony until his death, whereas Smith lost control of Virginia after only a brief presence. Smith died in England in 1631, Champlain in Quebec on Christmas Day, 1635.

Smith and Champlain were not only the greatest leaders and leading writers of their respective colonies; each was also a first-rate cartographer. Their works provide not merely exploration narrative but maps and guides to the parts of North America known to Europeans in the early seventeenth century. They reach beyond the linear knowledge of the empiricist traveler toward a two-dimensional representation and control of the land surface that was the basis of colonial domination. Reading *A Map of Virginia* or *The Description of New England* entails reading the text *and* examining the map. And this verbal/visual intertext involves not only maps but also images: Powhatan on his throne and the classicized Susquehannock warrior (adapted from John White via Theodor deBry) on the 1612 map of Virginia, and the five scenes of Indian life and of Smith's heroic battles with Opechancanough and with the Paspehegh chief in the tableau published with the *Generall Historie* (fig. 1). Champlain was an even more accurate and assiduous map maker and had been employed as a cartographer on his Caribbean voyages and on his first trip to Canada in 1603. His large-scale 1612 map of New France shows both Lake Ontario and Niagara Falls, based on his Indian informants' information, and the future Lake Champlain, the Gulf of St. Lawrence, and the New England coast from his own exploration. It was likely a source for Smith's map of New England. As Thoreau noted in *Cape Cod*: "Most of the maps of this coast made for a long time after betray their indebtedness to Champlain. He was a skilful navigator, a man of science, and geographer to the King of France" (1009). Thoreau also claimed that Smith and Champlain were the only visitors who correctly described Cape Cod as a sandy, barren place, rather than as a densely wooded land with fertile soil.

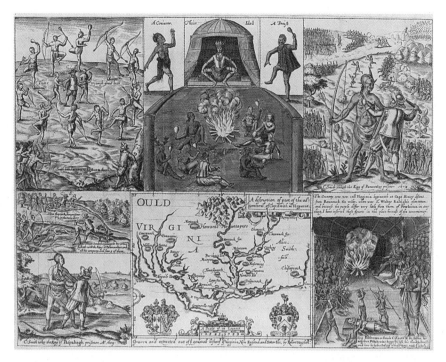

FIGURE 1. John Smith, Map of "Ould Virginia," from the *Generall Historie*, 1624. Top right panel has the caption, "C. Smith taketh the King of Pamaunkee prisoner, 1608." Bottom left has the caption, "C. Smith takes the King of Paspahegh prisoner, 1609." Top left shows "Their triumph about him" and below that, "C. Smith bound to a tree to be shott to death, 1607." Bottom right reads: "King Powhatan commands C. Smith to be slayne, his daughter Pokahontas beggs his life his thankfullness and how he subjected 39 of their kings." The illustration was done by Robert Vaughn, who copied the Indian scenes from Theodor deBry's *Virginia* of 1590. (Beinecke Rare Book and Manuscript Library, Yale University)

Smith's books feature illustrations printed alongside the maps, but Champlain integrates images of events into the cartographic representation at the place where they occurred. The harbor charts he drew during his coastal explorations of Norumbega and Quebec show, in miniature, Indian dwellings, fields, and fishing weirs; they employ a legend of letters to indicate the site of anchorages, watering places, and skirmishes between the French explorers and the natives (note the letters of the legend in the canoes and by the two slain Mohawks in fig. 2). These

FIGURE 2. Samuel de Champlain, "Deffaite des Yroquois" [defeat of the Iroquois], from *Les Voyages du Sieur de Champlain*, 1613. (From the copy in the Rare Book Collection, University of North Carolina at Chapel Hill)

charts are astonishingly accurate—one can locate the harbors by shape alone, claims mariner and historian Samuel Eliot Morison in his biography of Champlain. In addition to these charts, Champlain drew several illustrations of battles in which he participated, in a naive yet clear style. The juxtaposition of map and picture without regard to scale was common at the time, but Champlain is distinctive for creating a narrative storyboard effect by combining map and description, image and narration to complete a discursive mastery of the land and its inhabitants.[5] It has been suggested that his skill at ethnographic observation may derive from his first career: "From an anthropologist's point of view his chief merit was his ability to observe detail, which perhaps reflects his training as a cartographer."[6]

This neat complementary relationship between ethnography and ethnological illustrations can be problematic, however. Because all we have are the engravings in the books, we cannot with certainty attribute the illustrations to the hand of Champlain or of Smith. Comparisons reveal that the engravers of each had recourse to the popular deBry engravings published in the *America* series in the 1590s. For Smith's *Generall Histo-rie*, for example, the engraver took an image from John White's depic-tions of Indian customs reproduced in the deBry volume, which in-cluded Hariot's *A Briefe and True Report* (fig. 3), and inserted Smith into the scene (fig. 1, upper left panel). Although White had represented "A Religious Dance" and the caption in deBry suggests that it is a summer-time fertility festival, after Smith is grafted onto the scene it becomes a savage dance of triumph held to intimidate a captive. The dancers who carried leafy branches and gourd rattles in the original now hold bows and arrows and clubs. In the White/deBry version the three figures in the center of the circle are "three of the most beautiful virgins," whereas Smith and two captors replace them in the Smith version. The "tall posts carved into faces resembling those of veiled nuns," as the caption de-scribes them, disappear from Smith's illustration, replaced by the tree to which the captain is bound in the image at the bottom of the frame. This manipulated and manipulative image has been used to perpetuate the idea of American Indians as savage captors and torturers, for it has been adapted several times in illustrations for volumes of captivity narratives, such as John Frost's.[7] The substitution of the captive Smith for the beautiful virgins might be seen as the converse of Smith's insertion of the story of the virgin Pocahontas, who saves him from death in the account of his captivity in the 1624 *Generall Historie*, but is not men-tioned in either earlier version. These are just two examples of a pattern whereby Smith's self-possession and autobiographical independence are revealed to be a ruse, an impression created by the manipulation of many other individuals, both allies and rivals, whose words and representa-tions are recast and focused on Smith himself. In *The Proceedings of the English Colonie* and its later version in the third book of the *Generall Historie*, Smith collected or simply attributed short testimonial and narrative accounts from other colonists that tell of his exploits from an "objective" but rarely critical third-person perspective. These attribu-tions differ slightly in the two versions and in at least one instance cannot be accurate (1:214, note 10). In Champlain, we will see an in-verse process: his illustrations and narratives placed him as if in the eye of a hurricane, deflecting attention and blame onto surrounding figures so as to leave Champlain as a stable yet self-effacing center.

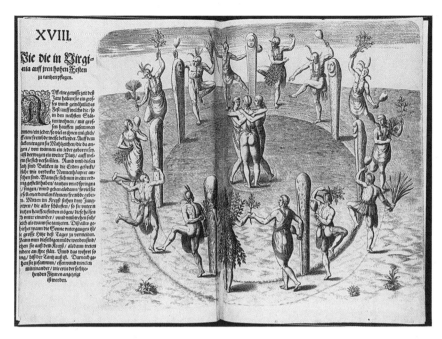

FIGURE 3. "The dances at their great feasts," from Theodor deBry's illustrated edition of Thomas Hariot's *A Briefe and True Report of the New Found Land of Virginia*, published in Frankfurt in 1590. The engraving was done from a watercolor by John White. (National Library of Canada, NL-19255)

Many students of American literature and history have a basic familiarity with John Smith and an impression of him that almost certainly includes notions like egocentric, ambitious, industrious, ruthless, and self-congratulating. Perhaps this will change in light of the highly inaccurate portrait of him as the hero of the animated Disney feature *Pocahontas*. The popular historical image of Champlain is virtually the opposite: modest, patient, a negotiator who put the success of his colony ahead of his own fame and fortune. These two men, whose career paths, historical significance, and bibliographies are so uncannily similar, are perceived to have personalities that are polar opposites. Yet, of course, these personalities are only the artifacts of the two contrasting strategies of representation. In his images Champlain did not try to dominate the scene; rather, he worked subtly and avoided leaving the impression that his narratives were constructed to promote his own interests in the colonial project. Smith, on the other hand, wrote mostly from England

and tried repeatedly to present himself as the man whose skills were essential to the success of upcoming colonization projects. I wish to argue that the leadership style each portrayed in accounts of his activities in America was largely a consequence of his conception of the Indian leaders who treated with and fought against him. Each projected an ideal of independence and self-possession; each claimed that the success of the colony lay on his shoulders, but this only concealed the influence of his Native American counterpart. Moreover, each presented himself as a commander of the same type as this counterpart, when in fact his situation was quite different.

Champlain's style was better suited to the economic basis of the Quebec colony than was Smith's to Virginia. New France was built on the fur trade, an activity that required good relations with Indians who killed the beavers and carried the pelts great distances to market. Champlain, although he often clashed with fur-trading interests, nevertheless built an initial base of trust with the Montagnais and Hurons, which ensured safe passage for French traders. Champlain held on to his leadership for more than twenty years because he facilitated the most profitable way to exploit Quebec's resources, whereas Smith's downfall can be attributed to his unorthodox economic vision, which resisted tobacco, the product that proved to be foundational for Virginia. Though a Native American plant, tobacco required no cooperation from the Indians, only their land. Smith's success at winning concessions from Powhatan was no longer valuable once the colony could feed and defend itself from the natives beyond the "fall-line." That Smith, like King James, was hostile toward tobacco and feared that Virginia might be too dependent on it partly explains why he never was able to return to the colony to reclaim his leadership. John Rolfe, who had taken Pocahontas for his wife, took up the "tawny weed" also; he imported seeds from South America to improve quality, and the market in tobacco boomed. Smith complained in *The True Travels* that in Virginia "everie one is so applyed to his labour about Tobacco and Corne, which doth yeeld them such a profit, they never regard any food from the Salvages; nor have they any trade or conference with them, but upon meere accidents and defiances" (3:216). The skills that Smith used to save the colony in its first

Henry adams accused Smith of fabrication?

years were no longer deemed important. John Seelye has cast Smith as a scorned prophet, writing that the rejection of "The authoritarian, fortress-dominated colony that was Smith's ideal" in favor of a tobacco monoculture was a mistake, because "By the end of the century Virginians had converted the Indian weed and Indian rivers to an economy of waste, one requiring a system that depended on the labor of slaves" (86–87). Smith's ideas for profitable colonial industries also fell on deaf ears in New England. In the *Description of New England*, Smith had imagined that the northern Anglo-American colony would thrive on the fisheries of the George's Bank, but the fur trade proved to be more profitable than fishing for the Plymouth colony.[8]

Arguably, Smith and Champlain also represent the colonial genesis of minority cultures and literatures within postcolonial nations, Champlain of French Canada and Smith of the Old South. But attitudes toward Champlain do not divide along regional or language lines, and his status as a founding father is not limited to Francophone Canada, though it is not pervasive. In his biography of Champlain, Morris Bishop made a frank appeal for his subject as Canada's national hero: "This book is, in some small way, an act of admiration and love. The author's chief hope is that it may arouse in others an answering admiration and love for the founder and father of Canada, the patron of her spirit, her Hero" (x). Canadian historians Marcel Trudel and Narcisse-E. Dionne also celebrate Champlain, though others such as Bruce Trigger are more critical.[9] In any case, judging by the number of places named for him, Champlain is less of a hero in Quebec than is Jacques Cartier, the first Frenchman to attempt to colonize Canada.

Smith's reputation, on the other hand, has long been tied to sectional interests. In 1867 Henry Adams published an essay in the *North American Review* accusing Smith of fabricating the tale of Pocahontas saving his life.[10] This was the culmination of extensive research designed to discredit the South and aid the Union war effort. John Gorham Palfrey, author of a five-volume *History of New England* (1858–92), invited Adams to write the essay because it "would attract as much attention, and probably break as much glass, as any other stone that could be thrown by a beginner,"[11] and Adams in a letter to Palfrey admitted that

political model

he was writing a piece of propaganda, "a rear attack, on the Virginia aristocracy, who will be utterly gravelled by it if it is successful" (1:287– 88). There was a great deal at stake, for "By the mid-nineteenth century Captain John Smith was as well known to Americans as any figure from American history, save, possibly, George Washington."[12] Smith's reputation suffered from this and from the 1890 work of Lewis L. Kropf, who claimed that the Transylvanian adventures in the *True Travels* were also fabricated. Laura Polyani Striker in 1953 and Philip Barbour in the 1980s have recuperated Smith's autobiography as fact, and since then, American academic opinion has been again divided on largely regional lines. Northerners, among them Francis Jennings, Gary B. Nash, and Karen Kupperman, have denounced Smith's treatment of the Indians (though all agree that the worst abuses occurred in the aftermath of the 1622 massacre at Jamestown, long after Smith's departure). Defenders of Smith include his editor and biographer Philip Barbour and J. Leo Lemay, author of the most recent book-length study of Smith, which makes a case for his hero status as strongly as Bishop does for Champlain. It would be unfair to attribute this to anti-Yankee chauvinism, however. Southerners understandably embrace Smith as a Virginia counterweight to the long-standing dominance of New England Puritan literature in the Early American field.

All defenders and some detractors of Smith acknowledge him as a prototypical American hero: proud, self-reliant, and disdainful of class privilege. Smith deserves the credit he receives as a founder of American pioneer ideology, as one can sense in this passage from *A Description of New England*: "Who can desire more content, that hath small meanes; or but only his merit to advance his fortune, than to tread, and plant that ground hee hath purchased by the hazard of his life?" (1:343). The issue of Smith's character and his status as a model American should arise not only from the question of whether or not he was a liar, whether or not a brutal imperialist, but also from his role among the jealous, greedy, and class-riven Jamestown colonists, and the way in which his texts recount and enact his strategies to maintain power there. Like the Revolutionary Founding Fathers for whom he serves as a typological forebear, Smith is a *political* model. The Virginia texts demonstrate the turbulence of a

why did he construct his texts in this way?

democratic society sensitive to public opinion and demagogic leadership. In the "starving time" of 1609, just after Smith's departure, mar-
tial law was imposed to quell mutinies in fractious Jamestown. Smith
himself was first brought ashore in Virginia as a prisoner and later
threatened by Gabriel Archer with hanging, only to rally his supporters
and defeat John Ratcliffe in the election for president of the council. He
was always sensitive of his public image, not only among his readers but
also among the other colonists. His rugged individualism was constructed, in part, from the reports of his exploits ostensibly written by
others. The Captain Smith persona was and is created through these
reports much like the image of a politician in American democracy, at
least since the propagandistic campaign biographies of the Jacksonian
era. Yet Smith biographers and critics rarely discuss the issue of why he
chose to construct his texts in this way, or whether his subordinates Anas
Todkill, Thomas Studley, William Phettiplace, and others really did
write the chapters attributed to them, and if so, at whose request.[13]
Smith shows not only the idealistic side of American democracy, but its
less attractive, contentious side as well. As Hannah Arendt has written:
"the well-known arguments of the Founding Fathers against democratic
government hardly ever mention its egalitarian character; the objection
to it was that ancient history and theory had proved the 'turbulent'
nature of democracy, its instability" (225). The first years of the Virginia
colony form part of this turbulent history just as Roman history does,
and Smith's status as a founding father represents not only his contempt
for class privilege but also his cunning political technique, an aggressive, despotic style that mirrors his image of his adversary Powhatan.

Compared with Smith, Champlain projects an image of a colony in
serene consensus, a small, close-knit group that submitted to a benevolent ruler. Champlain was not the leader of a colony until 1608 (the
same year Smith was elected president of the council), and ever after that
he was obliged to enforce fur trade monopolies granted by the Crown to
La Rochelle merchants the de Caen brothers and to the Company of the
Hundred Associates. Smith wrote his *True Travells* and most of his other
works in the third person, grammatically reflecting attention on himself. By contrast, in his early texts Champlain disguises his subordinate

status by effacing both himself and his commanders from his discourse. *Des Sauvages* is related mostly in the first person plural, and Champlain's name never appears after the title page.[14] Where the first person singular pronoun does appear in this brief text, Champlain is not narrating his exploits but giving his impressions of the Indians. After 1618 Champlain gave up exploration, and in his 1632 work he presents himself more like Smith, as the man on whom the fate of the colony depended. Still, in reading his works one is struck by this independent yet self-effacing style, which suppresses politics as it hides the author's subjectivity and turns one's attention away from the colonists and toward the Indians.

Along with the economic, the historiographic, and the political contrasts between Smith and Champlain there is, of course, religion. It is tempting to equate Champlain's secure leadership of the colony of New France to the authority of Catholicism in the French court and colonies, and to equate Smith's fractious power struggles in Virginia to separatist strife in seventeenth-century England. However, one must consider the political and religious aspects of the colonies separately before comparing them. In 1615 Champlain chose the Recollets from his hometown of Brouage to accompany him to Quebec, and this order, which included Gabriel Sagard, was the dominant religious presence until 1625, when Champlain acquiesced to the Jesuits' request to begin missions in Canada. Huguenots (and some Catholic fur traders) were opposed to Champlain not because they wanted a role as missionaries in his colony, but because they opposed the colony altogether. Huguenots owned many of the fishing and trading vessels that frequented the St. Lawrence, and their business, trading directly with the Indians at the shore, proceeded just fine without the additional expenses of the royal mandate to bring new settlers to Champlain's colony. The de Caen brothers, who were granted the trading concession in 1621, had strong Protestant ties and did little to support Champlain. Protestant traders were able to flout the ban against their faith that was instituted in 1627, so if they felt a real threat, it was an economic not a religious one.

Smith too was caught between the religious factions in the colonies. Though he was less patrician and more self-disciplined than a stereo-

was an Anglican Smith Powhatan
was not a
Puritan.

JOHN SMITH AND SAMUEL DE CHAMPLAIN   63

typical Virginia Cavalier such as William Byrd II, he was not a Puritan.
As is clear in his pamphlet *New Englands Trials* (1622), Smith was
enthusiastic about the Plymouth colonists' prospects not because he
supported their religious goals, but simply because he thought they
were well situated and well organized to exploit the potential wealth of
the coastal cod fisheries. Smith offered his services to the Plymouth
colonists and was rejected, probably because he was an Anglican who
did not share their separatist views.

We have still failed to account for the contrasting images of Smith
and Champlain's personalities and Indian policies. The "national character" explanation reduced to the difference between tobacco and the fur
trade. Regional chauvinism and the political structure of text and colony explained the uncertain status of Smith and Champlain as "founding fathers." And although both leaders faced opposition from members
of antagonistic religious sects, they were essentially secular in their
motives and actions. The fourth axis of cultural difference, and the most
suggestive, was that between the Indian nations among whom Smith
and Champlain traveled and their respective leadership. Here again,
geographic influences were important. The native nations around Quebec and Jamestown were all Algonquian peoples, but the different cli-
mates had produced different subsistence strategies and demographic
patterns. The rich agricultural potential of Virginia allowed for a relatively dense and stable population that supported Powhatan's opulence
and enabled him to consolidate an "empire" of tribute nations, a situation Smith described: "his will is a law and must bee obeyed; not only as
a king but as halfe a God they esteem him" (1:174).[15] In Quebec, the
Algonquians relied more on hunting and trade for their subsistence;
each winter they dispersed in small groups of a few families each to hunt
moose, beavers, and other game. No despotic rule over a large population was possible, and in any case Champlain traversed a region far larger
than the Chesapeake area as he traveled up the St. Lawrence and Ottawa
Rivers and around Lake Ontario.

For the most part, this contrast between Smith and Champlain must
be drawn out of their own writings and the colonial history around
them, but Champlain is also represented in Native Americans' own

history. At the beginning of his autobiography, Black Hawk, the Sauk leader famous for his defiance of U.S. troops in Illinois territory in 1831–32, recounts a history of the encounter of his ancestors with a French explorer in the lower St. Lawrence who, though unnamed, could well be Champlain. Although it is also difficult to identify this encounter in Champlain's narratives, it resembles several episodes. According to Black Hawk, the Great Spirit appeared in dreams to both the French leader and to Black Hawk's great-grandfather, foretelling the arrival of a white man on the banks of a great river and designating him as a father to the Sauk. The Frenchman used his wealth of trade goods to anoint Na-na-ma-kee, a younger son of a chief, as his chosen leader, awarding him clothing, guns, cooking pots, and a medal such as English colonists commonly gave native leaders in the eighteenth century. What most strongly suggests that this Frenchman is Champlain is that he uses trade to establish a position of trust and backs it up with promises: "having given them a large quantity of goods, as presents, and every other thing necessary for their comfort, he set sail for France, after promising to meet them again, at the same place after the twelfth moon" (44).

Already we can see a contrast between the self-conscious authority in Smith's Virginia, codified in councils and elections and jealous of its prerogatives, and a leadership in Quebec that presented itself as based on exchanges and mutual recognition with local Amerindian leaders. Smith and Champlain were formed in the images we have of them, the images created in their texts, by the influence of local Indians. The way each saw himself was a function of his impression of the Indian leaders who were his counterparts. This is not a direct reflection, however, but a process of misinterpretation. Smith fashioned himself after Powhatan and Opechancanough and imagined that he should become a leader in their style, when in fact his authority in the Jamestown colony was more democratic, in the good and bad senses, than despotic like the Powhatan he portrayed, and thus his psychological doubling with the two chiefs did not help him to maintain his control. Smith felt that he resisted and outwitted Powhatan, but it may have been Powhatan who controlled and created Smith in ways neither could be conscious of, given the enormous cultural difference between them. John Seelye appears to share this view when he writes of "a paradoxical dimension" in Smith's texts: "For Powhatan did nothing to Captain Smith that was not a reversal of what Smith intended for him, the Indian King, like his River, merely reflecting back the Captain's own countenance" (78). Ethnohistorians have suggested that Powhatan sought to use the English colonists to support his dominance in the region, or, what may amount to the same thing, that he offered to protect them in exchange for a steady supply of metal tools.[16] As pointed out in Chapter 1, Powhatan successfully enforced a monopoly on European trade goods; William Strachey wrote that "He doth by keeping us from trading with them monopolize all the Copper brought into Virginia by the English" (107). Champlain dealt with a series of less powerful regional chiefs in Quebec and fashioned himself a leadership style based on consensus and negotiation, such as he tried to achieve among the several tribes. If Champlain's style was more successful than Smith's (though he did make many mistakes), it was because he had fewer challengers to his authority, but also because the Indian leaders he dealt with held political positions that more closely resembled his own—a commander of small resources caught amid many powerful forces.

Smith internalized what he perceived as Powhatan's great power and cunning, but he did not revere him as a king. Smith was not a nobleman and complained in his writings that the power and privilege given to the gentlemen at Jamestown were unjust because they were not supported by practical skills or hard work. His image of Powhatan is in part a legitimation of his own claim to a power that transcends English class hierarchy. Christopher Newport, Smith's commander on the voyage to Virginia, did regard Powhatan as a king, and the differences between the two men's images of Powhatan demonstrate both the degree to which the ethnocentric gaze created an Indian that responded to the perspective of the observer and the opportunities that Powhatan had to learn how best to deal with each. Smith's second meeting with Powhatan (the first after his captivity) occurs when Newport sets out "to perfourme this strange discovery, but more strange coronation" (1:234; 2:181) of Powhatan and his kingdom.[17] Newport hoped to secure the allegiance and protection of Powhatan by conferring on him a European legitimation of his rule. Smith, as the president, argued against this project as a waste of time and supplies, but the council overruled him. Smith went to invite Powhatan to his own coronation, but Powhatan refused to come to the English fort, though he acknowledged his status as king: "If your king have sent me presents, I also am a king, and this my land, 8 daies I will stay to receave them. Your father is to come to me, not I to him, nor yet to your fort, neither will I bite at such a baite" (1:236; 2:183). Smith passed this message to Newport, who arrived with gifts to carry out a coronation ceremony. It was, according to Smith's reporter Anas Tod-kill, a farce: "But a fowle trouble there was to make him kneele to receave his crowne, he, neither knowing the majestie, nor meaning of a Crowne, nor bending of the knee, indured so many perswasions, examples, and instructions, as tired them all" (1:237; 2:184). Newport attempted to anglicize Powhatan, and to make him a tributary to the English king, by giving him a bed, basin, and cloak, much as Champlain acknowledged Na-na-ma-kee with gifts, but with quite different results. Champlain (if it was he) altered the Sauk power structure and improved his own status; Newport sought to cause Powhatan's power and his own to reinforce one another, to exchange ideals of monarchy, but he failed to communicate and failed to reap any benefit. Smith saw in Powhatan the cunning and skill by which he distanced himself from the dupe Newport and that he needed to outwit Newport, Ratcliffe, and Wingfield and gain control of the colony. His image of Powhatan was best summarized by the Indian Weraskoyack, who at the opening of the following chapter of *The Proceedings* says, "Captaine Smith, you shall finde Powhatan to use you kindly, but trust him not, and bee sure hee hath no opportunitie to seaze on your armes, for hee hath sent for you only to cut your throats" (1:244; 2:193). It was Powhatan's Machiavellian cunning more than his despotic rule that served as an effective model for Smith, and it was in the subsequent episode, the one Weraskoyack was warning about, that Smith and Powhatan emerged as psychological doubles, equally resourceful, egotistical, and suspicious.

Much of the scene at Werowocomoco is a dialogue between Smith and Powhatan and is therefore one of the most memorable and dramatic parts of Smith's writings. However, the reader should not imagine that this dialogue is a transcription of an actual conversation. There is no evidence that Smith in his two years in Virginia, including the three weeks in captivity, learned to speak Powhatan's dialect of Algonquian with such fluency as the dialogue displays. We should read the dialogue as a construction by Smith and/or Anas Todkill, even if one of the English *truchements* who did speak the native language well—Thomas Savage or Henry Spelman—was present to serve as an interpreter. The two voices are alter egos that converge on the same fears and desires; each recognizes in the other the desperate determination he has in himself. Powhatan drives a hard bargain for corn, asking forty swords for forty bushels. Smith is equally determined to either get a better price or simply steal the food. Powhatan has come to understand the threat Smith poses, a threat identical to the one that Smith heard from Weraskoyack: "for many doe informe me, your comming is not for trade, but to invade my people, and possesse my Country" (2:195; 1:247). Yet Powhatan also knows how necessary he is to the English: "what will it availe you," he asks, "to destroy them that provide you food? what can you get by war, when we can hide our provision and flie to the woodes, whereby you must famish by wronging us your friends" (1:247; 2:196). Smith needs Powhatan because he knows the English look to him as the only man who can deal with the Indian leader and because only Powhatan can summon the delivery of such large amounts of food. The enemies are bound to one another by common interests. Smith calls Powhatan his father, Powhatan pleads to Smith as his friend, but the conference is, we learn, merely a stalling tactic to enable Powhatan's men to prepare to attack Smith, kill him, and then flee, and for Smith's men to break the ice that blocks their barge from reaching the shore where they can attack Powhatan. The confrontation in the Virginia winter is a seventeenth-century cold war, where each side views itself through the frame of the threat posed by the other, and an ideology of polar opposition conceals many similarities between the two.

Champlain met and interacted with so many Indian leaders in his wide travels in Canada that there is no one who stands out as his counterpart or double, unless Na-na-ma-kee can be regarded as a synthesis of them all. The Micmac chief Membertou, leader of a band that lived near

Port Royal, plays a major role as an ally of the French in Champlain's Acadian narrative and is even more important in the 1616 Acadian memoir of the Jesuit Pierre Biard. On the St. Lawrence, however, Champlain tried to befriend each chief he met as a means of gaining assistance in his effort to penetrate farther west and north toward other nations and richer beaver hunting. One example of this process is the meeting with the Algoumequin sagamore Tessoüat at the Ile des Allumettes, near the site of modern Ottawa, in 1613.[18] The two did have more than a passing acquaintance, for it seems that Tessoüat had met Champlain far downstream at Tadoussac on his first visit to Canada in 1603, and when he sees him again is "tout estonné de me voir, & nous dit qu'il pensoit que je fusse un songe, & qu'il ne croyoit pas ce qu'il voyoit" (2:278) [much astonished at seeing me, telling us he thought I was a ghost, and that he could not believe his eyes].[19] Champlain, as is his usual tactic with the nations he passes through, offers a promise and asks a favor in return: "je leur fis entendre par mon Truchement que le subject de mon voyage n'estoit autre que pour les asseurer de mon affection, & du desir que j'avois de les assister en leurs guerres, comme j'avois auparavant faict" (2:283) [I explained to them through my interpreter, that the object of my journey was none other than to assure them of my affection, and of my desire to aid in their wars, as I had done previously]. Though he admits that the previous year he had not fulfilled his promise to go to war against the Iroquois, he nevertheless reiterates the promise and makes a request: "que je desirois voir une nation distant de 6 journees d'eux, nommée Nebicerini [Nipissing], pour les convier aussi à la guerre; & pource je les priay de me donner 4 Canots, avec huict sauvages pour me conduire esdictes terres" (2:284) [that I desired to visit a nation, distant six days' march from them, called the Nebicerini, in order to invite them also to go on the war-path, and that for this purpose I asked them to give me four canoes, with eight Indians to take me to that region].

Champlain, unlike Smith, does mention the interpreter, Thomas, through whom he is able to converse with Tessoüat and his nation. Indeed, the encounter soon focuses not on the two leaders but on a second *truchement*, Nicolas Vignau, who had spent a previous winter with Tessoüat's people.

Tessoüat at first agrees to provide the four canoes and the guides but then changes his mind and tries to dissuade Champlain from continuing his journey, warning of dangerous rapids and of the sorcery and poisonings that the Nebicerini nation could inflict on him. Tessoüat's true motive, Champlain was probably aware, was to preserve his status as middleman on the Ottawa River trade route, so that he could exact a toll from the Hurons and Ottawas coming downstream and from the French going upstream. As Sagard, when he followed Champlain's route through the Ottawa valley several years later, put it, "ces Epicerinys ne veulent pas mener de François seculiers en leur voyage, non plus que les Montagnais et Hurons n'en veulent point mener au Saguenet, de peur de descouvrir leur bonne et meilleure traitte, et le pays où ils vont amasser quantité de pelleteries" (110) [these Epicerinys are not willing to take lay Frenchmen on their journey, any more than the Montagnais and Hurons are willing to take them to the Saguenay, for fear of revealing the rich and most profitable source of their trading and the country to which they go to collect most of their furs (87)]. In this respect, Champlain and Tessoüat are doubled like Smith and Powhatan; each is trying to preserve a monopoly on trade. Champlain's impetus for northern exploration came from Vignau, who had told Champlain that he had traveled upstream and north all the way to Hudson Bay and had seen a captive Englishman, part of Henry Hudson's lost expedition of two years earlier. Champlain worried that the English might threaten the French trade advantage and wished to investigate. But Tessoüat and his people, seeking to prevent Champlain from forging trading relationships with upstream groups, swear that Vignau never went beyond their nation, that he had been lying to Champlain, and they attack the young man and insist that he be killed for his lies. Champlain, though very angry, prevents them from doing so.

The encounter between Smith and Powhatan was based on mutual mistrust, and dialogue was a screen for military maneuvers. The relationship between Champlain and Tessoüat was based on the mutual trust implied in the performative speech act of a promise. Champlain and Tessoüat exchanged promises, only to break them and seek a new equilibrium based on new promises. Champlain understood and followed Native American customs insofar as he recognized that a leader maintains his power largely through his generosity, creating goodwill obligations with the value of his gifts. Champlain tried to dissimulate on his own broken promises by telling Tessoüat's people "qu je les avois jusques à ce jour estimés hommes, & veritables, & que maintenant ils se monstroyent enfans, & mensongers, & que s'ils ne vouloient effectuer leurs promesses, ils ne me feroient paroistre leur amitié" (2:288) [that till then I had held them to be men and true to their word; but that now they were showing themselves children and liars, and that if they did not wish to keep their promises, they should not pretend to be my friends]. The narrative thus shifts the blame from Champlain, who did not fulfill his promise to go to war against the Iroquois the year before, to Vignau, who promised to lead Champlain to Hudson Bay when in fact he did not know how to get there. Champlain tells Vignau "s'il avoit veu ceste mer, que je luy ferois donner la recompense que je luy avois promise, & s'il ne l'avoit veuë, qu'il eut à me le dire sans me donner d'avantage de peine" (2:290) [that if he had seen this sea, I would have the promised reward given to him, and that if he had not seen it, he must tell me so, without giving me any more worry]. Champlain's text, though it does not collect praise around his heroic figure, is careful to shed blame, to direct it outward and thereby preserve his own credibility.

Let us now turn to the accounts of two battles that are fundamental to the reputations of Smith and Champlain and that are represented in the works of each by an engraving. The battles are perhaps the greatest moment of courage displayed by each of these "founding fathers" and the greatest success in the Indian relations policy pursued by each. Coincidentally, both events took place in the same year, 1609 (New Style, Smith's in January would be 1608 Old Style),[20] at a place that would later be made famous once again as a battlefield: Smith's at Pamaunkee (a Civil War battle site) in January, Champlain's on the lake to which he gave his name, near the site of the future Fort Ticonderoga (site

of pivotal battles in the Seven Years' War) in July. Smith's exploit is
described in the ninth chapter of *A Map of Virginia* and of the third book
of the *Generall Historie*, Champlain's in the ninth chapter of the second
part of *Les Voyages*.

Smith's confrontation with Opechancanough is also preceded by a
dialogue that reveals the mutual dependence of the foes: "You know my
want, and I your plenty, of which by some meanes I must have part,
remember it is fit for kings to keepe their promise" (1:251; 2:200).
Whereas Champlain made promises and then deferred them, Smith
turns the promise toward his foe and sharpens it with an implied threat.
The Powhatans bring some corn, but again the negotiations are a stalling
tactic, for "not long after came the king, who with a strained cheerefulnes
held us with discourse, what paines he had taken to keepe his promise; til
Master Russell brought us in news that we were all betraied: for at least
6. or 700. of well appointed Indians had invironed the house and beset
the fields" (1:215; 2:200). In a speech to his men Smith hesitates over a
strategy for how to neutralize his counterpart Opechancanough and
secure the food they came to trade for: "Should wee beginne with them
and surprise the King, we cannot keepe him and defend well our selves. If
wee should each kill our man, and so proceed with all in the house; the
rest will all fly: then shall wee get no more then the bodies that are slaine,
and so starve for victuall" (2:201; 1:251–52). Smith recognizes that he
will have to hold Opechancanough hostage to get his "victuall." His
solution is to remove the conflict from the scale of two mismatched
armies to the individual scale of a contest between two leaders. He
challenges Opechancanough to a duel and bets his trade goods against
the Indians' corn that he will win. It was Smith's most audacious act, to
scorn danger in the face of odds he describes to his men as follows: "As for
their fury it is the least danger; for well you know, being alone assaulted
with two or three hundred of them, I made them by the helpe of God
compound to save my life. And wee are sixteene, and they but seaven
hundred at the most" (2:201; 1:252). Smith emphasizes the overwhelming odds to stress his overwhelming strength. If he is equal to three
hundred, his fifteen soldiers with guns can handle the other four hun-

dred. In the illustrations surrounding the "Map of Ould Virginia" Smith takes the two chiefs prisoner in single combat, but where he is shown as a prisoner at least half a dozen Indians surround him.

There was a precedent in Smith's experience for this tactic of reducing warfare to individual combat. The *True Travells* includes the story of besieging the Turkish army in the Balkans, when a "Lord Turbashaw [the misnomer contains the word "pasha"] did defie any Captaine, that had the command of a Company, who durst combate with him for his head" (3:172). Smith is chosen by lot and kills Turbashaw, then another Turk named Guralgo, cutting off both heads for trophies. Smith had the Turks' heads emblazoned on his coat of arms and in his exploration of the coast of New England named a group of islands off of Cape Ann the "three Turkes heads" (2:419). The blending of chivalric combat and savage warfare, the display of the loser's head being customary for each, was irresistible for Smith and a key element of the projection of his own rule through that of Powhatan and Opechancanough.

Whether Smith would have triumphed in hand-to-hand combat we cannot know, for he writes that Opechancanough tried to ambush him, asking him to exit his compound to fetch a present, where two hundred bowman were waiting, arrows cocked. Angered by this, Smith, in the scene pictured in the upper right-hand panel of the "Map of Ould Virginia" (fig. 1 above), "in such a rage snatched the King by his long locke in the middest of his men, and with his Pistoll readie bent against his brest. Thus he led the trembling King, neare dead with fear amongst all his people" (2:202; 1:252). The illustration portrays the two levels of conflict: between the sixteen English and seven hundred Pamaunkee, and between Smith himself and Opechancanough. The English have superior firepower in each fight. The group of Englishmen with their rifles, above Smith's pistol on the right-hand side and at the top of the frame, are holding their own against charging Pamaunkee because the majority of the latter just stand by chatting, each holding his idle long bow. These masses, however, are only in the background, awaiting and decorating the outcome of the true contest. Opechancanough dominates the picture, standing facing the viewer in the exact center in a pose that again appears to have been copied from another one of John White's

fiesty Smith

watercolors reproduced by Theodor deBry. Although a dwarf beside his opponent, the fiesty Smith has control of the situation. He has his foe by the hair, as is the Indian style of fighting (see Smith's ethnographic account in *A Map of Virginia*, 1:167), and his pistol aimed awkwardly through his own helmet directly at Opechancanough's face, on a line that continues toward the tip of the chief's long bow. Whether due to his actual height relative to Captain Smith's or to the cut-and-paste method of the engraver, Opechancanough's great size is proportional to the scale of his humiliation before his people. Nearly the same poses appear in another frame at the opposite corner of the tableau published in the *Generall Historie*, where Smith conquers Paspehegh with his sword rather than his pistol.[21]

Throughout the episode, all attention is focused on Smith and Opechancanough. In a harangue to the Pamaunkees, while holding his foe by the hair, Smith delivers an ultimatum: "But if you shoot but one Arrow to shed one drop of bloud of any of my men, or steale the least of these Beads, or Copper . . . I will not cease revenge (if once I begin) so long as I can heare where to finde one of your Nation that will not deny the name of Pamaunk" (2:202; 1:253). This statement of the worthlessness of the savage horde, whereof any number of dead or wounded is just punishment for one drop of English blood, and where one white man claims the power to mete out such vengeance, is the converse of that which drives the plot of Joseph Conrad's *Lord Jim*, where Jim chooses to save his own life rather than assist the eight hundred Muslim pilgrims on the damaged ship. It also evokes the savagist belief that Indian war and vengeance are insatiable, and that therefore the "savages" will respond to no threat less than one of total annihilation. We have seen that Newport imagined Powhatan and Opechancanough to be kings in the European manner, but it is equally true that Smith adopted, in front of the Indians, a persona that he believed to be fittingly savage. Smith is his own best Indian. Every quality of civil and military life that he ascribed to and admired in Powhatan and his people—bravery, cunning, obedience—Smith prized in himself and expected from his subordinates. It is Opechancanough, however, who in hindsight is the best double for Captain Smith, because he too, according to many reports,

[handwritten marginalia: "openhance araugh = "he whose soul is white""]

experienced captivity and used it to represent his power. Just as Smith was captured by the Turks, Opechancanough was captured by Spaniards around 1560 and returned with Jesuits who tried to establish a mission in Virginia. The name Opechancanough or "he whose soul is white" was bestowed on him. He continued to fight the English after Smith's departure and finally was shot in the back in 1646.[22]

The illustration of Champlain at the 1609 battle against the Mohawk (fig. 2 above) is, according to one of his biographers, Samuel Eliot Morison, the only portrait that exists of him, and, unlike Smith, he is drawn to the same scale as others in the frame. Champlain's own "army" is made up not of colonists but of Indians, the Montagnais of the Quebec region. The expedition began when two chiefs, Ochasteguin and Yroquet, arrived with a band of two hundred warriors to hold Champlain to one of his promises. Ten moons ago, or the previous summer, he and his commander du Pont had promised to go to war with them. The Indians had been frustrated by traders who made the same promise with the motive of gaining safe passage to interior villages, where they could trade for pelts at a more advantageous rate. Champlain, with the selfless manner so dear to him, took it on himself to make good the Frenchmen's promise so as to preserve good trade and relations. His ulterior motive, however, was to see the Great Lakes, a possible link to the southern ocean and a route to China. Unfortunately, the Algonquins head south up the Richelieu River, not southwest up the St. Lawrence, and Champlain is disappointed to discover that his boat is halted by rapids: "cela m'affligea, & me donna beaucoup de desplaisir, de m'en retourner sans [a]voir veu un grandicime lac, remply de belles iles, & quantité de beau pays, qui borne le lac, où habitent leur ennemies, comme ils me l'avoient figuré" (2:79) [I was distressed, and I was particularly sorry to return without seeing a very large lake, filled with beautiful islands, and a large, beautiful region near the lake, where they had represented to me their enemies lived]. Nonetheless, he decides to continue with his allies, only two other Frenchmen accompanying him.

From this point until the moment of the battle, Champlain fills much of ten pages with descriptions of the preparations for war. He describes them in a general sense, as elements of an ethnographic portrait or *mœurs des sauvages*. For in Champlain's texts, this ethnographic material is not set apart, as Smith does in the "Proceedings" part of *A Map of Virginia*, but spread throughout. This is another way in which Champlain's narrative works constantly to distend the presence of his subjectivity at the center of the text and/or the historical events, to scatter the focus that so obsesses Smith. However, Champlain does participate in these customs as part of his participation in the war effort. He tells of the credence the warriors place in their dreams as auguries of the battle, then recounts a dream in which he saw the Iroquois drowning in the lake. On telling his allies of his dream, "Cela leur apporta une telle creance qu'ils ne douterent plus de ce qui leur devoit advenir pour leur bien" (2:95) [This gave them such confidence that they no longer had any doubt as to the good fortune awaiting them]. Champlain's dream is, in effect, a promise translated into another cultural idiom.

Champlain delighted in describing the customs of the Indians and subtly inserting himself into this vision of their culture. This does not mean that he was a more accurate observer of the Indians than other colonial writers, or that he sought to minimize his impact on their behavior, like an anthropologist doing fieldwork. Champlain did not really respect the customs he engaged in, but he knew the importance of playing along. He scorned the Montagnais' lack of army discipline, particularly their failure to post sentries at night. His view of the battle as beneath the dignity or gravity of European warfare and the mock heroism that presents so casually his own bravery are typical of the French representation of Indian war as I analyze it in Chapter 6. Champlain's description of the battle plan of the Montagnais commander shows a rigid planning and discipline at odds with nearly every other account of Native American warfare I have read, except, interestingly, Smith's, and suggests that Champlain's leadership among his Indian allies may have been more influential than his narrative admits:[23]

> . . . les chefs prennent des bastons de la longeur d'un pied autant en nombre qu'ils sont, & signallent par d'autres un peu plus grands, leurs chefs: Puis vont dans le bois & esplanudent une place de 5 ou 6 pieds en quarre, où le chef, comme sergent major, met par ordre tous ces

bastons comme bon luy semble: puis appelle tous ces compagnons, qui
viennent tous armez, & leur monstre le rang & ordre qu'ils devront
tenir lors qu'ils se battront avec leurs ennemis. (2:88–89)

[. . . the chiefs take sticks a foot long, one for each man, and indicate by
others somewhat longer, their leaders. Then they go into the wood,
and level off a place five or six feet square, where the headman, as
sergeant-major, arranges all these sticks as to him seems best. Then he
calls all his companions, who approach fully armed; and he shows
them the rank and order which they are to observe when they fight
with the enemy.]

The method of representing people by an equal number of sticks is a
Native American form of writing described by many colonial authors
including Christopher Columbus, Jean Bernard Bossu, Antoine Le Page
du Pratz, John Lawson, and Cadwallader Colden (see Chapter 4 below).
That the sticks are used to set out a geometric plan for battle is an
innovation unique to Champlain, however. This is an instance where so-
called savages, supposedly incapable of abstract thought, nonetheless
employ a system of representation that requires a subtle intelligence.

As represented in Champlain's illustration (fig. 2), the battle trans-
pired in a manner similar to European custom. The two armies camped
within sight of one another yet waited until the morning to begin
fighting. Champlain watched the Iroquois march out of their barricade,
then his allies advanced out of the trees: "pour me donner passage ils
s'ouvrirent en deux, & me mis à la teste, marchant quelque 20 pas
devant, jusqu'à ce que je fusse à quelque 30 pas des ennemis, où aussitot
qu'ils m'apercevrent, & firent alte en me contemplant, & moy eux"
(2:99) [to make way for me they divided into two groups, and put me
ahead some twenty yards, and I marched on until I was within some
thirty yards of the enemy, who as soon as they caught sight of me halted
and gazed at me and I at them]. The scene unfolds with the solemnity of
a duel, yet Champlain does not face off one-on-one against a fearsome
savage chief like Opechancanough. He does not tower over his soldiers
like a demigod, equal in strength to all of them together, and the
soldiers are not loyal colonials but Montagnais and their Algonquin and

Huron allies. Champlain stands in the center of the picture, yet he is tiny, one among many; neither he nor any of his foes dominate the scene as do Smith and Opechancanough. His heroic act is over in one shot, enough to kill two and wound a third of the unnamed Mohawk war chiefs, at which the rest of the army flees. It is clear enough that his gun, which the Iroquois had never before seen, is the true hero of the episode. Champlain is only the agent.

Champlain drew himself at the center of an ostensibly typical Indian battle, yet just as the form of the battle shows signs of Champlain's strategic direction, the representation of it betrays clues that it is not an independent production of Champlain's hand like his harbor charts. Palm trees are shown in the background, which, of course, do not grow on the shores of Lake Champlain. Also, the Indian warriors are depicted naked, though Champlain elsewhere describes the Montagnais as wearing clothes made of pelts and pictures them clad in armor woven from bark (see plate, 3:135). Evidently, the engraver completed the plate for *Les Voyages et Descouvertures* based on a sketch by Champlain and filled in some details based on his own preconceptions. François-Marc Gagnon has identified the engraver's model as one of deBry's illustrations for the captivity narrative of Hans Staden, which has palm trees to suit its Brazilian setting and where the canoes are also flat-bottomed, more like dugouts or pirogues common in the south than like birchbark canoes.[24] Champlain presents himself as a modest, cooperative leader and as an independent, self-sufficient author and illustrator, but on close examination each of these images is exposed as motivated, and Champlain no longer seems so guileless even next to the self-aggrandizing Smith.

So even the stark contrast between the egotistical Smith and the modest Champlain is an effect of the structure of their narratives and of their motives in relations with the Native Americans. Smith's text is centripedal, gathering and pulling information and attention from all directions toward his persona in the way Powhatan attracted obeisance from a confederacy of surrounding tribes. Champlain's is centrifugal, placing his persona at the center but directing our attention away from him toward the Indians and his French comrades, so that the credit for his knowledge may reflect back on him, while the blame for his broken promises rests with others. Smith engages in negotiations that conceal threats to take by force what he would ostensibly obtain by trade. For Champlain the process of trade itself, rather than corn, is the fundamental goal, and he achieves it by trading promises of future gifts and assistance. Much as the two individuals may have differed as human characters, it would be wrong to reward Champlain as a bright light of humanity in the shameful history of white relations with the Indians, while condemning Smith for the violent confrontations that took place in Virginia after he left it. Each pursued a policy that made sense in the context of how he understood Native American culture and power and what his colonists needed for their survival; each portrayed himself as a colonial leader in a manner consonant with his image of Native American leadership.

CHAPTER 3

Travel Narrative and Ethnography

Rhetorics of Colonial Writing

The writings of John Smith and Samuel de Champlain are of interest both for their eyewitness narratives of initial European settlement and exploration in parts of North America and for their accounts of American Indian life. In later exploration narratives by the likes of Louis Hennepin and the Baron de Lahontan, John Lawson and Jonathan Carver, these two genres, travel narrative and the description of manners and customs of the Indians, are explicitly marked off from one another, and the relationship between the two becomes a means for the author to assert his knowledge and extend its scope. In these texts two different ways of looking at the American land and native cultures, though in many respects epistemologically incompatible, were brought together in a formal hybrid that persisted for centuries. This hybrid form contained the epistemological contradictions; it organized partial knowledge so as to make it appear complete, and to enable colonials to impose a sense of order and control over the land and the Indians. It functioned as a discourse, in the sense given to the term by Michel Foucault, as an intellectual or theoretical construct that served practical ends in the administration of colonial power. Through this rhetorical bifurcation in exploration-ethnography texts, highly laudatory representations of loyal, brave, and independent-minded natives could inhabit the same texts as deceitful, drunken "Ignoble Savages." Indians involved in the fur trade or in colonial wars were frequently portrayed in exploration narratives as degenerate, corrupted by alcohol or by the lucre of profit. Yet elsewhere in the same volume, tribespeople could be presented in ethnographic descriptions as if living in a world of cultural purity, undisturbed by the colonial invasion that had brought the writer to America. The improbable combination of exploration narrative and ethnographic description survived until the late nineteenth century, when the discipline of anthropology emerged as a new claimant for the authority to represent other cultures.

My interpretation of the exploration-ethnography genre proceeds by deconstructing such binary oppositions as the degenerate versus the noble Indian, oppositions through which colonial American texts are commonly defined and interpreted. I begin with the large-scale features of books and genres and conclude with the small-scale tropes that organize the details of descriptions of the Native Americans, because whereas Hennepin or Lawson separate narrative from description explicitly, and others like Champlain do not, all shift between the two techniques and employ certain tropes from each.

First, I will look at the epistemological and historical foundations for each genre. Exploration narrative depended on the veracity and autonomy of the eyewitness narrator, an empiricism that arose in the seventeenth-century philosophy of Francis Bacon and John Locke and the liberal individualism of the bourgeois public sphere. The travel narrator's empiricism is the same as that which supported the truth claims of the early English novel. In contrast to this individualism and innovation, ethnography arose from Europeans' sense of cultural universality and depended on long traditions of intellectual authority. It can be traced back to classical portraits of the cultural Other by Tacitus and Herodotus. The clash between these two epistemologies, or claims to knowledge, may seem crippling to the coherence of texts that combined them, but the persistence of the hybrid genre suggests that in practice the two forms worked together dialectically. The contrast represents, in

Indians set apart from Judeo-Christian history OR bound into it.

a metaphoric way, the facts of travel on the rivers and in the forests of New France, and there were a few texts, such as Lahontan's, that cleverly interrogated the division between that which was known from specific eyewitness experience and that which was known by generalization from secondhand reports.

The second dialectic, operating in both the exploration narrative and the manners-and-customs genre, departs from the opposition between the Noble and the Ignoble Savage, which has sometimes been perceived as organizing all representations of Native Americans in European texts since the eighteenth century.[1] I will argue that this Manichaean view is too simplistic, that the most sensitive accounts of American Indians thematize the very problem of such a good/bad opposition, and that the Noble Savage transcends it through a capacity to be both savage and humane, both foreign and familiar to European culture. More useful for understanding the exploration-ethnography text than the Noble/Ignoble dichotomy is the manner in which American Indians were either set apart from Judeo-Christian history or bound into it. On the one hand was a romantic or racist primitivism that maintained that the *sauvages américains* were radically new, possibly nonhuman, and certainly without a place in historiography. On the other, many writers proposed different nations from the Bible and classical history as ancestors of the Native Americans. Scythians, Phoenicians, Carthaginians, and the Lost Tribes of Israel were all candidates, but the precise genealogy is less important than the consequences of an anthropology, such as that of the eighteenth-century Jesuit Joseph-François Lafitau, that seeks evidence for incorporating the Indians into the biblical genesis and into Western history. This opposition between a resemblance to peoples of Europe's classical history and imagination and the negation of qualities that Europeans saw in themselves and in their past could be viewed as an earlier version of recent conflicts between views of Native American culture that stress a radical difference and those that assert cultural commonalities. Both versions lead to a final dialectic, operating on the smallest, most basic scale in writings about the Indians, between the tropes that I call "substitution" and "negation." Insofar as the large-scale dialectics can be broken down into moves of substitution and negation, these two concepts are the best tools for interpreting the representations of Native Americans in colonial writing.

Exploration Narrative

A protagonist writes a narrative in the first person of his life and travels, of dangerous encounters with strange people in unfamiliar places. He or she survives, returns home, and publishes the story, inviting others to learn from these experiences. This outline describes both the colonial exploration narrative and the early novel, particularly those of a picaresque or autobiographical style such as Daniel Defoe's. Exploration narratives employed devices that the early novels imitated in their effort to pass for the experiences of real people. In his preface, John Lawson explains his knowledge of his topic, Carolina, and his motives for writing about it: "I not only surveyed the sea-coast and those parts which are already inhabited by Christians, but likewise viewed a spacious Tract of Land, lying betwixt the Inhabitants and the Ledges of the Mountains . . . the Discovery of which being never yet made public, I have, in the following sheets, given you a faithful account thereof, wherein I have laid down every thing with impartiality, and truth, which is indeed, the duty of every author, and preferable to a smooth style, accompanied with falsities and hyperboles" (6). Lawson declares that he has transferred to paper ("in the following sheets . . . laid down every thing") all that he has seen ("surveyed" and "viewed") and that this account stands as a visible and verifiable record. The reason this text will be of interest is because it contains new information "never yet made public," and in writing it the author is fulfilling a sort of contract with the reader, his "duty" to divulge his discoveries and to do so with "impartiality" and "truth." These claims resemble those employed by Defoe ten years later when he published *Robinson Crusoe*. In the half-page preface to the novel the unnamed editor asserts that Crusoe tells his story "with modesty, with seriousness" and that he believes the narrative "to be a just history of fact." The value or interest that motivates "making publick" this "private man's adventures in the world" is its remarkable novelty: "the wonders of this man's life exceed all that (he thinks) is to be found extant." In Lawson, the wonders of Carolina, a "healthful Country" and "as pleasant a Country as any in Europe" (6), resemble the benign fertility and familiarity of Crusoe's island, which in spite of its tropical latitude proves ideal for the cultivation of English grains.

Thus Defoe used the same rhetoric to claim factuality for his novel as Lawson did to support the veracity of his account of Carolina. The cycle of fictional texts imitating, and thereby undermining, the techniques of substantiation used by travel narratives began long before Defoe. As Percy Adams has shown in *Travelers and Travel Liars*, all the devices of empirical authority and verisimilitude that characterize true travel narratives were successfully used to validate not only novels but also fabulated voyages by clever "travel liars," including Hennepin and Lahontan. William Wood in 1634 was conscious of the skepticism with which travel narratives were read when he wrote near the beginning of *New Englands Prospect*: "I would be loath to broach anything which may puzzle thy belief, and so justly draw upon my self, that unjust aspersion commonly laid on travellers; of whom many say, 'They may lie by authority, because none can control them' " (sig. A3). Wood thus located the weakness of empiricism as a technique for validating exploration narrative, more damaging to it than to travel narratives about places already well known to Europeans.[2] With few or no corroborating witnesses for his accounts of recently discovered lands, the explorer could "lie by authority."

That early novels employed the truth claims of the exploration narrative does not prove that travelers are flagrant liars, but that these rhetorical devices carried great power and that the explorers wielded great authority. In these texts, readers invested their belief in the accuracy of a single man's report of huge tracts in distant lands, and frequently they also invested money as "adventurers" in colonial projects to exploit the possibilities they read about. Exploration accounts and promotional tracts promised utility for the reader who might travel to, trade with, or invest in colonies in those areas. Descriptions of indigenous peoples promised a fulfillment of less practical, less conscious desires, of myths readers held about their past and their societies. Books that kept the two genres separate enabled each kind of desire to flourish and prevented the contradictions between them from surfacing.

Let us look up close at the rhetorical tools that validate the exploration narrative, the tools used by Lahontan, Hennepin, and all our other explorer-ethnographers, and at some instances where they manipulated them to create plausible stories of exploration that probably did not take place.

The travel narratives employ temporal, spatial, and perspectival tools. First, a *chronologically linear narrative* connects real time with the diegesis and suggests that if every consecutive day is accounted for, the narrative must be truthful. It also ensures that a reader shares the suspense of adventure into the unknown by preventing unfamiliar phenomena from being explained through the benefit of hindsight or learned references. The journal or log is the form toward which this convention strives, although the repetitive and limited scope of the ship's log required embellishing before publication. Second, a *spatially linear and continuous narrative* induces an isomorphic relation between traveler and landscape. If the continuity of the route is preserved in its description, later travelers and mapmakers will have no difficulty fitting the explorer's account into the previous images of the world, and there will be no gaps where the narrator might jump into an imaginary or utopian setting. And third, the *traveler is the narrator is the author* of the account, and this focus ensures the independence of his subjectivity and protects against challenges to his veracity or to his freedom of movement and interpretation of phenomena.

How are these criteria established and maintained?

The first is established through codes that mark the act of writing as contained within the linear time of the narrative. Writing becomes an episodic routine alongside other routines of travel, and the discourse is produced in temporal (and spatial) proximity to the things described. Chronology can thereby easily organize diverse phenomena. As William Dampier explained in introducing his *A New Voyage Round the World* (1697), one of the most popular English travel narratives of its time and one inspirational to Defoe, who adapted it into a novel by the same title, his narrative "is composed of a mixt Relation of Places and Actions, in the same order of time in which they occurred: for which end I kept a Journal of every days Observations" (3). John Lawson entitled one section of his book "Journal of a Thousand Miles Travel among the Indians, from South to North Carolina" and reported on every day from December 28, 1700, to February 23, 1701. The journal or diary is an ostensibly private form of writing, a reflexive narrative. The information is not addressed to a reader but simply stored away for future reference. It therefore maximizes verisimilitude because the writer has no reason to fabricate; he has no one to fool but himself. Lawson and Dampier claimed the accuracy of a journal written on the spot but obviously revised and prepared their texts for the reading public. The published book is no longer an official or personal or strictly utilitarian text, yet it retains some of those forms' claims to veracity.

Some scholars consider the ship's log to be the foundation of the exploration narrative genre. Pierre Berthiaume writes, "Mais reprenons les choses au début, par l'étude du compte rendu manuscrit d'exploration, qui paraît d'autant plus en continuité avec le journal de navigation que l'instrument de la découverte est fréquemment le navire" (100) [But let us take things from the beginning, by the study of the actual manuscript of exploration, which appears all the closer to the journal of navigation since the instrument of the discovery is frequently a ship (my translation)]. A few observations on the maritime travel narrative can help us put American land travel narratives into perspective. In its utilitarian form, the ship's logbook records information about wind, weather, soundings, sightings, and views of land. One of the most successful adaptations of the log form in a *récit de voyage* is Louis-Antoine de Bougainville's *Voyage autour du monde*. Bougainville's skillfully edited narrative includes the conditions of each anchorage his ships made, expressed in the traditional maritime form as the depth in fathoms ("brosses") and the quality of the bottom brought up by the anchor or sounding lead. Bougainville rewrote his journal for a popular audience, but this information on the anchorages, along with the distance traversed between daily sextant observations expressed in latitude and longitude, constitutes a residue of the ship's log in the captain's narrative and validates the empirical origins of both. In the pseudonymous publisher's note to *Gulliver's Travels*, Jonathan Swift tried to use these details to legitimate Gulliver's narrative without actually providing any, claiming that the manuscript originally contained "innumerable Passages relating to the Winds and Tides, as well as to the Variations and Bearings in the several Voyages" and that he has excised these in order to "fit the Work . . . to the general Capacity of Readers" (xli).

A less extreme means of containing the act of writing within the time of traveling is the epistolary form adopted by Lahontan and Bossu, by Charlevoix in his *Journal d'un voyage*, and by Bacqueville de La Potherie in the first volume of *Histoire de l'Amérique Septentrionale*. The epistolary form fulfills the first code of travel narrative by keeping the explorer in the land he is writing about and enabling the text to travel from there to the reader via a correspondent. It is an outdoor version of Samuel Richardson's theory of "writing to the moment." Not only does this maintain temporal and spatial continuity, it keeps the traveler away from the metropole, where special interests might invite misrepresentations of the New World, and yet still allows him to pay some attention to his reader's questions and needs. The Jesuit Pierre François-Xavier de Charlevoix traveled from Montreal to New Orleans in 1720–22 and wrote a semiofficial report that was nonetheless cast as letters to the duchess of Lesdiguières. The letters include frequent comments on the logistical imperatives of such a correspondence, which depended on free moments for composition and on returning travelers to carry the letters. Such interruptions as "On vient de m'avertier qu'il faut m'embarquer, je finirai cet article à mon premier loisir" (189) [I am just now informed I must embark, I shall conclude this article the first leisure I have (end of letter 11, 1:289)] inscribe the act of writing within that of traveling and subordinate the former to the latter, adding to immediacy and verisimilitude. This subgenre of "Letters from North America" reached its peak after the American Revolution, when Europeans like Thomas Anburey, the Abbé de Robin, and Brissot de Warville came to investigate the young nation and wrote letter-journals of their findings. These works, too, use the epistolary form as a device; their addressees are ciphers such as the "F.B." to whom Farmer James writes in J. Hector St. John de Crèvecœur's *Letters from an American Farmer*. The epistolary form appealed to authors and readers even if both realized that it was only a device, because it drew on a tradition of philosophical daring and candor, as in Voltaire's *Lettres philosophiques*.

The *Jesuit Relations* also originated as letters of a sort; although they are the single most valuable source for information about the Indians of the Great Lakes region in the seventeenth century, they do not satisfy either of the first two criteria I have proposed for travel narrative. Fathers Brébeuf, Le Jeune, Bressani, and others composed a collective narrative subject based in Huronia and at the other missions, and Huronia was at least a month's journey by canoe from Montreal. Correspondence could reliably be sent out only once a year and might not receive a response until the following year. The "Relation de ce qui s'est passé en la Nouvelle France en 16—" or "Relation of what happened in New France in 16—" was therefore a single letter, or a few from different missions, wherein the entire year's events might be narrated in one burst of writing just before the journey back to Montreal. Rarely does one of the Jesuits narrate a long journey undertaken on his own initiative (although Claude Allouez's pioneering explorations of the shores of Lake Superior and Lake Michigan and Marquette's trip down the Mississippi are notable exceptions), and most yearly letters are organized in a nonlinear fashion, often reduced to accounts of the number of missions, the number of missionaries and their progress in learning the native language, and the number of *sauvages* baptized.

Although missionaries rarely wrote exploration narratives, some of the classic *Relations* from the 1630s show the Jesuits struggling between the imperatives of chronological narrative and comprehensive description. For instance, Paul Le Jeune, in his *Relation de 1634*, expresses some anxiety that he would like the text to be better organized as an ethnographic catalog. There are chapters entitled "On their feasts" and on the Hurons' good and bad qualities, their beliefs and superstitions. Le Jeune entitled the final chapter "Contenant un journal des choses qui n'ont peu estre couchées sous les chapitres precedens" [Containing a Journal of things which could not be set forth in the Preceding Chapters] and in it apologized, "quittant une remarque je passeray à une autre qui ne luy a point de rapport, le temps seul servant de liaison à mon discours" [I shall pass from one observation to another which has no connection with it, time alone serving as a link to the parts of my discourse (*JR* 7:94–95)]. Both this and the preceding chapters contain anecdotes involving his own experience, but the missionary emphasis on self-abasement and self-effacement marks this text and most of the *Jesuit Relations* apart from the explorers' relations. The mission does not travel except to follow the natives' periodic removals to new maize fields and hunting grounds, and the missionaries are driven not by a quest for geographic knowledge but by religious motives, or occasionally by the reactions of their Indian hosts. Rather than as narratives of the experience of individual missionaries, we might better think of the *Jesuit Relations* as annual reports of a nonprofit organization written by the employees to the directors (to "V.R." or "votre reverence," the superior in France) but intended also for the consumption of potential contributors to the conversion effort.

The third criterion, the independence of the voyager-narrator, is also often frustrated. The romantic vision of an explorer is of one who goes where he pleases or who is entrusted with costly ships and supplies by a sponsor who asks him to complete a simple yet treacherous route. We imagine Columbus performing his mission for Ferdinand and Isabella, Sir Martin Frobisher setting out to find a northwest passage, La Salle promoting his plan to find and claim the mouth of the Mississippi, or William Byrd disciplining the vulgar Carolinians and forcing the boundary line westward. It rarely worked out so neatly. A famous traveler's narrative was sometimes not accepted as the authoritative account of the region or even of the voyage in which he took part. Frobisher's and Hernando de Soto's discoveries were both told best by subordinate members of the expedition, Dionyse Settle and the Gentleman of Elvas, respectively. Charles-Marie de La Condamine returned to France to find that his fame and scientific progress had been claimed by Pierre Bouguer, who had arrived back in France years earlier and presented the expeditions' findings before the Academy of Sciences. Lahontan's narrative was so hostile to the Jesuits and to the French colonial administration that he was never able to return to France. Henri Joutel's *Journal historique* (1713) recounts the expedition and fate of his much better-known commander, La Salle, who did not write a long narrative of his first expedition and could not write one of his second because he was murdered by his subordinates. Joutel's book is the best narrative of the 1684–87 expedition to find the mouth of the Mississippi River; it climaxes with the story of how he quelled the mutiny and completed the journey on foot from Matagordo Bay on the Gulf Coast of today's Texas to the French post at the mouth of the Arkansas River. Back in France, Joutel's book waged a contest for sales and for authority with LeClercq, Hennepin, and Tonti, each of whom had already published accounts of La Salle's first voyage. In a preface, editor M. de Michel made an appeal to veracity and the reader's whetted appetite, while still suggesting that the real interest of the narrative lay with its murdered leader: "on ne doit pas s'etonner, si apres ce qu'on écrit le Pere Hennepin Recollect [sic], le Chevalier Tonty et quelques autres, on expose encore ici un Journal Historique . . . [qui] a cela de particulier qu'il contient exactement ce qui arriva jour par jour à M. de la Sale dans ce funeste voyage" [it is not to be wonder'd, that after what has been writ by Father Hennepin, a Recolet, the Chevalier Tonty and some others, we here now publish an Historical Journal . . . (which) has this peculiar, that it exactly contains what hapned to Monsieur de la Sale, Day by Day, in that fatal Voyage (47–48)]. Joutel's modesty was tireless, despite a commander whose egotism and abrasiveness were well documented, and he claimed little authority for himself or his text. His linear account does not contain a separate ethnography, and although it does work into the narrative fascinating accounts of natives of the Mississippi valley, it holds one's interest more by the sheer drama of its plot than by exotic or critical portrayals of Amerindians.

Louis Hennepin, a member of the earlier expedition of La Salle down the Mississippi, responds quite differently to the threat to veracity posed by his subordinate position. His was the best-selling account of the La Salle expeditions, and for good reason. Hennepin borrows and embellishes freely. His first effort, the *Description de la Louisiane*, includes a *mœurs des sauvages* [manners of the Indians] at the end and centers around his captivity among the Sioux. This episode is corroborated by Daniel Greysolon, Sieur Duluth, who wrote of rescuing Hennepin and his two companions and returning them to Michilimackinac. However, Henne-

pin does not mention that he was not the leader of the party La Salle sent
to explore up the Mississippi.[3] In 1697, after most members of the
expedition had died, Hennepin published a second, revised version,
which collected for himself all the heroism and leadership of the others,
lifting an account of the journey down the Mississippi from an account
by Father Zenobe Membré. Hennepin claimed to have made the trip to
the mouth of the river and back two years before La Salle did, and in just
forty days, so as not to overlap with the time occupied in the chronology
by his Sioux adventure. Some exploration writers seemed to believe that
so long as the conventions of temporal and spatial linearity were respected, even fabulous tales might win readers' credulity.

Lahontan also wrote of a trip into the Minnesota area in the seventeenth century. His volume manipulates the techniques of empiricist
exploration narrative more cleverly than Hennepin's and still has scholars debating its veracity. In October 1688, Lahontan writes, he traveled
to the Baie des Puants (today's Green Bay) and met with a chief of the
Outagami (Fox) nation. He assured the chief that he did not plan to go
among the "Nadouessious ses ennemis" [Sioux, his enemies] nor engage
in the fur trade, but that "je meditois quelque découverte" (1:144) [I had
some discovery in my view (1:110)]. With Outagami guides, he quickly
passed over the Fox-Wisconsin portage and down to the Mississippi
River, then upstream to the mouth of "La Rivière Longue" [Long River].
Although the Mississippi downstream of the Wisconsin was known
from Joliet and Marquette's 1673 exploration and from La Salle's 1679
voyage nearly to its mouth, Hennepin's books were the only account of
an earlier voyage upstream to the Nadouessious lands. Lahontan specifically claimed to have passed the edge of what had been seen by Frenchmen, into what was known only second or thirdhand. Of the Long River,
the guides say "qu'ils n'avoient jamais été à l'entrée de cette Riviére en
Canot, que cependant ils m'assûroient qu'à vingt lieuës plus haut ses
bords n'étoient que des bois ou des prairies" (1:147) [that they had never
been in the Mouth of that River before, though at the same time they
assur'd me, that about twenty Leagues higher, the Banks of it were clad
with Woods and Meadows (1:112)]. When he meets the Eokoros, the
first of several nations living along the river, "ils étoient ravis de ce que
nous êtions venus dans leurs Païs, parce qu'ils avoient entendu parler des

François d'autres Nations Sauvages qui les loüoient beaucoup" (1:149) [they were infinitely well pleas'd with our arrival in their Country, for that they had heard the Savages of other Nations speak very honourably of the French (1:114)].

Lahontan exploits the dichotomy common in exploration narrative between the eyewitness account and the descriptive reports obtained from informants. He intends to convert the latter into the former. He and his guides "passant de Village en Village sans m'arreter" (1:149) [pass'd from Village to Village without stopping (1:114)], finding a friendly reception and an eager desire for "des coûteaux, des cizeaux, des aiguilles & du tabac" (1:150) [Knives, Cissars, Needles, and Tobacco (1:114)], but remaining on their guard against a possible surprise attack. In villages of the next nation, "trois ou quatres cens Essanapés accoururent nous recevoir, & après avoir dansé vis-à-vis de l'endoit où nous étions, ils nous appellerent & nous inviterent à gagner terre" (1:153) [three or four hundred Essenapes came running to the shoar, and, after dancing just over against us, invited us ashoar (1:116)]. The large number of natives, the joyous reception they give him, the desire for small trade items, and the underlying suspicion of violence are all common features of exploration narratives from Columbus to La Salle. As Lahontan continues upstream to the West, the native nations— Gnacsitares, Mozeemleks, and Tahuglauks—are increasingly numerous, powerful, and resemble Asian as much as other American cultures. The fabulous report resembles Lederer's of the natives around Lake Ushery. The Mozeemleks tell him of the Tahuglauks: "ces peuples portoient la barbe longue de deux doigts . . . qu'ils étoient coëffez d'un bonnet pointu . . . que leurs femmes ne se montroient point" (1:166) [Tahuglauk wear their Beards two Fingers breadth long . . . they cover their Heads with a sharp-pointed Cap . . . their women never shew themselves (1:126–27)]. He does not actually reach the Mozeemleks, enemies of the Gnacsitares and other downstream nations, but he learns of them and of the Tahuglauks from Mozeemlek slaves. He thereby expands the limits both of the New France known from firsthand exploration and the descriptions of lands obtained from others. The map in the book (fig. 4) is quite explicit about this epistemological boundary. The eastern half is labeled "Carte de la Riviere Longue" and the western half "Carte que les

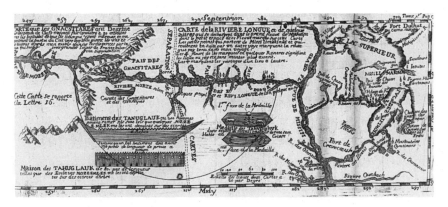

FIGURE 4. Lahontan's map of "La Rivière Longue," from *Nouveaux voyages . . . dans l'Amérique septentrionale*, 1703. (National Library of Canada, NL-19244)

Gnascitares ont dessiné" [Map that the Gnascitares drew]. A dotted line down the middle is the "separation de ces deux cartes" [separation of these two maps], and the point on the river where Lahontan turned back is marked with a fleur-de-lis.[4] The illustration on the western side of the line of a Tahuglauk boat carries a note claiming that it is 130 feet in overall length and manned by 200 rowers "s'ils sont tels que quelques Mozeemlek me les ont depeint sur des ecorces d'arbre" [if they are as some Mozeemlek drew them for me on birch bark (my translation)]. The Mozeemleks live beyond a mountain range on a salt lake drained by a river flowing west, suggestive to some later readers of the Great Salt Lake and to contemporaries of the passage through North America that explorers had desired for two hundred years and that Lederer and many others sought to satisfy.

Lahontan's westernmost voyage aroused a dispute among his readers and editors. Charlevoix referred to it as "le voyage sur la Riviere Longue, aussi fabuleuse que l'isle de Bataria, dont Sancho Pansa fut fait Gouverneur" [the voyage on the Long River, as fantastic as the island of Bataria, of which Sancho Panza was made governor (my translation)].[5] On the other hand, the river appeared on many maps of New France, including de Lisle's (fig. 6 below). Stephen Leacock, in his introduction to a 1932 edition of the *Voyages*, maintained that the Long River story is authentic and that the Tahuglauks were a misplaced band of Eskimo. Réal Ouellet, editor of the latest and definitive edition, attempts to corroborate the name "Gnacsitare" and other words that Lahontan transcribed with words from the Sioux language, and the landscape of the river with later accounts of the Minnesota river region by William Keating and Jonathan Carver. He explains a report from the Eokoros that they could muster up to 20,000 warriors as a misunderstanding on Lahontan's part, the Eokoros actually having referred to that number of bison. Milo Quaife, an early-twentieth-century historian of the Old Northwest region, attempted to separate true geography from fabulous tale through a comparison with Lamothe-Cadillac's description of a western river through the Sioux country, which resembles Lahontan's account of the entrance to the Long River.[6] Lamothe-Cadillac was commandant of the post at Michilimackinac and would have heard Lahontan's account when he returned there from the West. Lamothe-Cadillac wrote his "Mémoire" before Lahontan published the *Nouveaux voyages*, and because he does not mention the Eokoros or any of the other tribes along the river, or the possibility of an easy passage to the South Sea, Quaife believed this proved them to be Lahontan's inventions.

Another more obscure example of fabulated exploration is a short and enigmatic tale attributed to Matthew Sagean, which seems to elaborate on Lahontan's Long River episode.[7] Sagean told of a voyage up a river to the west of the Mississippi where he encountered the nation of the Acaanibas (which resembles both "cannibal" and the French name for an Abenaki band living far to the east, the "Canibas"), whose king claimed to be a descendant of Montezuma and whose people lived in a gilded splendor inspired by Spanish colonial wealth and dreams. The Acaanibas are said to carry on trade with another nation, a six days' journey farther west, which sports Asian features. Sagean's fantastic colonial topography linked the exotic riches of Central America with those of the Orient and located it in an area controlled by the French. After this suggestive opening, which was given credence by some hopeful French colonial officers, the narrative of Sagean's travels degenerates into a tale of piracy and intrigue between Quebec and New England during Queen Anne's War. That Sagean and Lahontan "fooled" so many officials, mapmakers, and historians can be attributed to the same sort of wishful thinking that breathed life into hopes for El Dorado.

English colonists demonstrated a similar desire to believe a doubtful story. Richard Hakluyt in 1582 and again in his 1589 edition of the *Principal Navigations* printed "The Relation of David Ingram." The text consisted of two versions, some fifteen pages each, of an interrogation in 1582 of this seaman who had returned to Europe from the coast of "Norumbega" in 1569. Sir Humphrey Gilbert, who was in the midst of promoting a colony in Newfoundland, was enticed by Ingram's descriptions of great wealth in the region. Ingram claimed to have been put ashore in the Yucatan by John Hawkins just a year earlier as part of an ill-fated group of English sailors,[8] and to have walked the three thousand miles or more across eastern North America. Ingram's account, unlike Lahontan's and Hennepin's, is not told chronologically and is not accompanied by a map or geographic details. Though he relates some plausible ethnographic descriptions, he also relates tales of plentiful pearls, silver, and rubies four inches long, of elephants and of "a Monstrous beast twise as big as an Horse, and in proportion like to an Horse, both in maine, hoofe, haire, and neighing . . . [which] hath two teeth or hornes of a foote long growing straight forrth by their nosethrilles."[9]

In spite of these apparent hoaxes, it would be wrong to assume that for the seventeenth- and eighteenth-century reader the New World was so bizarre and unknown that the imaginary was always indistinguishable from the real, or that any account of a monstrous beast was credible. Consider some of the maps of the region. Descelliers's world map of 1550 (fig. 5), which employs Cartier's explorations of Canada, separates clearly enough the known from the imagined. The Atlantic coast of North America is densely labeled with harbors and rivers. The interior, designated "terre incogneu quant a nous" or "land which is unknown to us," is illustrated with scenes of mountains, pygmies, a unicorn, and ostrichlike birds. The coast, with its densely indented and labeled rivers, bays, and points, is the result of the combined knowledge of many voyages and their narratives and is designed to guide future travelers to specific, real places. The interior is the locus of imaginary scenes not fixed to any spot but potentially filling the entire space and employs a different scale and mode of representation. Map and illustration are not connected by a narrative, as in Champlain's work, but are simply juxtaposed. The figures should be considered not for their plausibility or

FIGURE 5. Marvelous inhabitants in the interior of New France on the world map by Pierre Descelliers, 1550. (By permission of the British Library, C-18165)

realism by today's standards, but as hopeful yet reasoned speculation about what might be found in lands not yet explored. And we can see a change in the style of the imaginary between 1500 and 1700. Guillaume Delisle's 1703 map of "Amérique septentrionale" (fig. 6) belongs to a later style of cartography and a later style of the marvelous, yet imagined or speculative geography is still present and still distinguishable from the explored regions. It no longer takes the form of pygmies or ostriches transplanted from tales of other lands, but of a string of lakes leading straight west from the upper Mississippi valley and connected, via a long portage, to a river flowing straight south toward the "mer de l'ouest" (the Pacific Ocean), which so many explorers had hoped to reach by an easy passage through the continent. This is Lahontan's "Rivière Longue" as portrayed in his book and map published in the same year. Its features are so isolated and rectilinear that they look out of place next to the rest of the map. They extend out into what is now a blank, rather than a fanciful or bestiary, space of uncertainty and of hope—mapmakers and readers still recognized that this represented what they hoped to find as much as what was already known to exist. As we have seen, Lahontan's own map distinguished between eyewitness and secondhand knowledge represented on the map, and Delisle's map implies the same kind of separation, though without explicitly marking it.

The issues of authority and veracity in exploration narratives, and the techniques used to claim them, are complex and sometimes paradoxical. The independence of the narrator is required for an empiricist eyewitness accuracy, but an explorer in pursuit of his own glory lacks the disinterestedness that is another code for veracity. The "official" explorer, in his log or report, will frequently transcribe only place, distance, and time, the codes of spatial and temporal linearity, omitting all references to his own body. Similarly, the ethnography genre demands the effacement of the writer's bodily presence from the scenes of native life. Yet literary realism depends heavily on corporeal detail, and to achieve it a writer often had to abandon his detachment and officiousness. The cold of Canadian winters, the scourge of mosquitoes, the backbreaking difficulty of portages, and the stiffness and boredom of long-distance canoe travel are all rarely expressed by the French explorer-ethnographers in the bodily terms that are needed to convey them.

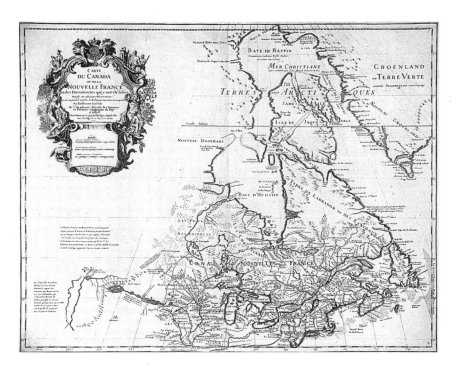

FIGURE 6. Map of North America by Guillaume Delisle, 1703, showing Lahontan's "Rivière Longue" stretching west from the Mississippi. (National Archives of Canada, C-22559)

Berthiaume, who as we have seen takes a practical and official view of the exploration narrative genre, significantly chooses Hennepin as an example of the effective use of this corporeality. He quotes a passage describing the cold discomfort of winter travel and admits: "L'imagination du lecteur a enfin de quoi se nourrir parce que l'imaginaire du rédacteur informe l'univers sur lequel, tel un romancier, il inscrit émotions et sentiments. Il est vrai que chez Louis Hennepin, une bonne part du récit relève plutôt du roman que de la relation du voyage" (105) [The imagination of the reader finally has something to feed on because the imagination of the chronicler fills in the universe in which, as a novelist, he inscribes emotions and sentiments. It is true that in Louis Hennepin, a large part of the narrative is more of a novel than a travel narrative (my translation)]. An effort to transport the reader through imagination to the place, rather than to transport the place through a metonymic text to the reader, draws the accusation of "romancier"—novelist or storyteller.

Berthiaume did not have to choose Hennepin to find an example of such corporeal realism (Joutel's evocation of standing all night in the water during floods in East Texas, when no dry ground was in sight, is even more effective), but that he did so choose is significant. Berthiaume justly claims that the plagiarized voyage down the Mississippi in Hennepin's 1697 book is identifiable because it violates the strict temporal continuity of the journal that is maintained in the accurate parts of his narrative. But by choosing one of the most notorious hoaxes (or "false topographies," as Percy Adams calls them) in the history of travel narrative, Berthiaume proves his point without need for recourse to his evidence. Hennepin's transgression of the principle of spatial and temporal continuity and factuality is used to taint him for also violating the code prohibiting the traveler's bodily presence in his narrative, a code that has shackled travel narrative and prevented it from becoming accepted as literature.

Joutel's reticence as a subordinate voyager who did not publish his own narrative (his journals were edited by de Michel and later by Margry) is thus rewarded. The independent and active presence of the traveler-narrator-writer damages credibility as often as it guarantees it. This is one reason why colonial writers added ethnographic manners-and-customs descriptions of the Indians to their texts. It relieved the pressure on their subjectivity and veracity, for it is a form that asserts authority without need for originality, by shifting from empirical to received knowledge.

Ethnography: A Venerable Genre

Whereas travel accounts still suffer from a reputation for fictions or embellishments, anthropology proclaims the authority of science when it describes the practices of the Natchez, Hurons, or another tribe. It also disguises the nature of its sources. We have seen how ethnohistory frequently uses a cut-and-paste technique that ignores the context in which material such as Grangula's speech was originally published. Anthropology, writes Johannes Fabian, "acquired its scientific and academic status by climbing on the shoulders of adventurers and using their travelogues, which for centuries had been the appropriate literary genre in which to report knowledge of the Other" (87). To impugn the veracity of sources such as Hennepin or Lahontan would shake these foundations, yet disciplinary boundaries have generally prevented this kind of dissonance; historians can discredit parts of Lahontan's text, literary critics can celebrate the creative genius of other parts, and anthropologists can cite virtually any part as documentary evidence.

Since the turn of the century, anthropologists have taken the job, formerly performed by colonists and explorers, of describing and interpreting the cultural Other for European readers. It is not only the situation of cultural contact that supports this comparison, but also the genres and traditions of writing that explorers and anthropologists have produced. Along with Fabian, another scholar who has perceived the common heritage of ethnography and travel narrative is Mary Louise Pratt. In an essay entitled "Fieldwork in Common Places," she uses two captivity narratives among primitive cultures in Brazil, one contemporary and one from the sixteenth century, to examine anthropology's assumptions about the relationship between the narrative of the ethnographer's experience and the description of the culture-object. Pratt, like Fabian, recognizes that "The practice of combining personal narrative and objectified description is hardly the invention of modern ethnography, however. It has a long history in those kinds of writing from which ethnography has traditionally distinguished itself. By the early sixteenth century in Europe, it was conventional for travel accounts to consist of a combination of first-person narration, recounting one's trip, and description of the flora and fauna of the regions passed through and the manners and customs of the inhabitants" (33).

Pratt cites some of the chapter titles from part two of *The Captivity of Hans Staden of Hesse in A.D. 1547–1555 among the Wild Tribes of Eastern Brazil*, including "How they are betrothed" and "What their dwellings are like." Although Pratt chose Hans Staden and Mungo Park, she could easily have used North American explorer-ethnographers Lahontan, Hennepin, Lawson, or Lescarbot to illustrate the long tradition of combining narration and description, travel narrative and ethnology, in this manner. Book 6 of Lescarbot's *Histoire de la Nouvelle France*, subtitled "Contenant les mœurs, coutumes, & façons de vivre des Indiens Occidentaux de la Nouvelle France" [Wherein are contained the Manners, Customs, and Fashions of Life of the Western Indians of New France], includes as its table of contents one of the most complete ethnographic catalogs:[10]

1. De la Naissance
2. De l'imposition des Noms
3. De la Nourriture des Enfans, & de l'amour des peres & meres envers eux
4. De la Religion
5. Des devins
6. Du Langage
7. Des Lettres
8. Des Vetements & Chevelures
9. De la forme et dexterité
10. Des ornemens du corps
11. Des ornemens extérieures
12. Du Mariage
13. La Tabagie
14. Des Danses & Chansons
15. De la disposition du Corps
16. Exercises des Hommes
17. Exercises des Femmes
18. De la civilité
19. Des vertus et vices des Sauvages
20. La Chasse
21. La Fauconnerie
22. La Pecherie
23. De la Terre
24. De la Guerre
25. Des Funerailles

[1. Concerning birth
2. Concerning the giving of names
3. Of the nurture of children
4. Concerning religion
5. Of the Sorcerers
6. Concerning language
7. Concerning letters
8. Concerning garments, and the fashion of wearing the hair
9. Of their form and dexterity
10. Of their bodily ornaments
11. Of exterior ornaments
12. Of marriage
13. Of banquets
14. Of dances and songs
15. Of their physical constitution
16. Of the pursuits of the men
17. Of the pursuits of the women
18. Of civilisation
19. Of the virtues and vices of the savages
20. Of the chase
21. Of falconry
22. Of fishing
23. Of the soil
24. Of war
25. Of funerals]

There is nothing particularly surprising about this list; what is remarkable is that after nearly four hundred years it looks so familiar. Pratt points out, after quoting a similar list from Hans Staden, "this discursive configuration . . . is the product neither of an erudite tradition nor of the rise of modern science, despite its similarities with contemporary ethnography" (34). The "Manners and Customs" organized in such catalogs remained the dominant mode of writing about American Indians through the nineteenth century. Thoreau wrote out a list of thirty-one topics similar to Lescarbot's, gleaned from three contemporary experts on the American Indians—Henry Rowe Schoolcraft, George Henry Loskiel, and James Adair—as an outline for his possible book on the Indians.[11]

Lescarbot was one of the best ethnographers of New France. Bruce Trigger, the dean of Canadian ethnohistorians, has observed, "the ethnographic writings of this early disciple of Montaigne deserve more careful attention than they have received to date."[12] Yet because Lescarbot organized the description of the Other through categories familiar to the European, a skeptic could argue, as many have of twentieth-century ethnographies, that he failed to do justice to the fabric of Amerindian culture. One such critic, J. M. Coetzee, whose study of ethnocentrism in colonial writings of South Africa, what he calls "The Discourse of the Cape," is influential for Pratt's work, has abstracted the typical chapter headings into a general formula:

> Although the framework of categories within which the travel writers operate is nowhere explicitly set forth by them, it is not hard to extract it from their texts. The list is roughly as follows:
>
> 1. Physical appearance
> 2. Dress: (a) clothing, (b) ornamentation, (c) cosmetics
> 3. Diet: (a) foodstuffs, (b) cuisine
> 4. Medicine
> 5. Crafts: (a) handicrafts, (b) implements
> 6. Technics
> 7. Weapons
> 8. Defence and warfare

9. Recreations
10. Customs
11. Habitation: (a) dwellings, (b) village organization
12. Religion and magic
13. Laws
14. Economy
15. Government
16. Foreign relations
17. Trade
18. Language
19. Character[13]

Any speculation on how the specific concerns or environment of Cape travelers affected the list of categories is less significant than the similarity of the categories employed in two different colonial theaters. Although the catalogs do not correspond exactly, the differences reflect more the time lapse between Lescarbot and Coetzee, during which terms like "Economy" and "Foreign Relations" became current, than any differences between native cultures in South Africa and North America.

Postmodern attacks on Enlightenment concepts of classification such as these chapter headings have gained such wide currency that there is little need to review them here.[14] As Pratt herself has written in an article on South African exploration-ethnographies, "Indigenous peoples are relocated in separate manners-and-customs chapters as if in textual homelands or reservations, where they are pulled out of time to be preserved, contained, studied, admired, detested, pitied, mourned."[15] Hypostasized descriptions within such a categorical formula preclude any analysis of the different organization of these spheres of life in indigenous cultures as compared to European societies and suppress the differences in even the most "universal" categories such as marriage. This common critique becomes less comfortable, however, once one realizes that the same encyclopedic categories predated the Enlightenment and endure in modern anthropology. Lescarbot's and Staden's tables of contents from 1557 and 1609 resemble those in ethnographies well into the twentieth century. Pratt compares Staden's text with ethnographies by Raymond Firth, Bernard Malinowski, and E. E. Evans-Pritchard, three well-known twentieth-century anthropologists who in writing up their fieldwork also maintained a division between personal narrative and professional ethnographic description. The categorization of spheres of social life and the segregation of cultural representations from actual colonial encounters, however ethnocentric, appear to be a consistent pattern of Western knowledge and power.

Coetzee argues, based on his list, that the "savage" Other is constructed from European man by differentiation from an ethnocentric model of universality: "The categories and subcategories of this framework constitute the samenesses that extend across all societies. They are the universals, while the observations that are filled in under the various headings constitute the *differentia* of societies, which in reports on the Hottentots tend to be the most remarkable *differentia*" (120). His article focuses on the idleness of the Hottentots, a characteristic that many writers observed infecting the white colonists as well, but which was hardly observed at all before 1652, when European leaders began to demand labor from natives and colonists. This scandal of idleness occurred in North America also. As William Wood wrote of the New England Indians, "much good might they receive from the English, and much might they benefit themselves, if they were not so strongly fettered in the chaines of idlenesse; so as they had rather starve than worke" (88). "Worke" is for Wood a concept derived from English society and its desires, which Indians could not fulfill. The conflict is an instance of the dialectic of substitution and negation examined below: the colonists substituted their notion of work for analogous but different behavior among the Indians, then used the difference to ascribe to the "savages" the negation of work, idleness.

Another aspect of the perverse power of the categories is their neat independence from one another. Clothing is not easy to separate from ornament in any society, nor is work distinct from play, and medicine and magic are deeply connected in American Indian cultures. Yet Lescarbot implies a discrete separation and a certain logic to the order of his chapters. For instance, he begins the chapter on marriage, "Apres avoir parlé des vétements parures, ornemens & peintures des Sauvages il me semble bon de les marier, afin que la race ne s'en perdre, & que le païs ne

demeure desert" (3:389) [Having spoken of the garments, gauds, ornaments and paintings of the savages, I think it meet to marry them, to the
end that the race may not die out, and the country remain uninhabited
(3:161)]. In his conceit, he suggests that the ethnographic object is
frozen in his text and can move only at his will, following a schematic
narrative through chapters 11, 12, and 13. Once the bride is dressed, the
marriage ceremony may proceed. Yet no particular marriage of any
Indian couple will be described; the chapter consists largely of moral
judgments and comparisons of "le licence de se prostituer" (the liberty
of prostituting oneself) among unmarried girls, as reported by Cartier
and André Thevet and observed by Lescarbot among the Souriquoi or
Micmac. The logic of the successive chapters is Lescarbot's own design
for the construction of "les sauvages de par-dela" considered in their
entirety, based on his limited experience and what few accounts had
been published before 1609. This singular, generalized *sauvage américain*
will live another life in Sagard, where the emphasis will be on its permis-
sive childhood and on the dances and songs or "festins." It will live again
in each subsequent ethnography. Rarely did an observer limit his description to the customs of just one nation, and rarely did he narrate a
specific marriage or healing ceremony involving named individuals.
More often he restated what he had read in previous accounts of other
tribes and synthesized it with his own observations, in an ongoing
process of copying and corroboration. Each chapter invoked the "ethnographic present" to create a singular, synthetic *sauvage* who stood in
for thousands of diverse individuals and communities.

　　Gabriel Sagard's *Le grand voyage au pays des Hurons* demonstrates the
odd attitude toward sources and empirical evidence on the part of many
explorer-ethnographers. The work is the first ethnography of the Hurons, based on Sagard's nine months of fieldwork in Huronia in 1623–
24, several years before the constant presence of *coureurs de bois* and missionaries introduced diseases and altered some traditional ways. Sagard
enjoyed the primacy that many anthropologists dream of, yet in his
book he copied many passages from Champlain and Lescarbot, even
though his own fieldwork was better than Champlain's and Lescarbot
had never visited the Hurons. That he employs many of the same cate-

gorical chapter titles (e.g. "Exercises ordinaires des hommes et femmes") is no surprise, yet he also copies or paraphrases several passages from Lescarbot's two chapters on the activities of the two genders. Still more bizarre (by today's standards of authenticity) are Sagard's borrowings in chapter 11, "De leur mariage et concubinage" [on their marriage and concubinage]. He denounces the freedom of young Hurons:

> . . . garcons et jeunes hommes de Canada, et particulierement du pays de nos Hurons . . . ont licence de se prostituer si tost qu'elles en sont capables, voir mesme les peres et meres sont souvent maquereaux de leurs propres filles, bien que je puisse dire avec verité, n'y avoir jamais veu donner un seul baiser, ou faire aucun geste ou regard impudique. (160)

> [. . . the boys and young men of Canada, and especially . . . those of the Huron country . . . are at liberty to give themselves over to this wickedness as soon as they can, and the young girls to prostitute themselves as soon as they are capable of doing so. Nay even the parents are often procurers of their own daughters; although I can truthfully say that I have never seen a single kiss given, or any immodest gesture or look. (121)]

Though Sagard insists that this is true of the Hurons, the rest of the quotation is copied from Lescarbot's chapter on marriage, which attributed this licentiousness primarily to the Brazilians: "Les filles du Bresil ont licence de se prostituer si-tot qu'elles en sont capables, tout ainsi que celles de Canada. Voire les peres en sont maquereaux" (3:390) [The maidens of Brazil have the same liberty as those of Canada to prostitute themselves as soon as they are able. Indeed the fathers act as their pandars (163)]. Lescarbot had never been to Brazil but no doubt read about it in the writings of Jean de Léry or André Thevet.[16] Thus each writer deferred to the description of a previous observer in a different region and claimed that it was true for the *sauvages* among whom he had lived, even if his own observations contradicted it. Sagard appears to have wished to verify a preconception of the *sauvages américains* as lewd and licentious, even though his authority, Lescarbot, used his account for a reproof not of the Amerindians but of the European explorers who accepted the offers of these "pimps" and, according to popular wisdom of the time, brought syphilis to Europe: "Dieu a severement puni ce vice par la vérole apportée des Espagnols à Naples" (3:390) [God has severely punished this vice by the pox, which was brought by the Spaniards from Naples (163)]. The desire to constrain the conception of the *sauvage américain* within a single, consistent formula prevailed over any sense of local differences and even over the importance of eyewitness observers' unique experiences. After all, where does the "Je" or "I" in Sagard reside if he has copied evidence from Lescarbot and presented it as if it were his own?

If Lescarbot and Sagard struggled with the difference between eye-witness observation and descriptive generalization of Indian cultures, Lahontan mastered this discursive relationship, using each genre to reinforce the other. His travel narrative is the "tome premier" or first book, which consists of twenty-five letters to "an old parent" in France. His ethnography and geographic and natural history descriptions are in the "tome second," entitled *Mémoires de l'Amérique Septentrionale.* The letters are dated and signed from places throughout New France and in Europe, yet it is highly unlikely that the twenty-five letters appear exactly as written nearly twenty years earlier, because there is a complex rhetorical relationship between the *Lettres* and the *Mémoires.* The *Lettres* profess to be partial, empirical information yet look forward to the encyclopedic *Mémoires*, at one point promising his correspondent that "après que je serai plus instruit du Commerce & du Gouvernement politique & Ecclesiastique de ce païs-là, je vous en donnerai des Mem-oires si exacts que vous aurez lieu d'en être contant" (1:19) [as soon as I am better instructed in what relates to the Commerce, and the Civil and Ecclesiastical Government of the Country, I'll transmit you such exact Memoirs of the same, as shall give you full satisfaction (1:15)]. The promise of a comprehensive knowledge to come applies also to the Indians: "Je ne puis vous informer sitôt des mœurs de ces Peuples, il faut du temps pour les bien connoître" (1:19) [As for the Manners of the People, I cannot pretend to describe 'em so soon; for a just Observa-tion and Knowledge of these things cannot be compass'd without time (1:15)]. Lahontan notes his correspondent's request for ethnography— "Vous me priez de vous faire une description des peuples Iroquois, & de vous mander au juste quelles gens ce sont, & comment ils se gouvernent" (1:29) [you require of me an account of the Iroquese, and would have me to present you with a just view of their Temper and Government (1:22)] —but insists that he has no time amid his duties to compile it.

Although the *Lettres* may be limited by time and inexperience, the *Mémoires* claim to draw on an inexhaustible collection of documents, suggesting the epistemological as well as rhetorical contrast between the two. At the opening of the second volume, we read:

> J'ai eu soin de faire des journaux très particularisez pendant le cours de mes Voyages; le detail en seroit ennuyeux pour vous, & la peine de les copier avant que de vous les envoyer demanderoit trop de tems. Vous trouvérez ici dequoi vous former une idée parfaite du vaste Continent de l'Amérique Septentrionale. (2:4)

> [In the course of my Voyages and Travels, I took care to keep particular Journals of every thing, but a minute relation of all Particulars, would be irksom to you, besides, that the trouble of taking a copy of the Journals, before I have an opportunity of shewing you the Original, would require more time than I can well spare. In these Memoirs you'll find as much as will serve to form a perfect Idea of the vast Continent of North-America. (1:204)][17]

The detail of his travels and experiences is so dense, Lahontan claims, that he is forced to produce a synthesis that subsumes the detail of time, place, or culture. The limited information of the *Lettres* refers rhetorically to the knowledge contained in a journal of infinite details, and the generalizations of the *Mémoires* also depend on this phantom storehouse of empirical facts.

For example, the passage quoted above from the third letter, "Je ne puis vous informer sitôt des mœurs de ces Peuples," continues, "J'ai été cet hiver à la chasse avec trente ou quarante jeunes Algonkins bien faits & très-agiles, expressément pour aprendre leur langue" [I have been this Winter at hunting with thirty or forty young Algonkins, who were well made clever Fellows. My design in accompanying them, was, to learn their Language (1:15–16)]. After another winter hunting with the Algonquins, the eleventh letter fulfills his correspondent's request for a description of the bear, dear, moose, and fowl of Canada and the Indians' methods of hunting them, as he observed those two winters. This descriptive writing is a foretaste of the *Mémoires*, where he returns to the topic. There, however, the implied presence of Lahontan as a witness to the Indians' hunting techniques recedes, and the extent of his knowledge grows to a "Table des Animaux des Païs Meridionaux du Canada" (2:38) [A List of the Animals of the South Countries of Canada (1:232)], followed by another for the northern regions and an "Explication de ceux dont je n'ai pas fait mention dans mes Lettres" (2:40) [A Description of such Animals or Beasts, as are not mention'd in the Letters (1:233)]. This encyclopedic totality extends also to the Indians, for whereas the two winters with the Algonquins were the only time Lahontan spent alone in a native band, and Algonquin was the only native language he learned, Lahontan claims: "Je connois mieux le genie des Sauvages qu'une infinité de François qui ont passé toute leur vie avec eux, car j'ai étudié leurs mœurs avec tant d'exactitude, que toutes leurs maniéres me sont aussi parfaitement connuës que si j'avois passé toute ma vie avec eux" (2:131) [I know the Humour of the Savages better than a great many French People that have liv'd among 'em all their Life-time; for I study'd their Customs so narrowly and exactly, that all their Conduct of Life is as perfectly well known to me, as if I had been among 'em all my Life-time (2:35)]. The *Mémoires*, in addition to the list of animals and fish, names forty-six "Nations sauvages du Canada" that are all described comprehensively, it is implied, in the generalized chapters on topics including "Mœurs & manières des sauvages," "Adorations des sauvages," and "Croyances des sauvages & les obstacles à leur conversion."[18] Though Lahontan's ethnographic encyclopedia does not have as many separate chapters as Lescarbot's, in the *Mémoires* he, like the other explorer-ethnographers, adheres to the ethnographic epistemology that omits specification of the tribes, individuals, and places described in favor of generalization. Customs are described in the present tense as if *all* the Indians have *always* practiced marriage, hunting, or medicine in that way.

In the early years of colonial contact with American Indians, the variety of tribes was acknowledged, but the diversity of cultures did not seem important. Only occasionally did an ethnographer address the possibility of a diversity of customs, usually to dismiss it, as when John Lawson wrote: "The Burial of their Dead is perform'd with a great deal of Ceremony, in which one Nation differs, in some few Circumstances, from another, yet not so much but we may, by a general Relation, pretty nearly account for them all" (185). Le Page du Pratz, who knew many Indian nations of Louisiana, acknowledged the presence of multicultural difference on a wider scale, while at the same time suppressing it:

> . . . on a remarquer que le caractère de ces Nations n'est pas le même, quoiqu'elles soient voisines les unes des autres; ainsi qu'on ne s'attende pas que dans la Description de leurs Mœurs on trouve une uniformité parfaite, ni que je rapporte toutes les différences. . . . Mon dessein n'est que de faire connoître en général par le caractère de ces Peuples, la route que l'on doit tirer pour en tenir un bon parti dans le Commerce. (2:307)

> [The character of these Nations is not the same, although they are the neighbors of one another; so that one should not expect to find in a description of their manners a perfect uniformity, nor will I report all their differences. . . . My design is only to make known, by the personality of these peoples, the route one generally must take in order to have an advantage in commerce. (my translation)]

Le Page du Pratz's ethnological writing includes many specifics, most significantly a great deal about the Natchez, a nation distinct among North American Indian cultures, and for which his text is the best extant source of information. Yet in this passage he wishes to amalgamate all descriptions as much as he can into a single "caractère" or personality, which might be useful for colonists and capitalists.

Based on Staden and later ethnographers, Pratt claims that these texts follow a "conventional ordering—narration first, description second" and that this order implies a hierarchy, "narration superordinate, description subordinate" (35). But neither mode can be called superior to the other because each claims a different kind of authority and yet depends on the other to support that claim. Furthermore, there is a continuum from texts that offered only ethnography without any narrative of the author's travels, such as Lafitau's, to narratives that inform the reader only of the land and not of its people. Lahontan's *Voyages* and *Mémoires* are roughly equal in length. Hennepin's *Description de la Louisiane* (1683) includes 312 pages of travel narrative and 107 pages of *mœurs des sauvages*. John Lawson, like many English colonists writing promotional tracts, added a survey of flora, fauna, and landforms to the exploration-ethnography duo. His *New Voyage to Carolina* (1709) consists of "A Journal of a Thousand Miles Travel among the Indians, from South to North Carolina" of 55 pages, then "A Description and a Natural History of Carolina" covering 104 pages, and finally "An Account of the Indians of North Carolina," 75 pages. Sagard in his *Grand voyage du pays des Hurons* reverses the proportion: roughly one-quarter of the text follows his voyage from France to Canada and then with Montagnais guides from Quebec to Huronia, and three-quarters is an ethnography describing, among many other topics, the "festins," "marriage et concubinage," and "croyances" (religious beliefs) of the Hurons.

Not every author segregated travel narrative and ethnography into separate parts of a published text, and the contrast between the two genres is significant not merely as a means of sorting texts into two groups, "voyages" and "manners and customs," but because it represents the epistemological processes of colonial knowledge. Some explorers and travelers, notably Champlain and Charlevoix among the writers of New France, interspersed ethnographic description throughout their texts in short sections. Yet it is still easy to recognize a shift between the two discourses. When the ethnographic Indian appears, he or she is not a single individual communicating with the Europeans in the diegetic time frame of the narrative, such as Tessoüat's negotiations with Champlain, but a plural, unnamed, and abstracted *sauvages américains*. Many exploration texts omit such confrontations like John Smith's with Powhatan and Champlain's with Tessoüat. These narratives exhibit the same sort of self-effacement as ethnography commonly does. Champlain's first narrative of Canadian exploration, *Les sauvages, ou, le voyage de Samuel Champlain* (1603), unrolls as a tedious enumeration of rapids, lakes, forests, "terres basses" and "élevées," "pays bons" or "mauvais" and the distances between each, and takes time out from this landscape narrative for a description of the eponymous "Sauvages," but never for an episode involving Champlain personally and corporally. Pratt has observed a similar phenomenon in South African colonist John Barrow's *Account of Travels into the Interior of South Africa in the Years 1797 and 1798*, commenting, "what is narrated proves to be a descriptive sequence of sights/ sites, with the travelers present chiefly as a kind of collective moving eye which registers these sights" and "Though he was travelling as a colonial official, charged with mediating disputes between Boer colonists and indigenous peoples, human interaction plays little role in his narrative."[19] Such disembodied narratives are rare in the literature of New France, but it is important to acknowledge this additional technique of not only separating exploration narrative from "manners and customs" discourse, but also suppressing information about interaction between travelers and natives.

What, beyond the inertia of generic tradition, motivated these explorers to divide their texts into a strictly linear, temporal narrative and an atemporal generalized description of the native peoples, flora, and fauna? Several reasons can be identified. For one, the skepticism with which travel and exploration accounts were received made it difficult for an individual writer to assert his veracity, and the *mœurs des sauvages* discourse relieved this pressure insofar as it depended not on the single observer's reliability so much as on a cultural construction of identity and difference. Moreover, in a depersonalized descriptive summary, the false expectations created by the exaggerated or fabulous reports of previous travelers, the division between preconceptions and actual firsthand experience, could be absorbed and dissipated. Disappointment with the reality of popular attractions such as the Greek and Roman ruins is a cliché of later exoticist travel narratives. It occurs as well in accounts of Niagara Falls, which did not fulfill the sublime expectations of visitors such as Peter Kalm and Margaret Fuller, whose preconceptions had been molded by exaggerated accounts beginning with Hennepin, who claimed that the falls were more than six hundred feet high.[20] The real thing failed to live up to these writers' romantic imaginings, built up from many simulacra before the journey. As Kalm put it, just after discrediting Hennepin, "This humour of travellers, has occasioned me many disappointments in my travels, having seldom been so happy as to find the wonderful things that had been related by others. For my part, who am not so fond of the Marvellous, I like to see things just as they are, and so to relate them" (84). Of course, Hennepin, Lahontan, and others had also claimed this empirical veracity. In encounters with the Amerindians, colonial travelers were forced to negotiate between the sensational tales of cannibalism and torture (and somewhat less sensational customs of marriage and funerals) with which many had been familiar before coming to America and actual experiences that may not have included observations of such activities. Disappointment, however, was rarely the result. Instead, the writer could use his ethnography to restate what he learned and believed before his voyage, adding to or changing it based on whatever he was able to witness. We saw this in action in Sagard's and Lescarbot's accounts of sexual practices. If general statements of fact are established by repeated trials and verifications, stereotypes arise from the repetition of statements heard or read but never verified. Karen Ordahl Kupperman has suggested that this explains the apparent contradictions in accounts of native behavior: "Some are full of praise when recounting events in which Indian steadfastness, courage, or honesty has been helpful, but give a formula lower estimate of Indian character when making a formal, abstract statement. It seems likely that, in telling of events, the writer is thinking of individual Indians whom he knows relatively well, but that the formal analysis of the native character calls forth the writers' preconceptions."[21] Yet it would be wrong to assume that all negative characterizations are expressions of prejudices and that favorable ones arise from experience. John Smith, for instance, was eager to describe his foe Powhatan as a cunning and ruthless "salvage" yet still saw these traits as potentially admirable in a leader and, consciously or not, imitated them.

Tzvetan Todorov, like Kupperman, proposes that the rigid separation between empirical and rational-synthetic, narrative and descriptive, *récit de voyage* and *mœurs des sauvages*, may have arisen from the gap between experience and myth. He uses for an example the division of Lahontan's text into its three parts and writes:

> The author's use of the three genres provides a good illustration of the requirements of primitivist exoticism: if one wants to idealize a

society, one must not describe it in too much detail; conversely, a description that is even slightly detailed lends itself badly to idealization. Lahontan needed to leave aside certain details of his own initial description in order to portray the Hurons as truly noble savages. (271–72)

Todorov employs an axis of near and far ("décrire de trop près" or literally "to describe too closely") to represent the separation between detail and generalization, actuality and idealization. Whereas the empirical travel narrative places Lahontan in close individual contact with the Other, the general *mœurs des sauvages*, the *Mémoires* in this case, is an aerial view, on a scale large enough to perceive or impose patterns on the raw data obtained during his sojourns among the Indians. The differences between Huron and Algonquin customs are no longer discernible in the scale of this map. If the travel narrative in the *Voyages* tells of details on a human scale such as a tree, the descriptive and synthetic account in the *Mémoires* shows only a forest. This metaphor of perspective explains the perpetuation of myths, but it also characterizes the point of view of objective science. Pratt writes of ethnography's scientific discourse as using the same trope of the bird's-eye view: "In terms of its own metaphors, the scientific position of speech is that of an observer fixed on the edge of a space, looking in and/or down upon what is other."[22] But estimating the degree of detail by the focal length is not always valid. Narratives of travels, however factual, are often lacking in the detailed descriptions that Lahontan's *Nouveaux voyages* has in abundance. As regards the landscape, a general assessment along the lines of "un très beau/mauvais fertile/stérile pays" [a very good/bad fertile/sterile land], such as Champlain provided in his first narrative, is a common style. On the other hand, the seventeenth-century ethnographies often demonstrate an excellent eye for detail in relating a particular ceremony or artifact, even if this is wrongly presented as true of all the Indians of the continent.

Rather than using this epistemic axis of proximity and distance, the rhetorical and generic technique that Lahontan and so many other explorers use can be better understood with an analogy taken from their own means of travel, by canoe. Canoe travel not only made it possible for

French colonists to explore far more of North America before 1763 than
the English did, it may also have influenced the modes of writing about
their explorations. These explorers knew the landscape as a waterscape, a
lacy network of rivers and lakes connected by portages. The forest in
between the waterways remained the domain of the Indians and the
game they hunted; it remained blank space on the maps or, more accurately, the "ground" for the "figure" of the lakes, rivers, and portages
shown on maps such as Delisle's. Even the resource most exploited by
the colonists, the beaver, inhabited not the forest but the rivers and lakes
and actually turned forest into lake with its dam building. The *mœurs des
sauvages* and the descriptions of landscape that often accompanied it are
not so much a retreat from immediate on-the-ground experience to an
overhead view as an extrapolation from what one *did* see to what one
would see behind the curtain of trees if one went in there. From the
limited perspective of an explorer in the wilderness, it enabled a shift to
the speculative power of a scholar in a library. It allowed for a network of
commerce and transportation to be extended into a continuous surface—
of knowledge of the land and natives through the natural history and
ethnography, and of control and ownership of the land through the maps
and surveys of Champlain, Smith, Lawson, or Thomas Jefferson. This
metaphor also conveys the importance of each genre to the other, for the
blank space on a map could be claimed only after it had been circumscribed by the exploration of rivers, lakes, coasts, or mountains.

The *mœurs des sauvages* or ethnographic discourse asserted the power of
knowing and comprehending native cultures through generalization.
The diversity of individuals' marriages and dances, for example, and the
motives of love or creativity behind them, were suppressed in favor of a
single formula for "Amours et marriages," as Lahontan called it. Events
and behavior demand to be *narrated* when their causes are known and
their consequences are deemed important. Because the barriers of language and culture prevented most colonists from understanding the
particular story behind the marriage of a native couple, they would
describe the visible ceremony as representative of all weddings.

To further understand how cultural difference constructs the discursive difference between the *récit de voyage* and the *mœurs des sauvages*,

consider how an Amerindian ethnographer might portray the manners
and customs of the French explorer or fur trader. The routines of wilderness travel, to the extent that they differed from Amerindian methods,
would receive close attention. We might read of cleaning weapons,
taking compass readings, writing in journals, saying prayers, arguing
about route finding and strategy, and of soldiers and servants doing
menial chores for their commanders. Each of these customs would be
described in one archetypal instance in the "ethnographic present" and
might be described by objective, outward features that would miss the
true purpose of the activities. The events important to the European
explorer, such as the discovery of a great lake or a valuable mine, might
not receive any attention at all. The behavior of travel, if it were an
Other's behavior, would be described, as the Amerindian Other is, not
narrated. It would no longer be travel narrative, but a "mœurs des
européens." On the other hand, in European explorers' own accounts of
their activities, the mundane tasks of setting up camp or mending
canoes are nearly always omitted, and one must read many narratives
before learning how time-consuming and important these tasks were.
Most explorer-ethnographers turn the narrative and descriptive eye outward, suppressing the bodily difficulties of wilderness travel so as to
present a seamless narrative of the landscape traveled through, and
omitting most accounts of encounters with Indians in favor of a generalized description.

The linear narrative suppresses not only repetitive, routine events in
favor of a synthetic description, but also familiar descriptions in favor of
the novel and unique. After the early days of the Huron missions, therefore, little ink is spent narrating the established routes along the St.
Lawrence and Ottawa Rivers between Montreal and Huronia or Michilimackinac; authors suppress familiar and repetitive information or resort
to descriptive summaries. But the temporal dimension remains. Exploration narrative, to attract the attention of readers in the late seventeenth and early eighteenth centuries, had to promise discovery of lands
that had not hitherto been described in print. Later travelers who stayed
within the known territory (such as Claude Lebeau and François-René
de Chateaubriand among French travelers in America) were forced to

add new dynamics of fiction and exoticism to keep the genre interesting. For North America before the Seven Years' War, travel narrative nearly always aspired to be exploration narrative. Discovery was privileged, and it was on the unknown frontier where it was possible. Thus Hennepin, Lahontan, and Sagean extended their voyages with fabulated accounts of imaginary locales. New Voyages/"Nouveaux voyages" was an overworked title, and other expressions using "new" were common, as in the titles of Hennepin's narratives, the first version in 1683, *Description de la Louisiane, nouvellement découverte au Sud Ouest de la Nouvelle France par ordre du Roy, avec la carte du pays, les mœurs & la maniere de vivre des sauvages* [Description of Louisiana, newly discovered to the southwest of New France by order of the king], and the second and expanded, embellished version, published in Utrecht in 1697, *Nouvelle découverte d'un très grand pays situé dans l'Amérique entre le Nouveau Mexique et la mer glaciale . . .* [New discovery of a very large land in North America, between New Mexico and the frozen sea . . .]. For the *mœurs des sauvages*, on the other hand, novelty was often a sham and copying earlier accounts was accepted practice. European travelers and readers sought the sensational in the "savage" but expected to find their preconceptions confirmed. Cannibalism, torture, polygamy all had to be included even if not actually witnessed.

The river and forest or figure and ground model is complicated by the fact that there is a version of travel narrative that fills in the empty forest. The exploration of "blank spaces" on maps, such as tempted Conrad and his Marlowe in *Heart of Darkness*, picked up in the eighteenth century after the frontiers between settlements and wilderness had become boundaries between colonies on the Atlantic coast, and only the unknown interiors remained.[23] Exploring a circumscribed but unmapped region was also a heroic endeavor that promised adventures of a singular, sensational nature and could be written up as *récit de voyage* and *mœurs des sauvages*. Narrative and description find an easy complementarity in this hybrid genre because what is found in part of the blank space is accepted as valid for the whole of it. Novelty has the power to induce generality. The first account of an unknown territory often characterizes that whole region, and a single village or nation encountered can represent all the region's inhabitants to the Eurocentric reader. The particular image is the origin of the general impression: Iowa is all cornfields, the Sahara is all sand dunes. The explorer is expected to look beyond what he sees, for he is asked to judge the opportunities the land offers for profitable exploitation by future travelers. Frequently these assessments were set apart in a description of the territory's potential for profit, such as Le Page du Pratz's survey of Louisiana or Wood's of New England. And when an explorer described what he looked for but did not find, he logically placed it in the space between or outside the route he traveled. The blank space survived, and though it might shrink, it continued to hold the hope of finding an El Dorado or a Northwest Passage.

In a nearly parodic example of this exploration trope, Le Page du Pratz cleverly played on fading hopes of finding mineral wealth in the unknown parts of Louisiana. The episode comes during some free time between his duties as officer and farmer: "je me disposai à faire un voyage dans l'intérieur de la Province . . . pour faire des découvertes dont personne ne parloit; pour trouver aussi s'il étoit possible, des choses que personne ne recherchoit. . . . Je voyageois pour m'instruire & pour l'utilité du Public; mais je voulois être seul pour me comporter à mon aise" (1:213–15) [I therefore resolved to take a journey through the country . . . . to make discoveries not mentioned by others. I wanted to travel both for my own instruction, and for the benefit of the publick: but at the same time I desired to be alone, without any of my own countrymen with me (133)]. Literally, the French says: "to make discoveries that no one has spoken of, and to find, if it was possible, some things which no one has searched for." This is a curious and paradoxical statement. Le Page du Pratz does not say that he is the first to visit this area, but rather he implies that he is the only person who has (or ever will) do so. Because each traveler's trip is different, perhaps one cannot help but "make discoveries not mentioned by others," and by going to a remote area Le Page du Pratz can fulfill the explorer's and ethnographer's dream to be alone among the natives and natural landscape. But on another level, it is self-defeating to "describe the thing that nobody has spoken of," for no one will be obliged to believe the description—there will be no possible corroboration.

Le Page du Pratz's journey in between the mapped and known parts of Louisiana is a fiction of a different kind than Lahontan's and Hennepin's, and even more clever at manipulating the rhetoric of exploration literature, because it includes a fail-safe device to prevent being exposed as a fabrication. Le Page du Pratz does not permit any other colonists to travel with him. He gives several reasons: first "Les François n'ont point tant de patience: ils ne sont point d'ailleurs assez forts . . . ils m'auroient tourmenté pour revenir" (216) [they neither have patience, nor are made for fatigue, would be ever teazing me to return again (133)]; second, he does not wish to be assassinated by these subordinates in a mutiny, as La Salle had been in 1687; and third, "Je ne voulois point . . . partager avec personne la gloire des connoissances que j'acquérerois & que je me promettois dans ce voyage" (1:215) [I didn't want to share with anyone the glory of the knowledge that I would acquire and that I promised myself from this voyage (my translation)]. Instead, he chooses ten Indian guides and designs a pattern for traveling that allows him to explore as much territory as possible. Most of the guides carry his bedding and provisions; three serve as scouts, walking a league or more ahead and to either side of him, and maintaining contact through smoke signals sent up three times each day. These *naturels*, as Le Page du Pratz calls the Indians throughout the *History of Louisiana*, serve as prosthetic extensions of his senses and knowledge; they are completely subordinated to his purpose of exploration.

From the outset of the discovery he is searching not for new native nations or for a river passage across the continent, but for things or objects. "Depuis mon arrivée à la Louisiane," he writes at the opening of the episode, "je m'étois appliqué à chercher des objets dont la découverte pût être utile à la Société" (1:213) [Ever since my arrival in Louisiana, I made it my business to get information in whatever was new therein, and to make discoveries of such things as might be serviceable to society (133)]. He even declares that he and his *naturels* "eviterons de passer chez aucune Nation . . . parce que je ne voyageois que pour découvrir des choses" (1:217–18) [will avoid passing through any native nation . . . because I traveled only to discover things (my translation)]. In the early stages of the trip, he expresses frustration that "Nous marchâmes quelques jours sans trouver aucune chose qui fixât mon attention . . . ma curiosité n'étoit point satisfaite" (1:225) [We marched for some days without finding any thing which could either engage my attention, or satisfy my curiosity (136)], disappointment that is only partly recompensed by the beautiful landscape, "un charmant Pays." Le Page du Pratz suggests that to bring back only descriptions or knowledge of places and peoples is quite different from, and less significant than, bringing back *things* of value. Yet we might also read this passage ironically as suggesting that the description of a valuable thing could be, in some circumstances, as valuable as the thing itself, at least for the colonial writer and for readers who will never go there or will never find it.

From this journey to an imaginary place, he will, of course, return only with descriptions, not objects. Le Page du Pratz discovers many commodities, but they are so much a part of the fabulous landscape that he cannot take them back to Louisiana or France. He finds gypsum but claims he has already processed it into plaster (1:232) and so has only the proof of its utility, not the mineral itself. He finds limestone that is not worth removing from the site. Finally, he finds only "indices" or indications of iron and gold, not the ore itself. The most interesting mineral discovery, however, comes when his "découvreur de devant," or the scout walking ahead, shows him "une pierre brillante & coupante: cette pierre étoit de la longeur & de la grosseur du pouce & aussi quarrée qu'un Menuisier auroit pû faire un morceau de bois de pareille grosseur" (1:236) [a shining and sharp stone, of the length and size of one's thumb, and as square as a joiner could have made a piece of wood of the same bigness (140)]. Some pieces are bursting out of the earth like tree stumps. He strikes some of this crystal against a flint and observes "beaucoup plus de feu que l'on n'en eût tiré avec le plus fin acier" (1:237) [it drew much more fire than with the finest steel (140)] without ever leaving even the slightest mark on the crystal.

These crystals are desirable to the Indians, too—"Mes gens en vouloient prendre & les emporter"—but Le Page du Pratz fears that "quelque Francois voyant ces pierres ne gagnât à force de présens ces Naturels pour découvrir cet endroit" (1:237–38) [My people wanted to carry some with them; but I dissuaded them. My reason was, I apprehended some

Frenchman might by presents prevail on them to discover the place (141)], thus either stealing his riches or exposing his fraud. He is able to prevent both catastrophes by telling the *naturels* that the crystals' aesthetic interest or fire-starting uses are less important than their value in some kind of industrial process:

> je les détournai de ce dessein en leur disant, "A quoi bon se charger de tout cela? j'avoue que ces pierres sont assez belles à la vûe, mais aussi elles sont plus dures que le fer ou l'acier le mieux trempé: avec quoi donc les travailler? Quel mérite enfin peuvent avoir ces pierres, si elles ne sont point travaillées? . . ." Je leur fis jetter les leurs comme des choses qui ne vallent pas la peine de les porter." (1:237)

> [I dissuaded them from this design by saying to them, "What good will it do to carry all that stuff? I admit that these stones are quite pretty to look at, but they're also harder than iron or the best-tempered steel. With what would one work upon them? What use can these stones have, if they are not workable? . . ." I made them throw aside their stones as things that were not worth the trouble to carry. (my translation)]

The crystal will become valuable only when work is done on it, and if nothing can cut it, it is doomed to remain a diamond in the rough. Yet the piece he describes is hardly rough, it is a perfect square, and others have "six faces bien égales & unies comme des glaces de miroirs, tres transparens, sans aucune veines, ni taches" (237) [six faces, even and smooth like mirrors, highly transparent, without any veins or spots (140)]. These remarkable crystals deconstruct the opposition between raw natural resource and finished manufactured product. He has found kernals of aesthetic perfection, so adamantine that they cannot be formed into the shape one needs, but must be found already in the perfect shape. The utility of these crystals would be limited by the number and size of the available pieces, and the colonists would be forced to accommodate their desires to the forms of the land, unlike the exploitation of lead and gypsum. Like the mythical Noble Savage who escapes the corruption of contact with colonists, the crystals remain pure and unchanged. They represent the contradictory desires to enjoy the aesthetic beauty of a natural setting and to exploit it for personal gain.

The rock crystals can also stand metaphorically for this entire episode of discovery within the *Histoire de la Louisiane*. Other parts of the text contain practical information about geography, Indian relations, and trade useful to the French colonists and perhaps even more to the English, who, just five years after the publication of Le Page du Pratz's book, obtained Louisiana as part of the spoils of the Seven Years' War. The preface to the English translation declares how the text has been abridged and rearranged so that "the nation may now reap some advantages from those countries" that "by right always belonged to Great Britain . . . by learning from the experience of others, what they . . . are likely to produce, that may turn to account" (ii–iii). Eager for words of such potentially valuable products, the translator included most of this tale of a journey where no one had gone before, even though Le Page du Pratz's enigmatic prairie is enclosed on all sides by a crystal wall of fiction and would be of no use to anyone except for the aesthetic pleasure of reading. Le Page du Pratz claims that he hid one small piece of this amazing rock in his pocket, and that he located the place, for his own possession of it, by using the rational system of latitude and longitude. He does not produce for us the numbers or the rock, however, for he wishes to exploit the secret as his own reward.

Exploration literature promised both wealth and *news*: new places, strange people, and new things. It recorded European penetration into the "virgin wilderness" of the New World and depended rhetorically on primacy, novelty, and particularity, though frequently the new adventures were to places known from (even copied from) previous voyagers' accounts, and occasionally new places were imagined. By contrast, the ethnographic genre was a discourse that suppressed novelty and was reluctant to be disrupted by new data that did not fit the paradigm. The *mœurs des sauvages* fed on all previous versions of the form to become ever more complete and authoritative. As an encyclopedia of Amerindian life, it invites comparison to the *Encyclopédie* of Denis Diderot and Jean le Rond d'Alembert, that of Pierre Bayle, and other eighteenth-century compendia that succeeded the cosmography of the sixteenth century. Within the French Enlightenment, one can detect a common epistemology in the two projects, including the following precepts: Reason is adequate to the description of nature because the two are organized in the same way; nature (or, in this case, primitive culture) will submit easily to exhaustive description because the grammar of encyclopedic categories, such as Coetzee's list, is universal and covers completely the phenomena; nature presents itself to the European consciousness unproblematically, with no more shame or dissimulation than the naked savage.

The *mœurs des sauvages américains*, which were rewritten by so many travelers, should be viewed as textbooks, compilations of a few new, firsthand reports (generally the author's own) added to the accepted knowledge found in the previous texts. As historians of science have shown, most research adds supporting evidence to accepted theories; only rarely does a researcher have the data, the insight, and the courage to challenge the assumptions that are reproduced from one report to the next. New areas and new nations of America were constantly being explored, but when faced with the option of either adding an appendix to describe the new and different customs of a recently contacted nation, or simply suppressing these differences to make the new nation fit the conventional pattern of the *sauvage*, most authors chose the latter. Therefore the accusations of plagiarism leveled against some travel texts should be considered in a new light. Citation of sources was, of course, not obligatory at the time, and if we view these texts as scientific reference works, it would still not be expected in a work of popular science writing.

The exploration-ethnography form flourished because the claims to authority of the two genres built on one another in spite of the internal contradictions. This is still true today. The interest of Le Page du Pratz or Sagard or Lawson as sources for anthropology is based in their descriptions of the Indians, whereas the assurance that each man really did see what he describes is found in their exploration narratives. However, to discern what these explorers learned from the Indians and what misconceptions they brought to America from Europe, it is necessary not only to compare each account with others of the same region, but also to understand the dialectical and paradoxical nature of these hybrid texts. So far we have examined the large-scale features of the texts' organization. But the dialectic between contradictory characteristics continues on the level of the ascriptions in the representations of the American Indians.

The Noble Savage

In the *mœurs des sauvages*, Enlightenment rationalism, the instrumental needs of imperialism, and the suppression of data that did not fit preconceptions all combined to produce a set of stereotypes comparable to that critiqued by Edward Said in *Orientalism*. The cultural Other might evolve, grow, or change through the inclusion of new peoples or the process of a diaspora forced on it by dominating powers, but the representation of the manners and customs of the Indian remains rigidly the same, even if it lags behind reality. In this sense, though in few others, the *sauvage* resembles the Oriental as an ideological stereotype within European culture. The power of Said's critique emerges when he shows how Orientalism still exerts its power-knowledge through the Western academic and diplomatic establishment. The popular myths about Indians found in early colonial texts are also still pervasive. Indians killed their elderly when they became too weak to travel. Indians buried a hatchet when they wished to end a war and fired an arrow with a white ribbon tied to it when they wished to declare one. Indians never spoke to a visitor until they had welcomed him with a meal and a pipe of tobacco. Indian women had no difficulty in labor, rejoining the traveling band just minutes after delivering a child. These are a few of the *mœurs des sauvages* recorded by colonial writers, and it is as difficult to find the first instance of each of these representations as it is to determine its accuracy.

The Indian of Wild West cartoons and movies, who utters war whoops more often than complete sentences, is giving way to idealizations of Native American spiritual or ecological values, which obscure the realities of Indians' urban and reservation lives just as the more negative images do. Whether in academic journals or in popular culture, myths of the Indian are unavoidable—an obstacle to a more sensitive and accurate understanding by the general public and even by native people,

who grow up with much of the same popular media. Moreover, a polemic with or differentiation from the myths of savagism necessarily
perpetuates them in a negative, repressed form. If one must write that
the Indians are not hairy and not cannibals, practice agriculture, have a
written language, and differ greatly from one tribe to another, as some
colonists began to do in the seventeenth century, this implies that readers used to believe that the Indians were all nomadic hunters, hirsute
beasts, cannibals, illiterate heathens.

There is a link between past and present stereotypes of the Indian in
the concept of the Noble Savage, which seems destined to flourish even
as less flattering myths fall into disuse. It is fruitless to identify an origin
for this bundle of stereotypes. Herodotus's descriptions of the Scythians,
so rife with the contradictions I believe are a strength rather than the
weakness of the Noble Savage, is one possible original. Tacitus's *Ger-
mania* is another, because the Germans are not only simple and virtuous,
but also show their moral strength by comparison with the corrupt
Romans who do battle with them.[24] Much has been written of the Noble
Savage. Hayden White, in the opening paragraph of an essay that offers a
provocative revisionist theory, goes so far as to say that "The theme of the
Noble Savage may be one of the few historical topics about which there
is nothing more to say. Few of the *topois* of the eighteenth century have
been more thoroughly studied" (121). White thus suggests that it is
passé as a subject of critical inquiry, and indeed the Noble Savage has
gone out of fashion since cultural critics have decided that it is just as
inaccurate, unfair, and racist as its shadow, the Ignoble Savage.

The unpopularity of the Noble Savage trope appears to have actually
made it less common in seventeenth- and eighteenth-century texts.
Critics of works containing some of what were once considered the most
famous Noble Savages have declared that they are in fact not to be found
there. Roy Harvey Pearce, in his study of savagism in the United States,
describes "Noble Primitivism" as a French myth perpetuated by the
French-Canadian-American Crèvecœur, whereas he claims that Anglo-
Americans such as Benjamin Franklin and Thomas Jefferson were wiser
and did not support the myth (139–42). Hoxie Fairchild's study of the
Noble Savage detects in the same Crèvecœur's 1801 work, *Voyage dans*

La Haute Pennsylvanie et dans le New York, a reversal of the idealizations in *Letters from an American Farmer* and comments, "his earlier praise of Indians was written merely in deference to a literary fashion from which, in this more soberly informative work, he feels himself free" (104). Antoine Adam, in an introduction to the Garnier-Flammarion edition of the *Supplément au voyage du Bougainville*, absolves Diderot from falling for the myth: "Diderot, à coup sûr, n'avait aucune sympathie pour la chimère du primitivisme et ne songeait pas à s'attendrir sur les vertus du bon sauvage" (26) [Diderot, one can be sure, had no sympathy for the chimera of primitivism and had no intention of lingering on the virtues of the noble savage (my translation)]. Or, take Tzvetan Todorov on Rousseau: "On voit maintenant combien est intenable l'idée que Rousseau serait un adhérant du mythe du bon sauvage" (313) [The idea that Rousseau subscribes to the myth of the noble savage is thus clearly untenable (280)]. Todorov claims that Rousseau does not see the *sauvages* he reads about in travel narratives as men living in his state of nature, but instead as humanoid animals, a view that makes Jean-Jacques seem a less perceptive reader of his sources than he was.

During the seventeenth and eighteenth centuries, the Noble Savage was more popular among the French than among the English, in large part because the French colonists in North America had more interaction with, more dependence on, and therefore more sympathy for the Indians. Also, the classicism that encouraged the comparison of the Indians with Greek and Roman ideals was strongest in France during the period when New France and Louisiana were developing most quickly, roughly 1630–1730. The Noble Savage also entered into the battle of the ancients and moderns as a modern challenger to the ancient monopoly on primitive virtues. Nonetheless, as the comments about Diderot, Rousseau, and Crèvecœur suggest, even in French scholarship the Noble Savage is a sort of ghost, a fleeting figure always present in the back of critics' minds, but never in what one is looking at or reading. Yet he must come from somewhere, and, indeed, we find him in the literature of New France, not only in the melodramatic or satiric characters like Lahontan's Adario, but also in the *mœurs des sauvages*. Characterizations such as Robert Rogers's Ponteach or Chateaubriand's Chactas are only one aspect of the theme, a later romanticist version. In exploration-ethnography texts, the Noble Savage arises from paradoxical generalizations that describe the Native Americans as selflessly generous and as hard bargaining traders, as chivalric warriors and as back-stabbing cowards, as indulgent parents and as careless infanticides.

Hayden White claims that the concept of nobility, not of the Savage, is the key element of the theme, and that this vision of Natural Man was employed in the years before the French Revolution to denounce the claims of European noble classes to a natural superiority: "The hidden or suppressed referent of the Noble Savage idea is, in short, that of 'nobility' itself. This concept of 'nobility' is implicitly characterized as 'savage' on the figurative level of the phrase" (131). For White, the oxymoronic quality of Noble Savage is fundamental to its purpose. This does not, however, preclude the existence of the Ignoble Savage, which, White claims, was used to justify the slave trade. The Noble and Ignoble each served different political purposes and, according to White, were generated out of different psychosocial processes. The Ignoble Savage arose from a "mode of contiguity," from a "horizontal" division between human and subhuman, and by positing the abnormality or degeneracy of the natives justified treating them as objects. The Noble Savage pertained to the "mode of continuity" and justified the replacement of the aristocratic class system by one based on wealth or merit. White's "The Noble Savage Theme as Fetish" encourages scholars to look at the Noble and Ignoble Savage not as a binary opposition, but as two themes with separate functions; his interpretation of the Noble Savage is consistent with the critical intent of Lahontan and others.

Understood dialectically, and drawing on White's definition, the Noble Savage becomes not the opposite of the Ignoble, but the sublimation or, to use Hegel's term, sublation, of the opposition between virtue and inhumanity, between "civilization" and "savagery." He is both cruel and kind, both stupid and clever, both godless and reverent. Furthermore, although the Noble Savage sometimes served to refigure Europeans' vision of their primitive past, it often served instead to justify a vision of the future in colonial America. One feature of an ideology is that it effectively suppresses contradictions, and contradictions contained in the Noble Savage helped colonial writers to justify learning from and imitating the Indians even as they believed the natives to be the savage foe of civilization. As Pearce observed in *Savagism and Civilization*, the Indian was frequently defined by Europeans as a negation: "The Indian became important for the English mind, not for what he was in and of himself, but rather for what he showed civilized men they were not and must not be" (5). Although this application of what I call the negation trope describes accurately many representations, the Noble Savage also enabled colonists to project positive ideas of what they wished to achieve in American society.

This dialectical Noble Savage is distinct from the romantic Noble Savage of the later eighteenth and early nineteenth centuries. The latter version commonly appears as a stoic chief mourning his own demise, such as Rogers's Ponteach (Pontiac), Lydia Child's Hobomok, Chateaubriand's Chactas (actually the French spelling of Choctaw), or Jefferson's Logan. These figures frequently were (or at least were named after) dangerous foes who had been defeated on the battlefield and were effectively neutralized in literary representations that showed them accepting their disappearance as a natural destiny. Lahontan's Adario was also based on such a figure, the Huron headman Kondiaronk, known to the French as "Le Rat" (which, indeed, means "the Rat"), and this transitional figure preserves some of the paradoxical nature of the dialectical Noble Savage. Kondiaronk had disrupted a peace between Denonville's French forces and the Iroquois by attacking a group of the latter and suggesting to them afterward that the cease-fire was a ruse by the French to lull their defenses. This "treachery" led to a devastating Iroquoian attack on Montreal in August 1689.[25] Yet in spite of this, Kondiaronk resumed his position as a key ally of the French, and on his death, during the conference for the French-Iroquoian peace treaty of 1701, he was buried with great pomp at Montreal. Lahontan transformed Le Rat of his *Voyages* into Adario of his *Dialogues*, and though it is an exaggeration to refer to Adario as Tzvetan Todorov and Richard White have ("the model for all the noble savages who followed him in European literature"),[26] he does initiate a series of Native American literary characters who challenged the values of European and colonial society after their namesakes could no longer mount a military challenge in the woods and fields.

The dialectical Noble Savage, however, does not often reside in a single noble character; rather, he arises from the observations of explorers and travelers wherein nobility is the more believable for being tempered with the realities of human cruelty. Thus Kondiaronk was once a traitor yet still came to be eulogized as a hero. The noble is meaningful, after all, only in contrast with the ignoble or cruel, and if understood as a reference to the European nobility, the word suggests not a pacific angel, but a proud knight. William Smith, in *Historical Account of Bouquet's Expedition against the Ohio Indians, in 1764*, gives ample space to descriptions of the cruelties of the "savages." Yet when Bouquet forces the enemy to surrender POWs, we read of "a scene, which language indeed can but weakly describe. . . . The scene I mean, was the arrival of the prisoners in the camp, where were to be seen fathers and mothers recognizing and clasping their once-lost babes" (74–75). In a book devoted to the campaign of General Bouquet and his soldiers, the representation of mothers, babes, and the sentimental family ties among them comes as an abrupt shift. In a text laden with the discourse of civilization and savagery, this scene presents the uncomfortable fact that "sisters and brothers unexpectedly meeting together after long separation, [were] scarce able to speak the same language, or for some time, to be sure that they were children of the same parents!" (76) and that these children, "having been accustomed to look upon Indians as the only connexions they had, having been tenderly treated by them, and speaking their language . . . considered their new state in the light of a captivity, and parted from the savages with tears" (80). The strict separation between civilized and savage disappears in this scene of familial attachment, and the polarization of Noble and Ignoble Savage dissolves as well. This nobility is not infused in a single semifictional chief but is common to this group of Indians, whom Smith holds up as moral models: "These qualities in savages challenge our just esteem. . . . Cruel and unmerciful as they are, by habit and long example, in war, yet whenever they come to give way to the native dictates of humanity, they exercise virtues which Christians need not blush to imitate" (77–78). Their sentimental virtues are noble not as a perfect abstraction but through the stark contrast with the image of the merciless warrior, a contrast equally relevant to European society, which condoned both love and war.

As we will see in Chapter 6 and in the Epilogue, Smith's was one of a small group of texts appearing in English after the Seven Years' War that advocated Indian methods of warfare as essential for successful military action in the American backcountry against native or colonial armies. Richard Slotkin has written of William Smith's book: "It suggests that the proper way to live in America is to imitate the Indian, and, conversely, that the Indian's patriotism, independence, and love of liberty make him the model of the ideal American" (231).[27] The most important effect of the Noble Savage is therefore not the image of an elevated chief or romantic primitive, but the plurality of Indians whose nobility resembles what colonists valued most in themselves. In these American Indians, such as those represented by John Smith and by Lahontan, we can see some origins of the modern individualized subject and his/her role in a representative democracy. We have the Enlightenment visions of sexual liberation and of a social hierarchy based on merit and achievement. Less optimistically, we can see the realpolitik of war, domination, and assimilation of neighboring peoples and the American tradition of individualized violence and vengeance. The future meets the past in the representation of the Amerindian, and as well as a twentieth-century future one can discover past futures, for the vision of the Indian was always bound up with the colonists' ideas of what kind of society they wished to create in Canada and the United States. The Noble and Ignoble versions of the Savage are not in a complementary opposition where each is of equal importance and of similar provenance. The Noble Savage is a more complex, fully developed ideology than the Ignoble, and its nobility, like that of the American colonist who internalizes the Indian he demonizes, lies in the successful synthesis of oppositions.

Willful Anachronism: The Premiers Temps Trope

The Noble Savage, a forward-looking utopian image, is best thought of not in opposition to the Ignoble Savage, but as a counterpoint to the backward-looking historical view that placed the *sauvage américain* in comparison with various peoples of the ancient world. I will call it the *premiers temps* trope after Lafitau's subtitle, "comparées au mœurs des premiers temps" [compared with the customs of primitive times]. To understand the logic of this approach, one must appreciate the methodology of cultural scholars before the development of the scientific or geologic scale of time. For instance, recall Book 6 of Lescarbot's *Histoire de la Nouvelle France*, from which I quoted the list of ethnographic categories: "Contenant les mœurs, coutumes, & façons de vivre des Indiens Occidentaux de la Nouvelle France comparées à celles des anciens peuple de pardeça: & particulièrement de ceux qui sont en même parallele & degré" [Wherein are contained the Manners, Customs, and Fashions of Life of the Western Indians of New France, and a comparison of them with those of the people of the old world; and particularly with those who are in the same parallel and degree]. Principles of symmetry within a circumscribed space and time on the earth are inviolable for Lescarbot. The Old and New Worlds are simply over there and over here, "pardela" and "pardeça." Time is either ancient or contemporary but never prehistoric; it always remains within the parameters established by classical and Western history. Lescarbot constantly holds the Old World up to the New; all history and culture is a potential source for comparison, all is on the same level of knowledge, a characteristic of the Renaissance episteme as defined by Michel Foucault. A description of a custom Lescarbot has observed among the *sauvages américains* is sure to evoke a comparison to a Roman, Greek, or barbarian practice or belief. When he notices that the American Indians do not wear hats, for instance, he informs us that "Tous les anciens ont eu cette coutume d'aller à téte nuë, & n'est venu l'usage des chapeaux que sur le tard" (3:373) [All the ancients had this custom of going bareheaded, and the use of hats came in but late (3:134)]. He is particularly inclined to draw comparisons with the Gauls, as if he wanted to see in the Indians the ancestors of his own French people and provide a reason why France's claim to this part of America should be respected by England, Holland, and Spain.

Lescarbot does not conclude that the American Indians are the descendants of migrants from somewhere in the Mediterranean world, he merely notes the common features of the two cultures. But theories that the ancestors of the Native Americans had migrated from some part of Europe or Asia began to appear soon after the discovery of the New World and grew in influence well into the nineteenth century. According to Cornelius Jaenen, Jewish, Carthaginian, Canaanite, Ophiric, Phoenician, Trojan, and Egyptian migrants were all proposed.[28] Whereas Lescarbot drew comparisons between the Amerindians and the Gauls, English colonists were fond of a theory that the Welsh king Madoc had settled America in the twelfth century. Tartars and other East Asian peoples were also suggested, a theory that coincides with the belief of today's anthropologists. The coincidence is deceptive, however, for in the eighteenth century there was no concept of an Ice Age neolithic prehistory during which such migrations could have taken place over thousands of years. Philological, racial, and ethnological comparisons, not archaeological or climatological findings, served as evidence for these theories, such as Lamothe–Cadillac's list of similarities between the Algonquians around Lake Huron and the Hebrews, both of whom enforce a taboo against menstruating women, marry widows to their brothers-in-law, and so on. The Hebrew theory, first proposed, according to Jaenen, by Joannes Lumnius in 1567, and the subject of a pamphlet debate in seventeenth-century England, saw a resurgence in the nineteenth century as the Ten Lost Tribes origin elaborated at great length by James Adair in his *History of the American Indians* (1775) and embraced by missionaries such as Elias Boudinot.

Lescarbot and Lafitau were the chief French practitioners of this effort to assimilate the Native Americans into the Judeo-Christian West's view of itself. This approach was not exoticist, but more nearly the opposite, and it was not a phenomenon of the eighteenth-century Enlightenment so much as of the Renaissance. For Lafitau and Lescarbot, the *sauvage* did not exist on the far side of the Fall or any other insurmountable barrier such as "progress" or the "arts and sciences"; instead, the cultural discontinuity posed by the discovery of pale-skinned people living a primitive life in a northern wilderness had to be accommodated with the Scriptures and the learned classical texts that contained human history.

The *premiers temps* theory asserted that the Europeans sailed back in time on the way to the New World, and that the people found there were barbarians like those who lived at the margins of the great ancient civilizations. Today, anthropologists often view their work as the study of human prehistory, but for Lescarbot and Lafitau there was no prehistory—all was explicable within the texts of scholastic canons. If the *sauvage* was always already within the history of the Occident, it could not threaten the concepts of human nature or civilization as it did for Rousseau. It could only pose challenges to the various colonial powers, which might learn from them, convert them, or exploit them. Lafitau wished to show that Europeans could learn from the Americans, not just about their origins, but as the Athenians and Romans learned or should have learned from the Spartans and barbarians when their own societies became decadent and weak. A process of decay pervaded this paradigm, as in this passage:

> Que les Sauvages ayent eu autrefois une éducation aussi rigoreuse [as the Lacedemonians], cela est encore sensible par les restes qu'ils en avoient conservez jusqu'à nos jours, & dont j'ai fait voir la ressemblance avec les Initiations aux mystères des Payens . . .
>
> Ce qui fait un nouveau motif de probabilité, c'est que cette Education des Crétois & des Lacédémoniens avoit été prise des Barbares, qui avoient en premier lieu habité la Grèce, & qu'elle se trouvoit parfaitement conforme aux mœurs des peuples de Thrace & de Scythie. (1: 599–600)
>
> [It is still obvious by the vestiges remaining today of the early education among the Indians that they formerly had as rigorous a system of education (as this). I have shown the resemblance (of their system) with the pagan initiations into the mysteries . . .
>
> A further indication of the probability (of my assumptions) is (the fact) that this Cretan and Spartan form of education had been taken from the barbarians who had, in the first place, inhabited Greece and that it is perfectly in conformity with the Thracian and Scythian customs. (Fenton and Moore's parenthetical insertions)]

Lafitau's belief in a decay from Spartan virtue to Roman decadence, or classical glory to modern weakness, and from the purity of the early Church to the dissent of the Reformation, here acquires another analogy, as the Amerindians' education has degenerated from its own primitive purity. Because Lafitau believed that the *sauvages américains* were most likely descended from the Scythians, this noble primitivism has the same locus for New World as for Old World peoples and refers back to Herodotus.[29] Yet because many different analogies were available in classical history, the various lessons drawn from the primitive Americans were contradictory. Robert Johnson, a promoter of the Virginia colony, also compared the Indians with his own people's forebears but concluded in favor of the moderns: "how much good we shall performe to those . . . will easily appeare, by comparing our present happiness with our former ancient miseries, wherein we had continued brutish, poore and naked Britanes to this day, if Julius Caesar with his Romane Legions (or some other) had not laid the ground to make us tame and civill" (14). The Romans were decadent compared with the rugged Spartans, yet enlightened and cultured compared with the ancient Britons. Seventeenth-century British imperialists identified themselves with the Romans in Johnson's allegory.

More often, however, the *premiers temps* trope was used to elevate the American Indians to a level that would offer lessons to colonial societies. Lafitau follows Hayden White's definition for the Noble Savage while ignoring its irony when, in the dedication to the Duc d'Orleans, he writes of the *sauvages américains*:

> . . . sous ces apparences incultes & grossieres vous verrez par-tout chez ces Peuples un amour pour la Patrie gravé dans les cœurs, un passion naturelle pour la gloire, un grandeur d'ame, nonseulement à l'épreuve du péril, mais même au-dessus de malheur, un secret impenetrable dans leurs deliberations; &, quand il s'agit d'éxecuter, un mépris de la mort né avec eux, & fortifié par l'education. Toutes ces qualités, MONSEIGNEUR, dont vous trouverez le principe en vous-même. (1:ii–iii)

> [. . . under this crude and uncultivated exterior, you will see everywhere, among these people, a love for their native land imprinted in their hearts, a natural passion for glory, a greatness of soul, not only at the test of peril, but even rising above misfortune. In their deliberations, they preserve an impenetrable secrecy. When it is a question of execution, they show an inborn scorn of death, strengthened by training. All these qualities, My Lord, of which you will find the elements within yourself, will arouse your understanding and praise.]

The trope connecting the Indians with classical virtues was enormously popular. An anonymous tract of 1755, *State of the British and French Colonies in North America*, said of the Indians, "In short these people are considered by the judicious Americans, both English and French, as equal, if not superior to either the ancient Greeks or Romans, for generosity, integrity, justice, policy in government, firmness of mind and courage" (82).

In recent attempts to interrogate the evolution and preconceptions of their field of writing, anthropologists have sought out precursors for the modern ethnography among early texts of colonialism. Lafitau's *Mœurs des sauvages américains comparées aux mœurs des premiers temps* has been identified as one of the most prescient anticipations of comparative ethnography. Articles by William Fenton, Michel de Certeau, Alfred Métraux, and Michèle Duchet have examined Lafitau's pioneer status in the field. His effort to establish a genealogical link between the Amerindians and the "barbarians" of ancient times based on similarities in dress, language, and customs reflects modern anthropological methods, even if his belief in the universal presence of religion and marriage along Christian models clashes with today's views. Lafitau actually anticipated twentieth-century paradigms by taking the same poles and inverting them. Whereas today social scientists might look for elements of native "pagan" beliefs in local customs of Christian worship, Lafitau, based on his belief in a single, Mosaic origin of civilization and a single revelation of the faith, finds elements of Christianity among the American Indians. Duchet observes that *Mœurs des sauvages américains* is neither a relation nor a description, but a comparison. The two elements of the comparison, the *sauvages américains* and the barbarians of the *premiers temps* before the rise of Greek civilization, are both artificial categories constructed so as to maximize the desired correspondence between them. The Americans include those of Brazil, Mexico, and Peru, whom Lafitau read about in others' relations, as well as the Iroquois he knew firsthand, who serve for the bulk of the examples. The peoples of the *premiers temps* are by definition known only secondhand: "Les sources seront tous les textes qui parlent de coutumes oubliées et de peuples dispersés ou disparus; la Bible, l'Iliade et l'Odyssée, et, s'il faut, la 'fable' ou 'Mythologie'" (614) [The sources will be all the texts that talk of forgotten customs and of dispersed or disappeared peoples, the Bible, the Iliad, the Odyssey, and, if necessary, "fables" or "mythology" (my translation)], writes Duchet. Like an anthropologist, Lafitau drew on both his own fieldwork and the accounts of other observers, and he described the patterns of life of our earliest ancestors from the viewpoint of a modern scholar who stands outside the time of these people and theorizes about broad patterns of culture.

Of these recent studies, the most provocative is de Certeau's; it goes beyond merely situating Lafitau as a precursor of anthropology, to examine his *Mœurs des sauvages américains* as a crux in an early-eighteenth-century shift in the relationships between time, history, and writing. De Certeau devotes much of his essay to the frontispiece of Lafitau's work (fig. 7), which shows a female scribe writing descriptions of images of *sauvages*, guided by Father Time. De Certeau argues that Lafitau does not just describe but *reads* Native Americans: "What Lafitau wants to see are *objects* pregnant with meaning. . . . He wants to read signs" (42, de Certeau's italics). Lafitau's achievement is not simply to interpret the Americans through the evidence of antiquity, but to use each to illuminate the other by creating an epistemological complementarity:

> But there is a difference of function between the ancient *things* and the savage *customs*. The first have primarily the value of relics, the second primarily that of "clarification" *(lumières)*. Archeology presents to be *seen* what ethnology permits to be *explained*. Lafitau writes: "I admit that if the ancient authors gave me some light to support various happy conjectures concerning the Savages, the Customs of the Savages gave me some light to understand more easily and to explain several things which are in the ancient Authors." (Lafitau 1:3–4; de Certeau 46, de Certeau's italics)

Lafitau's American history does not refer to the empirical authority of artifacts (archaeology had not yet emerged as a field of study), only to that of ethnological observations—from the field or from classical and colonial texts. The customs of the *sauvages américains* become a static text. This move liberates the writer of history from her sources by adding

FIGURE 7. Frontispiece from Lafitau, *Mœurs des sauvages
américains comparées au mœurs des premiers temps*, 1724.
(National Library of Canada, NL-19245)

such nontextual documents, and de Certeau cites Lafitau as among the
first historians to claim the power of writing, by which he means writing
that creates history rather than deriving it from other texts. "Writing
alone remains productive at a moment when the presence of antiquity,
paternal tradition, collapses . . . the mother/writing, celibate machine,
must generate another world and make a new beginning" (50). Ironically, this Jesuit, a counter-Reformation activist whose classical education was so omnivorous as to mold nearly all his impressions of the New
World, becomes not a hidebound traditionalist but an avatar of the

modern era, although de Certeau does acknowledge that Lafitau used his radical methods to support a Christian dogma of monotheism and monogenesis. De Certeau also admits that the complementarity of ancient and savage is not fair to the latter, that "the *living* (Savage) permits the *dead* (ancient) to 'speak,' but the savages are not heard except as voices of the dead, echoes of mute antiquity" (61). Lafitau has in common with Lescarbot and with later anthropologists the rhetorical silencing, hypostatization, and metaphorical killing of the cultural Other, who becomes a part of an ethnographic catalog rather than a living person.

According to de Certeau, Lafitau "makes a star out of a new hero of history: the power of writing" (50). Or, more specifically, "the Canadian travel narratives (from Champlain to Lahontan), describe at length the heroic trials of the writer (where and when one wrote, in spite of the cold, during a brief stop, with the sap of a tree, etc.)" (51). Yet de Certeau fails to note that Lafitau uses Champlain's and Lahontan's writings not for their travel narratives but for their *mœurs des sauvages*, and in these parts of the texts the heroic presence of the writers is effaced to better display the synthetic portrait of the Other. Lafitau is the best anthropologist among them because he so completely hides his subjectivity.

Why should Lafitau have been singled out among the many observers of New France as the one most like later ethnographers? After all, the descriptions of the Indians by many earlier travel writers, such as Sagard, Hennepin, and particularly Lescarbot, contain the same protoethnographic elements and often employ the same method of comparison to the ancient barbarians, a strategy actually more common in the sixteenth and seventeenth than in the eighteenth century. Before celebrating Lafitau as a writer of history, we should wonder why he did not write of his own personal travels and experiences in Canada. He stands out from the other writers of this study because his career more resembles that of an anthropologist. He was educated in rhetoric, philosophy, and theology in some of the best schools in France, and in 1712, at age thirty-one, he left for Canada to do his "fieldwork" as a missionary among the Iroquois at Sault St. Louis (Kahnawake or Caughnawaga) near Montreal. After five years, he returned to France and wrote up his findings (*Mœurs des sauvages américains* was published in 1724). He spent two more years in Canada, from 1727 to 1729, as superior of the same mission, then returned to Paris to work as procurator for the Jesuits in New France. He lived out the rest of his life in the metropole as a bureaucrat and a scholar.

Lafitau's life story, therefore, was as quiet and unobtrusive as that of a twentieth-century academic. He was neither a soldier who fought against the people he studied nor an official charged with developing the colony, whereas Champlain was both. He did not write a history of the colony in which he lived, as Lescarbot and Charlevoix did (although he did publish a *Histoire des découvertes et conquêtes des Portugais dans le Nouveau Monde* in 1733), nor did he write a narrative of his travels in Canada. It appears that he did not travel far beyond Sault St. Louis. He was a missionary, but he did not write of his work converting and baptizing the heathen as earlier Jesuits had in the *Relations*. Lafitau's work appeals to ethnographers as a precursor because it does not contain admixtures of exploration or missionary narrative, because Lafitau obeys the rhetorical codes of later anthropologists by suppressing his own personal experience and the scene of verbal dialogue between himself and his native informants, turning the Native American into a silent relic of his own culture.

Negation and Substitution

In the Noble Savage and in the *premiers temps* approach, which reached its strongest expression in Lafitau, we have examined the two dominant tropes for the representation of the Native Americans. I have attempted to show that the ideology of the Noble Savage is constituted through the sublimation of apparently contradictory attributes ascribed in such statements as "De religion on n'en recognoist aucune parmy eux. Ils ont quelque congnoissance de l'immortalité de l'ame" [One recognizes nothing of religion among them. They have some understanding of the immortality of the soul (my translation)].[30] These two sentences enact the tension between the two tropes of negation and substitution, such as are employed in the Noble Savage. The Noble Savage is, as

Hayden White demonstrated, a reversal of European values and social structures. Yet the negation of values is itself a deployment of cultural categories. The Savage has no religion because he is not (and cannot be, according to some) a Christian; yet he has a religion because the Bible tells us that all peoples were created by God and have religion. The power to take away *and replace* the elements of "savagery" and of "civilization" is fundamental to colonialism. The two parts of this ideological and rhetorical dialectic are what I call the tropes of negation and substitution.

Negation of the qualities cherished in the European self constitutes an Other through difference, as Coetzee described. Yet this different Other is not necessarily less civilized than the European, for the negation of negative qualities creates a favorable image. The trope of negation should not be considered a rhetoric of an inscrutable Otherness or of an ethnocentric suppression of "humanity." Descriptions employing negation contributed to the foundations of Enlightenment cultural relativism and to the romanticist Noble Savage. Nor should it be viewed as limited to any one period of conquest and colonization. Other scholars have called attention to the negation trope, notably Margaret Hodgen in her study of Renaissance anthropology (194–201). She quotes many instances of it in the sixteenth century, the most famous of which is Michel de Montaigne's essay "On Cannibals":

> C'est une nation, diroy je à Platon, en laquelle il n'y a aucune espece de trafique; nul cognoissance de lettres; nulle science de nombres; nul nom de magistrat, ny de superiorité politique; nul usage de service, de richesse ou de pauvreté; nuls contrats; nulles successions; nuls partages; nulles occupations qu'oysives; nul respect de parenté que commun; nuls vestements; nulle agriculture; nul metal; nul usage de vin ou de bled. Les paroles mesme qui signifient la mensonge, la trahison, la dissimulation, l'avarice, l'envie, la detraction, le pardon, inouïes. (235–36)

> [This is a nation, I should say to Plato, in which there is no kind of commerce, no knowledge of letters, no science of numbers, no title of magistrate or of political superior, no habit of service, riches or poverty, no contracts, no inheritance, no divisions of property, only lei-

surely occupations, no respect for any kinship but the common ties, no
clothes, no agriculture, no metals, no use of corn or wine. The very
words denoting lying, treason, deceit, greed, envy, slander, and for-
giveness have never been heard. (110)]

Montaigne, of course, never traveled to America, and many of these
negations are untrue. Native Americans, including those whom Cartier
and others had already encountered when Montaigne wrote the essay in
the 1570s, had clothes, agriculture, corn, and commerce. Montaigne
was probably aware of this, too, but wished to mock the neo-Platonic
philosophy that society is defined by certain essential elements. In the
last sentence he goes still further, to question the concepts behind words
in our languages. Negation is always already substitution, because by a
cultural variant of the hermeneutical circle, one can only imagine the
absence of such social structures as hierarchy and kinship by substituting an absence for a presence. Coetzee's list of categories also exposes this
process. European travel writers assert that the Savage has no law or
religion only after creating a context for the discussion of the category.
This is the thought experiment that created the Noble Savage, who both
has and does not have hierarchy, law, money, government, and other
elements of "civilized" life.

Although the existence of these two tropes has received some attention in recent scholarship, it is as hard to agree on names for them as it is
to separate them. Stephen Greenblatt in *Marvelous Possessions* discusses
them as contributing to the related paradox of European discoverers who
admit they know nothing of the native peoples, then confidently claim
to know everything, "to assume transparency, to rush from wonder—the
experience of stunned surprise—to possession or at least the illusion of
possession. . . . On the one hand, there is a tendency to imagine the
Indians as virtual blanks—wild, unformed creatures, as naked in culture
as they are in body. On the other hand, there is a tendency to imagine the
Indians as virtual doubles, fully conversant with the language and culture of the Europeans. These tendencies seem like opposites, but they are
in fact versions of one another" (95). Greenblatt approaches negation
and substitution through the problem of communication with the Indians. Negation: they have no language. Substitution: they have a lan-

guage, and we can understand it. However, this approach obscures a study of the gestures, guesses, and false assumptions by which European and Indian actually communicated at the moments of early contact, a study of great importance that has yet to be done, if in fact it is possible. Also, in this passage Greenblatt uses the categories of sameness and difference, tropes that do not exactly correspond with substitution and negation, are less accurate because even more interdependent and inextricable, and belong more to a cultural than a rhetorical register.

Negation and substitution may also appear to be analogous with the more historicized themes of Noble Savage and *premiers temps*, but these two pairs do not correspond so easily either. The Noble Savage results, I have argued, not from the negation of negative aspects of European civilization, but from the suppression of contradictions that often take the form of negations and substitutions, such as the two sentences from Bouton cited above. The *premiers temps* epistemology is just one possible substitution. Comparisons of the *sauvages* with a contemporary European population were also common. In 1664 Pierre Boucher, governor of Trois Rivières, Quebec, wrote of the natives:

> . . . & il est bien rare de voir parmy eux de ces esprits buses & grossiers, comme nous en voyons en France parmy nos paysans: Ils craignent plus une simple reprimande de leurs parens ou de leurs Capitaines, que l'on ne fait en Europe les roüs & les gibets: car vous ne voyez point de desordre parmi eux, quoy que les peres & meres n'ayent point de chastiment pour leurs enfans, nonplus que leurs chefs pour leurs inferieurs, que des paroles de reprimande . . . (96)

> [The Indians in general are quick witted, and dullness and boorishness, such as we see among our peasants in France, are very rarely to be seen among them. They stand more in awe of reprimands from their parents or chiefs than people in Europe do of the rack or the gallows; and you see no want of order among them, although the fathers and mothers have no punishments for their children, nor the chiefs for their inferiors, except words of reproof. (53)]

Boucher observed the absence in Canada of phenomena familiar in France: insolent peasants, beggars, and troublemakers. From this observation he attributed to Indian society a negative quality, a lack of disorder, constitutive of a positive European concept, government, which the "savages" lacked by definition. The result is to propose the existence of some force of social order that works as a substitute for government, a force that can be perceived by the negation or absence of anarchy. The passage also suggests a greater obedience among the Indians to the word, to spoken commands, an aspect of a certain utopia of language in the New World that I will explore in the next chapter. Because Governor Boucher had to deal with the problems he describes, his idealized *sauvage* is the product of a practical imagination, not a distant view like Montaigne's. English writers often made a move analogous to Boucher's, comparing the Indians with the Irish, a liminal, "savage" people whom the English colonized before sailing to America.[31] European colonists appreciated the virtues of Native American life only after they had preserved and protected their own cultural pride by denying to the Indians what they prized (or deplored) in themselves. Categories such as Lescarbot's chapter titles or Montaigne's litany of negations served as a template for such substitution.

The term "Other," which I have used occasionally with some trepidation, is overused in literary and cultural theory. The psychoanalytic definition, which insists on the fact that the Other is constituted by and within the Self through projection, has given way to nondialectical uses of the term, which deny the action of substitution and negation by insisting on an almost metaphysical cultural difference. Viewed next to today's debates and differences, the Native American of the seventeenth century seems the "other-est" of Others, and this causes too many readers to look for evidence that the early European conquerors denied the Indians both humanity and cultural particularity and called them beasts, and to overlook the ways in which the American Indians were viewed as human beings *comparable* to Europeans through a pattern of substitutions and negations. The explorer-ethnographers learned a great deal about their own society through comparisons with those of the Indians, and it is necessary to recognize, in both contemporary scholarship and colonial writing, the apparent contradiction between these two approaches, between negative and substitutive, forward-looking utopian and nostalgic *premiers temps* descriptions of the Indians, not as two distinct theories of cultural representation, but as constitutive of a paradoxical rhetoric that operated in colonial writing.

This chapter has sketched out a series of oppositions: travel narrative and ethnography, narration and description, figure and ground, Noble Savage and *premiers temps*, and finally negation and substitution. These categories are generic, rhetorical, topographic, historical, and epistemological. Each can be used to interpret in a different way the texts of discovery and description of North America in the seventeenth and eighteenth centuries, and each is dialectical, existing in tension with its antithesis, neither of which can be identified as the dominant or more accurate or more sensitive mode of portraying Native Americans and America. All are susceptible to deconstruction. In the following chapter the concepts of negation and substitution are applied to the issues of Indian clothing, money, and writing, three aspects of culture especially susceptible to misunderstanding through substitution, particularly important for locating New World peoples within Judeo-Christian cosmology and vital for colonists' successful trade and negotiation with the Indians.

CHAPTER 4

Clothing, Money, and Writing

The words *sauvage* and *nu* (naked) have long been closely associated. The "savage's" nakedness has multiple resonances. By an allusion to the Book of Genesis, nakedness signifies the innocence of the first humans before the Fall into shame, sin, and modesty. In a secular version of the myth of origins, it represents the absence of culture and the equality of humans at birth. Yet Adam and Eve in the State of Nature were not innocent because they lacked vice; they did not even know what it was, any more than an Algonquin in the fifteenth century knew what a European was. Both Eden and the State of Nature give rise to a hermeneutical circle, one of the most tightly wound instances of the dialectic of negation and substitution.

The State of Nature (itself a contradiction if "state" is defined as a political entity) is paradoxically both the negation of civilization and the substitution of innocence for sophistication. The innocence we attribute to this State of Nature, if not the entire concept, is an artifact of our status as observers, quite different from the experience of those in that state we observe. Jean-Jacques Rousseau, in the *Discours sur l'origine et les fondements de l'inégalité*, described the State of Nature as "un état qui n'existe plus, qui n'a peut-être point existé, qui probablement n'existera jamais" (151) [a state which no longer exists, perhaps never did exist, and probably never will exist (44)]. Interpreters of Rousseau have pointed to this passage to emphasize the hypothetical status of the State of Nature and to counter the notion, embraced at times by Rousseau as well as his readers, that it was a condition society had been in or could return to, or a state that might be witnessed among peoples in America or other colonial settings. But regardless of the correct interpretation of Rousseau's writings, the New World natives lived their lives in the state to which they were accustomed, and European observers had to reconcile their notions of primitive life, such as the naked or illiterate *sauvage*, with what they found in North America. Often a dissonance arose between claims that the Indians did not have clothing, agriculture, or writing and observations that they in fact did have these markers of civilization.

Pelts as Clothing, for Trade, and as Hair

As some indigenous peoples do live most of their lives naked, their nakedness must signify some positive aspects of their culture, not just the negation of characteristics of clothed Europeans. In the sultry tropics of Tahiti or the Amazon, long before the development of a discourse of anthropology to analyze and constitute the characteristics of primitive culture, nudity signified an elemental relation between humankind and its natural surroundings, a removal of the insulation between humans and nature. This is Diderot's thesis in the *Supplément au voyage de Bougainville*—that social practices in Tahiti followed natural laws. Virtually all Native North American peoples, however, did wear clothes, and in the cold forests of Canada, no one could survive for long without them. Indians wore a variety of animal skins and covered their own skin with shell belts and jewelry, bear grease, tattoos, and paint.[1] European observers therefore could not simply ascribe to them a primordial innocence or an absence of cultural acquisitions but had to explain the difference of clothing and to consider whether such tattoos, pelts, and paint were clothing, or ornaments, or an unfamiliar new code of social signification akin to writing.

All cultures represent identity through clothing, for it serves as an instant visual sign of belonging in a society, even if also divided into more specific codes for class, gender, occupation, and other identities. In seventeenth-century Europe, clothing was strictly determined by social and marital status, age, sex, and occupation. The classes of society were differentiable by their raiment, and sumptuary laws often enforced these distinctions, prohibiting people from wearing the clothes of someone above their station. To the degree that this system of sartorial significa-tion operated smoothly, it disguised its own functioning. Rather than status determining dress, dress effectively represented status, so that in practice it was true that "the clothes make the man." During the eigh-teenth century, however, with the rise of a wealthy bourgeoisie, the authenticity of clothing as a signifier of social status became more prob-lematic. When European colonists encountered the American Indians, they expected to find a similar system of differences in clothing that coded status. They did find such a system but in the process were forced to reconsider the definition of clothing, and Diderot's is just one example of the profound conclusions that could result from such reconsideration.

European clothing was apparently also a strong mark of identity for northeastern Algonquians, for Roger Williams translated the Narragan-sett word for Englishmen, "Wataconûog," as "Coatmen" (52). He also wrote in the chapter "Of Their Nakedness and Cloathing" in *A Key in to the Language of America* that, "While they are amongst the English they keep on the English apparell, but pull of[f] all, as soone as they come again into their owne Houses, and Company" (113). Nonetheless, colo-nists believed that efforts to convert Indians into Christians or clients would be aided by persuading them to adopt European garb. James Axtell remarks that clothing as a sign of cultural status was crucial to the process of conversion or acculturation: "So important was European clothing as a badge of 'civility' that an Indian's degree of acculturation could almost be read in his appearance."[2] To abandon savage nakedness for clothing was sufficient to change one's culture; the clothes really did make the man, or so Cartier believed in 1534 when he took back to France the two sons of Donnacona, leader of a nation on the Gaspé Peninsula, claiming that "nous desirons mener avec nous deux de ses fils, et qu'en apres nous retournerions en ce part" (66) [we wished to take two of his sons away with us and afterwards would bring them back again to that harbour]. The cultural appropriation was quickly accomplished through a change of clothes and ornaments: "Et ainsi nous fimes veter à ses fils a chacun une chemise, un Sayon de couleur, et une tocque rouge leur mettent aussi à chacun une chaine de laiton au col, dont ils se contenterent fort, et donnerent leurs vieux habits à ceux qui s'en retournaient" (67) [And we dressed up his two sons in shirts and ribbons and in red caps, and put a little brass chain round the neck of each, at which they were greatly pleased; and they proceeded to hand over their old rags to those who were going back on shore]. These two captives, Taignoagny and Domagaya, were not, however, so easily transformed as Cartier thought. When the discoverer of French Canada returned the next summer he expected the boys to guide his party up the Hochelaga (St. Lawrence) River, but instead they ran away to rejoin their people and tried to persuade Cartier not to sail upstream, but to turn around and go home. In this first encounter, clothing as a cultural signifier was manipulated by creative intercultural wearers and misread by the Europeans.

In this chapter I will be concerned not with the acculturation of Indians through the imposition of European clothing, writing systems, and cash economies, but with the importance for the French and English colonists of American Indian clothing, commodities, and signification practices. Visual marks of cultural identity such as clothing and tattoos, objects of ritual exchange such as wampum belts, and objects used as trade currency such as beaver pelts and wampum beads were all signifiers that colonists had to read and understand if they were to be successful in their relations with the Indians. Clothes, money, and writing were for the Indians not divided into three separate spheres but interrelated on the same register, and therefore Europeans were forced to *read* natives' apparel, their gifts, and their writing as languages. Discussion of these various signifying practices will therefore not treat them separately, as in the ethnographic catalog, but move from one to another as their connections become apparent.

Because in the northern forests native clothing consisted of pelts and tanned hides, clothing was inextricably tied up with exchange and

profit, with the very motive of European colonies in New France and
New England. This was doubly true due to the little-known fact that it
was not just by trapping, shooting, or trading that Europeans obtained
the beaver pelts used to make hat felt, but by stripping the natives of
their clothes. Charlevoix explains why this was necessary:

> La voici: le Castor Sec est la Peau de Castor, qui n'a servi à aucun usage:
> le Castor Gras est celle, qui a été portée par les Sauvages, lesquels,
> après l'avoir bien grattée en dedans, & frottée avec la Moële de certains
> Animaux, que je ne connois point, pour la rendre plus maniable, en
> cousent plusieurs ensemble, & en font une manière de Mante, qu'on
> appelle Robe, & de laquelle ils s'enveloppent le Poil en dedans. Ils ne la
> quittent en Hyver ni le jour ni la nuit; le grand Poil tombe bientôt, et
> le Duvet reste & s'engraisse, & en cet état il est bien plus propre à être
> mis en œuvre par les Chapeliers. (99)

> [The dry beaver is its skin before it has been employed in any use: the
> green beaver are such as have been worn by the Indians, who, having
> well tawed them on the inside, and rubbed them with the marrow of
> certain animals, with which I am not acquainted, in order to render
> them more pliant, sew several of them together, making a sort of
> garment, which they call a robe, and in which they wrap themselves
> with the fur inwards. They never put it off in winter, day or night; the
> long hair soon falls off, the down remaining and becoming oily, in
> which condition it is much fitter to be worked up by the hatters.
> (1:157)][3]

Adriaen Van der Donck a century earlier had written: "After the hairs
have fallen out, or are worn, and apparently useless, we get the articles
back and convert the fur into hats, before which it cannot be well used
for this purpose, for unless the beaver has been worn and is dirty and
greasy, it will not felt properly—therefore those old peltries are most
valuable" (113). Lahontan specified just how valuable in the *Mémoires*,
where he quoted the prices paid for different grades of beavers (castors):
for "Castors d'Hiver" (in the winter or "hiver," the beaver's coat is
thicker than in the summer), 4.10 livres; for "Castor sec ou ordinaire"
(dry or ordinary), 3 livres; and for "Castors gras" (greasy beaver), 5 livres.

For the *coureurs de bois*, the 50 percent premium paid for the greasy beaver pelts transformed the methods of their enterprise. Le Page du Pratz describes the lure of profits in "castor gras" with an anecdote about one Tissenet, a Frenchman of noble birth who went to Canada to earn his fortune. He followed advice to journey far into the wilderness and locate nations that had not yet been contacted by traders and was delighted to find that by offering "bagatelles dont ils furent enchantés, n'ayent encore rien vû de semblable" (2:304) [trinkets with which they were enchanted, never having seen anything of the kind (my translation)], he could obtain "Castor Gras, ce Castor est celui qui a servi aux Naturels pour les couvrir; il vaut le double de celui que l'on nomme Castor sec, qui est l'ordinaire" (2:305) [greasy beaver, from beavers that the Indians have used to cover themselves; it is worth twice as much as the kind that is called dry beaver, which is the regular kind (my translation)]. The episode acquires irony from another story that precedes it. Tissenet and his party were held captive and threatened with scalping if they did not surrender all their goods. But the clever trader awed the attackers into submission by removing his "chevelure" (wig or scalp) and offering it voluntarily. The Indians were astonished that a scalp of hair could be removable, although Tissenet took it for granted that their beaver garments were expendable. In this tall tale Le Page du Pratz interrogated the distinction between hair and clothing, and between the fur of one's own and the fur taken from others.

As Tissenet learned, interaction with the natives was essential for success in the early years of the fur trade, and it was worth the effort to journey ever farther afield to find the valuable preworn pelts. This was the motive driving some explorers such as Radisson and his partner the Sieur des Groseilliers. Indian middlemen could play an important role by buying their relatives' and neighbors' clothes, and traders often married into tribes in order to secure access to their robes. According to a memoir in the French Archives de la Marine:

> Les coureurs de bois font souvent mille bassesses auprès des sauvages
> pour avoir leurs castors; il les suivent jusques dans leurs chasses, ils ne
> leur donnent pas même le temps de faire sécher et de préparer leurs

peaux. Ils essuient les railleries piquantes, les mépris et quelquefois les coups de ces sauvages, que ne sauroient assez s'étonner d'une avidité si sordide, et de voir les François venir de si loin avec tant de fatigues et de dépenses pour ramasser des castors sales et puants, dont ils se sont habillés et dont ils ne font plus de cas.

[The *coureurs de bois* often committed a thousand base acts with the savages in order to obtain their beaver-skins; they followed them even in their hunting expeditions, and did not even give them time to dry and prepare their pelts. They endured the stinging jeers, the contempt, and sometimes the blows of those savages, who were lost in wonder at covetousness so sordid, and at seeing the French come from so great a distance, with so much fatigue and expense, in order to gather up dirty and foul-smelling beaver skins, with which they clothed themselves, and which they no longer valued.][4]

This sort of behavior scandalized the Indians' sense of propriety, for they recognized the value of their clothing not through selling it but in the prestige to be accrued, in certain situations, from giving it away. Clothing and other personal effects were interred with the dead by many nations that believed the deceased would need these things in the afterlife. Also, when Claude Lebeau gave an account of the departure of his trusted guides from their village, the farewell involved an exchange of clothing:

Chacun de leurs amis voulant avoir un gage de leur amitié mutuelle, s'empressoit à changer de vêtemens avec eux, desorte qu'étant sur leur Départ, ils se trouvèrent dépouillés en moins d'une heure, plus de vingt fois de differents Habillemens, soit couvertures, mitasses, souliers, haches, ceintures &c. car chacun, à proportion du degré d'estime qu'il avoit pour eux, ne croyoit pouvoir mieux leur donner des marques de sa considération, qu'en se faisant honneur de posseder quelque chose qui leur ait appartenu. (2:87)

[Each of their friends, wanting to have a token of their mutual friendship, implored them to exchange clothes, so that at the time of their departure they found themselves stripped in less than an hour more than twenty times of different items; blankets, leggings, shoes, hatch-

ets, belts, etc. Because each one, in proportion to the height of esteem
in which they held him, knew of no better way to show his consideration than by doing himself the honor of possessing something that
had belonged to them. (my translation)]

The special value that the Europeans placed on beaver pelt garments to
the exclusion of other things must have mystified Indians in the early
encounters. By the time the fur trade attained larger and more competi-
tive dimensions in the eighteenth century, with the establishment of
English posts on Hudson Bay, worn beaver or "castor gras" became a rare
and insignificant segment of the market. Most Indians replaced beaver
garments with those made from other skins and especially with the
traders' wool clothing. With beaver pelts as with cotton to the south,
America was regarded by the European colonial economy as the source of
the raw materials for clothing and the market for some of the finished
product. This pattern of exchange was, of course, very different from the
Indians' production and exchange of clothing, which was more local and
subsistence-based.

  Thus the beaver pelt trade enacted the dialectic of negation and
substitution. Relieved of the smelly, greasy pelts that kept him warm,
the *sauvage* became, after all, naked man in the primitive "state of nature." Yet in being denuded rather than discovered naked, the representation of the *sauvage* could not sustain the quality of innocence as a
corollary of nakedness. William Wood described this substitution con-
cisely, expressing regret that English traders "to uncloathe them of their
beaver coates, clad them with the infection of swearing and drinking,
which was never in fashion with them before" (68). Another episode
from Cartier, prior to the kidnapping of Domagaya and Taignoagny,
demonstrates that even in a primal discovery, the natives were not in an
Edenic innocence. Rather, the supposedly primal encounters create a
naked image, innocent and vulnerable to the explorer's penetrating gaze
and associative mind. At Cartier's landfall in Newfoundland he found
the natives "nous faisant signes qu'ils étaient venus pour trafiquer avec
nous; et ils nous montrèrent des peaux de peu de valeur, dont ils se
vêtent" (52) [making signs to us that they had come to barter with us;

and held up some furs of small value, with which they clothe them-selves]. Cartier actively pursues this investment in de-vestment, send-ing some of his men with "couteaux et autres ferrements" (knives and other iron tools) to make an exchange that appears to be a great profit for both parties:

> Et eux, voyant cela, descendirent partie d'entre eux à terre, avec des peaux, et ils trafiquèrent ensemble; et ils montrèrent une grande et merveilleuse joie d'avoir et de recevoir lesdits objets de fer et d'autres choses, dansant et faisant plusieurs cérémonies, en jetant de l'eau de mer sur leur tête avec leurs mains. Et ils nous donnèrent tout ce qu'ils avaient, tellement qu'ils s'en retournèrent tout nus, sans rien avoir sur eux; et ils nous firent signe que le lendemain ils reviendraient avec d'autres peaux. (53)

> [Seeing this, they sent on shore part of their people with some of their furs; and the two parties traded together. The savages showed a mar-vellously great pleasure in possessing and obtaining these iron wares and other commodities, dancing and going through many ceremo-nies, and throwing salt water over their heads with their hands. They bartered all they had to such an extent that all went back naked without anything on them; and they made signs to us that they would return on the morrow with more furs.]

The Native American is first seen not naked but clothed and becomes naked only after an exchange in which he ironically removes his inno-cence as he removes his clothing. Cartier has not reached the origin of mankind, but he belongs to the first stage of exchange between Euro-peans and indigenous peoples, where each side's commodities hold such a great luxury value for the other side that trading seems like an ex-change of gifts (which it likely was for the natives), and where the Europeans accuse the Others of not knowing the intrinsic value of pre-cious metals.[5] It is only after he strips the Indians that Cartier can ascribe to their nakedness a cultural absence, a space for substitution by European culture. The originary innocence is already past, for these Canadians are not only not naked, there is already a value associated with their clothes. The cultural value of nakedness as a negation of civilization is preempted by the exchange value of nakedness as declothed. The reason Cartier failed to reach the geomythical origin is that French and Portuguese fishermen had been in the area harvesting the rich stocks of cod on the Grand Banks, processing their catch at seasonal camps on shore and carrying on a secondary business of trading for pelts with the natives. The fishermen did not write narratives of their activities, but they did influence the reception given Cartier.

The same sort of nonprimal encounter occurred when the Pilgrims landed at Plymouth and met first Samoset, who spoke to them in English he had learned from fishermen and explorers, and then Squanto, who had been taken captive to England and returned. Seasonal trade preceded settlement everywhere in northeastern North America, because even where Europeans had not gone ashore, trade goods dispersed along native distribution networks. History and ideology, however, implant an image of originary settlement by Cartier in Canada and the Pilgrims in New England. The latter are portrayed as an agricultural colony gratefully accepting the Indians' thanksgiving gifts of food, but it was beaver pelts that paid for Plymouth's essential supplies from Europe.

In the cold boreal forests, a perverse competition was carried on between beavers, Indians, and colonizers for the essential use value of warmth, and the Indians were deprived of necessity to make a luxury for European gentlemen far away. Charlevoix claimed, incorrectly, that before the fur trade the Indians had not hunted beavers: "Il paroît que les Sauvages du Canada ne les molestoient pas beaucoup avant notre arrivée dans leur Pays. Les Peaux de Castors n'étoient pas celles, dont ces Peuples faisoient plus d'usage pour se couvrir" (104) [It appears that the Indians of Canada did not give them much disturbance before our arrival in their country. The skins of the beavers were not used by those people by way of garments (1:164)]. Skins, which did not merit recognition as civilized clothing, were, ironically, the most essential protection from the elements for the Indians and the most ostentatious luxury clothing when made into a hat by Europeans. In eighteenth-century Europe, the beaver hat signified status even more distinctly than other parts of the wardrobe: "Men and women could be instantly placed within the social structure according to their hats; meticulous etiquette prevailed about how the headpieces were worn and the sweeping gesture with which they were removed and parked so that they would mark their owners' station in life. The precise technique used in doffing a beaver expressed minute shadings of deference."[6] As the profit motive drove whites to obtain the skins from Indians and beavers alike, one might expect to find them discussed in similar terms, and indeed we shall see in the next chapter that the beaver was regarded as a human culture and described ethnographically. Charlevoix inscribed the values of utility and ornament on the beaver itself when he described the beaver's outer guard hairs as those "qui donne la couleur à la Bête. . . . qui ne lui sert que d'ornement" (95–96) [which gives the animal its color. . . . serving only for ornament (1:153)], while its inner hair, the source of hat felt, was its source of warmth.

The significance of furs and fur-bearing animals, and the contrast or confusion between fur and clothing, thus profoundly affected the confrontation of Europeans with the natives of northeastern North America. An Indian wearing clothes made from marten (a species related to the sable) was clad in a commodity reserved for royalty in Europe, connecting the top and the bottom of the Europeans social hierarchy and providing an impetus for the Noble Savage.[7] Yet pelts were not fully clothes to the explorer's eyes, as they simply covered one's skin with another's and seemed more like raw materials than finished garments. Because they were keen to obtain the beaver pelts that had been clothing, the *coureurs de bois* were inclined to view the Canadian human and beaver as two animals wearing the same skin. This dehumanizing regard seems more plausible given the fact that Amerindians of the mid-Atlantic region wore deerskins as a disguise to allow them to approach and kill other deer.[8]

Confounding skin and pelts was common in the representations of Native Americans, not only in terms of animal versus human or naked versus clothed, but also of bare skin versus furry skin. Thevet in 1558 entitled a chapter of his *Les singularitez de la France Antarctique* "Contre l'opinion de ceux qui estiment que les sauvages sont pelus" [Against the Opinion of Those Who Believe That the Indians Are Furry (my translation)]. He testified from his own experience at the French colony at Rio de Janiero that the Indians of South America were born as free of hair as European babies and plucked what little grew on their bodies in adulthood. Yet the impression of the *sauvage* as hairy, which corresponded to the medieval legend of the Wild Man, persisted. LeClercq in 1691 was still correcting popular belief:

> C'est une erreur qui n'est que trop commune, dont il est à propos de desabuser le Public. Il faut avoüer qu'on se persuade trop facilement dans nôtre Europe. . . . les croïant tous velus comme des ours, & plus inhumains que les tygres & les leopards. Il est bon cependent, pour corriger une idée si grossiere, si injuste & si peu raisonnable, qu'on sçache la difference qu'il y a entre nos Sauvages, & quantité d'autres Peuples feroces & cruels . . . puisqu'en effet nos Gaspesiens ont moins de poil que les François. (31–33)

> [There is one error which is only too common, and of which it is desirable to disabuse the public. It is necessary to admit that some persons in our Europe are persuaded too easily. . . . they even believe these people to be all hairy, like the bears, and more inhuman than the tigers and the leopards. It is well, however, to correct an idea so stupid, so unjust, and so unreasonable, and one should know the difference which exists between our Indians and any number of other ferocious and cruel peoples . . . as a matter of fact our Gaspesians have less hair than the French. (82)]

Le Clercq left room for readers to continue regarding the "other ferocious and cruel peoples" as hairy and bestial, but he wished to establish "his" Gaspesians, whom he was thrilled and proud to find worshipping the figure of a cross, as not hairy but human, innocent, and receptive to Christianity. Lafitau again corrected the error in his third chapter, which begins:

> L'idée qu'on se formoit autrefois des Sauvages, étoit d'une espèce d'hommes nuds, couverts de poil, vivant dans les bois sans société comme des bêtes, & qui n'avoient de l'homme qu'une figure imparfaite. . . . Les Sauvages, à l'exception des cheveaux & de sourcils, que quelques-uns même ont soin de l'arracher, n'ont pas un poil sur le corps. (1:104)

[The idea formerly held about the savages was of a species of naked
man, covered with hair, living like an animal in the forests without
social organization having only the imperfect appearance of man. . . .
The Indians, except for their hair and eyebrows which some even take
care to pull out, have not a hair on their bodies.]

To be hairless, when naked, is to be innocent and virtuous and to belong
at least potentially to the civilized-white-European-human species, the
species that trades for other species' pelts. That the Indians were naturally hairless or no more hairy than Europeans must have been difficult to
accept, for the misconception that the Indians were furry like animals
was corrected again and again by colonial writers. As editor William
Fenton observed (1:88 note 2), Lafitau's comments echo passages in
Sagard, Lescarbot, Le Jeune, and Du Creux, as well as LeClercq's above.
We can only assume that many readers continued to believe savages to be
hairy well into the eighteenth century, as corrections of this falsehood
remained so common.[9] By the seventeenth century, few doubted that the
Indians were humans, but the uncomfortable realization that they had
less body hair than Europeans served as a visible figure for the self-critical
primitivist notion that the *sauvage* was actually more civilized than the
European, the critique delivered most stingingly by Lahontan. Charlevoix even attempted to rectify the conflict by writing, "leurs Enfans
naissent avec un poil rare, & assez long par tout le corps, mais qui
disparoît au bout de huit jours" (311) [their children are born with a long
thin hair all over their bodies, but which disappears in eight days (2:91)],
a proviso that restores both innocence and bestiality to the origin. Later
in the eighteenth century, amid the "Dispute of the New World," there
arose a new misperception to be corrected that was a near reverse of the
former. This was the belief that the Indians grew no beards, a corollary of
the notion that "they lack ardor for their females."[10] John Long corrected
Lahontan and Lord Kames on this issue, citing James Adair and Robert
Rogers to support his contention that the Indians "are not naturally
imbarbes" (194). Long may have been trying to dispel fears that the
American climate could be emasculating for Europeans.

To the confusion over fur and beards, we must add the issue of skin color. Although the degrading epithet "redskins" became common in the nineteenth century, it was not used before the late 1600s, and the literal translation "peaux rouges" never became common in French. Earlier French colonists described the natives as "olivâtre" (olive) or "basané" (tanned), and there was widespread agreement that this color was acquired, not innate. For example, Pierre Boucher observed, "Ils sont bazanez, les enfans qui naissent sont blancs comme des François, & cette couleur bazanée ne leur vient qu'avec l'aage" (92) [They are swarthy: but new-born children are as white as French ones, that swarthy colour only coming to them as they grow up (51–52)], and Sagard, "Toutes les nations et les peuples Américains que nous avons veus en nostre voyage, sont tous de couleur bazanée . . . non qu'ils naissent tels: car ils sont de mesme nature que nous" (179) [All the American nations and tribes that we saw on our travels are of a tawny colour all over . . . not that they are so at birth, for they are of the same nature as ourselves (136)]. Among English writers John Josselyn concurred, writing that the Indians of New England were "of reasonable good complexions, but that they dye themselves tawnie" (90). Charlevoix described the natives' color in derogatory terms even as he said it was acquired:

> La couleur des Sauvages ne fait point, comme pleusieurs se sont persuadés, une troisième espéce entre les Blancs & les Noirs. Ils sont fort basanés, & d'un rouge sale & obscur, ce qui est plus sensible dans la Floride, dont la Louysiane fait partie: mais cela ne leur est point naturel. Les fréquente frixions, dont ils usent, leur donne ce rouge. (310–11)

> [The colour of the Indians does not as many believe, constitute a third species of men between the blacks and the whites. They are very tawny and of a dirty and obscure red, which is more sensible in Florida, of which Louisiana makes a part; but this is not natural to them. The frequent frictions they use is what gives them this copper complexion. (2:90)]

Karen Kupperman observes that, contrary to later racisms, the seventeenth-century English were primarily interested in skin color as an acquired or manipulable feature of peoples, not an essential one.[11] It became a topic of lively debate in seventeenth- and eighteenth-century Europe whether the colored complexions of humankind represented separate races and separate origins, as Buffon contended, or the effects of climate, as Montesquieu believed. In fact, since the voyages of discovery, Europeans had worried about whether their skin or that of their children would turn darker under the tropical sun.[12] Conversely, because southern Canada was at roughly the same latitude as France and had a colder climate, there was widespread agreement that the American Indians' red-brown skin color was not so from birth, and not a consequence of the climate, but was gradually acquired. The *sauvage* in Canada at least was therefore in essence and origin white "like us." This helped to assuage fears that creoles would become darker than Europeans. In addition, for those seeking support for the theory of monogenesis, and for some *premiers temps* theorists, the effort to recuperate the *sauvages américains* and account for their origin as a lost tribe of Hebrews, or possibly even a lost party of European voyagers, demanded some evidence of racial commonality. And finally, the exoticist critique of French society promoted by Lahontan, like the *premiers temps* theory of Lafitau, demanded as a point of departure an essential equivalence between the two peoples.

This sense of a shared racial origin was assisted by the fact that Canadians went about clothed rather than naked and displayed a consciousness of the value of their pelt clothing as a commodity in trade with the Europeans. But did this shared value for clothing entail a shared sense of modesty? Pilgrims Edward Winslow and William Bradford reported that Tarentine (Abenaki) women had not a prelapsarian innocence, but a virtuous modesty, for they "sold their coats from their backes, and tyed boughes about them, but with great shamefastnesse (for indeed they are more modest than some of our English women are)" (59). Marc Lescarbot, too, insisted on the shame of the naked body deriving from the Fall of man but evinced some conflict and confusion on the issue: "Le vétement donc n'est pas seulement pour garentir du froid, mais pour la bien-seance, & pour couvrir nôtre pudeur. Et neanmoins plusieurs nations anciennement & aujourd'hui ont vécu, & vivent nuds sans apprehension de cette honte, bien-seance, & honneteté" (3: 372) [Clothing then is not only to defend us from cold, but also for decency, and to cover our shame: and yet both of old time and to-day many nations have lived and live naked, without knowledge of this shame, decency, and honour (3:131)]. This comment confounds a series of opposing values associated first with nudity, from innocence to sexual scandal; with ornament, from beauty to vanity; and finally with clothing, from necessity to ornament. "Pudeur," the sense of shame, is "ours," held by European and Canadian alike, and Lescarbot implies that this is the reason the Canadians, unlike *sauvages* elsewhere, go about clothed and not naked. They may even be more modest than the Europeans. "Or les sauvages de la Nouvelle-France ont mieux retenu la leçon de l'honneteté que ceux-ci [the Europeans of ancient times]" (3:372) [But the savages of New France have better learned and kept in mind the lesson of decorum than these (3:131)]. The habits of the *sauvages* bear comparison not with innocent humanity in the Garden of Eden, but with the postlapsarian, pre-Christian barbarians, who were subject to temptation and sin. For Lescarbot, the danger of this challenge to the principle of original sin and to the idea that the Indians were bestial subhumans is less important than the notion that the *sauvages* of New France had more shame and therefore were more civilized than the liminal savages of ancient Europe and of other colonial areas. Frank Lestringant (84) has suggested by way of explanation that Lescarbot aimed to persuade French colonists to abandon Brazil, whose natives had been described as naked cannibals resistant to Christianization, and to redirect efforts toward New France.

In each of these three cases—clothing, body hair, and skin color—we see the dialectic of negation and substitution. First, the Indian is assumed to lack a certain characteristic of Europeans (he is nude, hairy, and copper-skinned or "basané"). Then this preconception is corrected by the observation that the Indians of Canada are actually clothed, hairless, and (at least at birth) pale-skinned. This lifts the *sauvages* out of bestiality and places them in the Judeo-Christian image of its own past. But finally, many of these virtues are withdrawn again, for the Indians are clothed only in skins, a version of hair; they are not really hairless but pluck their beards and hair; and their customs or environment give them red or brown and greasy skin. The Savage Other is bestial: naked,

furry, and red- or black-skinned. The Gauls, Scythians, or Lacedemo-
nians were pale, simply dressed, and not furry. The Native Americans
are either or both, depending on the exigencies of the observer. These
observers cannot be rigidly identified as adherents of an Othering or of
an assimilationist view, as promoters of the Noble Savage or the Ignoble
Savage stereotype, any more than the Hurons can be identified as an
ancient Semitic tribe and the Iroquois as vicious animals.[13]

Following the strategy of substitution within their erudite histories,
premiers temps writers look for ancient precedents to fill in the negations.
The *sauvage* is not naked and innocent but modestly clothed, not utterly
heathen but has an intuition of God. However, when Lescarbot considers
"Des ornements des corps" and "Des ornements exterieurs," in chapters
10 and 11 of Book 3, the pitfalls of this assimilative project become
clear. He collects citations from Pliny, the Bible, and Tertullian that
denounce the folly and vanity of ornament, much as does Nathaniel
Ward in "The Simple Cobbler of Agawam." Then he claims that Brazilians, the Floridians, and even the Canadians are guilty of abusing the
form given to them by God and nature. Lescarbot quotes from Tertullian: "il n'est pas en nous d'adjouster quelque chose à la mesure que
Dieu nous a donnée" (3:384–85) [it is not in us to add anything to the
measure which God has given to us (3:153)]. But soon after he qualifies
this: "Je ne veux pourtant blamer les vierges que ont quelques dorures,
ou chaines de perles . . . car cela est du bienseance, & toutes choses sont
faites pour l'usage de l'homme" (3:386) [Yet I will not blame the maidens who have some golden trinkets, or chains of pearls, or other jewels,
and therewith a modest vesture; for that is seemly, and all things are
made for the use of man (3:156)]. The "Indienne" suffers from the same
double standard as women today, condemned both for lack of modesty
and for failing to ornament her body to please men. Lescarbot also scorns
the Incas of Peru, whom he says festooned their bodies with gold, careless of the human cost of the dangerous mines; but he misses the essential equivalence between the gold that enticed the Spanish and the
beaver pelts that attracted the French colonials. In a complex cultural
irony, he again quotes Tertullian, who denounced Roman women who
adopted the fashions of the liminal barbarians by dying their hair red, as

the the Gauls and some Canadians do: "Elles ont honte de leur païs &
voudroient estre Gaulloises ou Allemandes, tant elles se deguisent"
(3:385) [They are ashamed of their country, and would be women of
Gaul or Germany, so much do they disguise themselves (3:153)]. Such
exoticism on the part of the Roman women is reprehensible, but the
reverse, the *sauvages* adopting the fashions of the Europeans, evidently is
not. And the genteel men of Europe who wore beaver hats are not
accused of affecting savage styles as these Roman women are, although
they are dependent on the *sauvages américains* for the beaver felt.[14]

In Lescarbot's classical humanist ethnocentrism, both savage and civilized are susceptible to the vices of ornament, but the Indians' clothing
is not worthy of the term; it merely functions to hide their shame. Roger
Williams used a more modern functionalist reasoning to arrive at a
similar portrait of Indian modesty. Whereas the chapter title "Of Their
Nakednesse and Clothing" suggests that the absence of clothing is as
remarkable as the clothing itself, Williams considers that a people who
so often go naked might have different reactions to seeing the nude
human form than European Christians do. Of Narragansett nakedness,
he writes: "Custome hath used their minds and bodies to it, and in such a
freedom from any wantonnesse, that I have never seen that wantonnesse
amongst them, as, (with griefe) I have heard of in Europe" (111).

Trade with the natives of Canada was based primarily on exchanging
the use value of guns, knives, and iron kettles with the European luxury
value for beaver pelts. But traders seeking higher profits tried to buy
pelts with European clothing and blankets, with ribbons and polished
metal trinkets, and, of course, with alcohol. As we saw in Le Page du
Pratz's story of Tissenet, the exaggerated dream that drew many into the
fur trade was that small items of negligible cost could be exchanged for
enormously valuable beaver pelts. As the Talon brothers had reported of
the Indians of Texas before extensive European contact, "they have not
esteem for gold or silver coins, preferring pins, needles, and bits of glass
or trade beads" (106).[15] Indians with furs to sell were not dupes: they
could drive hard bargains, and many of the Great Lakes area clients of
the French took their furs to the English to obtain better quality cloth
and tools at lower prices.[16] I cannot attempt to summarize patterns in

fur trade commodities or determine which Indians were most exploited
by traders, but it is important to observe that when pelts were traded for
European clothing or ornaments, cultural prejudices about ornament
and utility, exchange and use value, were called into question; the two
cultures shared an acquisitive desire for luxury and ornament. The common moral and racial heritage of the Europeans and the *sauvages* was thus
demonstrable, to the former, not only in virtues of modesty, but also in
the decadent, often gendered habit of denying nature and one's own
culture (the two are often synonymous) by ornamenting one's body.

Champlain, for example, suppressed any distinction between beauty
and vanity to focus on the value of the clothing and the universality of
vanity and ornament. The Montagnais and Algomequins or Ottawas
"sont ceux qui y prennent plus de peine, lesquels mettent à leurs robes
des bandes de poil de porc-espy, qu'ils taindent en fort belle couleur
d'escarlatte: ils tiennent ces bandes bien chere entr'eux" (3:133) [Above
all others our Montagnais and Algonquins are those that take the most
trouble with it; for they put on their robes strips of porcupine-quill
which they dye a very beautiful scarlet colour; they value these strips
very highly.] As for the women, Champlain describes ornamentation
that recalls the deadpan satire of Montesquieu's Usbek and Rica of *Lettres
Persanes* when they attend a French court ball. The young women of
marriageable age:

> . . . se montrent volontiers aux dances, où leurs péres, & méres les
> envoyent, n'oubliant rien de ce qu'ils peuvent apporter d'invention
> pour embellir & parer leurs filles, & puis asseurer avoir veu en des
> dances où j'ay esté, telle fille qui avoit plus de douze livres de pour-
> celaine sur elle[s]. (3:135)

> [. . . they like to show themselves at dances, where their fathers and
> mothers send them, forgetting no device that they can apply to bedeck
> and bedizen their daughters; and I can assure you that at dances I have
> attended, I have seen girls that had more than twelve pounds of wam-
> pum on them.]

Wampum was money in much of the Northeast, and for Adriaen Van
der Donck, as well, the aesthetic or moral aspects of natives' ornamentation were subsumed by the raw exchange value of what colonial trade

had transformed into a goldlike sign for wealth: "they wear a dressed dear-skin [*sic*] coat, girt around the waist. The lower border of this skirt they ornament with great art . . . tastefully decorated with wampum. The wampum with which one of those skirts is ornamented is frequently worth from one to three hundred guilders" (78). Roger Williams also remarked on the value of wampum clothing that adorned children, giving the word for the garment: "They hang these strings of money about their necks and wrists; as also upon upon [*sic*] the necks and wrists of their children. Máchequoce. *A Girdle*: Which they make curiously of one two, three, foure, and five inches thicknesse and more, of this money which (sometimes to the value of ten pounds and more) they wear about their middle and as a scarfe about their shoulders and breasts" (149).

Wampum made by coastal tribes had been a trade currency among inland natives before European colonization. The Dutch and others found great profits buying it up on the coast and selling it to the Iroquois for furs. Because wampam was an Indian analogue for gold, the natives could be held guilty of the same sin of vanity as Europeans who wore jewelry. LeClercq, in his 1691 *Nouvelle relation de la Gaspesie*, is an adherent of the *premiers temps* method, but he moves from the confusion of Lescarbot toward the critical primitivism of the eighteenth century, without arriving at a detached, relativist consideration of social customs as in the tolerant Roger Williams:

> Deplus, nous voïons aujourd'huy, sans aller chercher l'antiquité, que les femmes n'empruntent que trop souvent, par les mouches & par leur fard, une beauté que la nature leur a refusée. Aussi nos Sauvages, qui vinrent il y a quelque-tems en France, n'ont pû entendre sans s'éclater de rire, la raillerie de certaines Dames qui les prenoient pour des mascarades, parce qu'ils paroissent à la Cour, matachiez à la Sauvagesse: Elles n'ont point d'esprit, répondirent-ils à leur Interprete, & leur reproche est injuste, puisqu'elles ont elles-mêmes le visage tout moucheté de noir, comme nos Sauvages, dont il semble qu'elles portent toujours le deüil, par leur maniere de se matachier. (62–63)

> [Further, we see only too often in the present, without going to search antiquity, that the women, by their beauty-spots and their paints, borrow a charm which nature has denied them. Consequently our Indians, who sometime ago came to France, have not been able to

hear without breaking into laughter, the raillery of certain ladies who
took them for masqueraders, because they made appearance at Court
painted in the Indian fashion. "They have no sense," said these Indians
to their interpreter, "and their reproach is unjust, because they themselves have their own faces all mottled with black, like our Indians,
from which it appears that they are always in mourning, judging by
their manner of painting themselves." (97–98)]

Because each culture uses similar cosmetics, the Indians cannot understand why it is normal for one and exotic for the other. The basis of
social interpretation is entirely European, without any appreciation of
the different cultures that lie behind similar appearances. The Indians
are seen not as dressed in their own fashion, but as dressed up, masquer-
ading as themselves. And though the Indians have the last laugh at the
expense of the court ladies, they compare the makeup not to "our own
women" or "like us" but "like our Indians," suggesting their intense
alienation in France (or that LeClercq made up the entire episode). The
ethnocentrism is loud and clear at the end of this chapter, "Des habille-
ments & parures des Gaspesiens" [On the Clothes and Finery of the
Gaspesians], where LeClercq writes, "Ils sont si infatuez de leurs man-
ieres de s'habiller & de leurs maximes de vivres, qu'ils méprisent les
nôtres, & ne s'y peuvent du tout accoûtumer" (66–67) [They are so
infatuated with their manner of dressing, and with their own way of
living, that they disdain ours, and cannot at all accustom themselves
thereto (99)].

A more reciprocal, less ethnocentric appreciation of cultural assimilation through clothing would have to wait until some Frenchmen had
adopted native dress and been transformed into *sauvages*. Except for a
few early *truchements*, this came about in the second half of the seventeenth century as more *coureurs de bois* married Indian women and assimilated into local communities. Also, a few Europeans fled desperate settlements such as the early Jamestown and expeditions like La Salle's.
Henri Joutel, one of a handful of survivors (along with the Talon brothers) of the ill-fated 1684–87 expedition, encountered a couple of such
deserters of La Salle's previous and more successful exploration down the
Mississippi, among the Cenis nation on his trip back toward Illinois. At

the startling reunion, clothing and language are the factors by which Joutel determines whether or not the men have gone primitive. The first "C'etois un Provençal; il estoit nu comme eux [this is in Arkansas, not cold Canada] et, ce qui me surprit davantage, c'est qu'il avoit presque oublié sa langue, et ne pouvoit pas dire deux mots de suite" (Margry 3:342) [He was a Provençal, he was naked like them, and what surprised me even more, is that he had almost forgotten his language, and could not put two words together (my translation)].[17] Shortly afterward, Joutel is sitting with a group of Cenis (today known as Caddo) when another comes in and sits down silently. Not until he speaks does Joutel recognize that he too is French, or used to be, a second deserter of La Salle named Rutel or Ruter (Rutre in the Talon interrogation): "Il sembloit qu'il y avoit dix ans qu'il estoit Sauvage: il estoit nud et nu-pieds" (Margry 3:353) [It seemed that ten years had passed since he became an Indian; he was naked and barefoot (my translation)]. Joutel describes both as naked even though he had previously described the Cenis as more richly dressed and adorned than members of the other nations he had passed through. Naked, fully exposed to the European observer's gaze, both former Frenchmen appear savage. The reason why introduces another form of clothing popular in the Mississippi valley and highly significant in the discourse of the *sauvage américain*: "Mais ce que j'admiray surtout, c'estoit qu'il s'estoit fait picquer comme eux et marquer aux visage, de sorte qu'il n'avoit presque rien de dissemblable à eux, sinon qu'il n'estoit pas si alerte" (Margry 3:353) [But what I admired most of all was that he had had himself tattooed like them and marked on his face, so that there was almost nothing to distinguish him from them, except that he was not so alert (my translation)].

Piquage

Le *piquage*, or tattooing, is the negative limit of clothing. It implies the vanity of ornament without the utility or modesty of clothing and is an enduring mark of primitivism. Because through the fur trade Indians often adopted European dress, and traders took away the

Indians' former garments of beaver and other furs, there was the symbolic suggestion of a cultural reversal alongside the exchange of clothing. Traders' insatiable desire for pelts made them savage and Indians' adoption of wool clothing signified civilization. Tattooing mediated this reversal by reliably designating who was the "savage," and it resolved some of the European observers' confusion over what was clothing and what was ornament, who was dressed naturally and who vainly or barbarously, for as the negation of both clothing and modesty, tattoos, even on a European's skin, were a mark of savagery.

There are two angles from which tattooing and its relation to clothing can be examined to analyze cultural contact in colonial North America. First, tattoos were an analogue to clothing in the function of encoding status, but by their permanence they suggested a different, perhaps more authentic, type of social status. Second, tattooed skin as a radical antithesis to clothing emblemized the Native Americans' difference from the Europeans and offered a means of permanently representing an individual's place in this opposition. If clothing was one symbolic language available for "self-fashioning," as Stephen Greenblatt has termed the construction of identity during the Renaissance (without explicitly examining clothing but evoking the multiple meanings of "fashion"), tattoos were a quite different language. The difference between mutable (dis)guises and permanent, naked marks reproduced the supposed irrevocability of savagery. On the slippery slope of culture, backsliders into savagism could no more return to civilization than tattoos could be erased, yet this belief could not prevent some Europeans from transculturating and embracing the new life. A famous instance is the story of Gonzalo Guerrero recorded by Bernal Díaz del Castillo and employed by Greenblatt in both *Renaissance Self-Fashioning* (184) and *Marvelous Possessions* (140–41). Guerrero was shipwrecked in the Yucatan eight years before Cortes's invasion, married into a local community, and became a cacique or chief. When Cortes sent a letter to him asking him to aid the Spaniards in their conquest, Guerrero declined with these words: "Go, and God's blessing be with you. But my face is tattooed and my ears are pierced. What would the Spaniards say if they saw me like this? And look how handsome these children of mine are!"[18] Guerrero clearly is

happy and has no desire to leave his family, but the first reason he gives is
not his contentment but his tattoos, which make him ineligible for
European company. Instead, Cortes must use native interpreters dressed
in Spanish clothes. The result is a scandal. As Greenblatt describes it in
Marvelous Possessions: "Guerrero is for Bernal Díaz a disastrous instance of
the failure of blockage. The self had collapsed into the other: as the
Spanish put it in a report to the king, Guerrero had been made an
Indian" (141).

Descriptions of tattoos are more prevalent in narratives of Louisiana
and Virginia than in those from Canada, where many tribes evidently
did not practice *piquage*. In the early eighteenth century Lafitau observed: "Entre ces Sauvages Septentrionaux, quelques Nations ont plus
de goût pour ce Peintures Caustiques que d'autres; elles sont plus communes & d'un travail plus recherché à la Virginie, à la Floride, & vers la
Louisiane, que chez celles qui sont plus au nord, lesquelles en ont moins"
(3:38) [Among the Northern Indians, some tribes have more taste than
others for this caustic painting. It is more common and the work is more
delicate in Virginia, Florida and toward Louisiana than among those
who dwell more to the north who have less of it]. There is, however, an
engraving of an Indian with tattoos in Du Creux's *Historiae Canadensis*.[19]

Surprisingly, illustrations of the designs of tattoos and explanations of
their meaning are rare in the literature of colonial North America.
Graphic representations of tattoos on Native North Americans' bodies
begin with Theodor deBry's engravings of John White's drawings for
Thomas Hariot's *A Briefe and True Report of the New Found Land of Virginia* (1590). As befits engravings copied from drawings, it is not always
clear from the illustrations or the text whether these marks were en-
graved on the skin or drawn there. The caption to plate 4 reads: "Their
foreheads, cheeks, chynne, armes and leggs are pownced. About their
necks they wear a chaine, either pricked or paynted." The word "pounce"
or "pownce" means a design made with a powdered pigment. Hariot
may be referring to powder applied beneath the skin, or simply to
powders on the skin, and the first sentence is therefore as ambiguous as
the second. *A Briefe and True Report* generally emphasizes the ornamental
or honorific function of these marks, in that they appear in some of the

formal portraits of Indians of high status (plates 3–4, 6), though without any hint of precisely how their status is thus signified; they rarely
appear in the illustrations of Indian techniques and customs (plates 12–
22), which presumably portray commoners. The exceptional plate 23
depicts seven symbols resembling arrows or crosses that are marks of
identification, "rased on their backs, wherby yt may be knowen what
Princes subjects they bee, or of what place they have their originall."
This is a rare example of a visual representation and verbal explanation of
the tattoos that signified belonging or identity, such as Charlevoix and
others mention in print.

   Still more interesting is the appendix to *A Briefe and True Report*, "Som
picture of the Pictes." DeBry explained that these engravings were based
on the work of the same painter, John White, and that "I wold well sett to
the ende of thees first Figures, for the showe how that the Inhabitants of
the great Britannie have bin in times past as sauvage as those of Virginia."[20] The Britains apparently outdid the Indians in savagery just as
they would in civility, for in the pictures the Picts wear less clothing
and more elaborate tattooed designs. And though Hariot made only the
one attempt in plate 23 to interpret the language of native Virginians'
pouncing and painting, the pictured Picts bear a menagerie of creatures,
such as griffons, lions, and fish. The fame of the Picts for their body
painting continued in Lafitau, who wrote that this is how they got their
name (2:39). *Pictus* in Latin means picture, continuing the confusion
over whether the designs shown in deBry were painted on the body or
tattooed. The pictures seem as though they may have influenced the
description of Powhatans by William Strachey, although he made it clear
that these were tattoos: "The women have their armes, breasts, thighes,
showlders and faces, cunningly imbroydered with divers workes, for
pouncing and searing their skyns with a kynd of Instrument heated in
the fire, they figure therein flowers and fruicts of sondry lively kyndes, as
also Snakes, Serpents, Efts, etc., and this they doe by dropping upon the
seared flesh, sondry Colours, which rub'd into the stampe will never be
taken away agayne" (73).

   Piquage was frequently subsumed under a discussion of *peintures* or
painting. Gabriel Sagard segued from one to the other in a single sen-

tence: "Ils se peindent le corps et la face de diverses couleurs; de noir, vert, rouge, violet et en plusieurs autres façons; d'autres ont le corps et la face gravée en compartiments, avec des figures de serpens, lezards, es-cureux et autres animaux, et particulierement ceux de la Nation du Petun, qui ont tous, presque, les corps ainsi figurez" (192–93) [They paint their body and face in various colours, black, green, red, violet, and in many other ways. Others have their body and face marked in divi-sions, with representations of snakes, lizards, squirrels, and other ani-mals, and chiefly those of the Tobacco nation, who, almost all, have their bodies thus patterned (145)].[21] Roger Williams likewise saw body painting as a logical extension of painting on hides (see chapter 30, "Of Their Paintings"). Lafitau, who drew on accounts of indigenous peoples from all over America as well as the barbarians of the ancient world, also discussed it as a form of graphic art. After describing painting on animal skins, he noted: "ils en ont encore appris celui de se faire de magnifiques broderies sur la chair vive, & de se composer un habit qui leur coûte cher à la verité, mais qui a cela de commode, qu'il dure aussi longtemps qu'eux. Le travail en est le même que celui qui se fait sur les cuirs" (2:38) [They learned also that of making magnificent embroideries on living flesh and of making themselves coats which cost them dear in truth, but have this convenience that they last as long as they do. The work is the same as that which is done on leather]. For Lafitau, the only difference between painted leather and scarred bodies was that the latter happened to be live skin, not dead. He degraded the human surface to that of animal skins, which is in turn similar to parchment and to paper, a comparison reinforced by the strange notion that the costs—one in pain, the other in money—are somehow comparable on the same scale.

N. de Dièreville, a visitor to Acadia in 1708, wrote of tattoos he saw on Indians that consisted of mostly European symbols: "l'on en fait toutes sortes de Figures, des Croix, des Noms de Jesus, des Fleurs; enfin tout ce que l'on veut, & ces marques ne s'effaçent jamais" (176) [all kinds of Devices are reproduced, Crosses, Names of Jesus, Flowers; any-thing in fact that may be desired, & these marks never come off (170)]. Not only had these Amerindians apparently adopted European ico-nography, but also Dièreville went on to describe how some French

doctors took the "pelt" of one such Indian and put it on display: "J'ay vû
mourir à l'Hotel-Dieu de Paris un Sauvage qui étoit marqué de la sorte,
les Chirurgiens l'écorchent, & en firent passer la peau, sans que cela y
aportât aucun changement" (176) [I witnessed the death of an Indian at
the Hotel Dieu at Paris, who had been marked in this manner. The
Surgeons flayed him & had the skin dressed, without the slightest
change taking place in it (170)]. Even more than Lafitau's comment, this
anecdote reduces the Indian's body to the status of an animal's. But
Dièreville also told of French colonists submitting to the painful process
of *piquage*: "il faut qu'ils s'arment d'une grande patience, & d'un grand
courage: On est longtemps à le faire, & ils souffrent beaucoup à l'en-
durer. Quelques François en ont fait l'épreuve, qui pourroient en rendre
témoignage" (175) [they must fortify themselves with great patience &
great courage, it takes a long time to do, & they must suffer much pain
in submitting to it. A few Frenchmen have undergone this experience, &
can testify to this (169)]. Dièreville's account suggests that French colonists saw the Indians assimilating European motifs in their tattooing,
and conversely that some of the French had adopted the practice for their
own bodies.

A text from around the same time, attributed to Henri de Tonti, had
this sardonic comment on the fondness of the French officers and fur
traders for *piquage*:

> Ils se plaisent surtout à se faire piquer et il y en a beaucoup qui, au
> visage près, le sont presque partout le corps. J'en ai vu plusieurs et
> surtout un officier, homme de condition, dont vous pourriez connaître
> le nom, qui, outre une image de la vierge avec enfant Jésus, une grande
> croix sur l'estomac avec les paroles miraculeuses qui apparurent à
> Constantin et une infinité de piqûres dans le goût des sauvages, avait
> un serpent qui lui faisait le tour du corps dont la langue pointue et
> prête à darder venait aboutir sur une extrémité que vous divinerez, si
> vous pouvez.

> [They take great pleasure in having themselves tattooed, and there are
> many who have them all over the body save on the face. I've seen
> several and in particular one officer, a man of breeding whose name you

would recognize, who, as well as an image of the Virgin and the baby Jesus, a large cross on his stomach with the miraculous words which appeared to Constantine and an infinity of marks in the savage style, had a serpent which passed around his body and whose tongue pointed toward an extremity which I will leave you to guess.][22]

On the body of this soldier, each tattoo renders the others scandalous. The Madonna and Child might be a sign of piety if it appeared alone, but it is sacrilegious next to the savage markings. The latter likewise lose their status of valor when wrenched from their native setting. Finally, the snake pointing toward the penis is just plain obscene. Only the words of Constantine bring some ironic coherence to the tableau, for he represents the transition from barbarism to Christianity, the opposite of what this soldier has undergone. Tattoos here become a scene of transcultural contact that reconfigures the traditions of both colonist and colonized, and the status that the marks represent in one culture translate as a quite different status in the other.

Tattoos therefore, like the beaver pelt, had contrasting uses and values for the French and the Indians. Aesthetically neutral, *piquage* could adopt the symbols of Christian ornamentation as well as the hieroglyphics of the *sauvages*, and yet either way it remained somehow scandalous. It often denoted honor or status among the Indians, and Tonti's officer apparently was trying to translate some of this status into his own native hierarchy. But he would never be able to return to French society, for like Gonzalo Guerrero, the mark of the Other was on him. Tattoos are, of course, permanent, and the possibility of a permanent, visible signifier of social or cultural status was what made them so intriguing to French travelers and taught them of the possibilities of new kinds of social status signification.

Another description of tattoos inscribed on members of the La Salle expeditions comes from the Talon brothers. Eleven-year-old Pierre was sent as a *truchement* to live with the Cenis tribe mentioned above and remained with it for more than three years after La Salle was murdered and Joutel went on to Illinois. His two younger brothers stayed at the ill-fated castaways' encampment on Matagorda Bay and were captured by another band of Indians. All three received tattoos when they were adopted into the Indian communities:

> . . . comme quoy ils tombèrent au pouvoir des Sauvages, qui les marquent d'abord au visage, aux mains, aux bras et à plusieurs autres endroits de leurs corps, comme ils le sont eux-mesmes de plusieurs marques noires et bizarres, ce qu'ils font avec du charbon de bois de noyer pilé et destrempé dans de l'eau, qu'ils introduirent entre cuir et chair pas [*sic*] des incisions qu'ils font avec des épines forts aigües, quy leur faisoient souffrir de grandes douleurs, de manière que le charbon ainsy destrempé, se meslant au sang qui sort de ces incisions y forme des marques leur paroissent toujours, malgré cent remèdes que les Espagnols leur ont appliquez pour les tascher de les effacer. (Margry 3:615)

> [. . . they fell into the hands of the natives, they were first of all marked on the face, hands, arms, and several other parts of the body just as the natives themselves were, with various bizarre black markings. These are made using willow charcoal, powdered and stirred into water, that is introduced beneath the skin through cuts that are made with very sharp thorns, in an extremely painful process. The charcoal and water mixes with the blood that oozes from the cuts to form marks and characters that remain permanently visible, in spite of a hundred attempts by the Spanish to remove them. (112)][23]

This is not the only account to call attention to the pain and danger of infection in the technique of *piquage*. The Italian Jesuit Bressani, author of a short ethnography of the Hurons, wrote that tattooing and body painting were "certainly not barbarous" yet criticized them instead in the terms that Champlain used for the wampum ornaments: "when the painting [actually tattooing, as is clear from the context] covers a great part of the body, it is dangerous, especially in cold weather; and—either through some sort of convulsion, or for some other reason—it has caused the death of more than one, making him a martyr to vanity and a fantastic caprice, in the fulfillment of which they commonly give no sign of pain, although they experience it most acutely" (*JR* 38:251–53). Sagard also described the process and posited a similarity between "civilized" and "savage" tattooing while maintaining the cultural separation that Tonti's officer transgressed:

> . . . cela est picqué et faict de mesme, que sont faictes et gravées dans la superficie de la chair, les Croix qu'ont aux bras ceux qui reviennent de Jerusalem, et c'est pour un jamais; mais on les accommode à diverses reprises, pour ce que ces piqueures leur causent de grandes douleurs et en tombent souvent malades, jusques à en avoir la fievre, et perdre l'appetit. (193)

> [The method of pricking and fashioning it is the same as is used for fashioning and incising on the surface of the flesh the crosses which those who return from Jerusalem have on their arms forever, but they get them done on different successive occasions because these incisions give great pain and they often fall ill from them, even to the the extent of having fever, with loss of appetite. (145)]

One was never supposed to show the pain. Just as in torture, the insensitivity of the *sauvages* to pain was one of the most powerful elements of the popular stereotype, a notion that helped to rationalize the inflicting of great pain on the Indians. Pain is perhaps the only part of the repertoire of masculine, heroic achievements for which there is no visible sign to record in a name, a hieroglyphic, or a tattoo. But to the Europeans at least, tattoos did imply the pain of inscription. Though they do not describe their own pain in receiving their tattoos, the Talon brothers report that the Cenis, or the Texas-area Indians in general, tattooed their newborn infants: "if it is without defect and meets their approval, they mark it by incising the baby's tender skin. . . . They marked in the same manner the Talon brothers and the French children who remained with them. If a child cries very much during this ordeal they form a low opinion of its courage, and love it less" (126).

These marks on infants and on the French boys obviously signified identity or acceptance into the society, whereas those on adult males signified the status accruing from accomplishments at war or hunting. Le Page du Pratz provides a brief description of *piquage* that explains some of the different meanings the marks carried when inscribed on the bodies of men, women, and children: "Dès leur jeunesse les femmes se font piquer une raye sur le haut du nez en travers, quelques-unes sur le milieu du menton du haut en bas" (2:195) [From their early youth the women get a streak pricked cross their nose; some of them have a streak pricked down the middle of their chin (364)], an ornamentation that leads to an excessive vanity: "j'en ai vû qui étoient piquées par tout le haut du corps, le sein même étoit piqué par-tout, quoique cette partie du corps soit extrêmement sensible" (2:195–96) [I have seen some who were pricked all over the upper part of the body, not even excepting the breasts which are extremely sensible (364)]. The men also sport tattoos on the nose, but only warriors are entitled to wear more than this: "les Guerriers sur-tout n'ont garde de s'en priver: ceux qui se sont signalés par quelque fait d'importance, se font piquer un casse-tête sur l'épaule droite, & au-dessous on voit le signe hiéroglyphique de la Nation vaincue" (2:199) [the warriors especially rarely deprive themselves of them. Those who have distinguished themselves by some gallant exploit cause a tomahawk to be pricked on their right shoulder, underneath which is also pricked the hieroglyphic sign of the conquered nation (my translation)].

An indelible mark of savagery, *piquage* became instrumental in the exoticist critique of French society. Whereas the status of Frenchmen under the Ancien Régime depended on absent and arbitrary signifiers— a title, an estate, a family name—signifiers of Native Americans' social status were present and painfully visible on their own bodies. Moreover, tattoos usually signified not one's name or membership in a certain nation or clan, but achievements at war or hunting, the masculine virtues of Indian societies. Charlevoix did refer to inscriptions of an identifying mark of one's nation, as in the case of the Talon brothers, but insisted that this mark frequently lost its referentiality through the practice of adopting prisoners from other nations. For this reason the symbols described by Le Page du Pratz, signifying the nation that the bearer vanquished, were more common. Mere ornamentation was a factor, of course, but our attention is drawn in many explorers' accounts to the record of valor at war, a practice similar to the decals placed on a warplane signifying the number of enemy planes it had shot down or those on a football helmet signifying great plays made by that player. Because of these symbols, a warrior who had been captured and adopted into another tribe, a process we will examine in Chapter 6, could often retain the status that his tattoos recorded even as his name and kin were changed, for the feats of valor they represented were respected in most any community. Through *piquage* a radically different construction of subjectivity, a democratic, empirical society, where "all men are created equal" and men (but not apparently women) were judged by their achievements, could be a reality. Who one was became legible as what one had done. Tattoos were a form of "meritography" that offered a corrective to the nepotism and sycophantic flattery of European society and politics. The mythic egalitarianism of American culture was in part learned from America's native people.

The Louisiana soldier Jean Bernard Bossu provides in his first book some of the most provocative reflections on *piquage* as a critique of French status symbolism. His stories may be entirely fictional, but he cleverly combined the issues of transcultural adoption, meritographic status, and the ironic contrast between French and Native American symbols of prestige. Bossu in his first book wrote of his journey to the land of the Arkansas and told how he was adopted by that nation, which involved an identifying mark on his body: "Les Akanças viennent de m'adopter; ils m'ont reconnu pour guerrier & pour Chef, & m'en ont donné la marque; c'est un chevreuil qu'ils ont imprimé sur ma cuisse; je me suis prêté de bonne grace à cette opération douleureuse" (76) [The Arkansas have just adopted me. A deer was tattooed on my thigh as a sign that I have been made a warrior and a chief. I submitted to this painful operation with good grace (65–66)]. As he went to Louisiana rather late in its French colonial history, in 1751, and never was completely cut off from the settlements, Bossu had no opportunity or desire to fully adopt the Arkansas way of life. He simply wished to display his tattoos as a sign of adventure and bravery among his French peers, to adopt enough savagery to be exotic, but not alien. He also described in detail the pain and blood of the process and his fortitude in not showing the pain. Bossu was insistent about the credibility and honor signified through tattoos:

Si quelqu'un d'entr'eux s'avisoit de se faire piquer sans s'être distingué dans les combats, il seroit dégradé, & regardé comme un lâche, indigne de l'honneur qui n'est dû qu'à ceux qui exposent généreusement leur vie pour la défense de la patrie. Ils n'ont même de considération pour les fils des Caciques, qu'autant qu'ils sont braves. (102)

[If anyone should take it into his head to have himself tattooed without having distinguished himself in battle, he would be disgraced and considered a coward, unworthy of the honor due only to those who risk their lives to defend their tribe. Even the sons of chiefs are not held in special consideration unless they are as brave and virtuous as their fathers and their ancestors. (95)]

Not even the nearest native equivalent to noble birth entitled one to wear a mark of prestige. In an anecdote that follows, Bossu relates how he corrected the scandal of an Arkansas who had adopted corrupt European ways by trying to wear a mark of status he had not earned:

J'ai vû un sauvage qui, ne s'étant jamais signalé pour la défense de la Nation, s'avisa néanmoins de se faire piquer, ou calquer un marque de distinction, pour en imposer à ceux qui ne jugent que sur les apparences. Ce fanfaron vouloit passer pour un homme de valeur, dans l'intention d'obtenir en mariage une des plus jolies filles de sa Nation, qui, toute Sauvage qu'elle étoit, ne laissoit pas d'avoir de l'ambition. (102–3)

[I knew an Indian who, although he had never done anything outstanding in defense of his tribe, decided to have himself tattooed with one of these marks of distinction in order to impress those who judge others by outward appearances. This show-off wanted to pass himself off as a valiant man so that he could marry one of the prettiest girls of the tribe, who was ambitious even though she was a savage. (95)]

"Those who judge others by outward appearances" refers not to the French but to the Arkansas, unaccustomed to such deceptive counterfeiting of the minted skin of *piquage*, which evidently was more rare than impostors and violations of the sumptuary laws were in Europe. However, the young woman is implicitly compared to Europeans vulnerable to this deception because of vanity and ambition. Gender similarity here overrides cultural alterity. The scandal is resolved thanks to Bossu's own genius for social status in the French style, which can be lost as easily as it is gained. The "faux brave qui s'étoit induement décoré d'un Casse-tête sur la peau, sans jamais avoir *fait coup* à la guerre" (103, Bossu's italics) [this false hero who unjustly decorated himself with the tattoo of a tomahawk, without ever having struck a blow in battle (95)] is threatened with the forced removal of the skin that bears the bogus meritograph. Bossu offers to aid him with a secret of French medicine. Using opium, Spanish flies, and plaintain leaves, he anesthetizes the patient and removes the false meritography. With this miraculous cure, Bossu "surprit beaucoup les Jongleurs, qui ignoroient les propriétés des mouches cantarides fort communes dans l'Amérique Septentrionale" (103) [amazed the medicine men, who knew nothing of the properties of cantharides, although they are very common in North America (96)].

Implicit in Bossu's anecdote is an assumption that human nature is the same for the French and the Arkansas. Everyone is a little vain and thirsts after status and the admiration of peers. The difference is in the encoding of social status; among the Arkansas and many other New World peoples described in the exploration-ethnography texts, status was based on discrete accomplishments and represented in visible, permanent form. Through the meritographs of *piquage* the signification of status was transparent, that is to say, fully apparent to all onlookers regardless of their place in the status hierarchy. By contrast, one's position in the gossip mill of court intrigue for which the society of Louis XIV is famous was dependent on hearsay, opinion, and closely guarded secrets that would be trivial and imperceptible to a French peasant. The attraction of the "savage" system for French colonists, many of whom, like Bossu, were soldiers of limited wealth and power, is clear. Here one would be esteemed only for one's acts of bravery; no Indian warrior would be favored over another for a promotion because of his noble birth.

Bossu's anecdote also demonstrates that forcing indigenous peoples to assimilate colonists' culture is not the only way to exert power through the process of acculturation. Colonials also expressed their domination through their claim to be able to adopt only so much of native culture as pleased them, and to remain independent of it. The colonial self thought itself to be larger than and independent of any primitive Other, and therefore Bossu has the ability to select, inscribe, interpret, *and erase* tattoos on his own body or another's. We can assume that Bossu would be able to erase the tattoos from his own skin as well. He was able to do what the Spanish rescuers (we should call them the second captors) of the Talon brothers could not do not only because he made up the story but also because whereas the French boys' tattoos signified an irreversible decline into savagery, the Arkansas "faux brave" is inscribed with symbols wrenched from their context to serve in an allegory about European society. Here the tropes of negation and substitution are used to buttress colonial power. Bossu can substitute Indian prestige for European, raising himself in his peers' esteem by his tattoos, but he can also negate the substitution, returning himself from the absence of civilization back to his unmarked state.

As Bossu's manipulation of the Louisiana native cultures was intended to impress his French readers, so too did events in France comment on the representations of the Indians. Immediately following his erasure of the tattoos comes an explicit analogy between this episode of fraudulent meritography and the ambitious pursuit of symbols of bravery and honor by Frenchmen. Bossu states that

> Un officier du Régiment de l'Isle de France, étant devenu amoureux d'une Demoiselle à Paris en 1749, la mere de cette fille, dit qu'elle la lui accorderoit volontier s'il étoit décoré de la Croix de Saint-Louis. L'amour le porta aussi-tôt pour accelérer son marriage, à prendre de lui-même cette distinction, que le Roi seul peut donner.[24]

> [In 1749, an officer of the Ile de France regiment fell in love with a girl in Paris. The young lady's mother said that she would approve the marriage only if the officer were decorated with the Croix de Saint Louis. He was spurred on by love and a desire to be married as quickly as possible to award himself this honor, which only the King can grant. (96)]

A senior officer learned of his decoration, became suspicious, and exposed the fraud: "Le faux Chevalier fut jugé à avoir la Croix arrachée"

(192) [The false Chevalier was judged to have stolen the Cross (my translation)].[25] As the medal is easily removable, the crime of falsely wearing it is therefore all the more serious, and the overambitious officer was punished with twenty years' imprisonment.

Thus many French colonial observers saw in Native American tattoos what they failed to find in Native Americans' clothing, a system for the signification of social status. And although the pain and disfigurement of *piquage* contributed to the image of American savagism, the permanent record of valor inscribed through tattoos became an important part of the Noble Savage and part of American egalitarian ideology. In a few scenes where colonists had tattoos done on their own bodies, the cross-cultural inscription served as a mark of cultural reciprocity between European and colonized that actually only concealed the assumed superiority of the colonist, for whom the permanent bodily mark was only a temporary token of power and prestige.

Isomorphic Writing

In the anecdote about the Croix de St. Louis, the permanence of meritography is shown to be superior to social constraints permitting only certain individuals to wear certain designs. Yet the symbolic language in which the Croix de St. Louis signifies valor is taken for granted, and Bossu does not explain why the "faux brave" chose the tomahawk symbol. I now wish to shift the focus from the social role of tattoos to the signifying systems used in such paintings or inscriptions. When John Smith remarked in his *Map of Virginia*, "Many other formes of paintings they use, but he is the most gallant that is the most monstrous to behould" (1:161), he suggested that more was better and emphasized this rather than describe and explain the designs of the "paintings they use." Lafitau did likewise in his account of "pict-age"; "les grands s'y distinguoient par-là du commun peuple, à qui il n'étoit pas permis d'en avoir un si grand nombre que les gens de qualité" (2:39–40) [in this way the great were distinguished from the common people who were not permitted to have as many of these marks as people of quality.] For plate 3 of his second volume, Lafitau had copied one of deBry and White's Picts, as well as a collection of hieroglyphics supposedly used by American Indians. These identify a warrior named "Two Feathers" and record his exploits in war and diplomacy (fig. 9). His tribe and clan are signified by naturalistic drawings of the animal totems, but information about the number of warriors in the party he commanded and the number of scalps he took are recorded by the repetition of an icon or by a series of tally marks. In a semiotic system in which the number of marks denoted one's status by showing how many bison or enemy warriors one had killed, the number would be represented not with a numeral, for one could not change the tattoo of a numeral after an additional achievement, but by a series of marks: / / / drawn in connection with an icon that identified the marks as representing scalps or prisoners or the number of warriors one had commanded on a raid. Lafitau maintained that these symbols were used on trees and animal skins and implied that they might be used in *piquage* as well.

This principle whereby each of a set of persons, things, or events is represented in one-to-one correspondence by a set of signifiers is another of the most common tropes in the representation of American Indian cultures. It is perhaps an earlier version of the modern cliché about primitive people having no comprehension of the large numbers native to capitalist society. Popular accounts of latter-day "savages" recently contacted in the remnants of remote forests, such as the Tasaday of the Phillippines, almost invariably mention as proof of primitivism that the people's language has no word for any number greater than ten, eight, or even three.[26] Seventeenth-century colonists rarely expressed this cliché, however, and Roger Williams included in his *Key* Algonquian words for numbers up to 100,000. Rather than the the stultifying primitivism of a "lowest highest number," early American writers described an isomophic system of tallies suggesting that the Indians lacked the need for abstract numeric representation and instead used a more primitive system that contributed to a sublime awe of large numbers. Robert Beverley, in recounting the story of Pocahontas, wrote that Uttamaccomack, who accompanied her to England,

> ... had orders from Powhatan, to count the People in England, and
> give him an account of their Number. Now the Indians having no
> Letters among them, he at his going ashore provided a Stick, in which
> he was to make a Notch for every Man he see; but this Accomptant
> soon grew weary of that tedious Exercise and threw his Stick away:
> And at his return, being asked by his King, How many People there
> were; He desired him to count the Stars in the Sky, the Leaves upon the
> Trees, and the Sand on the Seashore, for so many People (he said) were
> in England. (pt. 1, par. 30)

England's power, both culturally and militarily, lay in its large population, Beverley suggested, and in the confrontation of the primitive with
civilization, the Powhatan is awed by numbers that he can only express
using a metaphor with the plentitude of nature. This metaphor is now a
cliché in representations of Native American natural religion.

But the trope could also be used to suggest that the Indians respected
the significance of individual things, people, and actions so much that
they could not subsume them into numerals. Bossu, for instance, described the Arkansas way of collecting members for a war party in a
manner that respects the will of each warrior. After a harangue describing the offenses that must be avenged, "Le chef ensuite prend un faisceau
de buchettes & le presente à l'assemblée; tous ceux qui veulent marcher
en prennent chacun une" (73) [The chief then holds out a bundle of
twigs to the assembly, and all those who want to fight enlist by taking
one (62)].[27] The next day those who have taken the sticks carry them to
the dance that continues the war preparations. Lafitau wrote of the same
practice: "C'est un morceau ce bois façonné, orné de vermillon, que
chacun des Guerriers marque de quelque note, ou figure distinctive, &
qu'il donne au Chef, comme un symbole qui le réprésent en personne, &
qui peut être regardé comme le lien de son engagement, tandis qu'il
subsiste" (2:186) [This is a small piece of wood, carved, painted with
vermilion, marked by each warrior with some note or distinctive figure
and given the chief as a symbol which represents him in person and
which may be regarded as the bond of his engagement, while he is
living]. Although this method amounts to signing one's name, Lafitau
does not acknowledge it as writing, but as a bond stronger than the

signature, for it represents not an abstract legal obligation but the person himself. The *sauvages américains* have no writing because they have something even better, a system that maintains the reference and truth lost from European languages. The Indians, of course, cannot miss something they have never had, but from the point of view of the Europeans, these methods of tokens imitate, and in certain ways surpass, writing; they represent the "savage" metaphysics of presence. It can be difficult to understand, however, how anyone with an adequate conception of numbers to think up such a scheme would actually need to use it. It would be truly useful only if the spatial arrangement of the markers was also significant, as in Champlain's account of the battle plan of his allied warriors at the 1609 battle against the Mohawk, or if there was a need, as in tattoos, to add to the quantity represented without erasing the previous sign.

Colonial writers also portrayed the weaknesses of such systems, as in the story of the famous Natchez Massacre of 1729, recounted by Le Page du Pratz and Bossu. Both were sympathetic to the Natchez, who played a role in the Louisiana colony similar to that of Canada's Hurons, the tribe best known, most idealized, and most quickly destroyed. The massacre was precipitated, according to both authors, by mistreatment from the French officer in the region, de Chepar, who demanded that they leave their village and, until they did, pay a tribute in the form of corn (which the French depended on). Bossu in his first narrative described the planning of the Natchez "soleil" or chief and reproduced his "harangue" to the nation. He knew that to defeat the French and their firearms, many allied nations would have to attack at the same moment:

> . . . pour en venir à bout, il faut préparer des paquets de buchettes égaux en nombre, en donner un à chacune, en garder un pareil; ils marqueront la quantité de jours qu'il faut attendre; tous les matins on coupera une buchette qu'on jettera au feu; lorsqu'il n'y en aura plus qu'une, ce sera le temps du carnage . . . (59)

> [To succeed in this, we shall have to prepare bundles consisting of equal numbers of twigs, one bundle to be given to each nation. Each morning of the waiting period, one twig will be cut up and thrown

into the fire. When there is only one left, they will know that the time
for the slaughter has come. (40)]

According to Le Page du Pratz, a Natchez woman who was in love with a
French soldier tried to sabotage the plan by stealing one of the sticks,
causing one party to attack alone one day early and thereby tip off the
French. Bossu wrote that she simply told her lover, who told de Chepar
and was punished for daring to suggest that the *sauvages* could pose any
threat to the French. De Chepar's hubris was tragic, for as contemporary
readers knew, the massacre took the lives of more than 200 colonists (Le
Page du Pratz claims 700 and Bossu more than 2,000). Christopher
Columbus (through his son's biography of him) told a similar tale of a
coordinated attack by the natives of Hispaniola that was to be timed by
the full moon. "But the Indians have no numbers by which to determine
dates or anything else that requires calculation; they can count only on
their fingers" (235), and so again, one overanxious cacique attacked too
soon, dooming the rebellion.

The method of tokens becomes even more like writing when each
token stands for a signified stored in memory. Cadwallader Colden,
whose book *The History of the Five Indian Nations* (1727 and 1747) consists in large part of speeches by the Iroquoian sachems at conferences
with the British colonial officers, explains how the Iroquoian leaders
memorized lengthy speeches, treaties, and policy statements:

> They commonly repeat over all that has been said to them, before they
> return any Answer, and one may be surprized at the Exactness of these
> Repetitions. They take the following method to assist their Memories:
> The Sachem, who presides at these Conferences, has a Bundle of small
> Sticks in his Hand; as soon as the Speaker has finished any one Article
> of his Speech, this Sachem gives a Stick to another Sachem, who is
> particularly to remember that Article; and so when another Article is
> finished, he gives a stick to another to take care of that other, and so
> on. (89)

The practice of diplomacy could be exact, egalitarian, cooperative, and
public in this way: one article, one stick, one person. The speaker, such
as Grangula whose orations are printed in Lahontan and in Colden, had a

job distinct from the chiefs or sachems. His oratorical skills were prized, and rather than embody the authority for whom he spoke, like a European envoy representing a king, he often used the method of tokens to guarantee the authority of the spoken words themselves. Amerindians too often were unable to enforce treaties, but this was not because they had no language for recording and preserving them. Many nations did have means for recording these texts, just as they did agreements among their own bands, and early French and English observers recognized this. John Lawson reported that an Indian orator relating his tribe's traditions made reference to a more sophisticated language of sticks: "To prove the times more exactly, he produces the Records of the Country, which are a parcel of Reeds of different lengths, with several distinct Marks, known to none but themselves; by which they seem to guess, very exactly, at Accidents that happen'd many years ago; nay two or three Ages or more" (187). Beverley was less colorful: "And they keep their account by knots on a string, or notches on a Stick, not unlike the *Peruvian Quippoes*" (pt. 3, par. 36). Beverley may have been stretching a valid analogy, for there is little other evidence that North American Indians used knots as well as bead belts, sticks, and reeds. Quipus were used by the Incas primarily for accounting and bureaucratic records, but according to Inca Garcilaso de la Vega, they could be adapted for historical annals as well: "In short they may be said to have recorded on their knots everything that could be counted, even mentioning battles and fights, all the embassies that had come to visit the Inca, and all the speeches and arguments the king had uttered" (331). Garcilaso insisted that quipus are not writing, but that Incan historians used their system to its full potential: "they had to use what devices they could, and treating their knots as letters, they chose historians and accountants, called quipucamayus, ('those who have charge of the knots') to write down and preserve the tradition of their deeds by means of the knots, strings, and colored threads, using their stories and poems as an aid" (332). Perhaps influenced by what they read of South American practices, European observers in North America emphasized the historical purposes of native semiology. Charlevoix, for example, described wampum beads strung on leather straps called branches and combined into larger "colliers" or collars:

Par le mélange des Grains des différentes Couleurs, on y forme telle figure & tel caractere, que l'on veut, ce qui sert souvent à distinguer les affaires, dont il est question. On peint même quelquefois les Grains: du moins est-il certain qu'on envoïe souvent des Coliers rouges, quand il s'agit de la Guerre. Ces Coliers se conservent avec soin, & non-seulement ils composent le Trésor public, mais ils sont encore comme les Registres & les Annales, que doivent étudier ceux, qui sont chargés des Archives, lesquels sont déposés dans la Cabanne du Chef. (210)

[By a mixture of beads of different colours, they form such figures and characters as they have a mind, which often serve to distinguish the affairs in question. Sometimes the beads are plaited, at least it is certain that they frequently send red collars when a war is in agitation. These collars are carefully preserved, and not only compose part of the publick treasures, but are likewise their registers or annals, and ought to be studied by those who have the charge of the archives, which are deposited in the cabbin of the chief. (1:320)]

The belts, like the calumet or peace pipe, were a form of writing for historical and diplomatic purposes, one that guaranteed the truth of what was said or what had happened, and/or the identity and intentions of he who bore it. Yet Charlevoix's statement is a bit of an exaggeration. The wampum belts that survive bear fairly simple designs, and it is more difficult to imagine them as written narrative history than it is the quipus. These sticks, wampum belts, and quipus were not the most sophisticated forms of writing produced by Native Americans, however. The Aztec and Mixtec pictographs of the era just before the Spanish invasion, and especially the partly phonetic Mayan language of the third to tenth centuries A.D., are all closer to our conventional definitions of writing than are wampum belts or the still-undeciphered Incan quipus. The extant literature of these languages is many times larger than that from the area north of Mexico. Yet our definition of writing is highly ethnocentric and works to exclude even these South American forms. We are inclined to view writing as "visible speech" (see deFrancis' book by that title) and overlook the degree to which even English and other European languages are not really written phonetically. A better way to understand the wampum belts and counting sticks, and other north-eastern American Indian writing systems such as those in the Lenape

Walam Olum and the Ojibway Midewiwin scrolls, or Aztec and Mixtec writing, is to compare them to musical notations or to the semiotic systems of mathematics and chemistry. These are not phonetic systems and there is no set form for translating them into speech, yet they are highly conventionalized and encode complex information.[28]

My purpose here, however, is not to prove that supposedly illiterate Indians did in fact use writing, but to study European reactions to and descriptions of systems of signification that confounded their notions of writing, money, and clothing as separate systems. For example, because the wampum in the belts was also used for money, particularly in New York by the Dutch buying pelts from the Iroquois, it was not only a sign for speech and a means of keeping accounts like a quipu, but also an object with its own "intrinsic" exchange value like gold. The wampum was so valuable that belts were frequently taken apart and the beads reworked into new belts for new conferences, which had the unfortunate consequence of destroying the records of old treaties.[29] Thus the archive was also the treasury, and the European observers could not but regard the exchange of collars as an exchange of bonds as well as or instead of an exchange of treaty documents. When the Iroquois concluded treaties with the French or English, the Europeans sometimes failed to realize that some of these gifts were significant not only for their exchange value but also because they actually recorded the language of the agreement. If they were unaware of Iroquoian writing techniques, English and French colonists might have believed that they could falsify the records of negotiations or even the treaties themselves without detection. The variance between La Barre's and Lahontan's versions of Grangula's speech may be an instance of this.

Colden's *History of the Five Indian Nations* devotes much attention to Iroquoian speech making and the writing techniques behind it. In a typical account of an Iroquoian oration, the Mohawk sachem Tahajadoric ("Tahiadoris" in some histories) addresses the English agents, weaving together a great deal of rhetoric about the power of the English and of the Five Nations and about the "covenant chain" that binds their alliance. (The metaphor of woven chains itself suggests wampum belts.) He reiterates the Iroquoian commitment to the war against the French and the suffering his nation has incurred in these battles. At the end of

each paragraph we read, respectively: " 'Here he gave a Bever. . . . Gives a
Bever. . . . Gives a Belt. . . . Gives one Belt. . . . Gives a Bever. . . . Gives a
Bever. . . . and gave a Belt. . . . We give two Belts, one for the Sun the
other for its Beams. . . . Gives two Bevers.' Lastly, He desired the
Magistrates of Albany to remember what he had said, and gave them a
Bever" (89–91).

As colonists interacted with the natives in trade and war, such ritual
gifts of valuable commodities were an enticing prospect. The Jesuits'
Relation of 1642 explained that "Les presens parmy les peuples font
toutes les affaires du païs: ils essuient les larmes, ils appaisent la colere,
ils ouvrent la porte dans les païs étrangers, ils delivrent les prisonniers,
ils resuscitent les morts, on ne parle quasi & on ne respond qu par les
presens: C'est pour cela que dans les harangues, le present passe pour une
parole" (*JR* 22:290–91) [Presents among these peoples despatch all
the affairs of the country. They dry up tears; they appease anger; they
open the doors of foreign countries; they deliver prisoners; they bring
the dead back to life; one hardly ever speaks or answers, except by
presents. That is why, in the harangues, a present passes for a word.] For
those who did not understand the meaning of such gifts in native cultures, one might suppose that presents such as Colden lists compensated
the traders and agents for the boredom of sitting attentively through
long speeches they did not understand. On a more theoretical level, the
pelts given at diplomatic affairs testify to the meeting between ad-
dressor and addressee, the "contact" in Roman Jakobson's semiotic template, whereas the belts are a record (for those who can read them) of the
text of what has been spoken and promised, the "message." Although
the symbolic language used on wampum belts may not be very specific,
there is an important functional difference between these and more
complex forms of writing. The sticks and wampum belts were not intended to be iterable as a text is; the uniqueness of the physical object
was essential to its significance in representing the presence of individuals and the declarations made by them.

Colden's book abounds in such exchanges, and his accounts of negotiations and speeches by British, French, and Iroquoian diplomats show
all three nations as duplicitous and the Iroquois as highly skilled at
equivocation. Cunning diplomacy required careful composition and

presentation of texts. We have seen that to memorize and record speeches the Iroquois represented each article with a stick, and in delivering them they accompanied each article with a beaver pelt or a wampum belt. Colden dissociates the function of such tokens as an aid to memory from their status as writing by dissociating the sticks from the wampum belts, and he separates the value of signification from money/exchange value by treating beaver pelts as separate from the wampum belts. His ethnocentrism lies in his insistence on maintaining clothing, writing, and money as separate modes of representation, whereas to the Iroquois and other Indians all belonged to the same register. Both pelts and wampum belts were also forms of money and of clothing, though their status as money was a consequence of the European invasion. As might be expected, it is the wealth to be obtained from such negotiations that excites Colden. Following the text of another speech, he comments, "Here we see the Mohawks acting like hearty Friends, and if the Value of the Belts given at that Time be considered, together with what they said on that Occasion, they gave the strongest Proofs of their Sincerity. Each of these Belts amount to a large Sum in the Indian Account" (107). It was a large sum in the English account as well, of course, and here the present is received as a deposit or bond that the Five Nations will stand by what they have declared. There was another instance, during a delicate period of détente between the two colonial powers, when the Iroquois dissembled a promise to not negotiate with the French. After presenting the text of this speech Colden pointed out, "They made the Governor a considerable Present of Furs, to shew their Respect to his Person; but they did not give one Belt to confirm any one Article: so that the whole of it is, according to their Stile, only argumentative" (139). Colonists often valued sincerity much less than the tokens of it, and this may explain the common refrain of colonial officials that they wish to bring about peace among all the warring tribes in a region. Not only did war divert energy from the pursuit of beavers, but also the process of concluding peace could bring a wealth of pelts to the European soldiers and traders.

In tattoos and in these valuable pelt tokens, European observers recognized a strong connection between sign and referent, meritograph and merit, word and deed. As the Talon brothers said, "celuy qui a le plus de ces chevelures estant le plus estimé de tous, et c'est en cela qu'ils font consister toute leur gloire" (Margry 3:616–17) [The brave with the most scalps is the most highly regarded, and their entire glory rests in their deeds (113)]. That the colonial observers refused to consider these techniques to be writing may be due to a reason they were not likely to admit to themselves—because they were *too* authentic, insufficiently arbitrary, iterable, and ambiguous. They did not have the qualities of indeterminacy and deferral characteristic of European writing. In these rudimentary semiotic systems we can see a primitivist origin for the logocentric ideal that Jacques Derrida identifies in *Of Grammatology* and *Writing and Difference* and that he credits Rousseau with developing in Western metaphysics. Rousseau read many of these travel narratives, which were hugely popular in seventeenth- and eighteenth-century France, and must have been captivated by the representations of such authentic and immediate relations between thing and sign, of a more direct relation to nature and its objects than was available to Europeans, for whom such relations were mediated by arts and sciences. Derrida detects in Rousseau a nostalgia for the innocence of the scene of the birth of language, for "a language of pure effusion, beyond the cry, but short of the hinge that articulates and at the same time disarticulates the immediate unity of meaning, within which the being of the subject distinguishes itself neither from its act nor from its attributes" (279). This subject could be the warrior whose meritographs unite his deeds, attributes, and identity. "The Savage Mind," in its seventeenth-century version, was characterized by a strict connection between sign and referent. The colonists' conviction on this point led to some absurd statements that demonstrated their confusion on the issues of Indian language and alphabetic writing. In introducing his "Petit dictionaire de la langue des sauvages," Lahontan wrote, "La Langue Algonkine n'a ni tons ni accens, étant aussi facile à la prononcer qu'à l'écrire, & n'ayant point de lettres inutiles dans les mots" (2:199) [The Algonkine Language has neither Tone nor Accent, nor superfluous dead Letters; so that 'tis as easie to pronounce it as to write it (2:288)]. How could it have superfluous letters when it had no indigenous written form? The phonetic perfection of the language was entirely the work of the Jesuit missionaries who had transcribed it.

Another version of the belief that Indians maintained a strong connection between sign and referent, an element of what Derrida terms the "metaphysics of presence," are statements about their excellent memory for natural objects and physical phenomena. Charlevoix, in an ethnographic digression on the "Character of the Indians of Canada," wrote, "Leur imagination tient du prodige, il leur suffit d'avoir été une seule fois dans un Lieu, pour en avoir une idée juste, qui ne s'efface jamais" (304) [Their imagination is a sort of prodigy; it suffices them to have been once in a place to have an exact idea of it, which is never effaced (2:81)]. Pierre Biard, writing of the Montaguets, Souriquois, and Eteminiquois of the Maritimes, concurred: "Ils ont fort bonne memoire des choses corporelles, comme de vous avoir veu, des qualitez d'une place, où ils auront esté, de ce qui aura esté fait devant eux, despuis vingt & trente ans, &c. Mais d'apprendre par cœur, là est l'escueil: il n'y a moyen de leur mettre dans la caboche une tirade rengée de paroles" (*JR* 3:72–73) [They have a very good memory for material things, such as having seen you before, of the peculiarities of a place where they may have been, of what took place in their presence twenty or thirty years before, etc.; but to learn anything by heart—there's the rock; there is no way of getting a consecutive arrangement of words into their pates.] Because a single visit left a permanent memory, successive visits would imprint similar but distinct ideas, in the Lockean sense, in an Indian's mind. Similarly, Rousseau maintained that at the origin of language each object, such as an oak tree, received its own name, and there were no generic terms. The Indian would be the best possible exploration narrator, for every place and experience could be recalled and represented accurately in a linear spatiotemporal order. He would be, however, the worst possible ethnographer, for he supposedly had no ability to synthesize and generalize using abstract concepts. And missionaries frequently complained that the Indians could not understand such concepts as the Resurrection or the Holy Trinity, as well as having difficulty reciting prayers and hymns.

Another instance of this ultra-empiricism is the writing and reading of a human or animal in the tracks that its feet inscribe in the ground. Indians' skills at tracking and route finding astounded the colonists, who often figured these skills as reading a text consisting of a line across a landscape. According to Lafitau, an Indian could read tracks with the same accuracy as the text on the conscription stick, where each sign referred unambiguously to an individual:

> Du premier coup d'oeil, ils diront sans se tromper, de quelle nation, de quel sexe, de quelle taille sont les personnes dont ils voient les pistes, & combien à peu pres il y a de temps que ces pistes sont imprimées. Supposé que ces personnes soient de leur connaissance, ils ne tarderont pas à dire ce sont les vestiges d'un tel ou d'une telle. (2:244–45)

> [It is certain that they perceive these evidences at places where we should not be able to see the least trace of them. At first glance, they will say without error of what nation, what sex and what stature are the people whose tracks they see and almost for how long a time these traces have been there. If these persons are of their acquaintance, they will not be slow in saying, "these are the tracks of such and such a man, or such and such a woman."]

Jonathan Carver may have copied this passage, for he wrote virtually the same sentence in English (328). Radisson similarly claimed that he and the Indians could recognize individuals by their tracks: "we discovered there abouts some tracks, judging to be our ennemy by the impression of their feet in the sand. All knowes there one another by their march, for each hath his proper steps, some upon their toes, some on their heele" (144). Lahontan reported much the same thing: "ils distinguent facile-ment si ces traces sont vieilles ou nouvelles; aussi bien que le nombre & l'espece qu'elles designent, & ils suivent ces vestiges des jours entiers sans prendre le change, c'est une vérité dont je ne sçaurois doutés après avoir été tant de fois le témoin" (2:177) [they can distinguish with a great deal of Facility between fresh Tracts and those of longer standing, and can make a just Estimate of the number and kind that made them. These Tracts they can follow whole days without being mistaken. This I have seen so often with my own Eyes, that there's no room left for the least doubt upon the matter (2:74)]. Lafitau and Carver echoed passages in earlier writers such as Lescarbot and Sagard, as well as Lahontan, suggesting that this issue, like that of the Indians' skin color, was one that explorer-ethnographers felt to be extremely important and wished to mention even if they had no firsthand evidence, as Lahontan claimed to have. Unlike conventional typographic writing whose origin or author is indeterminable, the writing of one's footprints always carries one's signature, and although there are techniques for covering one's tracks, it is impossible to walk a falsehood. The author of the track text is identifiable empirically, and the text clearly demonstrates the walker's intention or at least direction. Native Americans and European colonists could not understand each other at first contact, and many commentators have maintained that this caused Columbus and others to regard the Indians as being subhuman, lacking any language. But it is important also to recognize that seventeenth- and eighteenth-century explorer-ethnographers found in Native American signifying practices an ideal form of writing, one that better preserved memory and authority than did written French or English.

Writing Lessons

Even with the best interpreters, communication between the Indians and early explorers like Sagard and Champlain necessarily included some gestural sign language—they had to show as well as speak. The same was true for communication between native nations with different languages. Charlevoix recognized three separate language families, Sioux, Algonquian, and Huron (or Iroquoian), and wrote:

> . . . comme la plûpart des Sauvages du Canada ont été de tout tems en Commerce entr'eux, tantôt Alliés, & tantôt Ennemis, quoique les trois Langues Meres, dont j'ai parlé, n'ayent entr'elles aucune sorte d'affinité, ni d'analogie, ces Peuples ont néanmoins trouvé le moyen de traiter ensemble sans avoir besoin de Truchement; soit que le long usage leur donne la facilité de se faire entendre par signes; soit qu'ils se soient formé une espece de Jargon commun . . . (189)

> [. . . as the greatest part of the Indians of Canada have had at all times an intercourse with one another, sometimes as allies, sometimes as enemies, though the three mother-tongues of which I have spoken have no affinity or analogy with one another, these people have, not-

withstanding found means to do business together without having occasion for an interpreter; whether through long custom they have acquired a facility for making themselves understood by signs; or, whether they have formed a sort of a common jargon which they have learned by practice. (1:288–89)]

Inquiry into this aboriginal lingua franca could be fascinating but is beyond our means here. However, the implication that the natives were adept in sign language and might have tried to use it with the Europeans at first contact is suggestive. It might explain the confidence of Cartier and other explorers in interpreting what American Indians were trying to communicate at early contacts. The "savage" was by definition ignorant of writing and was supposed to possess consciousness without concepts or essences, only concrete particulars that could be seen and drawn. However, gestural language or ways of using objects symbolically often amounted to a form of writing, and there are scenes of surprise and scandal where Indians show a strong faculty for abstraction and representation. Sagard, troubled by his inability to explain the Christian concepts of Paradise or Resurrection to the Hurons, is also confused by some of the abstract concepts or absent objects he hears them discussing. Here is how he overcomes the problem:

> Et comme ils ne pouvoient par-fois me faire entendre leurs conceptions, ils me les demonstroient par figures, similitudes et demonstrations exterieures, par-fois par discours, et quelquesfois avec un baston, traçant la chose sur la terre, au mieux qu'ils pouvoient, ou par le mouvement du corps, n'estans pas honteux d'en faire de bien indecents, pour se pouvoir mieux donner à entendre par ces comparisons. (88)

> [And as sometimes they could not make me understand their conceptions they would explain them to me by figures, similitudes, and external demonstrations, sometimes in speech, and sometimes with a stick, tracing the object on the ground as best they could, or by a movement of the body; and they were not ashamed to make very unseemly movements in order to be able the better to make me understand by means of these comparisons. (73)]

Translation, the only means of making oneself understood across an enormous cultural abyss, necessitates a detour, a "discursion" (to coin a new term) by which figure supplements concept and incision demonstrates discourse. If one cannot be told, one must be shown, and showing is frequently a form of writing. Champlain, who favored colonization over conversion and integration over segregation as the best policy for New France, wrote his belief on this matter into the speech of an Indian who responded to a sermon as follows:

> . . . tu dis choses qui passe nostre esprit, & que ne pouvons comprandre par discours, comme chose qui surpasse nostre entendement: Mais si tu veus bien faire et d'habiter ce pays, & amener femmes, & enfans. . . . nous apprendrons plus en un an, qu'en vingt à oüyr discourir, & si nous ne pouvons comprandre, tu prendras nos enfans, qui seront comme les tiens: & ainsi jugeant nostre vie miserable, au pris de la tienne, il est aisé à croire que nous la prenderont, pour laisser la nostre. (3:145–46)

> [You say things that pass our understanding and that we cannot comprehend by words, as something beyond our intelligence; but if you would do well, you should dwell in our country and bring women and children, . . . we shall learn more in one year than hearing your discourses in twenty, and if we cannot understand, you shall take our children who will be like your own: and thus judging our life wretched by comparison with yours, it is easy to believe that we shall adopt yours and abandon our own.]

Effective assimilation depended on signs that could be seen and demonstrated, for a verbal profession of faith was either too hard to comprehend or too easy to counterfeit. The Indian in Champlain's story, by his naive insistence on the explicit visual over the shifting verbal, invites his own domination and assimilation by a colony that will inscribe itself into Canada. By comparison with this assimilation, Christian conversion is as feeble and incomprehensible as a word in a language one does not understand. Champlain wrote this before the Jesuits established the policy that missionaries must learn the native languages in order to make conversions or translations to God's word. They would also become hostile to the policy of integration and acculturation that Champlain

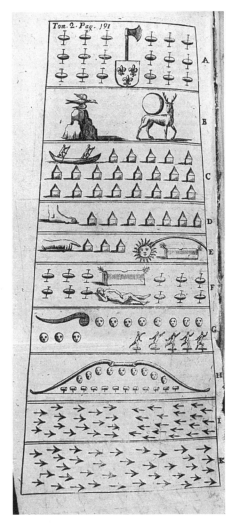

FIGURE 8.
"Hiéroglyphes des sauvages,"
from Lahontan, *Nouveaux*
voyages . . . dans l'Amérique
Septentrionale, 1703. (National
Library of Canada, NL-18987)

envisioned. But for Champlain, acculturation was a more reliable, because more visible, basis for colonization than was religious conversion.

We have already examined symbols that were written on the body
and carried signs of social status. A variation of the language of meritographic tattoos was also used for monuments inscribed on bark or on the
trunks of stripped trees at the site of a battle. Yet although *piquage* was
rarely described in detail or illustrated in an engraving, Lafitau, in the
plate mentioned above, and Lahontan (fig. 8) offered examples of this

"monumental" form of writing in the plates that illustrated the original editions of their works; Charlevoix and Deliette, among others, also described such glyphs but did not include illustrations. Lafitau explained, "Quand un Sauvage revient de Guerre, & qu'il veut faire connoître sa victoire au Nations voisines des lieux où il passe . . . il supplée au défaut de l'alphabet, qui lui manque, par des nottes characteristiques, qui le distinguent personnellement" (2:43–44) [When an Indian returns from war and wishes to make his victory known to the tribes neighboring on the places through which he passes . . . he supplies the lack of alphabet (which he does not have) with characteristic marks which distinguish him personally]. Lafitau here described a form of signature, such as the self-portrait of "Two Feathers" alongside the record of his exploits (fig. 9 below). But one page later, he added:

> . . . il exprime au-dessous de sa figure le nombre des guerriers qui composent le parti qu'il conduit, et au-dessous des guerriers le nombre des prisonniers qu'il a fait, et de ceux qu'il a tué de sa propre main. . . . Les guerriers sont réprésentés avec leurs armes, ou simplement par des lignes; les prisonniers par le bâton orné des plumes et par le *chichikoué*, qui sont les marques de leur esclavage. (2:45)

> [. . . he denotes below his face the number of warriors in the party which he is leading, and below the warriors, the number of prisoners whom he has taken. . . . The warriors are represented by their arms or simply by lines, the prisoners by the wand adorned with plumes, and the Chichikoüé (rattles) which are the marks of their captivity.]

Thus the function of enumeration is again simply a tally, a different register of signification from the marks of identification. Charlevoix, paddling down the Mississippi, also remarked on seeing such a monument:

> . . . nous aperçûmes sur le bord du Fleuve à droite un Poteau dressé; nous en approchâmes, & nous reconnûmes que c'étoit un Monument dressé par les Illinois pour une Expédition faite depuis peu sur les Chicachas. Il y avoit deux figures d'Hommes sans tête, & quelques-unes dans leur entier. Les premiers marquoient les Morts, & les seconds, les Captifs. (408)

[This day, we perceived a post erected, on the right side of the river, on taking a near view of it, we found it was a monument set up by the Illinois, on account of an expedition they had made sometime ago against the Chicachas (Chickasaw). There were two figures of men without heads, and some others entire. The first represented the dead, and the second the captives. (2:242–43)]

Again, there is an array of symbols to represent the quality of the achievement (the thing killed, subdued, or acquired) and repetition of the icon to indicate the quantity. Charlevoix's description is minimal, and there is no illustration of this monument. However, at the very end of his *Mémoires*, Lahontan provided an illustration of a "Hiéroglyphe" that purportedly narrated a battle between Seneca and French soldiers (see Figure 8 above). Ten panels are arranged vertically on a column or tree and proceed chronologically from top to bottom. The glyphs include a "cabane" or cabin to represent one day of travel to the engagement, a face for a warrior killed in the battle, and a mallet head for each one injured. Reuben Gold Thwaites, the editor of the first American edition of Lahontan as well as of the *Jesuit Relations*, described the drawing as "the work of a European quite unacquainted with Indian pictographs" (1:514), which is clear to the less-informed reader from several clues. Not only is the battle narrated a French victory (presumably one of the battles against the Iroquois in which Lahontan participated between 1686 and 1690), but also the panels include information about the French soldiers' experience, such as the number of days they traveled to the site, which the Seneca might not know and would have no reason to record. Also, the hieroglyph for a prisoner is a miniature of a nude in a classicist pose that looks like a birdbath and does not resemble any Indian style. The text is not an Indian history, but colonial history written in an alleged Indian language and thereby an authenticating history of the assimilated Lahontan, rather like Bossu's story of getting tattooed. Lahontan presents the purported writing of nonliterate Indians, but the story he tells in this writing is one of his learning from the Indians and of colonial violence against the Seneca. Lahontan's assessment of this hieroglyphic system does not ridicule its primitiveness but rather its complexity. As a nonalphabetic system, it has so many symbols that the language "est capable d'embarrasser extrémement l'esprit d'un Européen, ce qui fait que je me suis contenté d'aprendre les plus essentiels plûtôt par nécessité que par curiosité" (2:194) ['tis very perplexing to an European; for which Reason I have contented my self in learning only such of 'em as are most Essential; the knowledge of which I owe to Necessity more than Curiosity (2:88–89)].

Rousseau would later, in his *Essai sur l'origine des langues*, propose the following system aligning modes of signification with the stages of society's development: "La peinture des objets convient aux peuples sauvages; les signes des mots et des propositions, aux peuples barbares, et l'alphabet aux peuples policiés" (57) [The depicting of objects is appropriate to a savage people; signs of words and propositions, to a barbaric people, and the alphabet to civilized peoples (17)]. This represents a retreat from the prohibition against writing by savages but uses phonocentrism to maintain the primitive status of the *sauvages américains* even as it casts some Old World peoples under the same appellation.

Lahontan credited the Indians with teaching him about the limits and types of writing. He also theorized, more than half a century before Rousseau, three similar stages: "Les Chronologistes Grecs (qui ont divisé les tems en ἄδηλων: Ce qui est caché; μυδικὸν ἡρωικὸν: Ce qui est fabuleux; Ιζορικὸυ: Ce qu'ils ont eu pour veritable)" (2:90). [The Grecian Chronologers who divided the course of Time into three Periods, namely the ἄδηλον or that which is wrapt up in Obscurity, the μυθιχὸν, alias ἡζωιχὸν, or that which was the season of Fiction and Fables, and the ἱζοειχὸν which affords us true and creditable Actions (2:1)].[30] Not just historical stages, these are also genres of discourse, of which the first is oral (and therefore its past is unknown), the second is fiction, and the third is fact. The three reflect provocatively on Lahontan's own work, a combination of voices, facts, and fictions throughout.

Lahontan places himself in the position of the Greeks, "l'usage de l'Ecriture leur étant inconnu devant le Siége de Troye, il faut qu'ils s'en soient rapportez aux Manuscrits fabuleux des Egyptiens & des Chaldéens, gens visionnaires & superstitieux" (2:90) [the invention of writing being unknown to them before the Siege of Troy, they had no other

Standard to consult but the Fabulous Manuscripts of the Egyptians and
Chaldeans, who were a Phanatick Superstitious sort of People (2:1–2)].
Lahontan stands in the same relation to the Hurons, Iroquois, and Algonquins as the Greeks did to the Egyptians and Chaldeans. He has
discovered a race of primitives who write in hieroglyphics, who must
belong to an anterior stage of human social development, and whose
recent past may contain clues to the origins of his own culture. Yet he
can learn of their past only through their oral traditions, and, unlike the
Greeks Homer and Hesiod, who wrote cosmogonies based on oral legends, Lahontan feels an epistemological impasse:

> Or supposons que ceux-ci [the Egyptians and Chaldeans] soient les
> Inventeurs de cette Ecriture, comment pourra-t-on ajoûter foi à tout
> ce qu'ils disent être arrivé avant qu'ils eussent trouvé cette invention.
> Apparemment ils n'étoient ni plus éclairez, ni plus sçavans Chro-
> nologistes que les Ameriquains, de sorte que sur ce pied-là ils auroient
> été fort embarrassez à raconter fidèlement les Avantures & les Faits de
> leur Ancêtres. Je suis maintenant convaincu que la Tradition est trop
> suspecte, inconstante, obscure, incertaine, trompeuse & vague, pour se
> fier à elle; J'ai l'obligation de cette idée aux Sauvages de Canada, qui ne
> sçachant rapporter au vrai ce qui s'est passé dans leur Païs il y a deux
> cens ans, me font révoquer en doute la pureté & l'incorruptibilité de la
> Tradition. (2:90–91)

> [But supposing the Egyptians and Chaldeans to have invented the Art
> of Writing, what Credit can we give to the accounts of things that are
> said to have happen'd before the date of that Invention? In all proba-
> bility they knew no more of the matter than the Americans, and upon
> that score 'twas very hard for them to give a faithful Narrative of the
> Adventures and Exploits of their Ancestors. I am now fully convinc'd
> that Tradition is so inconstant, obscure, uncertain and fallacious, that
> we cann't pretend to rely upon it. And this Notion I owe to the
> Savages of Canada, who being at a loss to trace the truth of what has
> been transacted in their own Country but 200 Years ago, gave me
> occasion to call in Question the Purity and Truth of Tradition. (2:2)]

Later, he lashes out at the ultimate authority in writing, the Holy Scriptures, through an account of Indians' reaction to it:

> Quand je lui mettois devant les yeux les Révélations de Moise & des
> autres Prophétes . . . il me demandoit si mon Pere ou mon Ayeul
> avoient vû tous ces événnements, & si j'etois assez credule pour
> m'imaginer que nos Ecritures fussent veritables, voyant que les Rela-
> tions de leur Païs, écrites depuis quatre jours, étoient pleines de
> Fables. (2:122)

> [When I laid before him the Revelations of Moses and the Prophets . . .
> he asked me if my Father or my Grandfather had seen all these Events,
> and whether I was so credulous as to take our Scriptures for Truth,
> since the Histories of Countries writ but t'other day are found to be
> Fabulous. (2:27)]

Lahontan has become an Enlightenment skeptic, and he learned his
skepticism from the Indians. The natives' system of writing represents
only tangible objects and verifiable events, in contrast with their oral
history, which tells of vague and marvelous occurrences in a misty past.
The Indians were no doubt more confident of the truth of their oral
history than they were of the Bible, but Lahontan perceives an inconsistency and turns it into an empiricist critique of metaphysics similar to
Thomas Paine's attack on the Bible, which rejected all revelation as
hearsay. The influence of "primitive" peoples on Enlightenment philosophy goes far beyond romantic Noble Savages; it contributes to the
foundations of skeptical deism. An implicit adherent, though not a
theorist, of the *premiers temps* trope, Lahontan sees himself as doing ethnographic research into the accuracy of oral and classical history. He
believes that the epistemological standards demanded of contemporary
travel writers should be applied to the classical authors as well. If one
cannot trust oral history, how can one believe the Bible any more than
Indians' accounts of their origins, wars, and migrations? What is the
authority of classical literature arising out of oral traditions? Such skepticism invokes the truth claims of exploration narrative, where the author relates only what he sees along his path through the wilderness,
employs a memory as photographic as the Indians', and establishes by
documentary truth facts about America that were unknowable through
traditional Judeo-Christian history. The philosophical implications of

what Lahontan learns from the Indians are profound but tempt his readers to turn some skepticism toward his own narrative as well, particularly the secondhand information about inhabitants upstream on "La Rivière Longue."

Lahontan's skepticism is not unique. Lafitau, who as a Jesuit ridicules the freethinker Lahontan and his *Nouveaux voyages*, nevertheless shares his doubts about the written histories of times without writing, though less severely:

> les Athéniens eux-mêmes, ayant été des Barbares sans lettres, n'ont point eu d'Annales & des fastes . . . ont rapproché des temps bien éloignés de celui, où ils ont commencé à laisser quelquechose d'eux-mêmes à la posterité. La même chose arriveroit aujourd'hui à tous les Peuples barbares qui existent, s'ils vouloient ou si dans la suite ils pouvoient coucher par écrit quelque chose de leur histoire. Ils ont tous une tradition fabuleuse de leur origine, où l'on voit l'histoire de premiers temps déguisée, & ils la rapprocheroient indubitablement des temps où ils écriroient, faute de ne pouvoir rien dire des évenements arrivés dans un long enchaînement de siecles, qui sont pour eux dans un éternel oubli. (1:539)

> [the Athenians themselves, at that time unlettered barbarians (who) had no annals or records . . . have brought into comparison times very remote from those of their earliest written records. Today, the same thing would be the case for all the existing preliterate peoples if they were willing to or eventually could, write their history. They all have an origin myth in which the story of the first times is disguised and they bring it into comparison with the time when they are writing since they cannot tell anything of the events which took place in a long succession of centuries which remain, for them, in eternal forgetfulness.]

Lafitau interprets the *premiers temps* not as unknowable, but as merely disguised. Again, there is a complex interaction between European and Savage, history and prehistory. The *sauvages américains* are still without writing, but one can now set down something in writing of their history, for the French colonists (specifically the Jesuit missionaries) have imported writing and can do it for them. As well as recording Indian cosmogonies, they can also learn about their own European (pre-)history. In the conquest of the New World, when "they bring it into comparison with the time when they are writing," Lafitau, Lahontan, or Hariot/White/deBry and their Picts obliterate all the history between their present and the imagined barbaric past and appropriate the immediate history of the Amerindians for this imagined past. The intervening Dark Ages of European barbarism can be ignored. The colonial explorers have the advantage over the Athenians of viewing the prehistoric, preliterate past immediately; it is right in front of the observing traveler and protoethnographer.

Less than one hundred years later, when the "savages" were ideologically doomed to extinction as "vanishing Indians," the judgment of their history had altered considerably. Archeology had emerged as a field of inquiry, and thus a physical record as a form of writing about the past had become comprehensible. John Dunn Hunter described among the Plains Indians hieroglyphics very similar to those in Charlevoix and Lahontan, maps and narratives of battles on animal skins or bark. But additionally, Hunter reported writing of a more personal and specifically historical nature: "Their distinguished warriors register on skins all the remarkable incidents of their lives: which, with the exception of those they are buried in, are uniformly kept by their relatives as sacred relics and testimonies of honorable descent for many succeeding generations" (88). This is unquestionably writing, for the Anglo-American historian can read it, rather than writing the history of the Indians for them, or so at least Hunter hopes: "I have no doubt, more correct information, respecting the origin of the Indians, might be obtained from a comparison [of] the hieroglyphic characters of different nations and eras, than can possibly be arrived at from the analysis of their respective languages" (88–89). Much speculation had been made on the Indians' origin based on perceived similarities of their speech to the Hebrew, Welsh, and other Old World tongues. Thomas Jefferson, in *Notes on the State of Virginia*, had bemoaned the death of Indian languages because it meant lost opportunities for such comparisons and speculation, though he rejected archeological evidence as a clue to these questions of origin. Hunter, unlike Lahontan and Jefferson, insisted that the Indians did have writing that was a more reliable source of information than histories in the oral tradition, or philological speculation based on the analysis of spoken language. Yet many historians have doubted Hunter's own authenticity, placing him in the position of the mythmaker, not the skeptical reader.

We have examined some of the attitudes of the French toward Amerindian writing; we can complete the exchange by looking at scenes of the introduction of alphabetic writing to the Indians. This event cannot be dissociated from colonial conquest and conversion, from the imposition of European languages on native peoples and the suppression of local tongues. As the practical advantages of learning native languages, such as Lahontan's necessity of reading Seneca hieroglyphs, diminished with the increasing domination by the colonists, many American tribes were deprived of their language, often forbidden from speaking it in reservation schools. However, in the early years of European-Indian contact, many colonists and missionaries went to great efforts to learn Indian languages. The Jesuits' method of conversion did not impose a linguistic hegemony by forcing the heathens to speak French; in fact, it postponed teaching the French language for as long as possible. Although with very different motives, the Jesuit missionaries resembled modern anthropologists (including Claude Lévi-Strauss, as we shall soon see) who try to preserve the native culture they study by not infecting it with European writing. The missionaries lived in local homes, learned the local language as quickly as possible, and instructed their flock in catechisms translated into Huron and other local tongues. If an individual was judged sufficiently pious, the instruction led to a baptism that would be included in the lengthy stories of conversions in the *Jesuit Relations*. All this could come before the convert had learned any French. The Jesuits also recruited boys and girls to become students at the seminary schools in Quebec run by other orders, where they might learn French and Latin. The Recollets such as Sagard, by contrast, favored imposing French on their missions' subjects. Writing remained very important for the Jesuits. They wrote for the *Relations*, in their journals, in letters to one another, and as part of their efforts to learn the local tongues.

Thus, written language appeared as a secretive and sacred thing to the Indians. When the priests read prayers from the Bible, the Indians felt that they understood quite well what was going on—the "Black Robes" were reciting spells or singing sacred songs. This is the best interpretation they could give short of being fully indoctrinated into Christianity. When the Indians saw the missionaries writing, they reasoned that the priests were creating more of these magic papers. There was no way they could distinguish a priori between holy and worldly scripture, and so the missionaries were free to characterize the Indians' awe of writing as God-fearing or as superstitious, depending on whether they saw them reacting to the Bible or to a simple letter. James Axtell, in "The Power of Print in the Eastern Woodlands," has argued that the Jesuits had greater success than the English missionaries because their behavior with writing enhanced the Indians' perception that they had shamanic powers.

The Jesuits' work therefore required an excellent knowledge of native languages. Having been selected from among the best-educated young men of Europe, the Jesuits began to learn on their own and many progressed very quickly. Their methods were quite different from the adoption and immersion of the *truchements*. Jesuits maintained the primacy of writing and the centrality of the Holy Scriptures amid an oral culture. They compiled dictionaries and grammars and translated hymns, psalms, prayers, and catechisms. In the *Relation* of 1636, Père Jean de Brébeuf told what he had learned of Huron grammar and offered as an example the conjugation of a Huron verb. The verb he chooses is, strangely enough, *ahiaton*, "to write," one that he must have learned as the Hurons applied it to his own behavior (*JR* 10:120–23). In this case, the writing lesson is for Brébeuf. The task was larger than anticipated, and it proved very difficult "de vouloir comprendre de tous poincts une langue estrangere, tres-abondante, & autant differente de nos langues Europeanes qu'est le Ciel de la terre, & sans maistre & sans livres" (*JR* 10:54–55) [to endeavor to understand in all points a foreign tongue, very abundant, and as different from our European languages as Heaven is from earth,—and that without master or books]. Although he appreciated the language for its complexity, he still evaluated Huron, and the process of learning it, according to European standards. For classically trained Jesuits, to learn a language "sans livres" was almost unthinkable, and Brébeuf figured the difference in terms of heaven and earth (we can only assume which is which).

Lafitau expressed the Jesuits' confidence in their skills through the voice of the Indians. He wrote that the Indians considered Europeans incapable of learning their language "si l'on en excepte les Missionaires, qu'ils croyent devoir la posseder comme-eux-mêmes, parce qu'ayant le secours de l'Ecriture, ils se persuadent que tout est écrit, & que s'appliquant à la Langue par état, c'est leur faute s'ils la parlent mal" (2:480–81) [except the missionaries who, they think, should know it as they do because they have the help of the Scriptures (in which) they believe all is written and that, since it is their profession to apply themselves to language, it is their fault if they speak it badly]. According to Lafitau's disingenuous statement, writing is essentially no more or less than the Scripture (the word "écriture" signifies both in French), and the Holy Scriptures contain all the revealed knowledge of the world, including "barbarous" tongues. According to this religious-ideological fantasy, Jesuits already knew the Indian languages, just as God was omniscient and all the earth's people were descended from Adam and Eve. Such a passage comports with religious dogma yet is so patently absurd that it could only be placed in the mouth of the Other, who is stupid and ignorant, but also innocent as a lamb and the greatest hope of the future Church.

In other narratives by secular writers, the Indians' admiration for the skill of writing leads to a comic rather than an edifying scene. One instance is when Bossu narrates Monsieur de Belle-Isle's captivity among the Attikapas. The French officer saved himself by writing for help:

> Cet infortuné donna sa commission à ce Sauvage, & l'assura que c'étoit de l'écorce ou du papier qui parloit, qu'en le présentant au premier Chef des François de la partie d'où il venoit, il seroit bien reçu. Ce Naturel crût que cette lettre participoit de la divinité, puisqu'elle devoit parler pour lui, en arrivant chez les François. Les autres voulourent la lui ôter. Il se sauva, en traversant une rivière à la nage; & de peur de mouiller la lettre, il la tenoit en l'air.

[The poor man gave his commission to the Indian, assuring him that it was "talking bark" or paper. If the Indian gave it to the chief of the Frenchmen in his country, he would be well received. The native thought that the letter was a sacred thing since it was going to speak for him among the French. The others wanted to take it away from him, but he escaped by swimming across a river. He held the letter over his head to keep it from getting wet.][31]

The power of writing not only frees Monsieur de Belle-Isle from captivity, it ensures obedience from the Indians, who like the colonized everywhere are seen as lazy and recalcitrant, but superstitious and fearful. The letter possesses this Indian; he does not save the letter from the grasp of his companions, he saves himself by crossing the river and then the letter by holding it out of the water. Thomas Hariot claimed that the Indians regarded writing or books as animate objects that transmitted knowledge physically; he wrote of their reaction to the Bible: "And though I tolde them the booke materially and of it selfe was not of any such vertue, as I thought they did conceive, but onely the doctrine therein conteined: yet would they be glad to touche it, to embrace it, to kisse it . . . to shewe their hungrie desire of that knowledge which was spoken of" (40).[32]

Another scene is found in Claude Lebeau's *Voyage curieux et nouveau*. The opening chapters of the novel describe Lebeau's bourgeois Parisian background and his training as a lawyer, before his father disowned him and forcibly sent him to Quebec. After a year's work as a merchant's clerk, he becomes dissatisfied and recruits a couple of Hurons to help him escape to the English colonies in New York. When their small party encounters some Iroquois, one of the Hurons, Antoine, attempts to intimidate his nation's traditional enemies with the power of writing. He says Lebeau has the power to level mountains and smooth rapids by drawing maps of the terrain and then altering them. The *sauvages'* ignorance of writing is represented as an assumption that there must be a physical, concrete relationship between sign and referent, and that a change in one automatically entails a change in the other. This assumption follows on beliefs that the Indians can recall exactly every place they have been and read the tracks of animals and other people with unfailing accuracy. The band of Iroquois doubts this story, however, and to prove his case, Lebeau shows them his two diplomas from the law school in Paris, his "Lettres de Bachelier & de Licencié ès Droits de la Faculté de Paris" (1:193). Implausibly, the Iroquois accept these credentials and welcome Lebeau, celebrating their guest by dancing around a canoe paddle that bears his diplomas tied to one end.[33] Later in the novel, another band of Iroquois ask Lebeau to use the diplomas-on-a-stick to exorcise an evil spirit from a mountain grotto. Lebeau, who with Lahontan is the most creative practitioner of the French "Travels in North America" genre, exploits satirically the extreme cultural distance between a French lawyer and the Indians and the completely different codes for status in the two cultures. These comic scenes, though disrespectful of Native Americans' intelligence and traditions, do interrogate the idea of how textual material can carry social power and also conflate the credulous Indians with Christians who believe in the power of Scripture or of saints' relics.

In literary theory, the scene of the introduction of writing to "primitive" peoples demands mention of the critique of anthropologist Claude Lévi-Strauss by Jacques Derrida in *Of Grammatology*. The relevant chapter, "The Violence of the Letter," has helped to form influential postmodern ideas about the relationship between phonologic (alphabetic) writing, cultural contact, and violence. Much of what Derrida draws out of Lévi-Strauss about the ethnocentric suppression of alternative forms of writing applies to the literature of New France. For Derrida, Lévi-Strauss represents a revival of Rousseauism in the twentieth century and his *Tristes tropiques* is "at the same time *The Confessions* and a sort of supplement to the *Supplément au voyage de Bougainville*" (107). For his part, Lévi-Strauss revives the travel and exploration narratives of the seventeenth and eighteenth centuries. His multiple roles and positions as travel writer, anthropologist, scholar of political and social history, and scion of the French academic establishment repeat all that Lescarbot or Charlevoix were in their time. Moreover, *Tristes tropiques* encounters many of the same cultural issues and rhetorical problems as Lahontan's *Nouveaux voyages* and other texts examined above.

Lévi-Strauss's 1955 work integrates sections of ethnographic description (often adapted from his formal anthropological monographs) into a discontinuous narrative of his journey to South America. Lévi-Strauss consciously reenacts and in some respects inverts the archetypes of the exploration-ethnography genre. The chapter preceding "A Writing Lesson" (the one most important for Derrida) is a sentimental description of the Nambikwara entitled "Family Life." The chapter following presents, in the context of Rousseau's and later political theory, the fragile authority of their chiefs who rule by consent and charisma, much as North American native leaders are said to have commanded hundreds of years before.

Lahontan and others employ the divided form of *récit de voyage* and *mœurs des sauvages* to help evade questions such as where exactly he saw the panel of hieroglyphics and who wrote it. Lévi-Strauss does occasionally thematize, without ever fully confronting, the issue of his insertion into the cultures he has made it his work to study. As Derrida observes (and as Pratt might have), "a strict separation of the anthropological confession and the theoretical discussion of the anthropologist must be observed. The difference between empirical and essential must continue to assert its rights" (117). But the separation maintains itself only with difficulty. Between synthetic descriptions of familial love and of political consent, the traveling anthropologist bungles his entrance into the tribe with his gift of writing, making mistakes rarely committed by eighteenth-century travel writers, such as getting lost and misplacing his mule, camera, and personal belongings. Lévi-Strauss appears an unwilling and unprepared explorer of America, an anthropologist thrown out of his generic and rhetorical element.

The scene of "A Writing Lesson" resembles closely ones recounted by Jesuit missionaries and other protoethnographers in North America. The Nambikwara, like the Hurons, have a name for that which they cannot do, the act of writing. But the introduction of writing does nothing to enhance Lévi-Strauss's power among the *sauvages*, as Lebeau, Monsieur de Belle-Isle, Hennepin, and many Jesuits reported. Nor could he adopt native forms of writing for his own purposes, as Lahontan did. Quite the opposite: the Nambikwara chief acted out the behavior of a writer and reader in an attempt to enhance his own power over his band:

> I handed out paper and pencils. At first they did nothing with them,
> then one day I saw that they were all busy drawing wavy, horizontal
> lines. I wondered what they were trying to do, then it was suddenly
> borne upon me that they were writing or, to be more accurate, were
> trying to use their pencils in the same way as I did mine. . . . but the
> chief had further ambitions. No doubt he was the only one who had
> grasped the purpose of writing. So he asked me for a writing-pad, and
> when we both had one, and were working together, if I asked for
> information on a given point, he did not supply it verbally but drew
> wavy lines on his paper and presented them to me. (296)

He then attempts to use the power of writing to dictate the terms of
trade with Lévi-Strauss: "He took from a basket a piece of paper covered
with wavy lines and made a show of reading it, pretending to hesitate as
he checked on it the list of objects I was to give in exchange for the
presents offered me" (296). The introduction of writing does violence to
the Nambikwara's innocence, and Lévi-Strauss suggests that on a world-
wide scale literacy increases political despotism and instability: "The
villagers who withdrew their allegiance to their chief after he had tried
to exploit a feature of civilization (after my visit he was abandoned by
most of his people) felt in some obscure way that writing and deceit had
penetrated into their midst" (300). But the intervention of corrupting
colonial power through writing did not begin with Lévi-Strauss. He
relived the experiences of eighteenth-century explorers even more than
he realized, for a similar scene occurs in John Lawson:

> The next day, having some occasion to write, the Indian king, who saw
> me, believ'd that he could write as well as I. Whereupon, I wrote a
> Word, and gave it him to copy, which he did with more Exactness,
> than any European could have done, that was illiterate. It was so well,
> that he who could read mine, might have done the same by his. . . . He
> sent for several Indians to his Cabin, to look at his Handy-work, and
> both he and they thought, I could read his Writing as well as I could
> my own. I had a Manual in my Pocket, that had King David's Picture
> in it, in one of his private Retirements. The Indian ask'd me, Who that
> Figure represented? I told him, it was the Picture of a good King, that
> liv'd according to the Rules of Morality . . . (57)

Rather like following a track, the Indian king has the skill of following exactly the lines on a page, and as in Champlain's reported dialogue, he must be shown rather than simply told about the power of Europe. Once given "some lively carnal Representation" (58), instead of abstractions that cannot be represented, he will assent to the power of signs such as King David that might mean nothing to him. Lawson even adds that "a New-England Minister blames the French Jesuits" for the use of such "a lively Representation of our Christian Belief" (58) as a means of instruction. In the eighteenth century, teaching the Indians writing was bound up in the contrasting attitudes of Catholics and Protestants to the vernacular Scripture. In *Tristes tropiques*, writing is less a system of communication than a figure for the division between the technological West and the primitive *indigènes*. This is perhaps the reason why Lévi-Strauss does not recognize the Caduveo tattoos as writing in the sense I do here.

Lévi-Strauss holds to a Rousseauist primitivism and distrusts both bourgeois society and writing. Derrida's "The Violence of the Letter" interrogates these assumptions from the point of view of the threat that writing is seen to pose to transparent, self-present speech: "The scorn for writing, let us note in passing, accords quite happily with this ethnocentrism. The paradox is only apparent, one of those contradictions where a perfectly coherent desire is uttered and accomplished. By one and the same gesture (alphabetic) writing, servile instrument of a speech dreaming of its plenitude and its self-presence, is scorned and the dignity of writing is refused to nonalphabetic signs. We have perceived this gesture in Rousseau and in Saussure" (109–10). Derrida could have added "in Lahontan," as well as many other early observers of Indians. The American Indians' forms of writing might be called "servile instruments" of self-present speech. The exploration-ethnography texts scorn alphabetic writing by praising the transparency of Iroquoian belts and hieroglyphs that represent events or objects with a strict correspondence and avoid the arbitrariness that haunts Western metaphysics and writing. The false paradox that nevertheless acts out a coherent desire describes well the dialectic of negation and substitution in descriptions of the *sauvages américains*. We have seen Lahontan deny and then grant to hieroglyphic symbols the status of writing. And, of course, the same process obtains in many spheres besides writing. The denial and then grudging acceptance of the existence of Native American religion, clothing, and government all conceal a similar European dream and fear of its origins and of self-presence.

I have been perhaps already under the sway of Derridean poststructuralism in considering *piquage* and hieroglyphics as forms of writing. To it I also owe a sensitivity toward the valorization of speech and presence as a component of savagism. The eloquence, gravity, and long-windedness of Indian speakers, the polite attentiveness of listeners, and the "nobility" of their languages all contribute to the Western ideal of self-present speech that Derrida critiques.[34] But it is not only speech that holds these precious qualities. In his characteristic style, half mimicking, half criticizing Lévi-Strauss, Derrida questions the idealization of primitive societies, which supposedly do not suffer from the evils of writing: "the Nambikwara, who do not know how to write, are *good*, we are told. The Jesuits, the Protestant missionaries, the American anthropologists, the technicians on the Line, who believed they perceived violence or hatred among the Nambikwara are not only mistaken, they have probably projected their own wickedness upon them" (116, Derrida's italics).

Derrida deconstructs this situation of mutual misunderstanding and violence by arguing that writing is not the province of advanced societies, but of every society. Native Americans' forms of writing, though perhaps less efficient than alphabets, preserve better than alphabetic writing some of the ideals of truth, presence, and accuracy for which writing is prized by history. The logocentric ideals associated with Rousseau and Lévi-Strauss are found also in the exploration literature of colonial America. *Of Grammatology* does not discuss *piquage* or quipus, though its theory would define them as writing. Derrida's explanation of why the Nambikwara and other apparently illiterate societies do in fact practice writing is one of the most radical and difficult parts of *Of Grammatology*: "If writing is no longer understood in the narrow sense of linear and phonetic notation, it should be possible to say that all societies capable of producing, that is to say of obliterating, their proper names, and of bringing classificatory difference into play, practice writing in general" (109).

Derrida wishes to introduce a dialectical element into what he feels is an overly static structuralist theory of language as a system of phonological difference. In this system, no sign is metaphysically assigned to any referent, and there is no origin or grounded term in the interplay between signs and referents. Language operates only through the differential distinctions that our senses can make within the two fields. Lévi-Strauss endorsed this structuralist theory of language developed by Ferdinand de Saussure, whom Derrida critiques in the first section of his book, and proposed kinship as another such system of differences. For example, some cultures distinguish between maternal and paternal uncles with two words equivalent to the English "uncle." In "The Violence of the Letter: From Lévi-Strauss to Rousseau," Derrida plays with the notion advanced by Lévi-Strauss in *Les structures élémentaires de la parenté* (1949) that the prohibition on incest is the only universal in this system of arbitrary difference, the only fundamental link between nature (genetics) and culture (kinship). It is necessary to have a stable concept of identity to know to whom the incest taboo applies, and on this identity depends also the proper name and the grounds of Western metaphysics. Writing is so radical for Derrida because it deconstructs this metaphysics, as it continues to exist after composition and one can never with certainty identify its author. The proper name could function as a guarantor of individual identity only in an oral culture, where the speaker and the "parole" or utterance are always present. However, and this is the key point, it does not ensure identity, even in a supposedly very primitive oral culture such as the Nambikwara, because there is a taboo against speaking proper names. It is as if society prohibited proper names because it feared instituting a system of identity, and yet in the prohibition it unwittingly bound itself to a system of writing that was used to support other systems of identity such as meritography. Derrida draws on Lévi-Strauss's ethnographic observations to support his idea that the proper name is "always already under erasure." "For writing, obliteration of the proper classed in the play of difference, is the originary violence itself: pure impossibility of the 'vocative mark,' impossible purity of the mark of vocation" (110).

A prohibition on speaking the proper names of others, such as Lévi-Strauss observed among the Nambikwara, is common in indigenous American societies, and the particular ways this prohibition was observed among the Indians of Canada are of interest. Charlevoix noted that "les Sauvages" (as usual he is not more specific) never called someone by his proper name but instead used kinship terms (2:289). Sagard wrote that a Huron would tell him the names of others but not his or her own name.[35] Brébeuf added that the Huron would not say "brother" or "uncle," but always "my brother" and "my uncle." The *Relation de 1642* offers another example of how, among the Hurons as among other Native American peoples, a name is not a "proper" or permanent guarantor of identity but a shifting signifier of relations to others in a community:

> On donne le nom à un enfant quelque temps apres sa naissance, passant de l'enfance en l'adolescence, il change de nom comme les Romains changoient de robe, il prend un autre nom en l'aage viril, & puis encor un autre en sa vieillesse: si bien qu'ils en ont de rechange selon leurs aages, échapant de quelque danger ou sortant de quelque grande maladie: ils prennent un nom qu'ils croyent leur debvoir estre de meilleur augure que celuy qu'ils avoient. (*JR* 22:286–87)

> [A child's name is given to him shortly after his birth. When he passes from childhood to adolescence, he changes his name as the Romans changed their robes. He takes another name when he attains manhood, and still another in old age; so that they change their names according to their ages. When they escape a danger or recover from an illness, they take a name which they think will be of better augury than the one they had.]

So exactly what constitutes a proper name? Derrida claims that what Lévi-Strauss describes are not proper names, "The expression 'proper name' is improper" (111). Moreover, the functions of naming among the Native Americans are radically different from the "proper name," different in ways that the story of the Nambikwara does not explain but that Brébeuf suggests. The system of meritography, which we must now accept as a form of writing, inscribes not a proper name, in the strictest sense, but a collection of group identifying symbols and interpersonal affiliations, as well as the accomplishments of the individual's body. In connection with the plate showing the writing of "Two Feathers" (fig. 9), Lafitau described it this way:

> Le Sauvage donc, pour faire son portrait, tire une ligne simple en forme de tête, sans y mettre presque aucun trait pour designer les yeux, le nez, les oreilles, & les autres parties du visage; en leur place il trace les marques qu'il a fait pointer sur le sien, aussi bien que celles qui sont gravées sur sa poitrine, & qui lui étant particulières, le rendent connoissable, non-seulement à ceux qui l'ont vû, mais encore à tous ceux qui ne le connoissant que de réputation sçavent son symbole Hieroglyphique, comme autrefois on distinguoit en Europe une personne par sa devise, & que nous discernons aujourd'hui une famille par ses armoires. Au-dessus de sa tête il peint la chose qui exprime son nom: le Sauvage, par example, nommé le Soleil, peint un Soleil . . . (2:45)

> [The Indian, then, to make his portrait draws a simple line in the form of a head, hardly putting any marks on it to denote the eyes, nose, and other parts of the face. In their place, he traces the marks tattooed on his face as well as those engraved on his chest and which, being peculiar to him, render him recognizable not only to those who have seen him but also to all those who, knowing him only by reputation, know his hieroglyphic symbol, as formerly in Europe a person was distinguished by his coat of arms and today we distinguish a family by their armour. Above his head he paints the object which denotes his name. An Indian named the Sun, for example, paints the sun.]

The name is just one sign among many that contribute to the visible or written identity of this individual. This written name is not an arbitrary sign but an object that connects the individual with his achievements, just as in the material, iconic language of meritography, and much like a European nobleman's name connected him with the land he owned. As with tattoos, this representation tells a story about the person represented, making him legible to those who do not know him, for it expresses his relations to the common world of the hunt and of war. These representations erase, obscure, substitute for, or supplement the drawing of a face, the most accurate form of identification, but it is not clear that this constitutes a prohibition or "erasure." In his analysis of

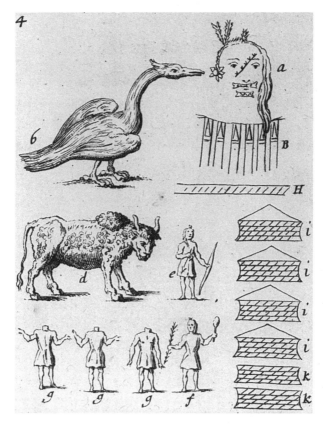

FIGURE 9. The "hieroglyphic painting" of Two Feathers, one of three panels from Book 2, plate 3 of Lafitau's *Mœurs des sauvages américains comparées au mœurs des premiers temps*, 1724. Lafitau's caption explains that figures *a–d* depict Two Feathers's facial tattoos or paintings, with the heron and bison standing for his tribe and family, while *f–k* represent the narrative of a war party he led. The tally in *h* gives the number in the party; *i* and *k* show that it was the sixth sortie in which Two Feathers participated and the fourth that he commanded. The three headless figures (*g*) represent scalps taken; *f* is a prisoner. (National Library of Canada, NL-18888)

Lévi-Strauss's episode with the Nambikwara, Derrida does not consider all the various ways in which writing can name or names can be written. The multiplicity of semiotic possibilities is implicit in his theory of writing, but his grammatology does not account for the diversity of indigenous forms of writing. Gordon Brotherston has criticized Derrida because "he has obviously taken little trouble with just those New World cultures that have so preoccupied his contemporary object of criticism, Lévi-Strauss" (67). And if the proper name is the most basic form of writing, then the different writing systems that humans use construct identity in different fields of difference, that is to say, in other cultures that might offer viable alternatives to Western logocentrism. According to American Indian autobiographers such as N. Scott Momaday and critics like Carter Revard, a multiplicity of shifting names is one aspect of the alternative ways in which American Indians define the self.

Structuralism and poststructuralism have taught us that languages are functional systems of differences, but they have suppressed the differences between languages as remote from one another as church Latin and Iroquoian wampum belts and the importance of these differences in intercultural encounters. Indian writing maintains unarbitrary, specific connections between signs and things or signs and events, even if these connections depend on the memories of tribe members, and even if proper names are not among these connections. Through the accounts of some European colonists, these connections contributed to the myth of lost presence, which imputed to the origin of writing the Fall of humankind, while also contributing to the paradoxical position of the Native Americans as both innocent and corrupt, naive and clever, illiterate and literate.

At the risk of failing to do justice to Derrida's critique, I wish to extend it from Lévi-Strauss to other twentieth-century anthropologists and popular writers who claim to have learned from seventeenth- and eighteenth-century colonialism how not to treat and think of the Savage Other, but who too often repeat the same prejudices. In "The Violence of the Letter," it is the prejudice dividing societies with writing from those without: "The traditional and fundamental ethnocentrism which, inspired by the model of phonetic writing, separates writing from speech

with an ax, is thus handled and thought of as anti-ethnocentrism. It
supports an ethico-political accusation: man's exploitation by man is the
fact of writing cultures of the Western type" (121). A similar scenario
was observed with regard to the Noble Savage, the renunciation of
which serves only to reinscribe the nobility of the irrepresentable Savage
at a further remove from the texts that represent him.

This chapter began with the beaver pelt, the most coveted object in
America north of the forty-third parallel for the European traders and
colonists from the mid-sixteenth through the nineteenth century. It is
therefore no accident that we find the beaver at the center of a web of
relationships of power, language, and value. Beaver pelts were clothing,
and their value as potential hat felt made them a money commodity. The
Indians were, in the eyes of the colonists, clad in money when they wore
beaver furs or wampum belts. Skins of animals and of Amerindians
served as the surface for writing, and beaver pelts and wampum could
themselves also function as written records. Surrounded by these multiple registers of value and meaning, it was inevitable that moral myths
about the origins of writing, of shame and clothing, and of money and
exchange emerged from the colonists' encounters with the American
Indians. Generally, Europeans imputed to the Indians the guilt or ambivalence that they themselves felt concerning advances in each of these
cultural technologies. In the next chapter, I will focus on the beaver
itself, prize and victim of the pelt trade. Even more than Indians, beavers
were ennobled as they were destroyed, and while colonial administrators
denounced and suppressed the pursuit and trade of pelts, beaver society
was held up as a model for Indian and colonist alike.

CHAPTER 5

The Beaver as
Native and as Colonist

La dépouille de cet Animal a jusqu'à présent fourni à la Nouvelle
France le principal objet de son Commerce. Il est par lui-même une
des merveilles de la nature, & il peut être pour l'Homme une grande
leçon de prévoyance, d'industrie, d'adresse, & de constance dans le
travail.

(Charlevoix, *Journal d'un voyage*, 94–95)

[The spoil of this animal has hitherto been the principal article in
the commerce of New France. It is itself one of the greatest wonders
in nature, and may very well afford many a striking lesson of
industry, foresight, dexterity, and perseverance in labor.

(1:151)]

I cannot refrain from smiling, when I read the accounts of different
Authors who have written on the œconomy of those animals, as there
seems to be a contest between them, who shall most exceed in
fiction. . . . little remains to be added to his account of the beaver,
beside a vocabulary of their language, a code of their laws, and a
sketch of their religion.

(Hearne, *Voyage from Prince of Wales Fort . . . to the Northern Ocean*, 149)

In the literature of New England, New Netherlands, and especially New France, one finds many brief but colorful accounts of the beaver. Nearly every travel narrative and natural history of the northern colonies in the seventeenth and eighteenth centuries included a few pages about this animal, which, as Charlevoix indicates, was as intriguing for its intelligence and social behavior as it was important for its economic value. Much more than an object of natural history, the beaver was to the French in Canada what sugar, tobacco, or spices were to other colonies. Its double status—as a natural and social marvel when alive, and as a valuable commodity when dead—caused representations of the beaver to become overdetermined with exaggerated and often contradictory ascriptions. A small, nonthreatening herbivore, the beaver was anthropomorphized, idealized, and sentimentalized in print even as it was killed by the thousands in the forests of North America, its pelts stacked, shipped, and traded in the pursuit of profit. Although Samuel Hearne was ridiculing the portrait of the beaver in one eighteenth-century work in particular, the *Wonders of Nature and Art*, his wry skepticism can be applied to many of these descriptions of an animal that was presented as a culture worthy of the attention given American Indians in the early ethnographic writings.

The beaver's function in literary representation is quite different from other animals famous in American literature. Whereas a single whale or bear became for Herman Melville or William Faulkner symbolic of natural or psychic forces locked in a struggle with Man, the portrayal of the beaver was ethnographic, not dramatic, and plural, not singular. When Lahontan, Charlevoix, and Le Page du Pratz described the life of the beaver, the representations were consonant with the descriptions of the Indians found elsewhere in their books, and it is in this context that the accounts of the beaver should be analyzed. The beavers' sociable life was represented in a timeless realm unaltered by humankind, much as ethnography is written in an achronic "ethnographic present" where the presence of the anthropologist is not apparent. The beaver's body and behavior were dismembered into assimilable or exploitable pieces, much as ethnography separated life into categories, including marriage and sexuality, clothing and ornament, health and subsistence, which deflected attention away from the creatural and cultural survival of the organic whole. The accounts of the beaver functioned in much the same way as the "manners and customs" of the Indians to rhetorically reconstitute the undisturbed indigenous life that was being destroyed by invading Europeans. By the latter part of the nineteenth century, if not sooner, rhetoric familiar from the trope of the vanishing Indian was also being applied to the beaver. "The beaver has gradually disappeared before the spread of civilization, which first settled along the shores of the Mediterranean. As each wave covered more of Europe, the range wherein the beaver existed perceptibly narrowed" (27), wrote Horace T. Martin in the beaver ethnography *Castorologia*; "North America remains the last stage on which are witnessed the scenes of a doomed culture" (29). Fur traders in the 1600s may not have imagined the beaver becoming extinct as it nearly did in the early twentieth century, but they did feel some anxiety over their dependence on a limited resource, an anxiety that fanciful portrayals of the beaver helped to assuage. And by the 1800s, the elegy for dying races was a trope that fit the beaver as well as it did the buffalo and the vanishing Indian stereotype.

Although the rhetorical method of ethnography was used for both, there is an important difference in the ideological function of the representations of the beaver and of the Amerindian. Whereas Native American society was represented as so antithetical to European that it was considered impossible to live in one without rejecting the values of the other, the social life of beavers supposedly resembled civilized and particularly colonial society. The cooperative, industrious, and nonnomadic beaver was often held up as a worthy model for colonists to imitate. Only one other American animal was so admired. Crèvecœur extolled "The well-known industry of bees, that excellent government which pervades their habitations, that never-ceasing industry by which they are actuated" (244).[1]

François-Marc Gagnon sees in the written and pictorial representations of the beaver in seventeenth-century New France a measure of the epistemic shift in natural history identified by Michel Foucault, from a discourse of similitude using analogies with the otter, fish, or lamb, to a discourse of representation that isolates the beaver as an autonomous natural object.[2] Nicolas Denys and Marc Lescarbot were still working in the Renaissance episteme that preceded natural history as we know it. Rather than an anatomical description of the beaver and an analysis of its niche in a system of nature, we find in these early colonial writers a presentation close to what Foucault has described as the typical form of histories for plants and animals in the seventeenth century: "the resemblances that could be found in it, the virtues that it was thought to possess, the legends and stories with which it had been involved, its place in heraldry, the medicaments that were concocted from its substance, the foods it provided, what the ancients recorded of it, and what travellers might have said of it. The history of a living thing was that thing itself, within the whole semantic network that connected it to the world" (129). Physical descriptions of the beaver often break up the animal into small parts and sort the pieces into the categories listed by Foucault, which are indicative of its dual status as natural marvel and as commodity; first, the organs and limbs are analyzed by their resemblance to those of humans or other animals and by their use for the beaver; second, the resources of the beaver are analyzed according to their value to Europeans. The beaver transcends Foucault's episteme, however, in the social characteristics that place it alongside contemporary ethnological thought.

European readers might have been more familiar with the beaver had it not been hunted to extinction in Western Europe. In England it had disappeared by the mid-fifteenth century.[3] As it was therefore novel to the colonists, anatomical analogies were needed to relate the beaver to more familiar animals and thus assimilate it to human uses. Charlevoix reported: "La Tête d'un Castor est à peu près de la figure de celle d'un Rat de Montagne. . . . Ses Jambes sont courtes, particuliérement celles de devant; elles n'ont guéres que quatre ou cinq pouces de long, & ressemblent assez à celles du Bléreau" (96) [The head of the beaver is very near like that of a mountain rat. . . . Its legs are short, particularly the forelegs, which are only four or five inches long, and pretty much like those of the badger (1:154)]. Denys wrote, in a passage copied almost word for word from Lescarbot: "il est à peu près de la longueur et grosseur d'un mouton, les pieds plus courts, ceux de derriere toillés ainsi qu'un oye, ceux de devant en forme de mains" (281) [It is almost as long and stout as a Sheep. The feet are short,—the hind ones webbed like a Goose, while those in front are like hands (362)]. In John Lawson's observation, "There Fore-Feet are open, like a Dog's; their Hind-Feet webb'd like a Water-Fowl's" (125). Adriaen Van der Donck also described the webbed feet but oddly extended the avian qualities of the beaver: "The hinder part of the body is short, much like that of a goose or swan" (114). Claude Lebeau ventured even further into the barnyard in search of comparisons: "Il a aussi les jouës & le bec d'un Liévre, la langue & la vessie d'un Pourceau" (1:316) [He has also the face and snout of a hare, the tongue and bladder of a pig (my translation)]. The most significant analogy, however, concerned the tail, which, due to its scaly covering and the beaver's facility in water, led it to be considered a fish. Charlevoix claimed that the beaver

> . . . nâge avec la même facilité que tout Animal Aquatique. D'ailleurs, par sa Queuë il est tout à fait Poisson, aussi a-t'il été juridiquement déclaré tel par la Faculté de Médecine de Paris, & en conséquence de cette Déclaration, la Faculté de Théologie a décidé qu'on pouvoit manger sa Chair les jours maigres. M. Lemery s'est trompé, quand il a dit que cette décision ne regardoit que le train de derriere du Castor. Il a été mis tout entier au même rang, que la Maquereuse. (96–97)

> [. . . swims with the same ease as any other aquatick animal. Besides, in respect of its tail, it is altogether a fish, having been juridically declared such by the faculty of medicine of Paris, in consequence of which declaration, the faculty of theology have decided that it might be lawfully eaten on meagre days. M. Lemery was mistaken in saying, that this decision regarded only the hinder part of the beaver. It has been placed all of it in the same class with mackrel. (1:154)]

"Le Castor est un poisson comme le Loutre" (281) [The Beaver is a fish like the Otter (362)], Denys stated baldly, extending the misclassification to another mammal. During Lent, that is to say during the Indians' late winter hunting season when all Canadians relied most on hunting for their subsistence, the beaver was therefore not taboo for the Catholic colonists. The relatively small beaver was not a common game animal, but the beaver-as-fish does demonstrate how the natural history of the time classified its objects by use and resemblance rather than by anatomical structures or ecological niches. The possibility that the tail might be Lenten fare whereas the rest of the meat was taboo (as the qualifier "all of it" suggests) underscores the process of dismemberment through which Europeans understood the beaver. Lahontan mocked such self-serving classifications after he learned from the Indians that beavers can live perfectly well away from water: "d'où je conclue que Messieurs les Casuistes ont grand tort de ne pas mettre les Canards, les Oyes, & les Sarcelles au nombre des amphibies aussi-bien que les Naturalistes" (1:139) [From whence I conclude, that the Casuists are out in not ranging Ducks, Geese, and Teals, in the number of Amphibious Animals, as the Naturalists are wont to do (1:106)]. The tail escaped any discourse of early comparative anatomy because it had no correlative among familiar species; it became a tool not only for the beaver but also indirectly for the French to use to reclassify it as a fish.

Like the whale, the beaver was valuable for products that had to be processed for the market. We saw in the previous chapter that the inner hairs of the beaver's fur provided the raw material for hat felt. Another beaver product, analogous to the whale's ambergris, was castoreum, a secretion highly sought after for medicines and cosmetics since the time of Hippocrates. As Charlevoix dissected it, it is "une matiere résineuse, mollasse, adhérente, mêlée de petites Fibres, de couleur grisâtre en dehors, jaunâtre en dedans, d'une odeur forte, désagréable & pénétrante, & qui s'enflamme aisément" (98) [a soft, resinous, adhesive matter, mixed with small fibres, greyish without, and yellow within, of a strong disagreeable and penetrating scent, and very inflammable (1:156)]. As with the beaver's tail, Renaissance naturalists regarded castoreum by reference to humans', not beavers', uses for it, and a history of misreadings and corrections ensued. Denys and Antoine-Denis Raudot/Antoine Silvy claimed that the source of castoreum was the "rognons" or kidneys.[4] Other early observers thought that it came from the testicles. Its strong odor recalled musk, and, after all, it was patriarchally logical that something of such value to man might issue from something of value to all men. As Thomas Morton wrote, "this beast is of a masculine virtue for the advancement of Priapus" (205). In reality, the castoreum glands are found in both the male and the female (which may explain why John Josselyn reported of the beaver that "the Indians say that they are Hermaphrodites"),[5] and the oil is used to maintain the water-repellent and insulating qualities of the fur. Not concerned with the beaver's own use of its fur, seventeenth- and eighteenth-century observers failed to perceive that these glands served the same purpose that Indians' sweat did when they wore beaver pelts—castoreum kept the beaver's pelt greasy. John Gyles, captive of the Abenaki in the 1690s, seems to have been the first writer to correctly observe that "With this oil and gum they preen themselves so that when they come out of the water it runs off them as it doth off a fowl."[6]

Le castor and its seminal castoreum gave rise to a provocative legend that signals hunters' tendency to dismember the beaver into parts incompatible with its organic survival. Both Pliny the Elder and the Greek naturalist Ælian recorded a legend, frequently repeated in bestiaries, and by Van der Donck among the colonial writers, that the beaver "understands the reason why hunters come after it with such eagerness and impetuosity, and it puts down its head and with its teeth cuts off its testicles and throws them in their path, as a prudent man who, falling into the hands of robbers, sacrifices all that he is carrying, to save his life, and forfeits his possessions by way of ransom."[7] In Ælian's economy, the beaver can give up all he has, all his wealth, and still remain viable, for there is no mention of his permanent injury or subsequent sterility leading to a decline in population. Yet the beaver is also portrayed as clever and opportunistic, for Ælian adds that when cornered, some who still have their testicles hide them inside their body (all beavers' sex organs, as well as the castoreum glands, are hidden beneath the skin) and stand up to show the hunters that their target has already been taken. Like the myth of the American sauvages being hairy, this misconception was perpetuated through repeated denials, beginning still in classical times. Louis Nicolas wrote, "Il n'est pas . . . vray de dire, et on amuse un pecheur par ces agreable menteries quand on dit que le castor se sentant pressé du chasseur, s'arrache les tezticules" [It is not . . . true to say, and one amuses a fisherman by these entertaining tall tales when one says that the beaver, feeling himself threatened by the hunter, tears out his testicles (my translation)].[8] Lahontan corrected the classical and Renaissance writers once again and began to overcome the utilitarian logic when he pointed out that "la matière que les Medecins appellent *Castoreum* ne réside point là [in the testicles], elle est renfermée dans une certaine poche que la Nature semble avoir faite exprès pour ces Animaux" (1:140) [for that which the Physicians call *Castoreum*, is not lodg'd in the Testicles, but in a certain Bag that Nature seems to have form'd on purpose for these Animals (1:107)]. Van der Donck was the most determined to debunk the myth, describing how with the help of "a discreet Indian" he dissected a female beaver and removed the cods that are the source of castoreum. Then, "for further certainty and assurance, that it was a female beaver, I removed four young from the body" (119).

These descriptions again imply that the beaver consists of independent parts including pelt, castoreum, and tail, and that colonists could take some parts and leave the animal unharmed, like milking a cow or buying an Indian's beaver pelt robe. In regard to the beaver castration myth, Charlevoix pointed out, "C'est de son Poil, dont il devroit alors se dépouiller, car au prix de sa Toison, le reste est presque compté pour rien" (99) [It is his fur he ought then to strip himself of, in comparison of which all the rest is of little value (1:157)]. As if the beaver had a choice between giving up its testicles or its skin!

Le castor, therefore, was not really represented as an animal any more than the *sauvage* was. It was a unique species set apart from the catalogs of flora and fauna compiled by Lawson, Lahontan, Charlevoix, Denys, and others. The beaver as an animal, suitable for comparison with more familiar animals, was only one axis of representation. More often the beaver was either a commodity resource or a humanlike culture. Nicolas Denys, the practical-minded colonist who devoted much of his *Histoire naturelle* to an exhaustive description of the fisheries industry, made this transition from anatomical to social in his description of the beaver: "c'est là tout ce que l'on peut dire de la peau & de la chair, qui n'est pas ce qu'il y a de plus remarquable en cet animal, mais son naturel laborieux & disciplinable, son industrie & son obeïssance dans le travail, en sorte qu'on aura peine à croire ce que j'en vais dire" (283) [That is all that can be said of the skin and the flesh. But these are not the most remarkable

things about this animal, which consist rather in its laborious and or-
derly nature, and its industry and obedience in work. These are such that
it will be difficult to believe that which I am going to tell (363)].

Thus the double reification of the beaver: it could not be presented as
an animal without being turned into a commodity, nor could its behavior be represented ethnographically without being assessed for its
labor power. I will consider the anthropomorphized beaver first, then
move on to how the image of the beaver and the actual trade for beavers
competed for the attention of the colonists of New France, and conclude
with two scenes of beaver observation that realign the relationships
between European writer, Indian trapper, and beaver.

Although the anthropomorphic portrayal of the beaver resembled
that of the Noble Savage in its ideological function—an elegy to compensate for or justify its imminent demise—it is quite different in its
content, and a similarity between the two was rarely proposed by colonial writers. Instead, the Indians were said to see themselves in the
beaver. Raudot/Silvy reported of the Indians: "Ils croient que ces animaux sont une nation; ils leur voient tant d'esprit, qu'ils ne peuvent
s'empecher de les comparer à eux" (letter 7) [They believe that these
animals are a nation. They see so much intelligence in them that they
cannot help but compare them to themselves]. LeClercq, too, remarked
that the Indians believed the beavers to be organized into nations.

The beaver's human qualities often evoked a sense of incredulity, such
as Denys's "qu'on aura peine à croire ce que j'en vais dire" [it will be
difficult to believe that which I am going to tell"]. When Dièreville, an
early-eighteenth-century visitor to Acadia, described how beavers drag
heavy logs to the water, he admitted, "Cela n'est pas facile à expliquer,
encore moins à comprendre, c'est cependant comme la chose se passe"
(131) [This is not easy to explain, & still less to understand; nevertheless, that is the way it is done (135)]. Lebeau, in comparing beavers to
dike-building Hollanders, claimed that the former also appointed Dyk-
Meysters, or inspectors of the dikes or dams, "pour voir si rien n'y
manque, & donner avis à la Societé s'il y a quelque chose à refaire. Mes
Sauvages m'ont assuré qu'ils s'assembloient pour cet effet, tenant con-
férence ensemble. . . . Je n'ai jamais été témoin de ces sortes d'Assem-
blées, je voudrois les avoir vûes moi-même pour y ajouter foi" (1:326–

27) [to see if anything is missing, and to give advice to the community if there is anything to repair. My Indians have assured me that they assemble for this reason, holding discussions together. . . . I have never been witness to these sort of Assemblies, I would like to have seen them myself to put faith in it (my translation)]. Finally, Lahontan, in a passage from the chapter in the *Mémoires* entitled "Chasse des sauvages," which Lebeau paraphrased, found such skill in the beaver's work that it could not be due to instinct:

> . . . je me hazarde de vous écrire sur ce sujet plusieurs particularitez, qui pourront peut-être vous faire douter de la sincérité de ma narration. Je commencerai par vous assurer que ces Animaux font ensemble une société de cent, qu'ils semblent se parler, & raisonner les uns avec les autres par de certains tons plaintifs non articulez. Les Sauvages disent qu'ils ont un jargon intelligible, par le moyen duquel ils se communiquent leurs sentiments & leurs pensées. Je n'ai jamais été témoin de ces sortes d'Assemblées, mais quantité de Sauvages & de Coureurs de bois, gens dignes de foi, m'ont assuré qu'il n'y avoit rien de plus vrai; ils ajoûtoient que les Castors se consultent entr'eux touchant ce qu'ils doivent faire pour entretenir leurs Cabanes, leurs Digues & leurs Lacs, et pour tout ce qui regarde la conservation de leur République. (2:156)

> [. . . I will venture to write to you many Particulars upon this Subject, which perhaps may make you doubt of the truth of my Narrative. I will begin with assuring you, that these Animals join together in a Society consisting of an Hundred, and that they seem to talk and reason with one another by certain bemoaning inarticulate Sounds. The Savages say they have an intelligible Jargon, by means whereof they communicate their Sentiments and Thoughts to one another. I was never Eye Witness of this kind of Assemblies, but many *Savages* and *Coureurs de Bois*, who are People worthy of Credit, have assur'd me, that there is nothing more true. They add, that they consult among themselves about what things they must do to maintain their Cottages, their Banks and their Lakes, and about every thing that concerns the Preservation of their Commonwealth. (2:56)]

Accounts of the humanlike qualities of the beaver, which authors thought their readers might find hard to believe or insulting to human

vanity, were often attributed to the Indians. As well as affording plausible deniability for improbable facts included in travel narratives that
advertised their veracity, this deferral enacted a new relation between
the ethnographic portrayals of the Indian and of the beaver. Whereas the
Indian serves as informant for the *mœurs des castors*, the beaver is constituted at a second remove from the European observer, and for once the
Indian assumes the powerful role of ethnographer. European is to Indian
as Indian is to beaver. Of course, the text we read is still in French
or English, and no eighteenth-century American Indian author has left
us a written description of the beaver. But in thus doubling the ethnographic gaze, the European texts both extend and undermine the authority of the ethnographic genre. The Indians apparently regard the
culture of the beaver through similar epistemological categories as the
Europeans use when they describe the Indians. And yet if the Indians'
notions of the beaver are wrong, the European's notions of the Indians
might be equally faulty.

But the colonial authors did not admit that the portrait of the beaver
was fabulated or even exaggerated. Rather, the *mœurs des castors* partakes
of the value placed on the marvelous in travel literature and on the
paradoxical formula, "strange, therefore true."[9] Deferring to the reports
of Indian informants was only sensible, as it was the Indians who hunted
the beaver and knew its ways. The description of the beaver was intended to be no less accurate than descriptions of the Indians, and when
Lahontan said that his information would test the credulity of his reader,
he intended his text to emerge victorious and strengthened from the
challenge.

The aspect of beaver life most subject to exaggeration was the scale of
the dam and lodge projects and the organization that this entails. Lebeau claimed that some dams were five hundred feet long, the product of
the work of one hundred beavers during six months.[10] According to
Denys, "Pour ce travail, ils s'assemblent jusques à deux, trois, & quatre
cens castors & plus, tant grands que petits" (285) [For this work they
assemble together as many as two, three, or four hundred Beavers, and
more, as well large as small (363–64)]. Charlevoix agreed: "ils sont
quelquefois trois ou quatre cent ensemble, formant une Bourgade, qu'on
pourroit appeller *une petite Venise*" (100, Charlevoix's italics) [there are

sometimes three or four hundred of them together in one place, forming a town which might properly enough be called a little Venice (1:159)]. An engraving in an Italian guide to America from the 1760s shows more than two dozen beavers living in a lodge that, revealed by an architectural cutaway, has three stories with five rooms on each.[11] The notion of so many animals working together betrays a strong desire among the writers, especially when one considers that in New France labor was in short supply and public works projects employing four hundred were not possible. Through the system of "seigneuries," the French colonial government granted land in a basically feudal system, but because land was plentiful in Canada and labor scarce: "les immense seigneuries ne sont pas mis en valeur. Les propriétaires hésitent à entreprendre des investissements coûteux, moulins ou chemins praticables, et les colons répugnent à l'harassant labeur du défrichement, 'très difficile à cause des gros arbres dont les forêts sont remplies' " [the large seigneuries were not improved. The proprietors hesitated to undertake costly investments, such as mills or roads, and the colonists recoiled from the hard labor of clearing land, "very difficult on account of the large trees with which the forests are filled" (my translation)].[12]

The beaver was uniquely equipped to clear land, and not only were its abilities exaggerated, but its methods were reported to resemble those of humans. Denys's account continues, "Pour mettre tous ces ouvriers en besogne, & bien faire leur travail, il leur faut un architecte & des commandans" (286) [To place all these workmen at their business, and to make them do their work well, there is need of an architect and commanders (364)]. This architect is said to be an elite specialist who travels from one project to another as his skills are needed! Bacqueville de La Potherie, in his account of a voyage to Fort Nelson in Hudson Bay, also wrote that "il y a un Castor qui commande & décide de tout" and that this architect commanded a division of labor: "Les uns taillent les arbres, d'autres font les fondations . . . & les autres prenant du limon avec leur queuë, en façon de truelle, en font le ciment des murailles" (341) [there is one beaver that takes command and decides everything. . . . Some cut down trees; others prepare the foundations . . . others, using their tail as a trowel, take mud and cement the walls with it (234)]. The praise of beaver architecture reached an apogee in Chateaubriand's *Travels in North*

America (1827). As one might expect from an ardent admirer of both American wilderness and antiquities of classical civilizations, Chateaubriand experienced a sort of revelation in the beaver: "on ne peut s'empêcher d'admirer celui qui enseigna à une pauvre petite bête l'art des architectes de Babylone" (736–37) [one cannot help admiring Him who taught a poor little animal the art of the architects of Babylon" (70–71)]. Beaver lodges became "Les palais de la Venise," complete with a portico, baths, and ten to twelve apartments on four stories, possibly influenced by Charlevoix, who also invoked Venice in the passage quoted above.

Labor power and organization are thus a key component of the fabulous accounts of the beaver, myths designed by and for the imagination of colonists. Whereas Indians living outside the colony tempted settlers to "go primitive," to abandon civilization for an unrestrained and exotic way of life, beavers, though also living in the forest, lived in a manner that French writers admired and wanted colonists to imitate. The Noble Savage was attractive for qualities suppressed by or alternative to those of the dominant classes of European society and therefore appealed to the individual who desired to escape it. The "Noble Beaver," on the other hand, represented dominant European values of work, planning, loyalty, and hierarchy. Charlevoix, addressing his correspondent, the Duchess of Lesdiguières, wrote:

> Voilà, Madame, tout ce que les Castors peuvent procurer d'avantages à cette Colonie pour son Commerce: leur industrie, leur prévoyance, le concert & la subordination, qu'on admire en eux, leur attention à se ménager des commodités, dont on n'avoit pas encore cru les Brutes capables de sentir la douceur, fournissent à l'Homme encore plus d'instructions. (100)

> [These, Madam, are all the advantages the beavers are capable of affording the commerce of this colony: their foresight, their unanimity, and that wonderful subordination we so admire in them, their attention to provide conveniences, of which we could not before imagine brutes capable of perceiving the advantages, afford mankind still more important lessons. (1:158)]

Charlevoix pointed to "Commerce" and not simply "Vie" (Life) or even "Prosperité," laying bare the raison d'être of the colony. But ironically, the beaver fur trade encouraged subversive behavior that mimicked the Indians as it destroyed the beavers, because the *coureurs de bois* had to seek out and adopt the life of the Indians in order to obtain the most high-quality pelts. Philippe Jacquin, in his excellent history of French-Indian relations in the fur trade, describes the impulse to freedom that colonists and authorities experienced in Canada: "le goût de vagabondage enracinés dans les comportements populaires, que la déchirure de l'immigration et la confrontation avec la société indigène conduisent à réactiver" (111) [the taste for wandering rooted in the populace, which the disruption of immigration and the confrontation with native society revived (my translation)].

Several scholars have suggested that European colonists expected the Indians to live as the poorest did in Europe and were shocked by ways in which their behavior instead resembled that of the European nobility.[13] The Noble Savage, particularly in Hayden White's theory of the trope, can be seen as the reaction to the failure to accommodate representations of the Indians to images of the poor and lower classes in Europe. Indian tribes wandered as poor beggars did in Europe, the colonial writers claimed, though they did not need to beg because they shared willingly among each other and with the newly arrived Europeans. Indian men hunted as only the rich were able to do in Europe, Lahontan and others observed, and like them they enjoyed a great deal of leisure when not hunting. The women tended to crops, but Europeans often overlooked this too when they denounced the Indians' refusal to settle down to a peasantlike agricultural subsistence. Europeans tried to view the Indians as serfs, for then they might be controlled as serfs were. Francis Jennings, in *The Invasion of America*, has also shown (46, 312) how the English colonists' rationale for attacking the Indians resembled that used against the Irish peasants during the same period.

In all these respects, the beaver offered a corrective to the anarchy of the colonial setting and the threatening vices of the Indians. Beavers built sturdy homes where they lived year-round and that sheltered their children from enemies and from the elements. Charlevoix scorned the Indians' dwellings, even the Iroquoian and Huron longhouses, as "construites avec moins d'art, de propreté, & de solidité, que celles des Castors" (334) [built with much less art, neatness and solidity than those of the beavers (2:127)]. In contrast to the Indians who were thought to be gluttons (a stereotype that ignored the substantial corn reserves of those tribes who lived in a climate where they could grow it), never saving food for lean times, Denys reported: "Le logement fait, ils font leur provision d'Hyver, car le castor ne mange point de poisson, il vit d'écorce de tremble qui est un bois fort leger; il abat un arbre, le couppe par tronçons de longueur pour ranger en son logis . . . aussi proprement que sont les bûches de bois flotté dans un chantier" (294–95) [The house having been built, they make their provision for the winter. For the Beaver does not eat fish. It lives on the bark of the Aspen, which is very light wood. He fells a tree, cuts it into sticks of a length to pile in his dwelling . . . They arrange it as precisely as the logs of wood are floated in a lumber-yard (367)]. According to Raudot/Silvy, Bacqueville de La Potherie, and Charlevoix, the Indians believed that the quantity of these stores was an accurate indicator of the severity of the coming winter. Though they could not practice agriculture, beavers did exploit a vegetable resource, timber, that the Canadian colonists were thought to be underexploiting. Charlevoix wrote: "Le Canada peut faire, & fait quelquefois avec les Isles de l'Amérique un Commerce assez considér-able. . . . Comme il n'y a peut-être pas au monde de Pays, qui porte de plus de sortes de Bois, ni de meilleure espèce" (91) [Canada is capable of furnishing many articles for a trade with the West-India islands . . . As there is, perhaps, no other country in the whole world, which pro-duces more sorts of wood nor of better kinds (1:145)]. Beavers were even thought to have more virtuous sexual practices than the Indians and than many colonists. In one of his verse passages Dièreville re-ported that

> Aprés qu'ils ont mis tout leur soin,
> A former ainsi leur demeure,
> Ils occupent chacun leur coin
> Sans jamais se quitter que l'un des deux ne meure.
> Ils gardent, dit-on, même au-delà du trepas
> Une fidelité si belle,
> Si le mâle perd sa femelle,
> Avec une nouvelle il ne s'accouple pas. (131)

[After they have devoted all their care
To building thus their home, each occupies
A corner, and they never separate
Until one, or the other, dies.
'Tis said that ever after they maintain
This beautiful fidelity, and if
The male should lose his mate, he does not with
Another then unite himself. (136)]

Whereas the Indian was thought to live "sans loi, ni roi" in an anarchic equality, the beavers maintained a hierarchical social order. Because industry was so valued by the beavers, there had to be some means of correcting indolence. Lahontan and others observed some beavers living not in island lodges, but in holes in the ground, and he called them "terriens":[14]

Ils les appellent des paresseux qui ont été chassez de quelques Cabanes dans lesquelles ces animaux habitent jusqu'au nombre de 80. . . . Ces Animaux faineans ne voulant pas travailler sont chassez par les autres, comme les Guespes par les Abeilles, & ils en sont maltraitez si violemment qu'ils sont obligez d'abandonner les Cabanes que la bonne race construit elle-même sur les Etangs. (1:140)

[They are likewise call'd by the Savages, the lazy or idle kind, as being expell'd by the other Beavers from the Kennels in which these Animals are lodg'd, to the number of 80 . . . the idle sort being unwilling to work, are expell'd by the others, just as Wasps are by Bees; and are so teas'd by 'em, that they are forc'd to quit the Kennels, which the better and more industrious Race huddles up to themselves in the Fens. (1:106–7)][15]

Raudot/Silvy, Denys, and Dièreville all described this punishment as the responsibility of the work chief, who from skilled architect could be thus transfigured into overseer. Denys wrote: "s'il manquent il les chastie, les bat, se jette dessus & les mord pour les mettre à leurs devoir" (288) [If they are neglectful of their duty he chastises them, beats them, throws himself on them, and bites them to keep them at their duty (365)]. Dièreville concurred, again in verse:

En traînant dans les Bois les arbres qu'ils abattent
Si quelqu'un par malice agit trop foiblement,
Les autres quittent prise, & vigoureusement
    Se jettent dessus & le battent. (133)

If one, by malice, does not work so hard
[In dragging through the Forests trees which have
Been felled, the rest let go their hold, to fall
Upon him lustily, & beat him well (137, first line my addition)]

Given the condition of laborers around 1700, this treatment does not necessarily detract from the positive image Dièreville gives of the beaver. Instead, it may represent the dream of a French nobleman who had witnessed the difficulties of ordering work in labor-poor Acadia. Dièreville continued by underlining the degraded existence of the "terriers" or "lazy beavers": "Il est de certains Castors que l'on appelle Fuïards, & qu l'on trouve par tout errans sans cabanner comme les autres, & ces Castors ne sont ainsi vagabons, que parce que ne voulant pas travailler, ils ont été battus & chassez par les sedentaires" (135) [There are certain Beavers, called vagabonds, to be found everywhere, roaming about without making huts like the others, & these Beavers only became wanderers like this, because they were unwilling to work, & had therefore, been beaten & driven out, by those who were established (138)].

Dièreville used the beaver to elaborate a vision of colonial society with all the hierarchy and social control of France. Not only were beavers not indolent like Indians, but they also maintained private property. A pond's inhabitants would use force to keep out other beavers, lending the community the characteristics of a nation-state:

Sous le toit bouzillé de sa loge aquatique,
    Chacun a son département;
    Ils forment tous séparément
    Une espece de République. (135)

[Under the roof of clay, in his
Aquatic lodge, each has his own
Department separate, though all
Join in a kind of Commonwealth (138)]

The early New England promoter William Wood described a somewhat more charitable treatment of outsiders: they are adopted as servants, "he is made a drudge so long as he lives there, to carry at the greater end of the logge" (28). If Dièreville used terms that anticipate the French Republic, Chateaubriand applied the militaristic romanticism of the Napoleonic era to the beaver. By his account, disputes between neighboring sovereignties led to strong punitive measures:

> La guerre n'est malheureusement point inconnue aux castors: il s'élève quelquefois entre eux des discordes civiles, indépendamment des contestations étrangères qu'ils ont avec les rats musqués. Les Indiens racontent que si un castor est surpris en maraude sur le territoire d'une tribu que n'est pas la sienne, il est conduit devant le chef de cette tribu, et puni correctionnellement; à la récidive, on lui coupe cette utile queue. . . . Quelquefois le différend est vidé par un duel entre les deux chefs des deux troupes, ou par un combat singulier de trois contre trois, de trente contre trente, comme le combat des Curiaces et des Horaces, ou des trente Bretons contre les trente Anglais. (739)

> [Sometimes there arises among them civil discord, independent of the foreign entanglements they have with the muskrats. The Indians say that if a beaver is surprised marauding in the territory of a tribe other than his own, he is brought before the chief of that tribe and punished for the purpose of rehabilitation; for a second offense, they cut off his useful tail. . . . Sometimes the quarrel is settled by a duel between the chiefs of the two troops, or by single combat, 3 against 3, 30 against 30, as in the combat of the Curiatii and the Horatii, or the 30 Bretons against the 30 Englishmen. (72)]

Today, beaver watchers know that the "castors terriers" are not the lazy outcasts of a workaholic society, nor the leisure class enjoying the weekend, nor a separate species as Lahontan suggested. Beavers build lodges in ponds for the safety they afford, and if predators do not threaten or if no suitable spot can be found, a beaver colony will live in a burrow on the bank. Most lodge dwellers also maintain dens on the shore, and kits more than a year old often live in these for the summer when their mother refuses to continue to accommodate them in the main lodge. The French observers probably saw some of these yearlings and called them vagabonds.

When Charlevoix wrote his semiofficial *Histoire de la Nouvelle France* (which includes his travel narrative, the *Journal d'un voyage*), he wished to identify ways to improve the colony's productivity, and he had most of the other texts I have cited as sources. Therefore, it is not surprising that he drew the most pointed lessons from the phenomenon of the lazy beaver:

> Ces prétendus Exilés sont apparemment ceux, qu'on appelle *Castors Terriers*, qui en effet vivent séparés des autres, ne travaillent point, & se logent sous Terre, . . . On les connoît au peu de Poil, qu'ils ont sur le Dos, ce qui vient sans doute de ce qu'ils se frottent continuellement contre la Terre. Avec cela, ils sont maigres; c'est le fruit de leur Paresse: on en trouve beaucoup plus dans les Pays Chauds, que dans les Pays Froids. (103–4)

> [Those pretended exiles are such as are probably called land beavers, who actually live separate from the others, never work, and live underground, . . . They are known by the small quantity of fur on their backs, proceeding, without doubt from their rubbing themselves continually against the ground. And besides, they are lean, which is the consequence of their laziness; they are found in much greater plenty in warm than in cold countries. (1:163)][16]

Charlevoix transferred from humans to beavers the popular climatic theory that inhabitants of warm or bountiful lands are less hard-working than those of cold, sterile places.[17] In beaver society even more easily than in human, these southerners could be classed as undesirables. Also, the "small quantity of fur on their backs" would make their pelts less valuable. Because of their indolent, antisocial, subterranean life, these lazy beavers reduced both the profit value of their pelts and their didactic value as a model for colonists.

In letter 4 of his *Journal d'un voyage*, the one preceding that about the beaver, Charlevoix outlined, as the title states, "Ce qui a empêché le progrès de la Colonie Françoise de Canada" [The causes which have prevented the progress of the French colony of Canada]. The description of the beaver may then be read as a prescription for improved colonial behavior. Many of the weaknesses of the colonists, some of which resemble the perceived vices of the *sauvages*, are answered by virtues of the beavers. Of the colonists, Charlevoix wrote: "Premierement on a été un tems infini sans se fixer: on défrichoit un Terrein, sans l'avoir auparavant bien examiné, on l'ensemençoit, on y élevoit des Bâtimens, puis, sans trop sçavoir pourquoi, le plus souvent on l'abandonnoit, & on alloit se placer ailleurs" (86) [In the first place, they were a very long time in fixing themselves; they cleared lands without having well examined them, they sowed them, and built houses on them, and afterwards frequently deserted them, without knowing why, and went to settle elsewhere (1:122)]. In this the colonists resemble both the Indians, whose agricultural technique involved cultivating fields for only a few years and then moving their crops elsewhere, and the "castors terriers" or land beavers who had been thrown out of the lodge. By contrast, the obedient and conformist beaver is deliberate and even democratic in the selection of sites for settlement, highly skilled in clearing the land of trees, and tireless in bringing both land and water under his control. The beavers serve as the model for the industrious and permanent settlers who were so slow to establish themselves in New France.

In his diagnosis of the social and economic ills of the colony, Charlevoix blamed the beaver trade, as many colonial officials had done for nearly a century. The institution of the system of "congés" or trading permits for furs in 1681 aimed to keep more colonists tied to the land and out of the woods, but it had the unintended effect of increasing illicit traffic to the English colonies. Lahontan identified the problem in his eighth letter, where he wrote, "Car il faut que vous sçachiez que le Canada ne subsiste que par le grand Commerce de Pelleteries, dont les trois quarts viennent des Peuples qui habitent aux environs des grands Lacs" (1:69) [for you must know, that Canada subsists only upon the Trade of Skins or Furrs, three fourths of which come from the People that live round the great Lakes (1:53)]. Charlevoix was less matter-of-fact than Lahontan; the language he used resembles the portrait of the lazy beaver. When a glut in the pelt supply drove prices down and drove

traders to the English merchants in New York, "les Vagabonds, qui
avoient pris du goût pour la liberté d'une vie errante & pour l'indépendence, resterent parmi les Sauvages, dont on ne les distinguoit plus, que
par leurs vices" (89) [the vagabonds, who had acquired a taste for a
wandering and independent life, remained amongst the savages or Indians, from whom they were no longer distinguishable but by their vices
(1:126)]. The life of these traders drew them closer to the Indians, and
Charlevoix claimed that they acquired many of the vicious traits of the
sauvages, particularly linking indolence to sexual promiscuity: "Ainsi
une partie de la Jeunesse est continuellement en course . . . d'y prendre
une habitude de libertinage, dont elle ne se défait jamais parfaitement:
elle y perd au moins le goût de travail, elle y épuise ses forces, elle y
devient incapable de la moindre contrainte" (89) [Thus one part of our
youth is continually rambling and roving about; it infects them with a
habit of libertinism, of which they never entirely get rid; at least, it gives
them a distaste for labor, it exhausts their strength, they become incapable of the least constraint (1:126–27)]. Each one of these vices is answered in the next letter by a virtue of the beaver: constancy, industry,
prodigious strength, and a firm social order. In reality, the *coureurs de bois*
worked extremely hard, and the beaver actually enjoys a great deal of
leisure once its dam is built. Charlevoix praised the beaver for its labor in
felling trees, but this is not the same as farming. John Lawson commented that the beaver could be a pest on a farm for the same reason: "If
you take them young, they become very tame and domestick, but are
very mischievous in spoiling Orchards, by breaking the Trees, and
blocking up your Doors in the Night, with the Sticks and Wood they
bring thither" (125).

Out of the beaver was fashioned a comprehensive ideology that both
encouraged behavior desired by colonial officials and warned of the
dangers of subversive behavior. Hunting beaver pelts was subversive not
only for the contact it necessitated among the *sauvages*, but also for the
great profits it could bring. Bourgeois merchants took most of this
profit, but entrepreneurial *coureurs de bois* could make huge sums as well,
which posed a threat to the dominant social order of the colony.[18] The
Indians whom the fur traders so resembled had also been corrupted by

the beaver trade, many colonial writers believed. Before contact with the
coureurs de bois (always to be distinguished from contact with missionaries), the hypostatized Noble Savages had no private property or *tien et
mien*, did not code status in wealth, were generous, did not overhunt
game, and did not find any great value in beaver pelts (did not even wear
them, says Charlevoix). Now they drive a hard bargain for the pelts and
trade them for liquor.

Many ethnographies included descriptions of methods of hunting
beavers—methods practiced by the Indians. Accounts of the Indians
often praised the primitive virtues of the "pure" culture, while denouncing vices introduced by the European traders, who often employed the
Indians to hunt beavers. The beaver was therefore doubly innocent, and
by making beaver hunting a part of the ethnography of Indian behavior
colonial writers could shift the blame for destroying this creature to
their mercenary employees and effectively conceal the fact that the destruction of idealized beaver life was their own responsibility. It is rare to
find a first-person narrative of a colonist hunting for beavers. Europeans
began to hunt in large numbers only toward the end of the eighteenth
century, when the method of using steel traps with castoreum as bait
brought European technology to the beaver hunt and ultimately threatened to make the beaver extinct.[19]

How much and in what way did the beaver trade change the lives of
Indians in the northern forests in the seventeenth century? James Axtell
believes that hunting for beavers and other fur-bearing animals disrupted the "delicate ecological balance" of the precontact era and took
up time previously spent at war or hunting for food.[20] Richard White
disagrees, contending that "The fur trade barely altered Algonquian
housing, transportation, and diet" (132). Colonial writers frequently
claimed that the fur trade had transformed Indian life, generally by the
degradation of primitive virtues, but the work behind the trade—beaver
hunting itself—was presented as an ethnological fact of Indian life in
its "natural" state. This deception seems to have put modern scholars
in conflict.

We have seen sensational facts about the beaver attributed to the
Indians, but what did northeastern Native Americans really think of the

beaver and its importance for their lives? The Iroquois cosmogony tells of a beaver (though in some versions it is a muskrat or an otter) who dives from the turtle's back to the bottom of the primordial sea to bring up the earth from which land is made. Lahontan suggested that the Indians may have domesticated beavers, and Van der Donck, too, said that it "is easily raised and will become as tame as a dog" (118). *Castorologia* cited Micmac and Algonquin legends of teeth six inches across to corroborate fossil evidence of a giant beaver, *Castoroides Ohioensis*. One of these accounts is from the Jesuit Paul Le Jeune, who reported Montagnais belief that "L'aisné des Castors, me disoient-ils, est peut-estre aussi gros que nostre Cabane" (*JR* 6:158–59) [The elder of the Beaver, they tell me, is perhaps as large as our cabin]. Then there are the accounts in which the Indians claim that the beavers live in nations, as they do.

One modern scholar of Native American responses to the fur trade, Calvin T. Martin, proposes a provocative and controversial theory of the despiritualization of Indian life amid the cataclysms of the European invasion, a process in which the beaver plays an important role. Martin argues that when fur traders urged the Indians to hunt beavers and other furbearers in numbers far greater than before and far more than their populations could sustain, the spiritual relationships between hunters and game were violated. Traditional beliefs whereby the spirit of an animal surrendered itself to a hunter who followed certain ritual preparations gave way to an all-out war between hunters and game, a war in which diseases afflicting Indian and beaver populations were weapons. Martin cites the *Narrative* of David Thompson, a Hudson Bay Company employee who traveled central and western Canada for thirty years in the late eighteenth and early nineteenth centuries. Thompson related a history told by Cree Indians near Lake Winnipeg that in the past, "the Beavers had been an ancient People, and then lived on the dry land; they were always Beavers, not Men, they were wise and powerful, and neither Man, nor any animal made war on them." Later the Great Spirit "ordered Weesaukejauk (the Flatterer) to drive them all from the dry land into the water; and they became and continued very numerous; but the Great Spirit has been, and now is, very angry with them and they are now all to be destroyed" (155). Martin's analysis suggests an ideological system linking colonizer, colonized, and exploited resource: the beaver was ennobled by those who wore it and profited from it, whereas those who were employed to kill it lost their former respect for the creature and grew to despise it. The account he cites continues by identifying the discovery of the technique of using castoreum as a bait in steel traps and indicates an awareness of the danger of destroying beaver populations:

> About two winters ago Weesaukejauk showed to our brethren, the Nepissings and Algonquins the secret of their destruction; that all of them were infatuated with the love of the Castorum of their own species, and more fond of it than we are of fire water. We are now killing the Beaver without any labor, we are now rich, but [shall] soon be poor, for when the Beaver are destroyed we have nothing to depend on to purchase what we want for our families, strangers now over run our country with their iron traps, and we, and they will soon be poor.
> (155)

If white traders were still not concerned about the devastation of beaver populations, native trappers were, and this late eighteenth-century account connects the tragic fate of beavers with that of Native Americans, much as the vanishing Indian trope would later do.

For their part, colonists were more likely to regard the Indians and the beavers as two parts of one system laid open for exploitation. Two exceptional beaver anecdotes from the mid-eighteenth century break down the ethnographic barrier that descriptions of the beaver had established against narrations of Europeans actually hunting the animal. An analysis of these scenes in Lebeau and Le Page du Pratz demonstrates how the ethnographic mode could become reflexive and the notion of Amerindians and beavers "naturally" cooperating to provide the colonists with commodities could be strained to the verge of irony.

Le Page du Pratz told of his observations of the beaver in a section of the *Histoire de la Louisiane* discussed in Chapter 3 above: the utopian excursion intended "pour faire des découvertes dont personne ne parloit; pour trouvait aussi s'il étoit possible, des choses que personne ne recherchoit" (1:213–14) [to make discoveries not mentioned by others . . . because I travelled in order to discover what no one before could inform me about (133)]. He thus created an originary space ideal for ethnography, as it was undisturbed by prior colonial invasion. Yet his desire to observe and describe the beaver leads blithely to violence and destruction. When his party first finds a beaver dam, "Nous nous cabanâmes à portée de la retraite des Castors, assez loin seulement pour qu'ils ne pussent voir notre feu: j'avertis mes gens de ne point faire de bruit ni de tirer, de peur d'effaroucher ces animaux" (1:244) [We set up our hut within reach of this retreat, or village of beavers, but at such a distance, as that they could not observe our fire. I put my people on their guard against making any sort of noise, or firing their pieces, for fear of scaring those animals (142)]. He forbids his native guides from carrying their guns as they go into a blind to observe the beavers at work. He induces an observation, however, by cutting a small trench through the dam to force the beavers to repair it, which they do in a well-organized team:

> . . . nous etions à la juste distance qu'il falloit pour n'être point apperçûs, & pour pouvoir les considérer: les uns faisoient de mortier, les autres le charioient sur leurs queues . . . sur la levée où d'autres restoient pour le prendre, le mettoient dans la rigole & l'affermissoient à grands coups de queue. (1:246–47)

> [. . . we (were) at the proper distance not to be seen, and to observe them. Some made mortar, others carried it on their tails . . . quite to the dam, where others remained to take it, put it into the gutter, and rammed it with blows of their tails. (143)]

His first experiment a success, Le Page du Pratz continues, "J'avois eu envie d'en tuer un, mais j'attendis au lendemain, parce que je leur préparois bien plus d'ouvrage que celui de la nuit & qui satisferoit plus parfaitement ma curiosité" (1:247) [I wanted to kill one, but waited until the next day, because I was planning something more than was the work of one night, and which would better satisfy my curiosity (my translation)]. He makes a larger breach in the dam to drive the beavers out of the lodge, whereupon "nous quittâmes la brêche, & allâmes nous cacher tous autour de l'Etang pour en tuer un seulement, afin de l'examiner de près" (1:248) [we went to conceal ourselves all round the pond, in order to kill only one, the more narrowly to examine it (144)]. He takes care, however, not to kill "l'Inspecteur des travaux" (1:249) [the overseer of the works] but instead a common laborer. With no apparent awareness of perverting his good intentions, Le Page du Pratz allows his urge for encyclopedic observation to lead him from a blind that kept the animals unaware of any human presence to killing one of the species and finally to breaking apart the lodge. As he puts it, somewhat paradoxically, "Je fis défaire le toit sans rien casser" (1:251) [I caused to undo the roof without breaking any thing (145)]. The episode demonstrates how ethnographic observation of beavers or Indians insists rhetorically on its innocence and nonintervention and yet entails the destruction of indigenous communities. Whereas elsewhere in his book Le Page du Pratz speculates on the best means for maintaining French control of Louisiana, and in one episode ruthlessly puts down a slave rebellion, in the encounter with the beavers he dons the cap of disinterested scientific inquiry that Mary Louise Pratt has termed the "anti-conquest," "a utopian image of a European bourgeois subject simultaneously innocent and imperial, asserting a harmless hegemonic vision that installs no apparatus of domination."[21]

The second episode is from the novel *Avantures de Sieur C. Lebeau, . . ., où voyage curieux et nouveau*. Claude Lebeau weaves impersonal observations of the beaver, which are mostly copied from Lahontan, into a narrative tale of observing firsthand its life and violent death. His sentimental scene reinforces the ideological portrayal of the animal as it shifts the blame for the extermination of beavers from the entrepreneurial French to the laboring Indians.

At the opening of the chapter, both narrative and travel are interrupted by a beaver dam. The river had been carrying Lebeau and his Huron guides very quickly, "desorte que nous eussions pu faire facilement quarante lieues dans un seul jour, si nous ne nous fussions souvent arrêtés par des Digues de Castors, que nous rencontrions de tems en tems" (1:315) [so that we could easily have made forty leagues in a single day, if we had not been halted by some beaver dams, that we encountered from time to time (this and following quotations from Lebeau are my translations)]. They float on in silence (for the dams apparently have not completely stopped the current), looking out for beavers. One of his guides,

Nicolas, shoots at one and injures it, but he cannot recover it, and the shot serves as a warning for many others to take cover underwater. The men disembark to lie in wait for their prey to resurface. Lebeau, intrigued by his literary preconceptions, goes into the woods, "dans l'esperance d'y voir peut-être travailler quelques Castors. . . . j'avançai doucement ventre à terre, pour voir sans être vû ces beaux Architectes nés, dont j'avois entendu dire tant de merveilles" (1:319) [in the hope of perhaps seeing some beavers working there. . . . I advanced slowly on my belly to see these gorgeous natural-born architects, of which I had heard so many marvels]. With such stealth, Lebeau the adventurer places himself in the discursive position of the ethnographer, who sees without being seen. He even suggests that to actually witness the beavers thus is exceptional, whereas secondhand accounts from informants are the norm:

> Car au moindre cri que font ces Sentinelles à l'approche des Hommes & des Bêtes, tous ces Travailleurs se jettent à l'eau & se sauvent en plongeant jusqu'au leurs Cabanes. J'avance ce fait pour l'avoir vû, ayant eu beaucoup de peine à le croire moi-même sur le raport que l'on m'en avoit déja fait, & si j'ai été, pendant un bon quart d'heure, assez proche d'eux sans être aperçu, il faut avouer que c'est un bonheur pour moi, ou un pur effet du hazard. (1:322)

> [Because at the least cry that the sentinels make at the approach of men or beasts, all the workers throw themselves into the water and seek safety by diving down to their lodges. I state this from having seen it, having hardly believed it myself on the reports that had already been made to me, and if I was, for a good fifteen minutes, close enough to them without being seen, I must admit that it was luck or a pure matter of chance.]

Again five pages later, when Lebeau believes that he hears the beavers talking, the scene of encounter confirms the fantastic preconception only by overcoming a strategic incredulity in the travel writer.

While author Lebeau digresses into the *mœurs des castors*, in part borrowed from Lahontan, character Lebeau lies on the ground observing, unaware that he is in turn being watched by his Huron guides. They too advance "ventre à terre" and are considerate of the writer's needs for a

while: "Ces Sauvages voyant que j'étois si attentif à regarder ces Animaux voulurent bien, pendant quelque-tems, me laisser jouir de ce
plaisir" (1:331) [The Indians, seeing that I was so taken with watching
the animals, wanted to leave me to enjoy this pleasure for a while], but
they eventually become impatient and fire at the beavers over Lebeau's
prone body. The relationship outlined above, where European described
Indian as Indian described beaver, is here reversed. Lebeau cuts in front
of the Indian informant to observe the beavers firsthand, and this puts
him in the line of fire of the Indians who are out to kill the beavers.
Caught in the cross fire, Lebeau casts himself as an innocent observer not
implicated in the fur trade and sentimentally deplores his guides for
crimes against beaverdom. In this scene motives of observation and
exploitation are set in conflict, whereas the typical representation of the
beaver put observation in the service of exploitation (either mercantile
or literary), describing the parts of the beaver according to their value
and use for Europeans, or relying on Indian hunters' reports of the
beavers' language, food storage, or democratic assemblies. His guides,
frustrated by an unsuccessful hunt, set about destroying a beaver lodge
with their hatchets:

> Si d'un côté j'étois ravis de cette expedition qui satisfaisoit la curiosité
> que j'avois de voir le dedans de ces maisonettes, d'un autre je fus
> extrèmement chagrin de voir la cruauté de mes sauvages, qui ayant
> trouvé trois petits Castors, pas plus gros que le poing dans un de ces
> Gîtes, froissèrent rudement le corps de deux de ces Petits contre la
> muraille de leur propre nid. (1:335)

> [If on the one hand I was delighted with this episode that satisfied the
> curiosity that I had to see the inside of these little cabins, on the other
> hand I was extremely mortified to see the cruelty of my Indians, who
> having found three little beavers, no larger than your fist, rudely
> crushed the bodies of two of these little ones against the wall of their
> own nest.]

Here we have a scene enacting the postmodern ethnographer's remorse at
the violence his penetrating gaze entails for its object. In this case, however, the perpetrator is the ethnographic object of the early seventeenth-

century colonists and many of the *Jesuit Relations*, the Hurons, and the victim is the second-degree object, the beaver. Lebeau therefore excuses himself from any of the ill conscience that anthropologists at least since Michel Leiris have often felt.

Lebeau's story erodes the separation between colonist, Indian, and beaver, just as his entire work, an action-packed tall tale that is nevertheless more geographically and ethnologically accurate than contemporary romances in American settings by the Abbé de Prévost and Alain-René Lesage, erodes the separation between travel narrative and novel. The scene with the beavers is one of ethnographic observation, not of hunting. A great fictional narrative of psychological reflection and spiritual pursuit of the beaver, the novel that would place the beaver in the same class as the whale and the bear, was not possible because the beaver was an ally, not a foe of colonization, and of course it never posed a threat to hunters' lives or limbs. The beaver continued to be one of Canada's most valuable resources into the nineteenth century, but as the bulk of the fur trade shifted into English hands and north to the inhospitable shores of Hudson Bay, the significance of the beaver for the ideology of settlement lessened.

The legends of the beaver survived, however. In the nineteenth century at least two books about the beaver were published that continued the range of discourses, from natural history to mythology and anthropology, that we have seen in the literature of New France. By emphasizing folklore, these books in a certain sense returned to Foucault's Renaissance episteme of natural history. One was Horace T. Martin's *Castorologia*, quoted above, and the other was by Lewis Henry Morgan, famous for his studies of the Iroquois and credited by some with founding modern anthropology, who published *The American Beaver and His Works* in 1868. An amateur scientist who made a fortune as a lawyer for railroad interests, Morgan wrote of observing the beaver during business trips to Michigan's Upper Peninsula. He explained the vagabonds or lazy beavers as those who have failed to find mates and are punished as "slave beavers" (135). By this time the fur trapper was as marginal a figure in the United States as the Indian, and his peculiar behavior and mythology was included in Morgan's work. The motive for Morgan's interest in the beaver can be found in his chapter on "Animal Psychology," where the beaver's profound intelligence is not a myth or a marvel, for "The popular mind has always been in advance of the metaphysicians with reference to the mental endowments of animals" (248). Morgan was an early animal rights activist who preferred to call animals "mutes." He believed that they were endowed with reason and the possibility of cultural evolution, such as the beaver's development of canals and perfection of the design of lodges. Bacqueville de La Potherie anticipated Morgan when he wrote "je ne sçai ce qu'en penseroient les Cartesiens s'ils avoient vû l'adresse avec laquelle il bâtit sa maison, elle est si admirable que l'on reconnoît en lui l'autorité d'un maître absolu, le veritable caractere d'un Pere de famille, & le genie d'un habile Architecte" [I do not know what the Cartesians would have thought of it if they had seen the skill with which it constructs its lodge, which is so wonderful that you recognize in it the authority of an absolute master, the true character of a paterfamilias, and the genius of a clever architect].[22] The stage theories that had come to dominate anthropological thought in the nineteenth century were in Morgan's work also applied to the beaver. Moreover, Morgan provided a new justification for representing the beaver more as a culture than as an animal, and for studying these representations within a history of ethnography as well as of natural history. The growth of colonial New France came at the expense of Native American cultures, and one of these cultures was that of the beaver, a kind, furry creature that, ironically, was believed to mimic the values of the colonists who sought to destroy it.

CHAPTER 6

War, Captivity, Adoption, and Torture

Europeans and Indians learned much from one another about war. From the Indians, colonists learned stealth, guerrilla techniques, and woodcraft. Indians learned from the Europeans about iron, guns, and powder, as well as about European-style military discipline and political manipulation. Yet the lessons colonists learned from the Indians go beyond such material or practical things. By studying the representations of Native American customs of warfare, and of the treatment of prisoners of war, we can see that some practices branded as "savage" actually originated with or resembled those of the colonists, and that other aspects of Indian war had a subversive attraction for the colonists, who often imitated them. This appeal was sometimes connected to the Europeans' past, such as the resemblance of Indian warriors' customs to codes of chivalric honor. At other points it resonates more with the future of American culture, as in an ethic of personal vengeance that encourages vigilantism or the potential for individual refashioning through adoption into an Indian family. The mimicry of Indian warfare had a potentially powerful impact, because, regrettably, warfare involved more colonists with Indians than did religion or intermarriage or possibly even trade.

War In/Outside History

To study Indian war, we must draw on both the ethnographic descriptions of it as carried on among Indians and the historical narratives of battles involving colonists. As we have seen, more French writers contributed to the former genre, whereas the English accounts are mostly from the latter. This disjunction adds to the problem, common in many areas of ethnohistory but especially acute with regard to war, of distinguishing "authentic" precontact customs from the effects of the European invasion. Although many French traders and officers fought alongside Indians in wars between tribes, we still must be particularly cautious about accepting any representations of the customs of war among the Native Americans. Along with trade, with which it was often linked, warfare was, of all the spheres of life in the catalog of the *mœurs des sauvages*, most immediately and irreversibly altered after contact. The introduction of guns, the wealth of the fur trade, and the decimation of the native population by disease could each alone have wrought enormous changes in the customs of war without even considering the shifting alliances and threats of the invasion. As one Québecois historian has written, "Les Européens prirent une part active au commerce indigène et participèrent à leurs combats, leur seule présence étant bien souvent la source de nouveaux conflits entre les populations autochtones" [The Europeans took an active part in native trade and participated in their combats, their very presence often being the source of new conflicts among the indigenous populations (my translation)].[1] Rather than the confrontation of two forms of war, European and Other, we must think instead in terms of the creation of a "savage" alternative to the techniques practiced in Europe, an alternative born of the European imagination, even if ingredients of it were indigenous to the New World.

John Smith and Samuel de Champlain were exceptional among colonial explorers in portraying themselves as locked with the Powhatans and with the Mohawk in a large-scale European-style war, and in describing Indian war as possessing some degree of logistical planning and subordination. "In Europe, soldiers fought opponents who were willing to accept battle under mutually advantageous situations and to forego actions in bad weather, darkness, or forested terrain" (32), writes Patrick Malone in a study of war in early New England; likewise, Champlain's allies and their Mohawk foes camped in close proximity the night before their battle and did not begin fighting until morning. Though there is some controversy among ethnohistorians on this matter, the two 1609 battles reviewed in the chapter on Smith and Champlain may well describe a precontact style of warfare that, ironically, resembled European strategies more closely than did the style that Europeans subsequently caused the Indians to adopt. This is the view of James Axtell. Olive Patricia Dickason agrees: "The guerilla type of warfare waged by the Iroquois, based on surprise and speed of movement, had become their preferred technique *after* they encountered firearms."[2] Similarly, Jacques Le Moyne de Morgues, who as a member of the Jean Ribaut/René Goulainé de Laudonnière expedition was among the first Europeans to encounter Amerindian nations in Florida, depicted in his paintings (in deBry's *Florida*, these are engravings 13 and 14) large armies of warriors massed around chiefs Outina and Saturiba. Thus the typically "savage" manner of warfare employing surprise and stealth tactics may in fact have been a response to the invasion of "civilized" warriors.

Yet Thomas Hariot, who at the Roanoke colony was among the first Europeans to contact the natives of that area in today's North Carolina, wrote that "Their maner of warres amongst themselves is either by sudden surprising one an other most commonly about the dawning of the day, or moone light, or els by ambushes, or some suttle [subtle] devises: Set battels are very rare" (37). Rare, he says, but we might assume that set battles on an open field were known, and it appears that both styles were practiced in aboriginal eastern America. Some other early witnesses describe both styles. Roger Williams wrote: "Their Warres are farre lesse bloudy, and devouring then the cruell Warres of Europe; and seldome twenty slaine in a pitcht field: partly because when they fight in a wood every Tree is a Bucklar. When they fight in a plaine, they fight with leaping and dancing, that seldome an Arrow hits" (180–81). Some writers who describe guerrilla tactics nevertheless also describe or include illustrations of palisades such as the Pequots built at

Mystic and the Oneida defended against Champlain's attack in 1615. Many nations may have had ongoing enmities that were acted out periodically in semiceremonial, mass field battles, where fighting was mostly hand-to-hand and casualties were few. When a more deadly strike was intended and surprise was possible, they would use guerrilla tactics. Champlain and perhaps Laudonnière were among the few explorer-ethnographers to participate in the former style of battle in North America. With so many tribes in so large a region and so few early eyewitness sources, it is difficult to construct an accurate image of indigenous warfare.[3]

In the ethnographic accounts, many writers contended that Indian war was not true war at all. The negation trope used in many of these representations denied to the Indians the very things wars in Europe were fought over: sovereign territory defined by borders, leaders with political careers to advance, ethnic divisions, standing armies, or revolutions. In romantic primitivist accounts, war was virtually unknown to the Indians. Crèvecœur's Frontier Man flees the dangers of the Revolutionary War and seeks refuge in an Iroquoian village because "They know nothing of the nature of our disputes; they have no ideas of such revolutions as this; a civil division of a village or tribe are events which have never been recorded in their traditions" (217). This utopian attitude was rare in the seventeenth century. More often, war did not disappear among the Indians, but was emptied of its ideological justifications and reduced to an essential hate and enmity. John Lawson wrote, "The Indians ground their Wars on Enmity, not on Interest as the Europeans generally do" (208). William Strachey concurred: "they seldome make warrs for landes or goodes, but for women and Children, and principally for revendge, so vindicative and jelous they be, to be made a dirision of, and to be insulted upon by an enemy" (104). By attributing to the wars of "savages" the base motives of vengeance and bloodthirst, colonists could support the ideology that European wars were fought for more rational, political reasons. Raudot/Silvy also denied any territorial motive in American Indian warfare: "Comme les sauvages ne veulent point envahir les terres n'y les bois de leurs ennemis, on ne peut douter que ce n'est que l'animosité, la haine, la vengeance et l'envie désordonné de tuër

des hommes ou de s'agrandir par les esclaves qui leur fait faire la guerre"
(letter 32) [As the Indians do not wish to encroach on either the lands or
the forests of their enemies, one cannot doubt that it is only animosity,
hate, vengeance, and the desire to kill men or increase their possessions
or slaves captured during war that makes them wage war]. Pierre
Boucher expressed a similar opinion: "La guerre qu'ils se font les uns aux
autres, ne se fait point pour conquerir des terres, ny pour devenir plus
grands Seigneurs, ny mesme pour l'interest, mais par pure vangeance"
(117) [The wars they wage against each other are not for conquests of
territory, nor for personal aggrandizement, nor yet for the furthering of
their interests in any other way, but merely for revenge (62)]. Occasionally this image of raw aggression was corrected. For instance, Lahontan
took exception to the notion that vengeance, not territorial disputes,
inspired Indian wars. He argued, "Les Sauvages se font la guerre au sujet
de la Chasse ou du passage sur leurs terres, parce que les limites sont
réglées. Chaque nation connoit les bornes de son Païs" (2:175) [The
Wars of the Savages are grounded upon the Right of Hunting, or of a
Passage upon such and such Grounds; for their Limits are adjusted, and
every Nation is perfectly well acquainted with the Boundaries of their
own Country (2:72)]. Or as Roger Williams had noted sixty years earlier
of the Indians of New England, "Nations are very punctuall in the
bounds of their Lands" (95).

We must see, therefore, contradictory descriptions of "savage" warfare as constitutive of its very possibility. They do not reveal the prejudice or ignorance of some writers and the careful observation of others,
nor a bifurcation into idealized Noble and devilish Ignoble Savage constructs, but are in fact essential to the representation of the *sauvages
américains*, which, as we have seen, worked to contain logically contradictory elements. Nowhere is this more true than in war, which in any
culture exposes the contradictions of human nature. The paradoxes of
war cluster also around the poles of substitution and negation, of the
mythical past of Western culture and the radical Other that threatens to
change it. War was sometimes seen as restrained by ideals of chivalry
and honor, ideals better realized in America than in Europe, and at other
times as a more vicious and rationalized process of killing than even

Europe had created. Captivity was represented as an allegorical struggle of good against evil, or as an opportunity for martyrdom, or as a secure exile in a welcoming community. European observers ignored these contradictions because each of the imperatives fed important ideological needs. They portrayed a society that was at once heroic and rational, chivalric and modern, diabolical and sentimental. As John Bartram wrote of the Iroquois, "They are a subtile, prudent and judicious people in their councils, indefatigable, crafty, and revengeful in their wars" (77). Bartram's comment echoes one in Colden, which he in turn quoted from Bacqueville de La Potherie: "When one talks of the Five Nations in France, they are thought, by a common Mistake, to be meer Barbarians, always thirsting after Human Blood; but their true Character is very different: They are the fiercest and most Formidable People in North America, and at the same time as Politick and Judicious as well can be conceiv'd" (xxi).

Representations of Indian War were not, of course, purely ideological and cannot be interpreted solely by reference to European history and self-images. The real differences between hunter-gatherer tribes of the north, generally Algonquian peoples, and the agricultural tribes south of the St. Lawrence and Great Lakes, especially the Iroquois, were very important. This regional and cultural dissimilarity may explain why Ribaut and Laudonnière report large armies of native warriors, which would scarcely have been possible in the more decentralized native communities of northern New England and Quebec. Agricultural nations had larger villages and greater political organization and subordination, were known for the torture to which they subjected prisoners, and for these reasons were usually more feared in war. The Iroquois were widely recognized as the most formidable fighting force in the Northeast, and not only by their enemies, the French.

Searching for the original customs of native warfare is bound to be inconclusive—more significant is the way in which colonists altered warfare to fit their purposes, both geopolitical and ideological. Wars fought with and against Indians in the frontier regions of northeastern America in the 1680s through 1760s were often driven by events in Europe. Unfortunately, colonial history as it is generally taught obscures these links—even the names of wars conceal them. What U.S. school-children are taught to call the French and Indian War is known in French (and in Anglophone Canada) as "La guerre de sept ans" or the Seven Years' War. This name makes clear that it was part of the struggle in Europe known by the same name, in which England and Prussia defeated France, Austria and Russia, Sweden and Saxony.[4] Without its victory in Europe, England would not have been able to force a settlement that awarded it all of France's North American colonies save the tiny islands of St. Pierre and Miquelon. The name French and Indian War implies that all the Indians involved were on the enemy side, which is false. French and Canadian historians are not immune to this practice either. The conflict beginning with Champlain's victory in 1609 and continuing throughout the seventeenth century is called the Iroquois Wars, although the enemy of France was the English more than the Iroquois.[5]

Following the ascension of William of Orange to the British throne, and continuing on and off for nearly a century, wars in New England and the Great Lakes region implicated the Iroquois and other native peoples in a colonial proxy conflict, the true causes and goals of which were often hidden from its mercenary soldiers and victims. Colden's *History of the Five Indian Nations* is a partial corrective to this: it brings Indian and colonial wars into the same historical narrative, though it represents Indian warriors and chiefs as antiquated, alternately barbaric and classical. Like the English translator of Le Page du Pratz, Colden declared that his work was intended to further English interests by educating readers about the importance of the colonies, the fur trade, and the Iroquois. In "The Preface to the Second Part," published in 1747, Colden told how, since the first part appeared twenty years earlier, "I have been informed, that a Publication, with a Continuance of that Work, would be acceptable there [in England]. I have the more chearfully complied with this Notice, because of the War threatened from France, believing that a Publication of this Kind may be useful, whether the present Inquietudes between the two nations end in a War or in a Treaty" (78). Colden's history facilitated, though it did not advocate, a cynical, instrumental use of the Iroquoian alliance in future English/French colonial wars. The

Iroquoian negotiators' speeches that fill much of the book frequently evoke the frustration of warriors who loyally followed instructions from Albany to attack the vital flow of pelts from the upper Great Lakes to Montreal but did not receive adequate support from their allies (none at all from the provinces other than New York) and were unable to negotiate on their own behalf. The governor of New France, Frontenac, had supposedly refused to conclude a peace with the Iroquois because "this can only be done by my Master, who lives over the great Water" (155), and the English commander, Colonel Foster, had told the Iroquois they must continue the war without any expectation of English military assistance. Colden commiserates: "Here we see these Barbarians, these Savages, as we call them, acting with the greatest regard to the Treaties they had entered into with their Allies, and that at a Time when the Exigences of their own Affairs, and when the faint feeble Assistance, which their Allies had contributed in the common Cause, would, among Christian Potentates, have been thought sufficient Excuse for their taking Care of themselves separately, in breach of the most solemn Confederacy they could enter into" (159). By substitution, Colden applies the political values of Europe to the Iroquois and shows how as allies they are being exploited.

Colden's book documents the Iroquoian role in advancing English colonial interests, but by foregrounding the eloquence of the speeches he reprints, Colden sometimes draws the modern reader's attention away from the historical importance of the occasions on which the speeches were delivered. Chapter 10 of the second part opens: "As by this time the Reader may be tired with the horrid Scenes of a barbarous War, it may be some Relief to observe the Indian Genius in the Arts of negotiating; and see how a barbarous People, without any of the Arts and Sciences in which we value our selves, manage their Interest with the most learned, most polite, and artificial Nation in Europe" (135). Rhetoric or negotiation is represented here as relief from, rather than an essential part of, the history of a war. Decanesora, the chief negotiator of the Five Nations, "resembled much the Bustos of Cicero" (140), a comment that contributes to the "denial of coevalness" implicit in the *premiers temps* trope.[6] Such portrayals were common because Indian wars were perceived to lie outside the course and concerns of Western history. A French colonial traveler who fought alongside Hurons or Montagnais learned about and participated in matters of ethnographic but not world-historical importance. This is part of the ideology that divides history (of the West) from ethnography (of the "rest"). The colonist fighting in Indian wars descends the sociotemporal slope toward primitive barbarism. Thus the Amerindians, and most of all the Iroquois, whose territory lay in such a strategic position, were condemned to be behind or beneath history, its victims but rarely its agents.

Colden is important because he is perhaps the only English colonial author before 1763 who represented any aspect of war from the Amerindians' point of view. A detailed account of the natives' practice of war written by an English participant observer as part of an ethnography is not available before the Seven Years' War, so I will rely mostly on French authors for the accounts of preparation for war, torture, and adoption that follow. Because the French and English sources come from opposing sides of wars and represent different forms of writing about them, disentangling the rhetorics of history, personal narrative, and ethnography is particularly difficult. Several of the narratives that have been central to this study, those of Champlain, Radisson, Perrot, and Lahontan, are among the most important sources for historians of the wars of the seventeenth century. But a reader unfamiliar with the dates and sites of the key battles in which these men participated, or the names of their commanders, could easily fail to recognize this and thus read these narratives solely for their ethnographic or autobiographical interest. For the French, unlike the English, firsthand experience and observation of Indian warfare predominate in the literature over the concerns of one's colony. Radisson, a native of France, defected several times from the French colony to the English and back; his knowledge of the Canadian land and native peoples made him extremely valuable as a mercenary in the Iroquois Wars and the battle for Hudson Bay. Lahontan, we have seen, went AWOL from the French colonial army. Even Champlain tended to be modest about how his participation in Indian wars helped secure furs for the French colonists and traders. The bargain of help at war in exchange for food or furs, which we saw Champlain initiating, continued well into the eighteenth century. Frenchmen were not afraid to submerge themselves in native communities, be it as soldier, trader, or missionary, and their ethnographic and historical accounts sometimes represented wars from the native point of view. Oddly, these efforts could be too successful; the writer's ties to the colony and its interests became obscured through ethnographic self-effacement, and the wars were represented as affairs of the *sauvages* alone. This tendency is found in Perrot and in the accounts of Perrot's activities by Bacqueville de La Potherie, as well as in the contention by many French writers that the demise of their allies, the Hurons, was due exclusively to the attacks of the Iroquois, not to diseases communicated by the Jesuit missionaries.

On the English side, the several histories of King Philip's War all present the fate of the English colonies as the primary concern and contain little or no description of Indians' motives and techniques in the war. These myopic accounts rarely included battles that took place outside New England and did not describe Indian warfare as distinct from war pitting colonists against Indians. Puritan colonists were reluctant to fight alongside Indian allies or adopt their techniques, because it symbolized a cultural surrender even if it might assist in an ultimate military victory. As mentioned in Chapter 1, Richard Slotkin's discussion of the many texts arising out of King Philip's War demonstrates how the Puritan colonists figured war with the Indians as a metaphor for conflicts within their own society: "The literary subject that best suited the demand of Puritan society for a vision of its unique experience, and the requirements of society's leaders for an appropriate vehicle of propaganda and doctrine, was the Indian wars" (67). Even Benjamin Church, who among all the Puritan writers and Indian fighters shows the best knowledge of native techniques, described these techniques within his violent heroic narrative; he did not discuss them ethnographically. Anglo-Americans finally internalized the virtues of "savage" warfare only with Daniel Boone and in Thomas Hutchins's primer on Indian warfare in *Historical Account of Bouquet's Expedition against the Ohio Indians in 1764*. The figure of the frontiersman, which Boone epitomizes, turns skills learned from the Indians against them in White-Red struggles. As Slotkin writes, "American writers prided themselves that their people could fight like Indians, as well as like redcoats—that they combined the best of a dual heritage."[7] Indeed, the American colonist claimed to have it both ways, to be "civilized" when facing the Indians yet possess "savage" virtues by contrast with Europeans. This is true also for the French who immersed themselves in native warfare, describing its causes and techniques in ethnographic detail, sometimes at the expense of a circumspect historical perspective on the conflicts.

The POW as Ethnographer

It is the Indian captivity narrative, an Anglo-American genre, that provides the basis for a contrast between the French and English colonies' attitudes toward Native American warfare, as well as a means of corroborating accounts of the Amerindian practice of adopting prisoners of war. In the article referred to in Chapter 3 for its illustration of the consistent taxonomy of ethnography from the sixteenth to the twentieth century ("Fieldwork in Common Places"), Mary Louise Pratt also notes that modern anthropology's ideal image of fieldwork bears certain similarities to (in fact, might be seen as a parody of) the position of the captive: "The experience of captivity resonates a lot with aspects of the experience of fieldwork—the sense of dependency, lack of control, the vulnerability to being either isolated completely or never left alone" (38). Captives were forced into an often brief but total assimilation of native ways and, unlike missionaries but like anthropologists, had no motive for changing their captors' ways, aside from securing their own deliverance. The foundational captivity narrative, Mary Rowlandson's, has become one of the most studied, most written about texts in early American literature. One of the reasons for its popularity is the ethnography included in it: "For the past three decades it has been, in excerpts, a staple of the classroom anthologies, in which interpretive headnotes customarily emphasized its importance in depicting Puritan trials and doctrinal orthodoxy on the colonial frontier. Yet in the 1990s Rowlandson's text is being reread as an ethnographic juxtaposing of two cultures, colonial whites and the indigenous Americans."[8] Such enthusiasm for Rowlandson is misplaced, because the ethnographic material in her narrative, notably the preparations for the Sudbury fight described in the "nineteenth remove," amount to a few tidbits compared with hundreds of pages of detailed accounts in the *Jesuit Relations*, in Lahontan, and in Lescarbot, to name only a few French texts.

Yet considered in the light of postmodern revisionist anthropology, the English captive has certain advantages over the French explorer-ethnographer. Ironically, his or her rigid ethnocentrism provides a valuable perspective on Amerindian practices, particularly those of adoption. Parts of ethnographies were often copied from earlier texts, and the absence of taxonomic ethnography from the captivity narratives (chapter 7, "Of Their Feasting, etc.," in John Gyles's is the only instance of this style in a captivity narrative from before the Seven Years' War), is compensated by an interested, embodied, eyewitness narrative voice of just the sort that is suppressed in ethnography. The New England captives' refusal to assimilate also responds to the problem of trying to distinguish original native techniques and customs of warfare from the changes caused by European invaders. In Rowlandson's or Quentin Stockwell's or even Radisson's highly specific accounts, it is apparent that the Indians were forced into desperate and improvised actions, that in the horrors of war, the traditional, "authentic," or even consistent custom was ephemeral. Therefore, it makes sense to discuss the captivity narratives, some of the best-known texts in colonial American literature, alongside French accounts of Native American warfare. By this approach, one can compare detached, synthetic descriptions of torture, adoption, and the preparation for war among Iroquoian and Algonquian peoples with captives' personal accounts of the same activities.

Chapter 1 examined possible reasons why there is no genre of captivity narratives in New France. Additional explanation can be gleaned from a comparison with the French colonists' representations of the Iroquois Wars. Because most Puritan captivities were consequences of King Philip's and Queen Anne's Wars, in their day the captivity narratives were read as news or intelligence reports from behind enemy lines; the personal narratives were also historical. This pattern continued in Ethan Allen's narrative, or, fictionally, in Melville's novel *Israel Potter*, where one sees the captivity narrative genre adapted to the purpose of propaganda in the Revolutionary War, as these captives are prisoners of the British, not the Indians. On the other side, French prisoners held in Boston were no doubt debriefed after they were ransomed or escaped, but their reports were rarely published. French reports of the colonial wars were more often written by soldiers like Lahontan who fought alongside Indians and lived with them voluntarily.

The English writers, as the contrast between Champlain and Smith suggested, are more ego- and ethnocentric than the French. For Puritan New Englanders, the state of war meant "us against the world." Although northern frontier settlements like Deerfield and Salmon Falls were almost indefensible, a siege mentality dominated; much of Rowlandson's challenge was to protect the habits and manners of her world from the assault of the Other. The enemy, be it a conspiracy of several Indian nations, of Indians and the devil, or of Indians, Frenchmen, and the devil, was not portrayed with cultural specificity—all was wilderness. The Puritan captive not only represented the entire sacred community in its figural captivity in the wilderness, he or she transported the objects and activities of the home into that wilderness. Just as Robinson Crusoe transformed his island into an English fiefdom with its castle, enclosed fields, and loyal serf Friday, Rowlandson carried on her domestic labor of sewing clothing in her new surroundings. The attitude of the French Jesuit was radically different. He had journeyed far into the wilderness to live in a heathen village, isolated from the colony, the French language, and often even his Jesuit brethren. The privations of the new environment were part of the holy suffering of his mission. If his reception turned from hospitable to hostile, the objective of captivity was not resistance and redemption, but martyrdom.

The only alternatives to Catholic martyrdom and Puritan redemption, both so deadly serious, are found in the captivities of Louis Hennepin and John Marrant, who verge on a parody of the genre, and of Elizabeth Hanson, whose Quaker tolerance breaks through the racist resistance of the Puritan captivities. Hennepin mocked the gravity of the Jesuit martyrs Isaac Jogues and Jean de Brébeuf. He escaped torture, but at one point in his 1683 book Hennepin remarked sarcastically that if a European monk suffered the trials and deprivations of starvation and weather that he had, that monk would be canonized (as Brébeuf was). Marrant's ordeal in the wilderness was precipitated by an encounter with the Reverend George Whitefield and followed the affective patterns of the Great Awakening. The young black musician experienced a conversion after he ran into the woods and became lost and hungry. He met an Indian who did not capture him but rather offered to take him back to his home in Charleston, South Carolina. Marrant refused and instead went to the Indian's community, where he learned the language and assimilated easily. When after many weeks a chief condemned him to death, Marrant converted his executioner to the Christian faith in a scene that resembles both the Smith and Pocahontas legend and the Old Testament story of Daniel in the Lion's Den.

Within Puritan literature, the demonization and misrepresentation of the Indians are symptoms of the rhetoric of election and biblical typology. When the Puritan historian Edward Johnson wrote apocalyptically, "Of the time of the fall of Antichrist, and the increase of the Gentile Churches, even to the provoking of the twelve Tribes to submit to the kingdom of Christ" (268), it is not clear if "the twelve Tribes" refer to the American Indians, biblical peoples, or both. Johnson goes on, "And further, behold, Kings, Rulers, or Generals of Earths Armies, doth Christ make use of in this day of battell . . . to defend, uphold and maintain the whole body of his Armies against the insolent, beastly, and bloody cruelty of their insatiable enemies" (270). The armies in this passage are figural, and their enemies may also be the Antichrist's forces and not any terrestrial army, but the same typological rhetoric in narratives of real wars and captivities creates an ambiguity about whether the diabolical enemy is the Indian, the papist Frenchman, or an abstract force of evil.

For the French, the enemy was real enough; the Iroquois were the object of frequent anxiety and terror. The isolated, discontinuous network of posts and settlements on the St. Lawrence was vulnerable to attack from the south. Lafitau recognized the reasons for Iroquoian power and wrote that this tribe "seul cause de la jalousie aux Nations les plus reculées, depuis l'embôuchure de fleuve St. Laurent & les côtes de la

Mer Océane, jusqu'aux bords du Mississippi" (2:178) [alone are a cause
of jealousy to the most remote tribes from the mouth of the Saint
Lawrence and the Atlantic coast to the banks of the Mississippi]. During periods of intense fighting, such as the 1680s, discourse about the
"Guerres des sauvages," usually not specific to any nation, often took on
a propagandistic anti-Iroquois slant. Hennepin, in the ethnographic
section of *Description de la Louisiane*, devoted the whole of the brief chapter "Manière de faire la guerre" [Manner of Making War] to the atrocities and domination of the Iroquois. Conversely, for the English colonists, hyperbolic tales of Indian cruelty generally involved the Huron,
Abenaki, or Algonquin allies of the French. The best-known example
would be *The Last of the Mohicans*, where James Fenimore Cooper made
the villain Magua a Huron and the most horrific scene the attack by the
French Indian allies at Fort William Henry; he had his favorite tribe the
Delaware eventually defeat the Hurons, when in truth it was the Iroquois who terrorized the Hurons and were the most important allies of
the English.

Even without the biblical figures, many of the captivity narratives of
the half century from King Philip's War to 1725 betray a deep-seated
ambivalence about the Amerindians and the French, confounding the
difference between them with their common status as heathen foes. As
Roy Harvey Pearce showed in one of the first important studies of the
genre, during the Seven Years' War captivity narratives became propaganda stirring up hatred of both the Indians and French, but even before
1725 the ambivalence was still strong. Mary Rowlandson wrote of her
son, "it might have been worse with him had he been sold to the French
than it proved to be in remaining with the Indians" (VC 54).[9] Perhaps
because this is the only reference to the French in the most-often-read
captivity narrative, it is not widely recognized that most of the hundreds
of captives of this period were held for longer by the French than by the
Indians, and that the French often ransomed captives from the Indians
only to hold them as prisoners of war. Rowlandson's remark was echoed
by captive John Gyles, who reacted with a fear of Catholics as paranoid
as any fear of Indians when he saw a Jesuit missionary attempting to
purchase him from his Indian captor: "The Jesuit gave me a biscuit
which I put into my pocket and dare not eat but buried it under a log,

fearing that he had put something in it to make me love him, for I was
very young and had heard much of the Papists torturing the Protestants,
etc., so that I hated the sight of a Jesuit" (VC 99). The paradox of savage
demons who treat captives with generosity and kindness, so evident in
Rowlandson and part of the larger enigma of the Noble Savage's merciless cruelty and familial tenderness, applied to the French as well. Cotton Mather, in Book 7 of *Magnalia Christi Americana*, called an invasion
force "half Indianized French and half Frenchified Indians" that took
more than fifty New Englanders into "the worst captivity in the world"
(VC 137). Yet a couple of pages later he admitted that of these captives,
"many more of them were bought by the French who treated them with
a civility ever to be acknowledged until care was taken to fetch them
home" (VC 139).

In the narrative of John Williams, *The Redeemed Captive Returning to
Zion*, the "popish captivity" (VC 208) becomes the true horror of the
tale, for the French reportedly used techniques far more sinister than the
Indians did to seduce him, his children, and his townspeople away from
Protestantism. At one point in the story Williams is able to neatly align
the threats of papists and savages. He is staying in the wigwams of
converts at Montreal, and his Indian master insists that he go to Mass. A
woman named Ruth, taken captive from her tribe during King Philip's
War and "now proselyted to the Romish faith" (VC 185), reminds him
that the commands of Scripture would have him obey his master. Then,
Williams reports, "My master took hold of my hand to force me to cross
myself, but I struggled with him and would not suffer him to guide my
hand; upon this he pulled off a crucifix from his own neck and bade me
kiss it, but I refused once again. He told me he would dash out my brains
with his hatchet if I refused" (VC 186). Less than a third of Williams's
narrative concerns his Indian captivity, and by the end the piece descends to the level of wartime propaganda, in which no accusation
against the Catholic enemy is too scurrilous to print.

Jesuits were, of course, not above propagandistic statements either.
The missionary Pierre Millet was held captive during 1690–91, when
the war was at a high point, just before William Phips's failed invasion
of Quebec. Many of the Iroquois wished to torture him in vengeance for
warriors killed fighting at Montreal and Fort Frontenac, but he was

protected by Oneida Christians favoring an alliance with the French, who concealed him in a series of safe cabins. Like Williams, Millet subsumed the opposition Civilized/Savage under Catholic/Protestant and even refused to be ransomed by the English. He accused the English of the sort of barbaric ceremonies usually attributed to Indians: "Les Chretiens d Onneiout que Javois baptisé me conserveroient la vie[.] Javois besoin de cet appuy, parceque le Anglois dit on avoient fait mon procez et mavoient desja fait brusler en Effigie" (*JR* 64:68–69) [The Christians of Onneiout whom I had baptised would preserve my life. I needed this support, because the English, it is said, had tried me and already burnt me in Effigy]. Later, when officially adopted in place of a late sachem, "Les Anglais ne furent pas contans de la decision des Onneiouts en ma faveur" (*JR* 64:92–93) [The English were not pleased with the decision of the Onneiouts in my favor]. Captivity was represented as the "Indian atrocity" par excellence, even though captives were frequently POWs held for ransom as in any European war. Rather than an utter negation of civilization, as Puritan propagandists such as the Mathers portrayed Indian captivity to be, it was frequently merely a substitution or adaptation of familiar wartime tactics to the American setting, which lacked standing armies, prisons, and executioners.

Trade and Alliances: Economies of War

Just as pelts were implicated in clothing, money, and writing, they were instrumental in war. We have seen in Colden how the beaver pelt bonds attesting to the sincerity of treaties could have a significant exchange value as well. In New France, the intercultural alliances of the fur trade were founded on wartime alliances. In his 1611 voyage, two years after his landmark defeat of the Mohawk, Champlain took part in a delicate series of negotiations and misunderstandings that illustrate how European influence on war also molded the practice of the fur trade. Champlain went to a rendez-vous with hundreds of Algoumequin (Ottawa) and "Ocheteguins" in order to gather a war party to march once again against the Iroquois. That summer, however, many French traders followed along, having learned of the assembly and of the trust Cham-

plain held among the Indians. While Champlain claimed to be interested first of all in exploration of the upstream lands (in the ever-hopeful
pursuit of a route through the continent to the Indies), he enjoyed gifts
of many beaver pelts in return for his assistance in the wars against the
Iroquois. Other Frenchmen were anxious to share in this wealth, although they had not fought in the wars. Champlain reported that the
Algoumequins were complaining of the "Basques et Mistigouches"
(fishermen and traders, many of them Basque and Norman) that "ce
qu'ils en disoient n'estoit que pour avoir & attirer leurs commoditez. Ils
me disoient tu as dit vray, ce sont femmes, & ne veulent faire la guerre
qu'a nos Castors" (2:121) [what they said was merely in order to obtain
possession of the Indians' goods. These said to me: "You have spoken
truly, they are women, who wish to make war only upon our beavers."]
Likewise, Champlain complained that while he risked his neck to secure
the allegiance, others reaped the profit of furs. The following summer,
when they saw the large camp of these Basques et Mistigouches, the
Algoumequins called Champlain aside and "ils me dirent qu'ils estoient
faschez de voir tant de François, qui n'estoient pas bien unis ensemble, &
qu'ils eussent bien desiré me voir seul: Que quelques uns d'entre eux
avoient esté battuz" (2:193–94) [they told me that they were displeased
at seeing so many Frenchmen, who were not very friendly towards one
another, and that they would have much liked to see me alone. They also
said that some of their people had been beaten]. Champlain had to
reassure them that the other Europeans were there with his sanction (a
declaration he bitterly retracted later when it was a question of losing his
concession for trade in New France). After a few tense days, the Algoumequins seemed satisfied, for "Peu de temps apres ils se resolurent
de faire quelques presents à tous les Capitaines des pattaches. Ils donnerent à chacun dix castors: & en les donnant, ils dirent qu'ils estoyent
bien marris de n'en avoir beaucoup, mais que le guerre (ou la plus part
alloyent) en estoit cause" (2:208–9) [Shortly after this they decided to
make gifts to all the captains of the patatches. To each they gave ten
beaver-skins, and in giving these they said that they were sorry they had
not more of them; but that the war to which the majority were on their
way was the cause of the small number].

The exchange economy of the fur trade was forced on the Indians by the Europeans. At the early stages of contact, as in Champlain's episode, colonists accepted gifts intended to secure allegiances as if they were free favors. French and later English colonists came to understand the importance of ritual gifts to maintain alliances and a client base in the fur trade, and the cost of these gifts, borne by the Crown, became a factor to consider in judging the true value of colonies.[10] If profits were drained by such overhead expenses, perhaps colonies were most significant not as investments but as a geopolitical competition with the other European powers, France versus Spain versus England, as was indeed the case by the time of the Seven Years' War.

Whether out of an acute cultural sensitivity or not, Champlain in the early 1600s shared with the Amerindians the belief that trade was not simply economic exchange, but entailed forging an alliance. Complying with the native practice of exchanging children to strengthen a trading relationship, he sent *truchements* to live among the nations with whom he traded. The Jamestown colonists did likewise with boys such as Henry Spelman. Champlain (like Smith) also became familiar with the Indian view of trading privileges as proprietary, the monopoly of the individual or the clan that had made the initial alliance. Sagard, who was at Quebec during Champlain's leadership and followed his path to Huronia, wrote:

> De mesme il fallait avoir la permission d'Auoindouan pour aller à Kebec, et comme chacun entend d'estre maistre en son pays, aussi ne laissent-ils passer aucun d'une autre Nation Sauvage par leur pays, pour aller à la traicte, sans estre recogneus et gratifiez de quelque present. (127)

> [Similarly it was necessary to get permission from Auoindaon to go to Quebec, and since each means to be master in his own country, they allow no one of another tribe of savages to pass through their country to go to the trading unless they are recognized as master and their favour secured by a present. (99)]

This practice mimicked the trade policies of Europe at the time, whereby monopolies on the fur trade in certain regions of New England, New Netherlands, or New France were granted to companies or even individuals. At the outset, before the monopoly was officially granted to the de

Caen brothers, Champlain, like a native chief, believed that he granted other French adventurers the opportunity to trade for pelts out of his own generosity.

Champlain may not have fully understood native customs, but he too wished to be respected for more than just his wealth and to engage in relationships that were more than merely economic. He wanted his readers to believe that it was his courage as discoverer and warrior that was being rewarded (more generously by the Indians than by the French court), not his kettles or axes. Champlain, in effect, adopted the native principle of status as a reward for achievement and then risked the status he had accumulated for the benefit of his fur-trading compatriots. This is another example of how portrayals of the Indians were not just savagist ideology but ways of life that Europeans had to understand and often adopt if they were to achieve their goals. Champlain assimilated himself into the representation of the natives' system of transparent signification, where word is supported by actions and promises must be kept. Although wealth was status in New France as elsewhere, "Les Mœurs des Sauvages de la Nouvelle France" introduced the subversive idea that there existed a society where it was based instead on deeds.

As other explorers and colonists were rarely aware of these rules governing trade in Amerindian society, they often created the impression that relations between local groups were more antagonistic than they actually were. An example is found in Joutel's narrative, where, during his trek from the Gulf coast near today's Galveston to the Mississippi, the explorer was in a desperate position and had to engage in a sham of the custom of concluding a trade alliance in return for military assistance. The routine proceeded like this: The French band arrived in a new nation, hungry and lost. The locals fed and sheltered the visitors with generous hospitality in exchange for a few ribbons. Joutel asked for a guide to lead him toward his goal. The Indians implored him to stay and go to war with them, using guns against their enemies who had none, and sweetened the offer with promises of houses and wives. From this point departed a dialectic of competing promises. Joutel repeated his request for a guide, promising knives and hatchets if the guide successfully led him to the next landmark, the Mississippi River or the first

French fort. The young men of the nation, not wishing to surrender this valuable trading partner to a neighboring village that had no right to it, answered with threatening tales of the hostile reaction that the next nation had in store for the small band of refugees. Joutel's desperation overcame his fear, and he countered with a more valuable promise deferred further into the future: "nous amènerions des hommes pour aller avec eux à la guerre; qu'alors nous destruirions touts leurs ennemis et mettrions la paix partout" [we would bring back some men to go with them to war, and then we would destroy all their enemies and establish peace everywhere (my translation)].[11] The final outcome was that one Indian agreed to serve as guide and in exchange for a few knives led the band just to the frontier of the next nation, where the guide turned back and the cycle began all over again. The accounts of John Smith and Jacques Le Moyne de Morgues illustrate the same principle operating in a context where the balance of power has shifted toward the invaders. Smith ignored the warnings and anger of Powhatan and traveled up the bay to the Susquehannocks. The French allied at first with Saturiba (this name also has many spellings, including "Saturouna"), then shifted their allegiance to his enemy Outina when it became apparent that Outina was more powerful. Later, when they learned that gold and peltry lay inland in the territory of enemies of Outina, they again regretted their choice of alliance. So the mercantilist practice of awarding a monopoly in the pelt or other trade to a company or wealthy individual, or of seeking to dominate trade and drive out competition, actually resembled Indian custom more closely than early colonists had imagined.

Honor and Individualism

One of the most important revelations to European observers of Indian war was the importance that they found was placed on preserving the life of each warrior. North American Indian warfare was on a small scale. Epic battles involving thousands, such as Hernán Cortés's siege of Tenochtitlan, are absent from the French and English literature of exploration and settlement. The techniques of war may have been extreme, but the tactics were cautious, for the loss of a warrior was a great blow to the village. This is why a few European explorers with guns could be so decisive and were so eagerly sought as allies.

French colonial writers were impressed to find societies in which each member was deemed a valuable asset, and the customs of marriage, war, and family all appeared to be organized so as to preserve the nations' populations. This discovery may have influenced the doctrines of Montesquieu and the Physiocrats, who believed that maximizing population was among the prime goals of statecraft. The *sauvages*, according to Lafitau, were appalled by the custom of duels, and

> Ils ne sont pas moins étonnez de cette indifférence que les Européens ont pour ceux de leur nation, de peu de cas qu'ils font de la mort de leurs Compatriotes tuez par leurs Ennemis. Chez eux un homme seul tué par un autre d'une Nation différente de la leur, commet les deux Nations & cause une guerre. Parmi les Européens, la mort de plusieurs des leurs ne paroît intéresser personne. (2:291)

> [They are no less astonished by the indifference of the Europeans for their fellow countrymen, by the slight attention paid by them to the death of their compatriots killed by their enemies. With them, one man killed by another of some tribe different from theirs, causes war between the two tribes. Among Europeans, the death of many of their own people appears to be of no concern to anyone.]

The descriptions of the grief that the death of even a single warrior would elicit in his home village demonstrate the value of the individual life. Lamothe-Cadillac, in a short *mœurs des sauvages* based on his time as chief of the post at Michilimackinac, wrote, "Ils ne parlent jamais de ceux qu'ils ont tué, ils ne parlent que de leurs morts" [They never speak of those whom they have killed, but only of their own dead].[12] Lahontan and Charlevoix both reported that as the war party returned to its village, they let out a series of cries, *He He He He*, to signify not the number of enemy warriors killed, but the number of casualties from their own party, whose mourning took precedent over any victory celebration.[13] This sent the women and children of the village into cries of grief even before the warriors reported the full outcome. When Mary Rowlandson witnessed the return of warriors from an attack on the town of Sudbury that had resulted in the death of more than thirty Englishmen,[14] she was surprised to see that "they came home without that rejoicing and triumphing over their victory which they were wont to show at other times but rather like dogs (as they say) which have lost their ears. Yet I could not perceive that it was for their own loss of men. They said they had not lost but above five or six" (VC 64). The loss of six would have been perfectly acceptable to the English in such a victory. The concern to avoid losing warriors in an attack appears to have been true across Native America. Le Page du Pratz reported that "le Grand chef de Guerre paye à la famille ceux qu'il ne ramene pas; ce qui rend ces Chefs plus soigneux de ménager leurs Guerriers" (2:437) [the big war chief pays the family for those he does not bring back, which makes the chiefs more careful in the management of their warriors" (my translation)]. Bossu, too, wrote of the conservative tactics of the "chef de guerre":

> Un Général qui remporteroit une victoire avec une perte de beaucoup de monde, seroit très mal reçu de sa Nation, parceque ces Peuples comptent pour rien la victoire quand elle est achetée au prix du sang de leurs parents & de leurs amis: aussi les Chefs de parti, ont grand soin de conserver leurs Guerriers, & de n'attaquer l'ennemi, que lorsqu'ils sont surs de vaincre.[15]

> [A chief who won a victory involving a great loss of men would be very badly received by his people. They consider absolutely worthless a victory bought with the blood of their friends and their relatives. Therefore, the chiefs are very careful to spare their warriors and to attack the enemy only when assured of victory. (165)]

Bossu employed the language of exchange to describe war, victory being "achetée" or bought, yet he also evoked the close ties of a small village, where a casualty would certainly be a relative or the relative of a friend.

Because the death of one was serious enough to motivate revenge, it would likely lead to the death of another, and the high value placed on individual life lead to an endless cycle of killing. Vengeance was thus logically incompatible with an effort to preserve or maximize the population, yet in practice it made a coherent part of the same ethic. After all, the problem of vengeance haunted Western culture as well. With this

absolute vengeance, war maintained an epic or chivalric purity, representing European nostalgia for its own past.[16] It was the means by which
young men proved their valor and worth. Here is Lafitau again, from the
beginning of the chapter "De la guerre":

> Les hommes, qui sont si desœuvrés dans leurs Villages, ne se font
> une gloire de leur indolence que pour donner à entendre qu'ils ne
> sont proprement nés que pour les grandes choses, & sur-tout pour la
> Guerre, laquelle exposant leur courage aux plus rudes épreuves leur
> fournir de fréquentes occasions de mettre dans son plus beau jour toute
> la noblesse de leurs sentiments et l'inébranlable fermeté d'une gran-
> deur d'ame vraïement héroïque. (2:161)

> [The men, who are so idle in their villages, make their indolence a
> mark of honour, giving it to be understood that they are properly born
> only for great things, especially for warfare. This exercise, which ex-
> poses their courage to the rudest tests, furnishes them frequent occa-
> sions to put in its brightest light all the nobility of their sentiments
> and the unshakeable firmness of a truly heroic greatness of mind.]

The Indian warrior here, though he might enjoy no privileges as a
member of an elevated class, is nonetheless imbued with a nobleman's
idle pride. Such polite abstractions as "sentiment" and "âme," or soul,
here translate with apparent ease from the European to the Indian world.
Do these passages by Lafitau constitute a critique of European society
and its wars? The individual autonomy combined with eye-for-eye vengeance perceived in Amerindian society leads to ambivalent conclusions.

Some observers saw in the *sauvages* an extension of the logic of war
that European armies were not yet able to countenance. Bossu, writing
of the efficiency of the strategy of surprise, used such a rational standard:
"les Sauvages font consister leur gloire et leur science dans cette sorte de
guerre; qui est presque toujours fatale à ceux qui en sont l'objet" [The
Indians are famous for their skill in this type of warfare which is almost
always fatal to the foe (64)].[17] Lahontan also expressed the single-
mindedness of Indian warfare and its motivations:

> . . . ils considérent les moyens de faire leur commerce de Pelleteries
> avec les François sans desavantage, & ceux de pouvoir chasser les Cas-
> tors durant l'Hiver sans courir aucun danger. Ils proposent sur tout à

leurs Alliez de ne finir point la guerre, qu'après avoir totalement détruit leur ennemis, ou les avoir obligez d'abandonner leur Païs. (2:187)

[The next thing that they have in view, is the carrying on of the Trade of Skins with the French without disadvantage, and the Hunting of Beavers in Winter without exposing themselves to danger. After all, they make this proposal to their Allies; that they shall engage not to put an end to the War till their Enemies are intirely destroy'd, or else oblig'd to abdicate their Country. (2:82)]

Descriptions of war contain both chivalry and rationality, both a rigid state control and a mercenary anarchy. It is difficult to determine if colonial writers have a favorable or a negative attitude toward such an extreme, rationalized warfare as Lahontan describes; it is susceptible to the same unresolved contradiction found throughout the *guerres des sauvages* between brutal aggression and calculated vengeance. Lafitau divided war accordingly into a "petite" or casual war that expressed the *sauvages'* natural aggressiveness and a more serious "grande guerre" that could involve many nations and that, ever in search of classical allusions, he compared to the Trojan War. But the distinction between instinct and custom was difficult to maintain. Nicolas Perrot inverted the common belief that "Indians ground their wars on enmity, not on interest" in a prejudicial account that nonetheless drew support from the well-documented value placed on individual warriors' achievements:

La vengeance des sauvages a plustost pour principe l'ambition que le courage; car il n'y a pas de gens au monde plus lasches qu'eux. . . . si l'ambition les excite à se venger, ils iront de guet-apend poignarder un homme au milieu de ses amis, et affronter une embuscade, quoyque persuadez de n'en pouvoir jamais revenir. Ils sont si hardis qu'ils approcheront du camp des ennemis de manière à les pouvoir compter. Mais toutes ces bravoures extraordinaires ne sont soustenües que d'une vaine gloire, ou d'une passion de s'attirer des loüanges pendant la vie ou après la mort. (76–77)

[The vengeance of the savages is more often inspired by ambition than by courage, for there are no people in the world more cowardly than

they are. . . . if ambition excites them to vengeance they will go
stealthily to kill a man in the midst of his friends, and to confront an
ambuscade, even though they are sure they will never return from the
undertaking. They are so bold that they can approach a hostile camp so
near that they can count their foes. But all these extraordinary displays
of courage are maintained only through vainglory, or from a passion to
attract praises to themselves, either during life or after death. (1:
142–43)

As with a kamikaze pilot, the greatest courage and self-sacrifice can also
be regarded as the worst cowardice. Perrot's statement, which may be
informed by time he spent with Sioux peoples west of the Mississippi,
recalls the custom of the "coup" among plains Indians. Touching an
enemy in his own territory and escaping to tell a "coup tale" earned a
warrior as much valor as a scalp did a northeastern Indian.[18] In light of
the meritographic honor accruing to individuals successful in war and
the lack of military subordination among the Indians, Perrot accused
warriors of acting only for their own interest. But Perrot did not consider the warrior's relation to the one whose life he was avenging, and his
criticism may arise from the uncomfortable fact that the Indian warrior
enjoyed much more individual autonomy than did a soldier in a European army, the kind of soldier Perrot was often trying to recruit from
among the Indians for battles against the English.

The means by which the instinctual and the political, Lafitau's
"petite" and "grande guerre," were reconciled reflects how early ethnographies served as experiments with Enlightenment individualism.
Among the *sauvages*, unlike in Europe, no one would be obliged to fight
in a war he did not support. A declaration of war could not be made by a
despot out of a vendetta or for self-aggrandizement; it would be sol-
emnly debated and assented to by a council of statesmen. The fighting
would be done not by an army of peasants commanded by noble officers
but by a cadre of young warriors whose actions and rewards fell on their
personal initiative.

In deliberating over and planning for war, Amerindians clearly did
engage in rational political discourse. Lafitau described the scene
this way:

> Le Conseil ne se détermine point à la Guerre, sans en avoir couvé long-
> temps le dessein, & sans avoir pesé toutes les raisons du pour & du
> contre, avec beaucoup de maturité. Toutes les Assemblées roulent sur
> cette matière. On y examine avec soin toutes les suites d'une entreprise
> de cette consequence. (2:170–71)

> [The Council decides on war only after considering the plan for a long
> time and weighing with mature consideration all the factors pro and
> con. All the assemblies treat this matter. They examine carefully all
> the consequences of an enterprise of this importance.]

One could only wish that all governments were so circumspect about
war. The description of the "conseil des viellards" (who all had to be at
least eighty years old, according to Lahontan) was an occasion to portray
the solemnity that was part and parcel of the popular stereotype of the
Indian. They never interrupted one anothers' speeches but waited pa-
tiently to consider every point of view. LeClercq turned this into a
criticism of European manners:

> . . . les Sauvages n'interrompent jamais celuy qui harangue; & ils les
> blâment avec raison, ces entretiens, ces conversations indiscretes et
> peu reglées, où chacun de la compagnie veut dire son sentiment, sans
> se donner la patience d'écouter celuy des autres: c'est aussi pour ce
> sujet, qu'ils nous comparent à des cannes & aux oyes, qui crient,
> disent-ils, & qui parlent tous ensemble, comme les François. (545)

> [. . . Indians never interrupt the one who is speaking, and they con-
> demn, with reason, those dialogues and those indiscreet and irregular
> conversations where each one of the company wishes to give his ideas
> without having the patience to listen to those of the others. It is,
> accordingly, for this reason that they compare us to ducks and geese,
> which cry out, say they, and which talk all together like the French.
> (311)]

This image of Indian oratory continued in eighteenth-century America,
as can be seen in the reprintings of Grangula's "harangue" and in the
even greater popularity of Logan's speech, which became a common
declamation piece (among the many reprintings of it was one by Thomas
Jefferson in query 6 of *Notes on the State of Virginia*). It was given early

impetus by Colden, who demonstrated it with many speeches that are frankly superior to Logan's.

When organizing a party of warriors the Amerindians were reported to use a language of tokens, as we saw in Chapter 4. In pointed contrast to the press gangs who kidnapped young men for military service in Europe, the American Indians relied on voluntary enrollment. Benjamin Church witnessed a similar system of recruiting soldiers for his efforts in King Philip's War, soldiers who became "Mr. Churches Indians, that offered their Voluntary Service to go under his command in quest of the Enemy":

> Then the Chief Captain step'd in between the rings and the fire, with a Spear in one hand and an Hatchet in the other danced round the fire, and began to fight with it, making mention of all the several Nations & Companies of Indians in the Country that were Enemies to the English; & at the naming of every particular Tribe of Indians, he would draw out & fight a new fire brand . . . The Captain of the Guard stept up to Mr. Church and told him, They were making Souldiers for him, and what they had been doing was all one Swearing of them, and having in that manner ingaged all the lusty stout men. (432–33)[19]

Mary Rowlandson described a similar ceremony in preparation for the Sudbury battle in the same war.

These warriors recruited through a voluntary enrollment retained a certain autonomy in battle. The warrior was portrayed as acting with individual freedom or in accord with instinct. The authority of the "chef de guerre" was consensual, and the solemn deliberation of the council did not impart to him the power of a commander-in-chief. Champlain wrote, "ce ne sont pas des gens de guerre, & d'ailleurs qu'ils ne veulent point de discipline, ny de correction, & ne font que ce qui leur semblent bon" (3:72) [for they are not warriors, and moreover they will not submit to discipline nor to correction, and do only what they like]; he later added, "Ils n'ont point de Chefs particuliers qui commandent absolument, mais bien portent-ils de l'honneur aux plus anciens et vaillants" (3:157) [They have no special chiefs with absolute command, but rather they pay honour to the eldest and bravest]. Any discipline or punishment within the fighting force was effected not by bodily force but by speech, "on luy remonstre par belles, & bonnes parolles, son debouir" (3:158) [they set him before his duty with fair and favorable words]. The advantages of discipline by consensus over that of coercion could be significant:

> Capt. Church inquired of some of the Indians that were become his Souldiers, How they got such advantage often of the English in their Marches thro' the Woods? They told him, . . . The Indians always took care in their Marches and Fights, not to come too thick together. But the English always kept in a heap together, that it was as easy to hit them as to hit an House.[20]

Using these tactics, without the mechanical discipline of a European army, successful action must arise out of a utopian identity between the individual and the general will. Yet few were ready to accord "savage" society this theoretical sophistication, which recalls Rousseau's *Social Contract*. Instead, there was simply a coincidence of consensus inspired by loyalty. As Charlevoix allowed, "tant il est vrai que parmi des Hommes, qui se conduisent par la raison, & qui sont guidés par l'honneur & le zéle pour la Patrie, l'indépendence ne détruit point la subordination, & que souvent l'obéissance libre & voluntaire est toujours celle, sur laquelle on peut plus sûrement compter" (269) [so true it is, that amongst a people who are guided by reason, and inspired with sentiments of honour and love for their country, independence is not destructive of subordination; and that a free and voluntary obedience is that on which we can always rely with the greatest certainty (2:25)]. Perrot wrote, "Le sauvage ne sçait ce c'est que d'obéir: il faut plustost le prier que de la commander; il se laisse néantmoins aller à tout ce qu'on exige de luy" (78) [The savage does not know what it is to obey. It is more often necessary to entreat him than to command him; he nevertheless yields to all demands made upon him (145)]. If Indian warriors were motivated to fight so effectively without any rigid military discipline or threat of punishment, then the Europeans' concepts of loyalty and patriotism had to be reformulated to account for Native American virtues. The most common response, however, was an application of the *premiers temps* trope that compared Indians to ancient peoples celebrated for battlefield valor—Spartans, Romans, Picts, or Gauls—and thus recuperated their bravery as somehow European in origin.

Because the *sauvages américains* had no political life on the model of the nation-state, the European invaders could not readily understand their wars and wavered between interpretations of Indian warfare as vengeance and as bestial or greedy aggression. On the one hand lay an economy of exchange, by which one can put a price on anything, including human life. The practice of "covering" for a murder by paying the family of the victim was the obvious example of this. On the other hand lay an economy of vengeance arising out of values of group solidarity and retribution, where only a life is worth a life, a system that to the Europeans recalled the Old Testament. To decide which system applied in a given instance required yet another economy of calculation and justification, one related to tribal and familial kinship. Europeans might not have understood Amerindian kinship systems but were often involved in this economy as it determined the fate of captives, who might be tortured in vengeance or sold to other Indians, the French, or for ransom. A captive became aware of his or her value, as Mary Rowlandson described: "the sagamores met to consult about the captives and called me to them to inquire how much my husband would give to redeem me. . . . I was in a great strait. I thought if I should speak of but a little, it would be slighted and hinder the matter; if of a great Sum, I knew not where it would be procured. Yet at a venture, I said twenty pounds, yet desired them to take less" (VC 62). Her ill-ease is evident. Life is no longer priceless. The passage calls the bluff on the biblical rhetoric of surrender and selflessness, of her potential martyrdom and the wrath by which God might revenge her death, for the allegorical power of her story is deflated to a simple bargain: she must name a price her captors will accept if she is to be redeemed.

The two economies, of vengeance and of compensation, not only governed the treatment of captives, who could be tortured or redeemed, but also the treatment of criminals. Captives such as Rowlandson understood the logic of their situation fairly well, but cultural differences could be especially acute in the area of justice and punishment. Whereas the autonomy of the Amerindian individual inspired comparisons with republican virtues, the unfamiliarity of this conception of the individual became apparent when it came to establishing responsibility for "criminal" actions. Charlevoix wrote: "En un mot, ces Amériquains sont parfaitement convaincus, que l'Homme est né libre, qu'aucune Puissance sur la Terre n'a droit d'attenter à sa liberté, & que rien ne pourroit le dédommager de sa perte" (272) [In a word, these Indians are perfectly convinced, that man is born free, and that no power on earth has a right to infringe his liberty, and that nothing can compensate the loss of it (2:30)], and though the passage continues by decrying their ignorance of original sin, it seems that what really bothered the Jesuit traveler was that "il n'y a presque point de Justice Criminelle parmi ces Peuples" (272) [they have scarce the shadow of criminal justice among them (2:29)]. Sagard and many other observers in New France reported that if a Huron murdered a member of his own family or village, no punishment would be demanded and others of the nation (who belonged to different families or villages) would not interfere. Rather, they would believe that the murderer must have acted with good reason. Furthermore, if the murderer's rational faculties were lacking, or even if he was drunk, the crime might be excused. As Charlevoix explained:

> . . . ils sont persuadés qu'une personne, qui n'est pas en son bon sens, n'est point réprehensible, ou du moins ne doit pas être punie . . . qu'un Sauvage en tuë un autre de sa Cabane, s'il étoit Yvre, & souvent fait-on semblant de l'être, quand on veut faire de semblables coups, on se contente de plaindre & de pleurer le mort; c'est un malheur, dit-on, le Meurtrier ne sçavoit pas ce qu'il faisoit. (273)

> [They are not only persuaded, that a person who is not in possession of his reason is not responsible for his actions, at least, that he deserves no punishment. . . . should an Indian kill another in his cabin, being drunk, which they often pretend to be when they harbour any such designs, they content themselves with bewailing the dead: It was a great misfortune, say they, but as for the murderer he knew not what he did. (2:32)]

What is more, "S'il étoit de sang froid, on suppose aisément, qu'il avoit de bonnes raisons, pour en venir à cette extremité" (273) [If the thing was done in cold blood, they suppose without difficulty that the person who committed it, must have had very good reasons before he proceeded to this extremity (2:32)]. The proper response to violence was guided not by judgment of and retribution against the individual found guilty, but by the negotiation of positions in a social universe. Lafitau described the quite different reaction that a murder by a sober assailant from outside the family would elicit: "L'affaire change bien de nature, si le meurtre a été commis à l'égard d'une personne d'une Cabane différente, d'une autre Tribu, d'un autre Village, & encore plus d'une Nation étrangère; car alors cette mort funeste intéresse tout le Public" (1:490) [The nature of the affair changes if the murder has been committed upon a person of another house, another clan or village, and still more of a foreign country for then this grievous death is a matter of concern to a whole people]. In this case, the murder could still be recompensed; the family and nation of the murderer would attempt to make up for the loss with presents, a symbolically prescribed list of sixty presents, many with symbolic functions of, for instance, smoothing the path between villages. As Lafitau described them: "les neuf premiers se mettent entre les mains des parent pour ôter de leur coeur toute aigreur et tout désir de vengeance. Les autres sont suspendus à une perche au-dessus de la tête du mort" (1:491) [the first nine are put into the hands of the kin to remove from their hearts all bitterness and desire for vengeance. The others are hung on a pole above the dead man's head]. Yet even these often failed to heal the wound, and such violence could touch off a blood feud and a war.

There was thus a rigorous principle based on kinship proximity, which recalls both the concepts of clan and phratry that would be developed by later anthropologists and the rigid boundary of inclusion and exclusion that characterizes the utopia and frequently also the modern nation, class, or family. If the killer and victim were members of the same group, there would likely be no punishment; if they were separated between clans within the same village or nation, the system of compensation might "cover" the crime; but if the victim belonged to an enemy tribe, his relatives and compatriots might send a war party out for vengeance. We saw above how the nations visited by Joutel and Hennepin emphasized their benevolence by comparison with the brutal violence practiced by their enemies. The representations of Amerindian cultures resembled the model of the utopia in European literature in this strict division between placid, egalitarian relations within the society and the fierce violence that reigned outside. As Bossu wrote,

> Les Sauvages sont très hospitaliers envers les étrangers avec qui ils sont en paix, bons envers leurs alliez & leurs amis; mais cruels & inéxorables envers leurs ennemis. Ils sont très surpris, & même scandalisés de voir à la Nouvelle Orléans nombre d'Anglois qu'on y attire pendant la guerre, pour y faire le commerce . . .[21]

> [The Indians are very hospitable toward strangers with whom they are at peace and are kind to their allies and friends, but they are cruel and unmerciful to their enemies. They are surprised and even scandalized to see Englishmen, who have come to New Orleans presumably to negotiate the exchange of prisoners, carrying on business affairs and wandering about in our settlements. (134–35)]

Although some observers, like Charlevoix above, commented on the inconsistent treatment of murderers, Bossu drew attention to the Europeans' own inconsistency in the relationship with their enemies in the two spheres of trade and war. The utopia represented among the *sauvages* is of a society of consensus and consistency, with no division between the political, social, and economic, or even between public and private, only between the interior and the exterior of the community. Richard White has described very well this cultural contrast in the attitudes toward killing:

> For the Algonquians there were two kinds of killings—deaths at the hands of enemies and deaths at the hands of allies. The appropriate response depended on the identity of the group to which the killer belonged. If the killer belonged to an allied group, then the dead were raised or covered [i.e. replaced by an adoptee or compensated for by gifts]. . . . For the French it was murder that demanded blood revenge; for the Algonquians, it was killings by enemies, killings which the French saw as warfare. (80)

Thus the natives did have consistent principles for dealing with killings, but rather than distinguish between killings in civil society and those in warfare, they distinguished according to the identity of the killer. This identity was a relational system rather than one of abstract rights and values. In this it differed from evolving republican theories, though in many other ways Indian customs contributed to Anglo-American republican ideology. Of course, a criminal justice system as such was impossible in the Indian communities, for a prison, with its enforced idleness, confinement, and separation of an offender, was impossible in a life of seasonal migrations. Captives and prisoners had to be either incorporated into a family or tortured and killed. One was either on the inside or the outside of the quasi-utopian space, either accepted, exiled, or dead.

Of course, the two different conceptions of punishing killers brought native and colonial cultures into difficult confrontations, as White illustrates with several episodes from the *pays d'en haut* (76–93). In another, earlier example, Champlain described an incident of the violence that wore at the edges of the European invasion and that forced two philosophies of justice to seek a "middle ground." It began with the death "de deux de nos hommes de l'habitation, qui perfidement, & par trahison, furent tuez par deux meschants garçons sauvages, Montaigners" (3:181) [of two of our men at the settlement who, through perfidy and treachery, had been killed by two wicked young savages, Montagnais]. The Montagnais had taken revenge after one of them was beaten by one of the two Frenchmen. Afterward, "se voyant privez de nostre conversation, & bon acceuil accoustumé" (3:189) [seeing themselves deprived of intercourse with us and of our customary welcome] by the French, the Montagnais offered to deliver up the two murderers, though continuing to urge the French to accept instead some valuable presents: "si mieux les François n'avoient aggreable pour reparation & recompense des morts, quelques honnestes presents des pelleteries comme est leur coustume, & pour une chose qui est irrecuperable: ce qu'ils prierent fort les François d'accepter plustost, que la mort des accusez" (3:190) [but that if the French would rather take, as reparation and compensation for the dead, some suitable presents of fur skins, as is their custom for a thing which is irrecoverable, they urgently begged the French to accept rather than to (require) the death of the accused]. This last phrase was not a reproach—the irrecoverable was meant to be replaced with presents of value. The murderer himself was offered as much as a gift, a sign of the giver's goodwill, as for the opportunity of retribution through punishing him. In this case, the Montagnais feared a war if they did not deliver up the killer, but they could not force him; they had to convince him to go for the benefit of the whole nation. One of the offenders did come to the colony to turn himself in, dressed as if for a wedding and accompanied by his parents. The Recollet missionaries were equally afraid of a war and therefore opposed executing the offender. For these missionaries, the living Indian was an asset, as the object of possible conversion he was as valuable to them as a scalp to a warrior. In the end the Recollets' self-interested mercy triumphed, the gift was accepted, the offender's life was spared, and the native system of justice apparently prevailed, awaiting the arrival of French ships to render another layer of "civilized" justice. When the ship arrived bringing Champlain, he was forced to accept this resolution of the case rather than risk a disruption of the fur trade. Champlain was angry, however, to see the murderer, Cherououny, later become chief of the Montagnais.[22]

Through issues of crime and justice, Champlain's and other explorer-ethnographers' texts examine philosophical questions of the freedom of the individual subject within the society or state. On the one hand, the *sauvages* are said to live without any law or system of justice, which leaves the individual with an existential freedom. Wrote Lafitau, "Un chacun regardant les autres comme maîtres de leurs actions, et d'eux-mêmes, les laisse se conduire à leur guise et ne pense qu'à soi" (1:485) [Each one, regarding others as masters of their own actions and themselves, lets them conduct themselves as they wish and judges only himself]. On the other hand, there demonstrably is a system of justice, but this system does not constrain the freedom of the individual "qu'à soi." Rather, it deconstructs the individual subject and replaces it by a system of relations of kinship and obligation. The freedom that so impressed the French observers in the years before the Enlightenment was not an individual freedom, that is, not an accumulation of actions and symbols around a stable subjectivity (although meritography did allow the signification of achievements on the body, which is not the same as the subject). Rather, the *sauvage américain* was free to redefine his position within the network of social relations: to remake it through adoption, to raise it through wartime valor, or to suspend it through drunkenness.

Captivity and Adoption

The adoption of prisoners of war is the most startling application of relational identity, and it is portrayed in very different ways by different exploration and captivity narrators. The precise rules for adoption are difficult to determine, but in any given case, the sudden changes of fate must have been nerve-racking if not positively heart-stopping. Pierre-Esprit Radisson, the lone secular French captivity narrator, appears to have accepted intuitively his shifting status. He stoically endured being tied to stakes at night shortly after his capture, complaining instead about the rancid meat he was served. Later, however, his captors turned kind: "Their behavior made me neverthelesse cheerfull, or att least of a smiling countenance, and constraine my aversion and feare to an assurance, which proved not ill to my thinking; for the young men tooke delight in combing my head, greasing and powdering out a kinde of redd powder, then tying my haire with a reddstring of leather" (32). A few weeks later he refers to his adopted family as mother, father, sister, and brother.

Gabriel Sagard, in his ethnography of the Hurons, was the first to portray as a typical practice the adoption of prisoners to replace those lost in a war. The Recollet was scandalized by the absence of proper European family behavior, particularly the parents who did not discipline their children. His reaction to the treatment of children taken captive proceeded along these lines:

> ... femmes, filles et enfants ... ils font rarement mourir; ains les conservent et retiennent pour eux, ou pour en faire des presens à d'autres, qui en auroient auparavant perdu de leurs en guerre, et font estat de ces subrigez, autant que s'ils estoient de leurs propres enfans, lesquels estans parvenus en aage, vont aussi courageusement en geurre contre leurs propres parens, et ceux de leur Nation, que s'ils estoient naiz

ennemis de leur propre patrie, ce qui tesmoigne le peu d'amour des enfants envers leurs parents, et qu'ils ne font estat que des bien-faicts presens, et non des passez, qui est un signe de mauvais naturel. (213)

[. . . women, girls, and children, seldom putting them to death, but saving and keeping them for themselves or to make presents of them to others, who have previously lost some of their own in war and make much of these substitutes, just as if they were actually their own children. These when they grow up go to war against their own parents and the men of their nation as bravely as if they had been born enemies of their own country. This shows how slight an affection children have for their parents and that they take account only of present, not past benefits, which is a sign of an evil disposition. (159)]

Beneath his reprobation, Sagard answers his own question. The children have no "propre patrie" [own country] because their concept of nationality does not pertain to where one was born or who one's parents are, only to the position one currently occupies in a small social system. As befits the stereotype of cultures without writing, the Hurons can only "read" signs of the present, not of the past. Together with the semiotic system of isomorphic writing examined in Chapter 4, this sense of belonging contributes to the metaphysics of presence built into the representation of the *sauvages américains* that would be so important to Rousseau and other philosophes. Family belonging was all the more important if it was not necessarily permanent. Lamothe-Cadillac was also struck by this apparent betrayal of kinship, writing of the adoptees:

... ce sont les premiers qui vont en guerre contre leur propre nation et qui tuent ou amènent prisonniers leur pères, leurs oncles ou autres parens indifféremment, comme s'ils ne leur estoient rien du tout, faisant plus de cas de la seconde vie qu'on leur a donnée que de celle qu'ils ont receue ce leurs pères et de leurs mères, qu'ils voyent souvent brusler et déchirer par morceaux.

[. . . they are the first to go to war against their own tribe, and kill or take prisoners their fathers, uncles, or other relatives indifferently, as if they were nothing at all to them, thinking more of the second life

which has been given them than of the life they received from their
fathers and mothers, whom they often see burned and torn in pieces.][23]

European colonists had a great deal of difficulty accepting that the
members of one's nuclear family, the basis in their own culture for name,
class, and inheritance, could change.

According to most observers, the practice of adoption was routine,
though there is not complete consensus on how it worked. Le Page du
Pratz, so detailed on other matters, simply said that the *naturels* tortured
and killed the male prisoners and adopted the women and children. But
in other texts, notably Lafitau's, men were also adopted by women to
replace the sons and husbands they had lost to war in a custom he calls
"resusciter" and Fenton and Moore translate as "to requicken." This was
never the only fate of prisoners, however, for torture always retained a
place. Lafitau implied that adoption was practiced only among the Hurons and Iroquois (although there are many reports of it among other
nations) and suggested that it conformed to the traditions of slavery in
the ancient world. He consistently referred to prisoners as "esclaves" or
slaves, even when adopted: "Une conduite si douce des Iroquois envers
leurs Esclaves, est l'effet d'une excellente politique; car ces Esclaves ne
voyant presque point de différence entre les Iroquois naturels & eux-
mêmes ne s'aperçoivent aussi presque point de leur servitude, & ne sont
point tentés de s'enfuïr" (2:309) [This gentle conduct of the Iroquois
towards their captives is excellent policy. For these captives, seeing
almost no difference between the real Iroquois and themselves, scarcely
notice their servitude and are not tempted to flee]. This enabled the
Iroquois to maintain "la supériorité qu'ils ont depuis si longtemps sur
les autres nations" [the superiority that they have so long had over the
other tribes], Lafitau explained, for "c'est ainsi que ceux-ci obtiennent
plus facilement les deux points qui leur sont les plus essentiels, qui sont,
de soûtenir leurs familles chancelantes, & de grossir leur nombre" (1:
310) [It is in this way that the Iroquois most easily obtain the two points
most essential for them, i.e., to sustain their tottering families and
increase their number].

Lafitau was no doubt thinking of the Roman Empire, which likewise benefited from the assimilation of conquered peoples. But he can also be read as anticipating the notions of the Physiocrats and even the later American ideal of the melting pot. This practice of assimilation could also apply to tribes that appealed to stronger nations for protection against powerful enemies, as the Tuscarora had when they became the sixth nation of the Iroquois in 1715. The practice of adopting entire tribes was also common in the lower Mississippi valley.

Adoption takes at face value the oft-betrayed principle that "all men are created equal," for it recognizes that the qualities of an individual are not essential, but are made up of the roles and actions he or she contributes to the social fabric. If the father of a family was killed, grief and mourning were called for, but the deceased's skills as hunter would be missed most, and these could be replaced. In the matrilineal Iroquoian system, a daughter was arguably even more valuable, and Lafitau affirmed that even a broken link in the bloodline could be repaired through adoption:

> Si l'esclave est une fille donnée dans une Cabane, où il n'y ait point de personne du sexe en état de la soûtenir, c'est une fortune pour cette Cabane là, & pour elle. Toute l'espérance de la famille est fondée sur cette Esclave qui devient la maîtresse de cette famille, & les branches qui en dépendent. (2:308)

> [If the captive is a girl, given to a household where there is nobody of her sex in a position to sustain the lineage, it is good fortune for this household and for her. All the hope of the family is placed in this captive who becomes the mistress of this family and the branches dependent on it.]

Although, as we have seen, the achievements of an individual were often inscribed on his body, the body is not a permanent, self-contained subject. Signifiers on a body are not really on that body but on the locus in the social system that that body fills, much as a job description in a bureaucracy. That job can be filled, and the same status assumed, by someone else, who really is not someone else at all but the same person.

As Lafitau continued: "Si c'est un homme qui ressuscite un Ancien, un Considérable, il devient considérable lui-même, & il a de l'autorité dans le Village, s'il sçait soûtenir par son mérite personnel le nom qu'il prend" (2:308) [If the captive is a man who requickens an Ancient, a man of consequence, he becomes important himself and has authority in the village if he can sustain by his own personal merit the name which he takes]. A certain level of cooperation and skill from the adoptee is assumed, which reaffirms the strength of the whole system.

A prisoner of war was generally awarded to a family that had recently lost a member, not always in war, but also occasionally to recompense a death due to natural causes. Nicolas Perrot, in a chapter on mourning, stated that on the death of a chief or other important member of the village, the community observed one year of mourning, "au bout de laquelle les parents s'assemblent pour adopter une personne capable de remplir la charge du mort, et qui soit du mesme rang. A l'égard des femmes, filles ou garçons, ils en usent pareillement, du mesme age et du pareil sexe" (36) [at the end of which time the relatives assemble to adopt a person who is qualified to assume the office of the dead chief, and who must be of the same rank. As for women, girls, or boys, a similar usage prevails, (the adopted one being) of the same age and sex (as the dead) (1:84)]. In Perrot's account, this adoptee was not necessarily a prisoner of war, and his or her adoption was not an alternative to torture or vengeance. This custom prolonged the life of the Jesuit Pierre Millet, for though a prisoner taken from Fort Frontenac, when he was adopted "on me fit un trait d'amy en me donnant pour un Capitaine mort de maladie depuis longtems, plutost que pour un de ceux qui avoient esté tuez à lattaque des francois" (JR 64: 90–91) [a friendly act was done me by giving me instead of a Chief who had died long before of disease, rather than for one of those who had been killed in the attack on the French]. Because he replaced a man of high status, he was accorded that man's respect, and as he did not replace a casualty of war, he was less likely to be tortured to avenge that death.

When prisoners of war were brought back to a village, the families who had recently lost members apparently regarded requickening and vengeance as alternatives equally satisfactory for assuaging their grief. Lafitau described the scene as follows:

> Un ancien déclare le partage qu'on en a fait, les Nations alliées, ou les personnes à qui ils sont donnez, & le nom de ceux ou de celles qu'ils doivent remplacer. On distribuë aussi en même temps les chéveleures lesquelles tiennent lieu d'un esclave, & remplacent aussi une personne. (2:271)

> [An elder declares the allotment made of them, the confederated tribes or the persons to whom they are to be given and the names of the men and women whom they are to replace. At the same time, scalps which take the place of a captive and replace a person are distributed.]

Scalps or other signs of vengeance, rather than the torture of the captive, might also recompense the grieving family. It was likely members of this same family who had urged the war party to go out seeking scalps and captives. Jonathan Carver may have copied Lafitau when he wrote, "A herald is sent round the village or camp, to give notice that such as have lost any relation in the late expedition are desired to attend the distribution which is about to take place" (343). Following the two economies of vengeance and replacement, there were two totally different means of compensating for the death of a family member.

Because the unit of subjectivity in Amerindian society was not the individual but the position in a network of kinship, war, and labor relationships, the name affixed to a certain position did not always refer to the same individual. The Jesuit Barthelemy Vimont, in the *Relation of 1642*, told how "Une mère ou un parent qui ayme tendrement son fils ou sa fille; ou quelqu'un de ses proches, le fait resusciter par une affection de le voir auprès de soy: transportant l'amour qu'elle portoit au deffunct, à celuy ou à celle que se charge de son nom" (*JR* 22: 288–89) [Mothers or other relatives who love a son, or a daughter, or any of their kindred, cause such persons to be resuscitated, through a desire to see them close by them, transferring the affection that they felt for the deceased to the persons who take their names]. Freed from the constraints of Europe's rigid class structure, the representations of the *sauvages* begin the propagation of American myths of equality and merit. One can "make a name for oneself" by associating with one's name achievements in war and hunting or by adopting a name that already bears these marks. The status of the name is insured against one's death, for in that event, the name will pass to another who can perpetuate or improve on it. Requickening or "resuscitation" goes beyond adoption—there is no question of the adoptee being less than a biological relative, because the kinship network is maintained unbroken when a new body replaces a lost one.

Information about adoption and requickening comes almost entirely from the French ethnographic writers, because few English captives understood as well as Millet did the customs that determined their fate. Most imagined only that it wavered between ransom and vengeance, or captivity and torture. In the narratives of New England captives, the protagonist's uncertain status was explained in terms familiar to European society. Moreover, during the wars that rocked the Northeast in the last quarter of the seventeenth century, the practice of selling prisoners to the colonists for eventual ransom or exchange became common enough that captors probably did not usually look at their captives with an eye toward requickening a dead relative. Still, the issue of who held claim to a captive was a sensitive one. The day after Quentin Stockwell was captured in Deerfield, Massachusetts, his captors stopped by the Connecticut River, and "There the Indians marked out upon trays the number of their captives and slain as their manner is. Here was I again in great danger. A quarrel arose about me, whose captive I was, for three took me. I thought I must be killed to end the controversy . . . they agreed to have all a share in me, and I had now three masters and he was my chief master who laid hands on me first" (VC 81). We cannot be certain if the three were jealous about getting a cash reward from the French or hoping to adopt Stockwell into their family, but it is interesting to see evidence of a meritographic language recording the attack on Deerfield. Later, Stockwell intervened to prevent the French from hanging one of his three masters, who called him brother and thanked Stockwell for saving his life.

Any captive is susceptible to the phenomenon of developing sympathy for his captors. Alden Vaughan and Edward Clark address this question (12–13) in abstract terms but do not mention the family relationship that the Indians fostered with their captives. Unlike Millet or Radisson, New England captives often failed to perceive it. Mary Rowlandson alternately evoked a familial tenderness between herself and her master and mistresses and then dismissed it as a relationship better explained by a comparison with slavery or material exchange. She reported that "My master had three squaws, living sometimes with one, and sometimes with another one" (VC 61) and named the three: the old squaw, Wettimore, and the young squaw. She lived most of the time with Wettimore, but, as with Stockwell's three masters, jealousy and money intruded. Toward the end of her captivity, Rowlandson writes, "By that time I was refresht by the old squaw with whom my master was. Wettimore's Maid came to call me home, at which I fell a-weeping; Then the old Squaw told me, to encourage me, that if I wanted victuals I should come to her, and that I should lie there in her wigwam" (VC 61). Here she sounds like an anxious child, yet at earlier points she represented herself as a slave or an orphan, always using the word "master," never father, brother, or husband. When she performed a sewing job and her client paid her with a knife, she reacted not as a capitalist entrepreneur but as a loyal serf: "I carried the knife in, and my Master asked me to give it him, and I was not a little glad that I had anything that they would accept of and be pleased with" (VC 48). When hungry, she circulated from one wigwam to the next seeking food, which the Indian ethic of hospitality and sharing made available to her from any family. Yet the proprietary interest of the master returned when her son was beaten and sold by his master for returning late from a visit to his mother. Rowlandson's captivity resonates with the memory of slavery in the United States, not with the intercultural family ties of more successful adoptees like Radisson, Mary Jemison, or John Jewitt.

Once one understands something of the northeastern Indians' customs of adoption and requickening, the captivity situation acquires a powerful new meaning, one rarely understood by the authors of the captivity narratives or by their critics. Adoption by an Indian band offered not just an escape from the strictures of colonial life, an escape that notorious transculturated captives such as Eunice Williams, Gonzalo Guerrero, and Mary Jemison embraced, it literally offered a new identity. If the Indians fully accepted such adoptees and did not expect that they would display the habits of their old life, or seek to return to it, it was because they had an existing system for the re-creation of the identity of a dead member of the band in the body of a new adoptee. That this has not been recognized may be because, although many captives write of being adopted into a family, few express an awareness that their new identity replaces that of a deceased member of the same family. It may be that Indian families did not often wish to confer such an identity on a European captive who had little prior knowledge of the necessary skills and customs to perform in the new identity. Yet when we take this ethnological fact and look again at the captivity histories, we get a profound new meaning for the potential to create a new identity in America.

The assimilation of adoptees could be difficult, for they both were and were not identical with their previous versions. As Lafitau wrote, "leurs parens & leurs amis pleurent les morts que ces esclaves remplacent . . . la vûë de ces esclaves rappelle un souvenir amer, et renouvelle la douleur qu'on a euë de les avoir perdues" (2:271) [their relatives and friends, are still weeping for the dead whom these captives replace . . . of whom the sight of these captives recalls a bitter recollection, renewing their grief in their loss]. This grief was both strong and sincere, and volatile and indeterminate, for it could be assuaged either by vengeance or by re-quickening. The choice might be delayed as the victim suffered, even though the body of the future adoptee might be harmed by torture. The family could starve and torture him for weeks, only to then heal, feed, and revive him so as to replace his dead counterpart. Many considerations might affect the decision, such as potential hunting ability, fertility, or the likeness in age and demeanor to the lost person. For example, Le Jeune's *Relation* for 1637 told of a captive awarded to a Huron named Saouandaouascouay, who hesitated over the fate of his new charge:

Mon neveu il faut que tu sçache qu'à la premiere nouvelle que je reçeus que tu estois en ma disposition, je fus merveuilleusement joyeux, m'imaginant que celuy que j'ay perdu en guerre estoit comme re-suscité & retournoit en son païs, je pris en mesme temps resolution de te donner la vie, je pensois desià à te preparer une place dans ma cabane & faisois estat que tu passerois doucement avec moy le reste de tes jours, mais maintenant que je te vois en cét estat les doigts emportez, & les mains à demy pourries, je change d'avis, & je m'asseure que tu aurois toy-mesme regret maintenant de vivre plus long temps. (*JR* 13:52–55)

[My nephew, thou must know that when I first received news that thou wert at my disposal, I was wonderfully pleased, fancying that he whom I lost in war had been, as it were, brought back to life, and was returning to his country. At the same time I resolved to give thee thy life; I was already thinking of preparing thee a place in my cabin, and thought that thou wouldst pass the rest of thy days pleasantly with me. But now I see thee in this condition, thy fingers gone and thy hands half rotten, I changed my mind, and am sure that thou thyself wouldst now regret to live longer.]

Handicaps resulting from mutilation were only one liability the pris-oner faced. If the grief for the dead one was recent or strong, the captive's death was assured, claimed Lafitau. Aged or crippled prisoners were usually killed; young, able-bodied ones were adopted; and the most elaborate tortures were reserved for prominent warriors. Lahontan con-curred that although a prisoner who could prove that he had never taken a life might be spared and adopted, "s'il y a des preuves que ce misérable prisonnier ait tué des femmes, ou des enfants durant sa vie, ces jeunes Bourreaux le ménent au Bucher où ils lui font souffrir ces cruautez atroces" (2:185) [If evidence be brought that the poor Slave has kill'd either Women or Children in his lifetime, the young Executioners lead him to a Woodpile, where he is forc'd to undergo the dismal Torments (2:80)].

The capturer also was recognized in the economies of adoption and torture. The warrior who took the prisoner got to keep his or her posses-sions; also, "La cabane à qui l'esclave est donné, doit répondre à ce present par un autre si elle lui donne la vie" (2:272) [The household to which the captive is given should respond to this present by another (given to the capturer), if it grants him life]. But if he were tortured, a "pleasure" enjoyed by the entire village except the family to whom the prisoner was offered as a replacement (most other commentators do not concur with Lafitau on this last detail), the payment devolved upon the whole village. Both the labor of capturing and the pleasure of torturing had a price. These details about the debts and obligations associated with adoption are from Lafitau, as most other *mœurs des sauvages* authors concentrate on the gruesome details of torture, not on the determination of who suffers, who tortures, and in whose name.

Hennepin articulated the conflicts of adoption particularly well, for, though a missionary, he was not eager for martyrdom when taken prisoner by the Nadouessiou nation, at the headwaters of the Mississippi. Hennepin was prone to exaggeration and histrionics, as La Salle's description of him and Hennepin's commercial exploitation of the experience in his publications suggest, yet historians agree that he really was a prisoner. Regardless of the veracity of his tale, he identified the conflicting impulses of wealth, revenge, and mercy that motivated his captors.

Hennepin first meets the Nadouessiou as an explorer and potential trader and follows the practices proven effective by other explorers like Champlain and Joutel; he offers six hatchets in return for hospitality. Together they smoke the calumet Hennepin carries, which assures him of a peaceful reception. But Hennepin realizes that this exchange, if extended to its logical conclusion, is not in his favor, for he is lost and powerless and his need for assistance is potentially infinite, while his supply of commodities is limited. He does not take on a productive economic role in his new home as Rowlandson did with her sewing. Like a paranoid tourist, he suspects his hosts of a deliberate and sinister campaign to gradually relieve him of all his articles of exchange: "ils se servoit d'autres Biays pour avoir les marchandises de nos Canoteurs petit à petit, n'osant les prendre hautement, comme il le pouvait, crainte d'être blamé par ceux de sa nation de lacheté que les plus braves ont en horreur" [(they) employed other devices to get by degrees the goods of our canoemen, not daring to take them openly, as he might have done, for fear of being accused by his own people of cowardice, which the bravest hold in horror].[24] The only motive for protecting him is to attract other Frenchmen who might follow his path and come to redeem him. As he was taken hostage on the Mississippi where it today borders Iowa, far from his captors' home, they are obliged to interrupt their war party against the Miami to take Hennepin and his guides back upstream. This suits those who want his "marchandises" but angers "le Chef du party nommé Aquipaguetin, qui avoit eu un de ses fils tué par les Miamis" (216) [the chief of the party named Aquipaguetin, one of whose sons had been killed by the Miamis (211)]. This chief theatrically demonstrates his grief and the revenge that motivated the war party, "il faisait gemir un de ses fils pour emouvoir les Guerriers à compassion & pour les obliger de nous tuer, et de poursuivre leur ennemis à fin de vanger la mort de son fils" (227) [one of his sons . . . he caused to weep . . . in order to excite his warriors to compassion, and oblige them to kill us and pursue their enemies to avenge his son's death (217)].[25] He also asks the French to contribute trade goods to "cover" the death of another relative whose bones he carries with him.

Once they reach the nation, Hennepin and his companions are treated exactly like adopted prisoners of war, as described in other accounts, "ils s'assemblerent pour déliberer de nous, ils nous distribuent separément, et nous donnerent à trois Chefs de familles, à la place de trois de leurs enfants qui avoient esté tué en guerre" (233) [(they) assembled to deliberate about us. They distributed us separately, and gave us to three heads of families in place of three of their own children who had been killed in war (220–21)]. Hennepin is ill and too weak to walk, and his adopted family cares for him. They carry him around on a sort of bier and prescribe treatment in the sweat lodge for his illness. Hennepin says that within a few weeks he became dearly beloved by his captors, who denounce those who stole his commodities and offer to repay him in beaver pelts. From helpless tourist, Hennepin transforms himself into savvy entrepreneur.

In discussing the adoption or torture of prisoners of war, we have passed over the crucial question of the production of these prisoners. What motivated warriors to take prisoners rather than scalps? At what point did the need for replacements or the thirst for vengeance motivate the organization of a war party? According to Lafitau and several others, it was the women who determined the fate of the prisoners, as it was generally men who were lost in war and whose labor power had to be replaced; in most accounts it is also women who press for wars in order that they might have these prisoners. Le Moyne de Morgues's engraving 18 in deBry's *Florida* shows a group of widows kneeling before the chief of the tribe, heads in hands. The caption reads, "The wives of the soldiers who have fallen in battle or died of disease assemble before the chief on a certain day. They approach him with loud demonstrations of sorrow. . . . They beg him to avenge the death of their husbands." Hennepin's tale of Aquipaguetin urging vengeance for the death of his son is therefore an exception in this regard. An account in the *Relation de 1642* reverses the cycle of vengeance and adoption by placing the onus on the adoptees themselves. Adoption becomes not the successful completion or balance of vengeance but its beginning, as "celui qui tirer le nom d'un homme tué en guerre s'oblige de venger son mort" [He who takes the name of a man killed in war is obliged to revenge his death (my translation)].[26] A macabre, accursed quest, where one dies before one is born and then must revenge one's own death!

Regardless of whether a prisoner was tortured or adopted, or in other words, whether the economy of vengeance or of recompense might prevail in a certain instance, the cycle of war continued. For the adoptee was still eligible, or obligated according to the *Relation of 1642*, to avenge the death of the individual whom he requickened, and the victim of torture had every expectation of being avenged by his compatriots. A prisoner's fate was oblivion. As Lahontan put it, describing the destruction and re-creation of identity that he toyed with himself: "Dès qu'ils sont liez, ils sont considérez comme morts de leur Parents, aussi bien que de leur propre Nation" (2:186) [As soon as they are put in Chains, their Relations and the whole Nation to which they retain, look upon 'em as dead (2:81)]. And if the prisoner should escape, "ils seroient méconnus même de leurs plus proches, & personne ne voudroit absolument les recevoir" (2:186) [they would be contemn'd by their nearest Relations, and no body would receive 'em (2:81)]. This, of course, freed the prisoner to assume a new identity, because his position in his former nation was suspended, awaiting vengeance or requickening, and he could not return to reclaim that former identity. Although Indian society was made up of relational rather than stable, individuated subjects, it did arguably offer more respect for a person's life than European society of that era or ours. A French soldier dead on the battlefield would be the subject of special mourning only because he subordinated his life to the pursuit of collective (or alien) geopolitical interests; he was means to an end. The Native American "guerrier," on the other hand, served his own interests, or in a war of vengeance and adoption that interest was embodied through the equivalence established in requickening. To many French observers, the *sauvages américains* demonstrated a great respect for honor and for human life, in spite of "barbaric" techniques of warfare and torture.

Torture

Torture takes a privileged place in nearly every ethnographic description of the Indians of northeastern America—it might be considered the northern equivalent of cannibalism, an obligatory part of the savagist representation. Although it did not find its way into the name that Europeans gave the natives and their locale, as "Carib" spawned "Caribbean" and "cannibal," torture was an almost inescapable part of writing about the Indians of the Northeast. Although no ethnohistorian has argued that it did not really occur, as W. Arens has for cannibalism, torture became so obligatory in colonial descriptions of the Indians that one suspects some writers of simply repeating what they had read and heard without ever witnessing it. On the other hand, there are many reliable and chilling firsthand accounts.

Torture is negative, destructive of flesh, of meaning, and of structured relationships between human beings. Nonetheless, it was potentially substitutive, because Europeans practiced it extensively in interrogations and punishment. European torture had little in common with that portrayed among the Indians, however. The Indian torturer did not go through the charade of extracting a confession or valuable information from the victim. Pierre Boucher was the only observer who claimed of the victim that "l'interrogeant de temps en temps de l'estat de son pays,

& des choses qu'ils desiroient sçavoir: & s'ils voyent qu'il leur dissimule quelque chose, il luy redoublent ses tourmens" (130) [he is being inter-rogated from time to time as to the condition of his country and other things that they desire to be informed of; and if they see that he is hiding any thing they increase his torture (67)]. Elaine Scarry theorizes torture as withdrawing from the victim his place in the world, the relations between his body and its surroundings. In extracting a bogus confession, the torturer destroys the truth of reference, and in blocking all sensory input save that of pain, he shrinks the victim's world down to the size of his body. None of this applies to the almost chivalric torture of the *sauvages*. Rather than deprive the victim of any national identity, the Indians' method of torture staged a contest of honor between the two nations.

Both torturer and victim tried to reinforce the links between the victim, his nation, and his past actions in order to celebrate his punish-ment and the honor being symbolically transferred from his nation to that of the torturers. Lafitau constructed this dialogue: " 'N'es-tu pas de telle nation ennemie de la nôtre, qui a tué plusieurs de nos pères, de nos frères, de nos femmes, de nos enfants, et de nos alliés?'—'Oui, vraiment,' dit l'esclave, 'et j'en fais gloire; je ne suis pas épargné moi-meme à vous faire du mal' " (2:302) ["Are you not of such and such a tribe hostile to ours, which has killed many of our fathers, our brothers, our wives, and our allies?" "Yes, truly" says the captive. "I am, and I glory in it. I have never spared myself in doing you harm"]. Rather than plead, lie, or promise, the victim's proper role was to defy and insult his captors, to taunt them with the truth of his crimes against them. Frequently, the victim's litany of his heroic achievements took the form of a death song or "chanson de mort," which was often rehearsed for members of his own nation before departing with a war party. Cadwallader Colden sum-marized the content of this "death song" when he told of the torture of an Iroquoian prisoner by Christian Indians in Montreal. The victim walked to the place of execution, "with as much indifference as ever Martyr did to the Stake. While they were torturing him, he continued singing, that he was a Warrior brave and without Fear; that the most cruel Death coud not shake his Courage; that the most cruel Torment should not draw an indecent Expression from him . . . that he had the comfort to reflect, that he had made many Frenchmen suffer as he did now" (122). This was a grotesque drama in which both parties played roles, for a victim who showed pain or did not sing a *chanson de mort* was the object not only of contempt, but also of real disappointment. Taking this code to an extreme, the imaginative and satiric Bossu recounted how a Monsieur d'Artaguette, sentenced to be burned to death by the Chickasaw,

> . . . échappa à ce supplice par un st[r]atagème assez singulier. Comme la langue des Sauvages lui étoit familière, il s'en servit en cette occasion pour invectiver contre ses bourreaux . . . *Vous êtes des chiens, puisques vous avez brûlé mes Chefs, je veux l'être aussi; je ne crains ni le feu, ni la mort, parce que je suis un véritable homme; faites-moi bien souffrir, car c'est ce que je demande.* Les *Tchikachas*, voyant sa résolution & sa fermeté, le prirent pour un homme extraordinaire, & lui accorderent la vie.[27]

> [. . . escaped this ordeal through a rather peculiar trick. Since he was familiar with their language, he shouted insults at the executioners. He untied himself and threw at them everything he could reach. "You are dogs! You have burned my chiefs, and I want to be burned too. I am not afraid of death or fire. I am a real man. I demand that you torture me." When the Indians saw his firmness of purpose and his resolution, they decided that he was an extraordinary man and granted him his life. (173)]

As in the tale of his own adoption and tattooing, Bossu demonstrates the resonance of "savage" customs on European manners by introducing a French character who takes part in these customs and yet defies them, claiming for himself a special privilege or power emblematic of his cultural superiority. I have never found any analogous account of mercy being awarded to an Indian victim, but the spirit of defiance or "fermeté" was valued so much that LeClercq, Lafitau, and several of the *Jesuit Relations* reported that witnesses of the torture of an especially firm victim would give his blood to their children to drink, smear it on their bodies, or eat small pieces of the victim's heart, hoping to acquire some of his fortitude. This practice partakes of the economic of cannibalism well known from Montaigne's "On Cannibals," whereby the power of the slain enemy could be incorporated by the eater.[28]

Whereas for seventeenth-century New England captives torture was an unspeakable horror from which they were fortunately excused, Jesuit captives Brébeuf, Jogues, and Millet were victims of it. For Jesuit writers and Catholic readers, the parallels between martyrdom and Indian torture worked in both directions, elevating Indian converts to the dignity of martyrs and winning missionaries respect within the Amerindian value system. The strength required to maintain one's honor and not show pain was ascribed to Christianity when Jerome Lalemant wrote,

> On nous a dit que les Hiroquois voulans brusler quelque prisonnier, luy demandent s'il prie, c'est à dire s'il est baptisé, s'il respond qu'il a receu ce divin Sacrement, ils perdent esperance de le faire gemir dans ses tourmens, se persuadans que la Foy donne de la constance à une ame. (*JR* 31:122–23)

> [We have been told that the Hiroquois, intending to burn any prisoner, ask him if he prays,—that is to say, whether he is baptized. If he answer that he has received this divine Sacrament, they lose hope of making him groan in his torments,—persuading themselves that the Faith gives constancy to a soul.]

In the account by Christophe Regnault of the martyrdom of Jean de Brébeuf in the *Relation de 1649*, there is an inversion of the common substitution trope of finding Christian correlatives for Indian customs; instead, Brébeuf's fortitude under torture resembles that displayed by the stoutest of native victims. Brébeuf complied with the custom of singing the *chanson de mort* by substituting a sermon for this song:

> Pendant tous ces tourments, le Pere de Brebœuf souffroit comme un rocher insensible aux feux et aux flammes, qui estonnoient tous les boureaux qui le tourmentoient. Son zele estoit si grand qu'il preschoit tousjours a ces infideles pour tascher a les conuertir; ses bourreaux indignez contre luy de ce qu'il leur parloit tousjours de Dieu et de leur conuersion. (*JR* 34:28–31)

> [During all these torments, Father de Brebœuf endured like a rock, insensible to fire and flames, which astonished all the bloodthirsty wretches who tormented him. His zeal was so great that he preached continually to these infidels, to try to convert them. His executioners

were enraged against him for constantly speaking to them of God and
their conversion.]

The fortitude of torture victims becomes one of the most powerful
elements of the representation of the *sauvage*, because the two different
cultures' visions of heroism so neatly coincide in the stoic, silent sufferer.
But by substituting his proselytizing sermon for the *chanson de mort,*
Brébeuf subverted the customs of torture, for his heroic forbearance did
not enhance the power of those who conquered him when he patroniz-
ingly claimed to suffer for their lost souls. In response, one of his torturers subverts Christian rites: "un miserable huron renégat, qui de-
meuroit captif avec les Iroquois, que le Pere de Brebœuf avoit autrefois
instruit et baptisé, L'entendant parler du Paradis et du St Baptesme
fut irité et luy dist, Echon, c'est le nom du Pere de Brebœuf en Huron,
Tu dis que le Baptesme et les souffrances de cette vie meine droit en
Paradis, tu irras bien tost, Car je te vais baptiser et te bien faire souffrir,
afin d'aller au plus tost dans ton Paradis: Le barbare ayant dit cela, prist
un chaudron plein d'eau toute bouillante, et le renverse sur son corps
par trois diverse fois en derision du St baptesme" (*JR* 34:26–29) [a
wretched huron renegade,—who had remained a captive with the Iroquois, and whom Father de Brebœuf had formerly instructed and baptized,—hearing him speak of Paradise and Holy Baptism, was irritated,
and said to him, "Echon," that is Father de Brebœuf's name in Huron,
"thou sayest that Baptism and the sufferings of this life lead straight to
Paradise; thou wilt go soon, for I am going to baptize thee, and to make
thee suffer well, in order to go the sooner to thy Paradise." The barbarian, having said that, took a kettle full of boiling water, which he poured
over his body three different times, in derision of Holy baptism]. Perhaps with reference to the famous martyrdom of Brébeuf, later French
ethnographers seemed inclined to regard Indian torture through a comparison with religious martyrs tortured for their beliefs. For example,
Lafitau likened the native victim's suffering to that of the martyr: "Cet
héroïsme est réel, et il est l'effet d'un courage grand et noble. Ce que
nous avons admiré dans les martyrs de la primitive Eglise, et qui était en
eux l'effet de la grâce et d'un miracle, est nature en ceux-ci, et l'effet de la

force de leur esprit" (2:280) [This heroism is real and the result of a great and noble courage. What we have admired in the martyrs of the primitive church which was, in them, the result of grace and a miracle, is natural to these people and the result of the strength of their morale]. Always anxious to find evidence of God's revelation among the American Indians, Lafitau here again relates them to the people of the *premiers temps*, this time not the barbarians but Christians. In a strange anticipation and yet inversion of deist philosophy, Lafitau naturalizes sacred suffering and finds in the creatures of nature the same virtues that God bestowed on the chosen people of the early church. The Indians acquired this fortitude through painful tests, such as two men holding a burning ember between their arms, and through acclimatization to cold and hunger. Though the *sauvages* suffer tortures bravely for a different motive, the missionary could also be tortured after their fashion and, he believed, for their salvation.

Torture destroys the body as a sensitive organism, and in its Native American version it paradoxically also destroys the fundamental relationship between mutilation and pain. The victim was obliged to conceal his pain by a code of honor that resembled the martyr's grace. Denial of the flesh was carried to an extreme if the torturer could not force a cry of agony in response to mutilation. Champlain described his Algonquin allies burning Iroquois all over their bodies, and though at first he reports, "les pauvres miserables sentans ce feu faisoient des cris si haut que c'estoit chose estrange à ouyr" [the poor wretches, feeling the fire, would utter such loud cries that it was awful to hear], further down the page he seems to retract this, stating, "Mais neantmoins ils endurent si constamment tous les tourmens qu'on leur fait, que ceux qui les voyent en demeurent estonnez" (2:136–37) [Nevertheless, they endure all the tortures inflicted on them with such constancy that those who see them are struck with astonishment].

Torture also destroys the relations of signification inscribed in the body, such as meritography. Surprisingly, in light of all the isomorphic techniques of signification we have seen ascribed to the Amerindians, there is no relationship described between certain mutilations or certain parts of the body and elements of revenge that the torturers wished to

inflict or signify. The improvised, Christian context of the special tortures inflicted on Brébeuf is exceptional. In typical accounts of Indian
torture, fingernails are pulled out, fingertips bitten off and burned in
pipes, tendons stretched and snapped, red hot hatchets hung in a neck-
lace against the victim's skin, the scalp is removed and hot coals placed
on the exposed skull, but the whole process follows a routine that does
not comment on the identity of the victim. If the body is frequently a
locus of social communication, the destruction of body parts in torture
seems to be not another means of inscription but a destruction or negation of the possibility of individual signification. The victim's valor as a
warrior, which often was visible on his skin in meritographs, gets appropriated by the torturers' nation *in toto*. The social capital accrued by one
warrior was taken and credited to the common account, quite differently
from the status of an adoptee. And though in state-sponsored torture
and capital punishment a similar pattern of collective vengeance is present, the supposed equivalence is a negative one, between the murder of
the victim and the execution of the murderer. In Amerindian society, the
practices of revenge and torture did not follow an economics of retribution calculated on an individual level. A murder within the group could
be compensated positively, with presents given by the murderers' group
to the victims' group, and the revenge of torturing a prisoner of war
came not from the death and pain avenging that suffered by a previous
victim, but from the acquisition and internalization by the torturing
band of the power the victim displayed while alive. Thus, even when
torture and vengeance were chosen over adoption and requickening, the
result was an increase in social value, not merely retributive destruction.
The American Indian customs are not comparable to capital punishment in the contemporary United States.

It is easy to propose explanations for the prominent role accorded
torture by explorer-ethnographers and missionaries. It is more difficult
to interpret the role of torture within Amerindian culture because ethnocentric reactions by the colonists were so strong. Missionary writers
deplored such barbarism, and the Jesuits had some success at suppressing the practice among the Hurons, but in their descriptions of torture
the sublime imagination of Christ's and the holy martyrs' suffering

clearly colored some of the most graphic portrayals, and the outrage shifted to sensationalism. Moreover, the self-righteous denunciations of barbarism shared by all Western cultures were hypocritical given the techniques and prevalence of state and church-sponsored torture in Europe. And this self-righteousness was far from harmless. Frequently, the commanders of American colonies cited the Indians' use of torture as sufficient justification to employ the same methods in defense of their colony. Champlain, in explaining his belief that the Montagnais prisoner in the episode outlined above should have been executed, wrote of the Indians, "ils jugeront que nous aurons peur & crainte d'eux . . . ils se rendront plus insolents, audacieux & insupportables" (3:212) [they would judge that we were in fear and terror of them, and that if we let them off so easily they would become more insolent, bold, and unbearable]. Lafitau regretted the French assimilation of barbarism, while he admitted its necessity:

> Les Peuples les plus doux sont forcez de sortir eux-mêmes hors des bornes de leur douceur naturelle, quand ils voyent qu'elle sert de prétexte à des voisins barbares d'en devenir plus fiers & plus intraitables. Les François en sont un exemple. Lorsque pour se venger des Iroquois, on leur a permis de traiter leurs prisonniers, comme ils traitoient les nôtres, ils l'on fait avec tant de fureur & d'acharnement qu'ils n'ont cédé en rien à ces Barbares, si même ils ne les ont surpassez. La vérité est, qu'il fallait en user ainsi. (2:289)

> [The gentlest people are forced to put aside their natural gentleness when they see that it becomes a pretext for barbarous neighbors to become prouder and more intractable. The French are an example of this. When, to avenge themselves on the Iroquois, they were permitted to treat their prisoners as the Indians treated ours, they did it with so much ferocity and zeal that they were, in no way, inferior to the barbarians but even surpassed them. The truth is that it was necessary to treat them this way.]

When given the opportunity, the more "civilized" French were also more barbarous than the Indians. Cadwallader Colden turned this French policy to propaganda purposes in *The History of the Five Indian*

Nations. He recounted how Frontenac sent a party to the Niagara peninsula to attack the Iroquois and applied a policy that Lahontan also noted
and reproved: "They surprised likewise a cabin, where they took some
Men and Women Prisoners; and four of them were publickly burnt alive
at Montreal. So far the Count Frontenac thought it more proper to
imitate the Indians in their most savage Cruelties, than to instruct
them, by his Example, in the Compassion of the Christian Doctrine"
(161–62). John Easton, a Quaker Rhode Islander, was a rare dissenter
who, in his history of King Philip's War, accused the Europeans alone of
torture: "It is tru the Indians generaly ar very barbarous peopell but in
this war I have not herd of ther tormenting ani but that the English
army Cote [caught] an old indian and tormented him" (13–14). Although European invaders misunderstood Indian warfare, they knew
how to use it and its "barbaric" techniques to their own "civilized"
advantage.

The confusion between wars of vengeance and wars of interest, wars of
political motivation and those to advance commercial interests, only
reproduced a similar obfuscation endemic to European wars and their
ideological bases. But the confusion of cultural contact did eventually
lead to the Europeans learning a great deal from the Native Americans.
The nexus of collective motivation, consensual command, and individual achievement in Indian war provided a model that Western political
thought has tried in vain to imitate. The Indians' techniques of guerrilla
warfare have caught on around the world, if they were not already
indigenous to oppressed peoples everywhere. The image of the sovereign
family governed by its own laws, protected from the savage exterior by a
code of violent vigilante retribution endures in American popular consciousness to this day and perhaps contributes to cycles of gang warfare
and domestic violence. What Richard Slotkin saw happening in Viet-
nam (562–64), I have tried to show can be construed from colonial
representations of Amerindians to apply to what occurs within our society. War is savagery, but savage war is part of our civilization.

Borders : Niagara, 1763

The Seven Years' War and the War of 1812 defined the border between the United States and Canada. The first was part of a transatlantic conflict in which England and France contested for valuable American colonies. The second was a war of territorial expansion with circumstantial ties to the Napoleonic wars, as the young, postcolonial nation fought against its former metropole and against Indians in the South and Midwest resisting further invasion of their lands. At no point along the more than three thousand miles of border between the United States and Canada is its history more palpable than on the "Niagara Frontier," as residents of western New York call it. From either bank of the river, citizens gaze across it with a different nationalistic regard, conditioned by a different war. The border, its monuments and narratives, can serve as a metaphor for the assymetrical divisions between French and English, American and Canadian, European and Amerindian in North American history and literature.

How was this border drawn? A straight line along the forty-ninth parallel, from Lake of the Woods in Ontario and Minnesota, to Blaine, Washington, has defined the western half of the border since 1818. This is a characteristically Anglo-American border similar to the line William Byrd II surveyed between North Carolina and Virginia, a straight line existing in theory before fact, conceived by geopoliticians before it was surveyed or explored and intended to prevent conflicts before they turned violent. But in the East, the frontier lies near the center of Canadian history and geography. The St. Lawrence has been the cradle of New France and of Canada, yet it also forms the international border from Kingston, Ontario (the old site of Fort Frontenac or Cadaraqui, established by and for La Salle with permission from Governor Frontenac in 1673), to the St. Regis Mohawk reserve near Massena, New York. These Mohawk are descendants of the bands who remained loyal to the English, whereas Caughnawaga (a name with perhaps more different spellings in its history than any other in this book) outside Montreal was established for French-speaking Catholic bands. It was at Kanawake that Eunice Williams lived from 1704, when she was taken captive along with her father John, until her death in 1785. John Williams wrote the most anti-French captivity narrative of the early eighteenth century, *The Redeemed Captive Returning to Zion*, while Eunice remained in her adopted family, a continuing embarrassment and curiosity to Puritan New England.[1] East of St. Regis the border is again a straight line through the forest. Bostonians and New Yorkers regard Vermont's Northeast Kingdom, the White Mountains, and northern Maine as a frozen wilderness, generally unaware of how different the border looks from the other side. For Québecois, the land south of the St. Lawrence and north of the border contains the heart of traditional francophone life, the river itself is the corridor of modern industry and urban populations, and only north toward the Laurentians and Hudson Bay does wilderness begin.

In the continent's industrial and historical middle, the Great Lakes form a natural barrier between the two nations. At three points between the lakes the two countries face each other across a river, but Sault Ste. Marie and Detroit were still frontier trading posts during the Seven Years' War, and the Anglo-Americans regarded them as enemy territory during Pontiac's rebellion in the 1760s. Indeed, by the Proclamation Line of 1763, the crest of the Alleghenies and Appalachians officially divided the English provinces from Indian territory, placing all the Great Lakes beyond the frontier from the Anglo point of view. Only along the Niagara River is the border the same today as it was between 1763 and 1812. The river must be the shortest with such a large flow in the world and forms an excellent natural barrier. It runs cold, clear, and fast for its entire forty-mile length. Only near Lake Ontario is it safe to cross over in a small boat without danger of being upset in a rapid or swept over the falls. Niagara Falls remains one of the most important tourist destinations in the world and one of the most canonical scenes for travel narrative, as it has been since the Abbé Bréhan de Gallinée first described it in 1669,[2] and Hennepin usurped him with a claim to primacy and a hyperbolic description of a six-hundred-foot drop.

The falls have formed where the Niagara Escarpment, running east-west across the entire Great Lakes region, intersects the river. At the edge of the escarpment on the Canadian side, overlooking orchards on the lakeshore and the gorge that has formed as the falls have eroded the escarpment and retreated upstream, stands a huge column surmounted by a statue of General Isaac Brock, British/Canadian hero of the War of 1812. Brock was killed on October 13, 1812, as he defended his position against U.S. troops, many of whom were shot as they tried to scale the cliff after crossing the river. The Canadian bank of the Niagara is lined with several smaller memorials to battles of this war, all celebrating the British forces that held the advance of the renegade Americans. On the U.S. side, however, there is no memorial for the battle of La Belle Famille, where five hundred soldiers died fighting the British and Iroquois on July 24, 1759. There is only Fort Niagara, a large medieval-style fortress restored to a combination of its appearance during the two wars. Although this is the only major monument the United States has dedicated to the battles of the war, the fort actually belonged to the British, French, and U.S. troops at different times in its history. La Salle built the first one in 1668, Denonville another in 1687 after his victory over the Seneca at Ganondagon (a battle recounted in detail by Lahontan), only to tear it down and retreat the following year. Here William Johnson and his Iroquoian troops besieged the French two days after the victory at La Belle Famille. Fort Niagara was crucial to the security of the overextended French colony, for without it fur traders would be forced to abandon Detroit as well and retreat to the Ottawa River–Lake Nippissing portage route followed by Champlain and Sagard in the early 1600s, when the Iroquois controlled the Niagara frontier.

Niagara, then, is at a geographic and historical nexus. The current border between nations, it has been in the past the border between nation and colony (United States and Canada), between two colonies and their languages (English America and New France), between enemy Hurons and Iroquois, and between East and Midwest in the heyday of the Erie Canal. The river marks a historical dissymmetry, however. Imperialist capitalism is accustomed to continual expansion, remembering only victorious battles, running over borders and erasing them in order to establish a newer, farther border that is quickly represented as the only one of any importance. To repeat Thoreau's words, "while we are clearing the forest in our westward progress, we are accumulating a forest of books in our rear," books "effectually forgotten and not implied by our literature and newspapers." Thus Canada remembers only the events of the last (and for the northern party, most successful) war fought on the border, in 1812–14, and the United States, which contains many earlier borders, does little to remember any of them.

The border, "la frontera," "la frontière," has recently become a critical term in literary and cultural studies. The work of Gloria Anzaldua and Ramon Saldivar deconstructs the geopolitical view of a border as a discrete line of secure division that separates cultures through the power of politically imagined communities. They see the border instead as a permeable region where communities challenge and resituate racial, linguistic, and cultural categories. Chicano residents on both sides of the Mexico–United States border regard it not as a line but a place with its own distinct culture. It is their hope that discrimination against Chicanos and the ignorance of Spanish and indigenous history and communities in the southwestern United States can be overcome through a new appreciation for frontiers as a space of intercultural contact, rather than a one-sided limit of Anglo-American expansion. Spaniards began settling the Rio Grande valley of New Mexico before 1600 and explored it in the 1540s, and therefore the Southwest has a colonial history even older than Virginia and New France.

The U.S.-Canadian border has not inspired a theoretical discourse of "la frontière." Lacking the urgency of poverty, massive migration, and intense cultural conflict, this border might be characterized by the absence of a difference. Canadians look at the border with ambivalence.

They might wish it to help inscribe a distinctive national character, but perhaps because the conflict between francophone and anglophone within the country is more salient, the border seems to call attention to its superfluity, to the homogeneity of middle-class anglophone North America. Yet as a geographic figure of inquiry into history and literature, the United States–Canada border can be a valuable impetus for bilingual and multicultural study. The forests of the Great Lakes and St. Lawrence valley were not the site of fantastic imperial cities like Cuzco, nor of epic wars involving thousands like Cortés's attack on Tenochtitlan, but they do have a native and colonial history that remains important. Arguably the need for Spanish studies is greater than for French, but it was against French colonialism and Catholicism that the New England Puritans who have maintained hegemony in American history and literature defined themselves in war from the 1680s to the 1760s.

If the Niagara River could serve as a geographic locus for this new paradigm, the end of the Seven Years' War would be the logical temporal divide. Although the European version of the war is named for the years 1756–63, the American seven years are properly from 1754, when George Washington explored and surveyed the west side of the mountains and ambushed the French, to 1760, when the French surrendered Montreal. Histories and curricula in U.S. literature most often choose 1789 or 1790 as the dividing point between colonial and nineteenth-century periods. This date makes sense historically in a nationalist narrative as the time when victory in the War of Independence was secured and the Constitution ratified; it makes sense for literature largely because the genre that matters most to the twentieth century, the novel, did not exist in America before Susannah Rowson and Charles Brockden Brown in the 1790s.

Nonetheless, a better boundary between periods would be 1760. It was the Seven Years' War that transformed the genres in which colonial American literature was most comfortable and provided the setting for many later classics. James Fenimore Cooper titled his best-known book *The Last of the Mohicans: A Narrative of 1757* and centered it around the "massacre" of the British troops by French and Indian warriors at Fort William Henry in that year. This notorious instance of "Indian atrocities" resulted in the death of only 40 or 50 English according to Francis Parkman (2:1193), whereas the British attack on Fort Carillon/Ticonderoga eleven months later saw 550 British die.[3] As Jane Tompkins has shown (94–119), *The Last of the Mohicans* inscribes the importance of racial, gender, and cultural definition and separation during the Jacksonian period. The most important division is, of course, between civilized and savage, but as in Puritan captivity narratives, French is an ambivalent signifier susceptible to assimilation with the "savages." The war also transformed the captivity narrative genre from the religious allegories of the Puritans into tales of assimilation such as James Smith's, Alexander Henry's, and Mary Jemison's, and on the darker side, Indian-hating and anti-French propaganda. As its ideological representations in literature, at historical sites, and in school textbooks all demonstrate, the issues of the "French and Indian War" are still present in U.S. culture.

The Vanishing Frenchman and the Exploring Englishman

In the previous chapter I noted the absence of ethnographic accounts of Indian warfare by English writers. The situation changes, and might even be said to undergo a reversal, after the Seven Years' War. The English, having won title to the coveted Ohio valley, perceived the need for ethnographic intelligence that Cadwallader Colden had expressed in the preface to his 1727 book about the Iroquois: "I know of no Accounts of them Published in English, but what are meer Translations of French Authors. This seems to throw some Reflection on the Inhabitants of this Province, as if we wanted Curiosity to enquire into our own Affairs, and that we were willing to rest satisfied with the Accounts the French give us of our own Indians" (ix). The French, having officially lost control of their network of trading posts and settlements, turned from realistic to romantic portrayals of American Indians, nostalgic figures who, by mourning their own passing are, in an allegorical reflection, mourning the departure of the French colonists. A reading of two texts from shortly after the Seven Years' War, Jean Bernard Bossu's second installment of his adventures and Jonathan Carver's *Travels*, will illustrate how French and English colonial writers exchanged strategies and styles as Ohio and then Louisiana passed to the English.

Bossu's first book, *Nouveaux voyages aux Indes Occidentales*, dealt with events prior to the Treaty of Paris. In 1770–71 the sardonic, rebellious soldier returned to Louisiana, ostensibly to retrieve his effects left there years earlier. A Spanish administration was at this time slowly taking possession of the colony, and much of Bossu's second book, *Nouveaux voyages dans l'Amérique Septentrionale*, is propaganda for the failed French claim to Louisiana. He does not resort to legalistic or nationalistic arguments, however; he speaks through the mouths of sympathetic Indians:

> Ces peuples m'ont paru consternés de cette cession; & n'ayant aucune connoissance du systême politique des Cours Européennes, ils m'ont réitéré ce qu'ils me dirent à mon premier voyage: que les premiers hommes blancs qu'ils virent ici, étoient des François; qu'ils les reçurent à l'exclusion de tout autre peuple; mais qu'ils étoient aujourd'hui fort étonnés de voir que nous les avions abandonnés, sans cependant nous en avoir donné aucun sujet. (110)

> [These people seem to me to be appalled by this cession. Having no acquaintance with the political system of European courts, they repeated to me what they had said on my first trip: that the first white men they saw here were the French whom they welcomed to the exclusion of all other people, but now they were astonished to see that we had deserted them without even giving any reason for it. (45)]

Bossu uses the Vanishing Indian trope, which would become so common with Anglo-American writers in the nineteenth century, but connects it to a Vanishing Frenchman, who surrenders Louisiana with much the same pathos of nobility in the face of injustice. The Allibamon (Alabama) chief Tamathlemingo is so loyal to the French that he refuses the presents offered by English traders: "Le Cacique ne voyant plus les François, se livra à tout son désespoir. Il ne voulut pas que les Anglois profittassent du Fort que sa Nation avoit bâti pour la nôtre. Il ordonna en consequence à ses gens d'y mettre le feu" (136) [The *Cacique*, no longer seeing the French, gave himself up to his despair. He did not want the English to benefit from the fort that his nation had built for us.

Accordingly, he ordered his people to set fire to it (54)]. Tamathlemingo
soon dies from his grief at the French departure and his immoderate
taste for liquor, receiving baptism from a French priest before expiring.

We saw in Chapter 4 that Bossu in his first book claimed to have
perfected a technique of erasing tattoos so that he might be able to
inscribe on his skin a sign of his adoption into the Arkansas tribe but not
be permanently marked by savagery. In that tall tale, the permanent
signifier of identity, so superior to European habits of deceit and disguise, became deceptive once more. In the second book are several episodes where Bossu employs such tricks to awe the Indians into submission. He uses a magnifying glass to start a fire. He and his sidekick, a
Gascon soldier nicknamed Sans-peur (Fearless), construct a large speaking tube to ventriloquize as the ghost of a murdered Frenchman and
frighten a village into delivering up the murderer.

But the most successful technique Bossu acquires is his role as a
medicine man. When he finds an Allibamon man lying apparently dead
of smoke inhalation, Bossu, in a comical scene reminiscent of Lebeau's
use of his law degree in an exorcism and of John Smith's treatment of
another victim of smoke inhalation, conceives a plan to revive him in a
theatrical manner: "je me décorai des marques glorieuses du Doctorat,
en m'attachant au menton une grande barbe postiche. J'endossai une
longue robe, faite de peaux de loutres cousues ensemble. Je couvre mon
chef d'un large bonnet, dont la pointe sembloit menacer le ciel" (148) [I
adorned myself with all the glorious distinctions of the Doctorate. At-
taching a long artificial beard to my chin, I donned a long robe made of
otter skins sewed together. I covered my head with a big cap, the tip of
which threatened the sky (58)]. In reviving the patient he proves the
superiority of European to Indian traditional medicine, and "Le bruit qui
se répandit de cette cure attira de tous côtés ce qu'il y avoit de plus habiles
Docteurs Indiens, qui vinrent pour me voir, & même me consulter,
comme la perle des Jongleurs" (151) [The report which spread about this
cure attracted from everywhere the most able Indian doctors who came
to see me and even to consult me as the best of medicine men (59)]. Bossu
attributes his power to a combination of technology and deceit. When an
Allibamon learns of the new vaccination against smallpox and uses it on

some of his tribesmen, only to see them die, Bossu intervenes to defend him from angry tribesmen and warns the Indians that "ils devoient en cela imiter les hommes blancs, plus éclairés que les rouges, qui n'ont pas l'*écorce parlante* pour s'instruire sur l'art de la Médecine" (171) [they should imitate white men who were more learned than the red who do not have the *speaking bark* to instruct them in the art of medicine (68)]. Bossu is not simply asserting a logocentrism or ethnocentrism. He does understand the difference between European and Native American medicine, as he reminds his correspondent, "Je vous ai dit que les Jongleurs font ici les fonctions de Prêtres, de Médecins, de Chirurgiens, & veulent se faire passer pour Devins" (175) [I have told you that medicine men here perform the duties of priests, physicians, and surgeons and want to be regarded as soothsayers (69)], but the distinction is lost in the will to colonial power: "tant que je passerois pour un grand jongleur, j'aurois une autorité absolue sur eux, & que je ne serois occupé toute la journée qu'à recevoir de présens" (112–13) [that so long as I was considered a medicine man I would have absolute power over them, and that I would be kept busy all day long just receiving presents (46)]. Because the French have lost Louisiana, Bossu has no political structure in which to exercise this power, but he attempts to capitalize on the French reputation for genius in Indian relations and argues that the colonist who can best control the natives should have the right to do so. If he can receive valuable presents without paying for them, he has turned back the clock to the first stages of contact, in which explorers like Cartier benefited from natives' customs of gift giving.

Bossu differs from the missionaries of the previous century in the nature and referent of his conviction of superiority to Amerindian culture. Whereas the Jesuits impressed the Indians with the power of writing, which they believed to be sacred, and tried to use this power to convert them to Catholicism, Bossu offered no religious justification for his deceptions. And whereas the Jesuit missionaries struggled to explain concepts like the Trinity, Heaven, and Resurrection that refer to abstract or absent referents, Bossu mounted a visual demonstration of his power. Guilty of what the Jesuits were often accused of, Bossu did not care if the Allibamons did not truly understand what the power of the doctorate was or how vaccines worked. Deception was now permissible, and though Indian religions were described by Roger Williams or by LeClercq through respectful comparisons with Christianity, Allibamon medicine was to be superceded by Bossu's French medicine, even though it did not fill the same role in life as medicine in Europe. It was not so much that technology had replaced Christianity as the rationale for seizing the land of the American Indians, as that colonization, knowledge, and control had each become its own justification.

In the mid-eighteenth century France began to try to buttress its poor record in the competition for colonies with an emphasis on leadership in science. As Mary Louise Pratt observes in *Imperial Eyes*, a traveler pursuing scientific research might claim the right to travel throughout the colonial world under the immunity of the "anti-conquest." The most ambitious project was the determination of a debate raging among cartographers concerning whether the earth is oblate (flattened at the poles) or prolate (pointed like a football). Maupertius, an adherent of the oblate theory, traveled to Lapland in 1736–37, and La Condamine participated in a larger expedition to Peru and the Amazon basin which consumed ten years, 1735–45. The king of Sweden welcomed the French travelers, whereas the Spanish colonial government in Peru warily granted permission for the scientists to enter territories whose geography and mineral resources had been carefully guarded secrets. Although these scientific expeditions with their delicate instruments and obscure geometrical concerns may seem distant from Bossu's jocular pranks, there is a connection between their innovations in travel, knowledge, and narrative. The scientist journeyed in an abstract space, as if at sea, and thereby claimed to ignore political and cultural boundaries; Bossu traveled in an America where the marvels of crocodiles, rattlesnakes, European medicine, and Indian customs suspended colonial conflicts and establishments. As translator Samuel Dickinson notes, Bossu wrote of traveling to Nachitoches and to the mouth of the Arkansas, both locations of French trading posts, but never mentioned these posts. The Indians in Bossu's text were restored to a fanciful innocence and the land to a plenitude more characteristic of the narratives of initial explorers than of colonial soldiers. Bossu also employed the rhetoric of the "anti-conquest," referring to himself in French in the third person as the prototypical colonial scientist:

> Il s'occupe à herboriser, tantôt dans des vallons, dans de forêts, tantôt sur les collines, ou dans des plaines incultes, bornées par des lacs & des rochers. Il fait les plus utiles réflexions dans une contrée où la nature a prodigué des richesses qu'elle a refusées aux autres parties de la terre. Outre les mines d'or & d'argent qu'elle y a placées, elle y fait croître les plantes les plus précieuses & les plus salutaires.
>
> . . . Tout présente ici de quoi intéresser le Philosophe, le Naturaliste, & le Commerçant.
>
> Le long séjour que j'ai fait dans ce pays, m'à mis à portée de le connoitre, & de m'instruire de tout ce qui concerne les usages & coutumes des peuples qui habitent les rives du grand fleuve de Mississipi. (189–90)

> [I spend my time collecting herbs, sometimes in valleys, in forests, sometimes on hills or in uncultivated plains bordered by lakes and rocks. I make the most useful reflections in a country where nature has lavished riches that she has denied other parts of the earth. Besides gold and silver deposits that she has placed here, nature grows here the most valuable and salutary plants.
>
> . . . All that the Philosopher, the Naturalist, and the Trader are interested in is present here.
>
> My long stay in this country has enabled me to understand it and to instruct myself in all that concerns the customs and habits of the people who live on the banks of the great Mississippi River. (74)]

In these "Rêveries d'un promeneur colonial" ["Reveries of a Colonial Walker"], Bossu, like Rousseau, combined a romantic idealism for the moral virtues of nature and of natural man, the American Indian, with a keenly cynical attitude toward political conflict. While the former is easily and widely recognized as symptomatic of impending romanticism, the latter also demands recognition; French writers in colonial America could not represent land that was no longer part of imperial New France, and Indians who were no longer loyal subjects, in the same manner as they had before 1763. Bossu and later Chateaubriand chose to turn back the clock and represent America as an Eden similar to that described by Columbus and other discoverers. The posts and settlements of Louisiana, which the French had worked so hard to build, disappeared from the literature, sacrificed to an attempt to legitimate the fallen colonial empire by attributing to it a natural innocence.

From Captain John Smith to Benjamin Church to Daniel Boone, the English colonists best acquainted with the ways of the Indians had employed their knowledge against those same Indians in violent conflict. During a period when trade was subordinated to war, this use of intelligence made sense. Thomas Hutchins's appendix, "Reflections on the War with the Savages of America," to William Smith's *Historical Account of General Bouquet's Expedition* (1765) was a systematic primer for frontier warfare, using the experience gathered on the successful mission to retake Fort Pitt and pacify the upper Ohio valley. James Smith, a captive of the Indians during most of the Seven Years' War, wrote in *A Treatise on the Mode and Manner of Indian War* (1812) that these lessons paid off in the following two wars: "the progress we had made in their art of war contributed considerably towards our success in various respects, when contending with Great Britain for liberty" (10). Slotkin and Pearce, reading Anglo-American texts of this era and later, have brilliantly analyzed the representations of savagism as a return of the repressed, where the frontier man is empowered to turn savage in order to exterminate the savages.[4] The dynamic is not limited to violent or negative behavior but includes, as we have seen, writing systems and woodcraft. The paradox of savage yet admirable aspects of Indian culture partakes of the suppression of contradictions inherent in the Noble Savage. For Anglo-American colonists, learning from the Indians remained for a long time a dangerous enterprise carried out subconsciously, because texts such as Hutchins's and James Smith's did not appear until after the Seven Years' War, when the Indians became partners and subjects, rather than the demonic exterior of frontier settlements. For the French, on the other hand, overtly learning from, imitating, and writing about the Indians had been accepted practice for a long time.

One prong of the effort to explore, assimilate, and subdue the "old" (at that time new) Northwest territory acquired in 1763 is represented in Jonathan Carver's *Travels through the Interior Parts of North-America in the Years 1766, 1767, and 1768.* Carver's effort was organized by his friend, the Seven Years' War hero Robert Rogers. The two had applied their skills at Michilimackinac after 1763, when Rogers was appointed governor of this conduit for the fur trade in the upper Great Lakes. In his popular book Carver broke with the tradition of Anglo-American travel and exploration literature, for his concerns were those of the writer more than the warrior or promoter. He was comfortable neither with the aggressive threats of Benjamin Church and John Smith nor with the mercenary promises of Champlain and Joutel. While living among the Naudowessie (his spelling of Nadouessiou), he writes, "The chiefs applied to me, and desired I would put myself at their head, and lead them out to oppose their enemies. As I was a stranger, and unwilling to excite the anger of either nation, I knew not how to act; and never found myself in a greater dilemma" (60). He chose instead to negotiate a peace between his hosts and their "Chipéway" enemies. Carver was the first secular Anglo-American writer to publish a full-fledged travel narrative and ethnographic text about the northern forests in the manner of the French texts that have formed the core of this study. His 550-page book, published in London in 1778, contains extensive natural history of flora and fauna, travel narrative interrupted by descriptions of all the lakes and rivers found on his map, erudite speculation on the origins of the American Indians, and narratives of battles in the Seven Years' War and Pontiac's rebellion. Only by deferring the demands for quick and violent action in favor of the needs of a historian and ethnographer could he emerge as the English answer to Charlevoix and Lahontan.

Detached description does not imply political disengagement, of course. Carver spent the last ten years of his life in London seeking compensation for the expenses of his travels and financing for another expedition, and his book grandly proclaimed its utility for English colonial management. He set out after the Seven Years' War "to make that vast acquisition of territory, gained by Great Britain, in North America advantageous to it" (i) and dreamed of finding a transcontinental Northwest Passage. Because he believed that "the French, whilst they retained their power in North America, had taken every artful method to keep all other nations, particularly the English, in ignorance of the concerns of the interior parts of it" (ii), Carver did not trust the French maps and reports of the area. The claim was disingenuous, however, for although Carver's map of North America was an improvement over its predecessors, the path he traveled followed established trading routes known to the French for nearly a hundred years and to natives, of course, for much longer. From Michilimackinac to Green Bay, across the Fox-Wisconsin portage, and down to Prairie des Chiens, he paddled in the path of Joliet and Marquette. When he wintered among the Naudowessie above the Falls of St. Anthony and returned eastward along the shores of Lake Superior, he retraced the steps of Louis Hennepin.

Carver followed the French in more than just their travel routes. Not the least important skill of the tradition in which he wrote is that of copying predecessors while simultaneously denouncing them. At the beginning of his ethnography he mentioned his most important sources, Hennepin, Charlevoix, and Lahontan. The first, Carver wrote, "fell very short of that knowledge which it was in his power to have attained from his residence among them [the Naudowessie]" (220), Charlevoix made geographic errors, and Lahontan told stories that were "delusions." The *Jesuit Relations* he pronounced useless because they had not been translated into English and because their information was "chiefly confined to the religious principles of the savage," a misinformed accusation. Like any good ethnographer, Carver claimed that his account was best because its subjects still practiced traditional customs in their original purity: "I am able to give a more just account of the customs and manners of the Indians, in their ancient purity, than any that has been hitherto published" (222), overlooking Hennepin's presence eighty-seven years earlier and subsequent contacts with French agents including Perrot. Among the sections copied from Lahontan are the calendar in chapter 4, "The Indian Method of Reckoning Time," and much of chapter 12, "Of their Marriage Ceremonies." In the latter, Carver finesses the problem of reconciling his observations with a previous body of ethnographic literature that differs from it, much as Sagard did: "Although I have said that the Indian nations differ very little from each other in their marriage ceremonies, there are some exceptions. The Naudowessies have a singular method of celebrating their marriages, which

seems to bear no resemblence to those made use of by any other nation I
have passed through" (372–73).[5]

After creating his text, Carver, like John Smith and the Baron de
Lahontan, felt qualified to undertake a major role in the English colonization of North America. However, the skills he advertised were not
military, but literary. Having failed to find the Northwest Passage, he
proposed setting out again, at nearly seventy years of age, on a round-
the-world voyage:

> I once made an offer to a private society of gentlemen, who were
> curious in such researches, and to whom I had communicated my
> sentiments on this point, that I would undertake a journey, on receiv-
> ing such supplies as were needful, through the north-east parts of
> Europe and Asia to the interior parts of America, and from thence to
> England; making, as I proceeded, such observations both on the lan-
> guages and manners of the people. (216)

Although this expedition was never organized, Carver was the most
ambitious explorer-ethnographer that English America had yet produced. In his writing, or at least in the book that bears his name, a value
for protoscientific knowledge took the place of the self-promotion of
John Smith and the land promotion of John Lawson, two of his leading
predecessors. In particular, ethnographic knowledge, which had been
given short shrift by most earlier English colonists, occupied a major
part of his book. Nonetheless, Carver, like Smith, was an explorer who
would have us believe that he did it all by himself and never lost sight of
his practical goals, though he failed to reach them. And like Hennepin,
his time among the Naudowessie was neither captivity nor adoption nor
exile, but fieldwork.

In examining writings by colonial explorers who spent extensive time
living among the Indians of North America, we have seen that many
discursive categories that ostensibly maintained a separation between
the two cultures actually allowed for some passage between them. Captivity, the Protestant's descent into the underworld, proleptically mimicked the role of the anthropologist in the field and subversively allowed
portrayals of the generosity and humanity of Indian captors. Adoption,

the converse of captivity, showed the Indians to be more receptive to outsiders, and more respectful of the truly important skills of living in the American wilderness, than were the Europeans. Indian warfare did not simply demonstrate the inhumanity of the *sauvage* but instructed English colonists in the ways of the forest, taught French colonists about the meaning of honor and individual autonomy, and revealed both peoples to be potentially savage in the heat of war. The Indians' supposed lack of writing, an apparently insurmountable proof of incivility, was undercut by the existence of semiotic systems that resisted the duplicity of European phonological writing. Within the representation of Indian speech, the "harangue" was appropriated by colonists to enhance their authority not only among the Indians but in colonial discourses as well. Finally, the fur trade did not always reinforce essential differences in the two cultures' sense of value but in fact encouraged questioning of the concepts of clothing, vanity, utility, and money and fostered in some colonists an understanding of Indian reciprocity. Even the line between human and beast was obscured in representations of the beaver that made this creature a model for productive colonial conduct.

In each case, for the colonist to "play Indian," to seek out some degree of assimilation, was possible and advantageous, though rarely did it enable Europeans to unlearn their prejudices of superiority. The slippery slope of savagism, the ideological truism that, as Crèvecœur put it, "children who have been adopted when young among these people can never be prevailed on to readopt European manners" (213), was in the seventeenth and eighteenth centuries not the empirical proof of original sin; it was an opportunity for adult colonists to venture across, however tentatively and temporarily, the cultural divide they had built and return with knowledge, power, and profit. Those who had "gone primitive," the lost Roanoke colonists, Bossu and Guerrero, Eunice Williams, and many others, were the object of fascination and allure. Writing narratives of their experiences was a means of realizing these assets. At least one Indian captive, John R. Jewitt, spent the remainder of his life promoting and selling his narratives; he even portrayed himself in a play based on his captivity on Vancouver Island.

If contemporary criticism and scholarship have failed to recognize the importance of the impulse of colonial American writers to "play Indian," it is not only because this impulse is embarrassing: childish, racist, backsliding, or in bad faith. It is also because academics are reluctant to cross their own boundaries. Historians and anthropologists pluck facts about the American Indians from explorer-ethnographers' texts without examining the interactions that each writer had with the Indians and the new perspectives on European culture that each drew from the experience. Anthropologists have recently critiqued the discourse of ethnography, but these studies nearly always refer to the twentieth-century canon of professional anthropologists, not to their eighteenth-century precursors. U.S. literary study continues to overlook French and Canadian texts even as it attempts to construct a new, more pluralistic canon of American literature. Rereading the seventeenth and eighteenth-century explorer-ethnographers can not only teach us about Euramerican-Amerindian relations, it can also reveal the influence that the representation of the *sauvage américain* has had on modern American culture through its ethics of individualism, tribalism, vengeance, and utopianism. Americans continue to play Indian and to adapt, reject, assimilate, and evaluate native cultures in the midst of dispossessing them.

Biographical Dictionary of Colonial American Explorer-Ethnographers

As the large number of little-known authors and texts discussed in this book may cause confusion for some readers, this list is provided as a reference guide for names and publications. The name commonly used in the text is in boldface. Each entry collects information on dates of birth and death, time spent in North America, titles of works and dates of their publication, and some additional facts where they might be helpful or interesting. For further information, the most useful reference work on the French colonial writers is the *Dictionnaire des œuvres littéraire du Québec*, ed. Maurice Lemire, vol. 1, *Des origines à 1900* (Montreal: Fides, 1980–87). For English colonial authors, the *Dictionary of American Biography* is a key source.

Claude-Charles le Roi, dit [a.k.a.] **Bacqueville de La Potherie** (1663–1736): Born in Guadaloupe, he took part in an expedition led by Pierre Le Moyne d'Iberville to take the fur-trading stations on Hudson Bay away from the English. The first volume of his *Histoire de l'Amérique septentrionale* (1722) tells of this expedition and includes some *mœurs des sauvages*. The second continues with ethnographic descriptions of the tribes of the Great Lakes and derives in large part from Perrot's memoir, which had not yet been published. The third volume is a history of the Iroquois Wars, and the fourth centers around the peace of 1701.

Robert **Beverley** (ca. 1673–1722): Planter, government official, and colonial promoter. His *History and Present State of Virginia* (1705) is divided into four parts: a history, a natural history and list of exploitable resources, an ethnography, and a geographic description of the colony.

Jean Bernard **Bossu** (1720–92): Soldier and colonist in Louisiana during 1751–57, 1758–63, and 1770–71. His *Nouveaux voyages aux Indes Occidentales* (1768; 2d ed., 1769) is a narrative of his first two sojourns in the colony, written in the form of letters to a friend in France. *Nouveaux voyages dans l'Amérique Septentrionale* (1777) takes much the same form and covers the 1770–71 trip. Some of his fanciful stories might be seen as initiating the southern tradition of humor and tall tales.

Pierre **Boucher** (1622–1717): Soldier, official, and finally governor of Trois-Rivières, Quebec, he first went to Canada in 1635 and lived there until his death. He was married briefly to a Huron convert, Marie-Madeleine Chrestienne. His *Histoire véritable et naturelle des mœurs et productions du pays de la Nouvelle France* (1664) was written during a short furlough in France as a defense of the colony and its potential. The short book is entirely descriptive— of the flora, fauna, productions, and natives of New France.

Jean de **Brébeuf** (1593–1649): Born into a noble family, he went to Canada in 1625 as one of the first Jesuit missionaries there. Like Paul **Le Jeune**, his coauthor for many of the *Relations* of 1634–36, he spent one year with the Montagnais before going to Huronia. He lived among the Hurons for nearly twenty years, until he was captured and tortured to death in an Iroquoian attack in 1649. He has since been beatified, and his relics are preserved at Quebec.

Jacques **Cartier** (1491–1557): Navigator popularly known as the "Founder of New France," he made three voyages to Canada—in 1534, 1535–36, and 1541–42—and wrote a short relation of each. The second voyage included the first European visit to Hochelaga, the site of Montreal.

Jonathan **Carver** (1710–80): A soldier in the Seven Years' War, his eyewitness account of the siege of Fort William Henry is one of the key sources in the debate over events there. Robert Rogers sent him on the trip that resulted in *Travels through the Interior Parts of North America in the Years 1766, 1767, and 1768* (1778), a great popular success. Comparison of this text with Carver's manuscripts reveals that much material was added by an editor, including some of the ethnography, and that much of the additional material was plagiarized from other, mostly French, writers. For more, see Epilogue.

Samuel de **Champlain** (ca. 1567–1635): Captain, explorer, and colonial leader, he first went to Canada in 1603 and was governor of the Quebec colony when he died there. He explored the Atlantic coast from Port Royal, Acadia, to Cape Cod in 1604–8 and the lower Great Lakes in 1615. For a list of his published writings, see Chapter 2.

Pierre François-Xavier de **Charlevoix** (1682–1761): A Jesuit, though never a missionary among the Indians, Charlevoix was in Canada in 1705–9 and traveled through Canada and Louisiana in 1720–22 on an official expedition in search of a route to the "Mer de l'ouest" or Pacific Ocean. He published a history of Christian missions in Japan and a history of the Caribbean island of St. Domingue as well as *Histoire et description générale de la Nouvelle France* (1744), of which the third volume is the *Journal d'un voyage*, the narrative of his 1720–22 explorations, with extensive ethnographic descriptions included.

Benjamin **Church** (1639–1718): New England military officer whose efforts were instrumental to English victory in King Philip's War of 1675–76. His pragmatic willingness to employ Indian soldiers and their techniques contrasted with the Puritans' religious interpretations of the war and the enemy. *Entertaining Passages Relating to Philip's War . . .* (1716) was a compilation of his memoirs published by his son, Thomas.

Cadwallader **Colden** (1688–1776): Scientist, historian, and lieutenant governor of New York, he came to America in 1710. A long career in public service was further embellished by correspondence with Carl Linnæus, Benjamin Franklin, Samuel Johnson, and others. He published many scientific papers as well as *The History of the Five Indians Nations Depending on the Province of New York* (pt. 1, 1727; pt. 2, 1747). This book is a history of the Iroquois in the colonial wars of the 1660s to 1700 and draws extensively on French writers such as Lahontan and Bacqueville de La Potherie.

Pierre **Deliette** or de Liette (d. 1729): Officer and colonial commander. He was the nephew or cousin of Henri de Tonti (see below) and author of a memoir about the Illinois country written in 1702 and signed "De Gannes."

Nicolas **Denys** (1598–1688): Merchant and fisherman in Acadia, he founded several settlements in today's Nova Scotia but several times ran afoul of the colonial authorities and was arrested. His *Description geographique et historique des costes de l'Amérique Septentrionale* (1672), notwithstanding the title, concerns Acadia exclusively, describing the coasts, their flora and fauna, and the techniques of fishing.

N. de **Dièreville**: A physician, of whom neither the dates nor even the first name is known, he went to Port Royal, Acadia, in 1699–1700 as a curious visitor. His *Relation du voyage du Port Royal* (1708) was originally written in verse and retains many verse passages amid its prose. It is not an exploration narrative, but rather an exoticist promotional tract, which includes fine descriptions of animal life and the natives' customs and cuisine.

John **Eliot** (1604–90): The best known and most committed Puritan missionary to the Indians, he sailed to New England in 1631. Eliot established "praying towns" and published a translation of the Bible into Algonquian (1661–63), as well as catechisms and edifying dialogues for use in missionary work.

Daniel **Gookin** (1612–87): Puritan colonist, first in Virginia (1630–44) and then in New England. His *Historical Collections of the Indians in New England* (1792) combines ethnography with missionary history, focusing on the work of John Eliot. *An Historical Account of the Doings and Sufferings of the Christian Indians* (1836) is a defense of the converts who were persecuted during King Philip's War. Both volumes were first published long after his death.

Thomas **Hariot** (or Harriot) (1560–1621): Mathematician, surveyor, and official historian of Sir Walter Raleigh's expedition to the Roanoke colony in 1585–86. His *Briefe and True Report of the New Found Land of Virginia* (1588) is best known in its illustrated and expanded edition published by Theodor deBry in 1590. This first volume in deBry's series on America featured engravings based on the watercolors by John White, who made two trips to the Roanoke colony.

Louis **Hennepin** (1626–after 1697): A Recollet friar, he went to Canada in 1675 and was chosen as one of three monks to accompany La Salle on his expedition to the Mississippi. He returned to France in 1681 and in 1683 published *Description de la Louisiane, nouvellement découverte au Sud Ouest de la Nouvelle France*, the first narrative of the expedition to appear and a huge success, with many subsequent editions and translations. He had not gone with La Salle down the Mississippi but instead traveled upstream and was taken captive by the Issati band of Sioux. In *Nouvelle découverte d'un très grand pays* (1697) and its second edition, *Nouveau voyage d'un pays plus grand que l'Europe* (1698), he embellished his story by claiming that he had accompanied La Salle to the mouth of the Mississippi and copying a narrative of that trip written by another Recollet, Zenobe Membré, and already published by LeClercq.

John **Josselyn**: A royalist opposed to Puritans, he visited New England in 1638–39 and 1663–71. Botanical, medical, and other scientific observations are the focus of *New Englands Rarities Discovered* (1672) and *An Account of Two Voyages to New England* (1674), which also include some ethnography.

Henri **Joutel** (ca. 1645–after 1723): He left Rouen in 1684 on La Salle's last expedition, which sailed into the Gulf of Mexico in search of the mouth of the Mississippi. Unable to find it, they were stranded in today's Matagorda Bay, Texas, where Joutel commanded the small settlement while La Salle went in search of help. His *Journal historique du dernier voyage qui fut M. de la Sale* is the narrative of the tragic expedition and the final desperate walk across Texas to the Mississippi and on to Canada, which he reached in 1688. It also tells of the murder of La Salle, which Joutel attempted to conceal for fear that he would be blamed for it. The book was published in 1713, toward the end of the series of narratives of La Salle's expeditions.

Joseph-François **Lafitau** (1681–1746): Jesuit missionary at Sault St. Louis near Montreal, 1712–17. Later he was named procurer in Paris for the Jesuit missions in New France and returned to Canada for a visit in 1727–29. His *Mœurs des sauvages américains comparées aux mœurs des premiers temps* (1724) eschews missionary history and travel narrative in favor of an exhaustive study of Native American customs compared with, and illuminated by, an enormous variety of sources from classical civilizations and literatures. Ethnographic material from the Iroquois among whom he worked predominates, but Lafitau also borrows from the *Jesuit Relations* and even accounts of the natives of South America. He also discovered ginseng in North America and wrote a treatise on that plant, as well as a history of the Portuguese discoveries and conquests in America.

Louis-Armand de Lom d'Arce, Baron de **Lahontan** (1666–1716): Soldier and officer, he traveled in Canada in 1683–93 (with a brief return to France in 1690–91). *Nouveaux voyages . . . dans l'Amérique Septentrionale* was published in The Hague, Netherlands (1702–3), and an English translation in London (1703). For more information, see Chapters 1 and 3.

Antoine **Lamothe-Cadillac**: Officer, then commandant of the French fort at Mackinac, 1694–96, and at Detroit from its founding in 1701 to 1711, when he was sent to Mobile in Louisiana. In 1695–96 he wrote a "Mémoire" that included an ethnography supporting the theory of a Hebraic origin for the

American Indians. It was first published in Margry's collection, and a translation was edited by Quaife.

Robert Cavelier, Sieur de **La Salle** (1643–87): Although the explorations he led produced some of the most popular and important exploration narratives and ethnographies of America in the seventeenth century, La Salle did not write one himself, and he is a somewhat mysterious and heroic figure. He went to Canada in 1666 and was inspired by Joliet, who reached the Mississippi in 1673, to undertake explorations of his own. He gained the favor of Governor Frontenac, who secured him a fort at the east end of Lake Ontario, and a monopoly on the western fur trade. In 1680–82 his expedition, including Hennepin and Tonti, established two forts on the Illinois River, and he traveled down the Mississippi to the sea. His last expedition, in 1684–87, was to find the Mississippi from the Gulf of Mexico but ended in disaster. In Texas some of his men mutinied and shot him, a story told by his brother Jean Cavelier and by Henri Joutel. Pierre Margry and Francis Parkman are only two of the many historians who have developed the figure of La Salle as a tragic hero of French exploration in America.

Réné Goulainé de **Laudonnière**: Huguenot navigator and historian of the ill-fated French colony at Port Royal, South Carolina, in 1563–65, led by Jean Ribault and including the artist Jacques Le Moyne de Morgues. His *Histoire notable de la Floride* (1586) is the best narrative of this colony.

John **Lawson**: Born in 1674, Lawson was killed by Tuscarora Indians in 1711. He traveled in Carolina during 1700–1709 and again from 1710 until his death. A surveyor, promoter, and land speculator, he was appointed surveyor-general of the province of North Carolina in 1708. His *A New Voyage to Carolina* (1709) is perhaps the best English exploration-ethnography text before the Seven Years' War.

Claude **Lebeau**: Virtually all that is known of him is from his picaresque novel, *Avantures du Sr. C. Le Beau, avocat en Parlement, ou Voyage curieux et nouveau parmi les Sauvages de l'Amérique Septentrionale* (1738). Independent sources reveal, however, that in 1729 he was transported to Canada as a prisoner, rather than emigrating voluntarily as his book maintains. Much of his ethnographic and geographic description is copied from Hennepin, Lahontan, and others, and certain episodes of his adventures are obvious fictions.

Chrestien **LeClercq** (ca. 1641–after 1700): Recollet missionary. He lived among the Indians of the Gaspé Peninsula of Quebec during 1675–83 and returned to France in 1686. The natives he wished to convert revered a cross symbol as a totem, which gave him high hopes of their potential as Christians. His *Nouvelle Relation de la Gaspesie, qui contient les Mœurs & la Religion des Sauvages Gaspesiens Porte-Croix* (1691) is a travel narrative, missionary relation, and ethnography similar in form to that of fellow Recollet, Gabriel Sagard. *Premier Establissement de la Foy dans la Nouvelle France, contenant la Publication de l'Evangile, l'Histoire des Colonies Françoises, & les fameuses decouvertes . . . de la Salle* (1691) tells the history of New France from a perspective favoring the Recollets over the rival Jesuits and includes the account of La Salle's expedition down the Mississippi by the Recollet Zenobe Membré.

John **Lederer**: A German who moved to Virginia in 1668. His three exploratory journeys into the Blue Ridge Mountains west of colonial Virginia were probably the first by any European in the area. *The Discoveries of John Lederer* (1672) was translated and published by William Talbot of Maryland, where Lederer took refuge from angry Virginians in 1671.

Antoine Simon **Le Page du Pratz** (ca. 1695–after 1758): Soldier and colonist, in Louisiana from 1718 to 1734. He published several articles on Louisiana in the *Journal Œconomique* in 1751, then his massive three-volume *Histoire de la Louisiane* in 1758. His detailed and sympathetic portrait of the Natchez is the best ethnography of that nation and one of the best of any tribe by a colonial author. The English translation, *The History of Louisiana* (1763, 1774), though incomplete, is still the only one available.

Marc **Lescarbot** (1570–after 1619): In the midst of a career as a lawyer, he visited Port Royal in today's Nova Scotia for twelve months in 1606–7. His *Histoire de la Nouvelle France* includes accounts of previous French colonies in America and appeared in three editions: 1609, 1611, and an expanded version in 1618. His comparative *premiers temps* method of ethnography anticipated Lafitau. His short collection of poems, "Les Muses de la Nouvelle France" (1618), has been called the first literature written in Canada.

Thomas **Morton** (ca. 1590–1647): Trader and colonist in New England, 1622–30 and 1643–47, interrupted by arrests and deportations back to England. Morton was the nemesis of William Bradford and the Plymouth colonists, because his trading post interfered with their business and his Anglicanism with their religious doctrines. His *New English Canaan* (1637) has a sympathetic and romantic description of the manners and customs of the Indians, as well as a description of the natural commodities, and a history of the New England colonies.

Nicolas **Perrot** (1644–1717): Went to New France at age sixteen and worked as a lay servant to missionaries, then as a fur trader. His knowledge of native languages and customs earned him assignments as a negotiator with Indian allies of the French during the Iroquois Wars. His efforts were recorded with admiration by Bacqueville de La Potherie, and his writings also served as a source for Charlevoix. His own text, *Mémoire sur les mœurs, coustumes, et relligion des sauvages de l'Amérique Septentrionale*, was not published until 1864. It takes a grimmer, more cynical view of Indian customs and frontier life than most exploration ethnographies.

Pierre-Esprit **Radisson**: Went to Canada in 1651 and worked as a fur trader, along with his brother-in-law, Médard Chouart, later called Sieur des Groseilliers. They were taken captive by the Iroquois in 1652, the beginning of an incredible series of adventures too long to summarize. He worked for both the French and English colonies and helped to establish the first posts on Hudson Bay. The manuscripts of his *Voyages* are obscure on some points, invaluable on others, and were nearly destroyed before being published in 1885.

Antoine-Denis **Raudot**: Intendant (a post of nearly equal power to the governor) of New France during 1705–10. *Relation par lettres de l'Amérique Septentrionale* (1904, ed. Camille de Rochemonteix) was attributed by that editor to Antoine Silvy, but it is now generally agreed to be Raudot's work.

Robert **Rogers** (1731–95): The first English colonist to build a career as fur trader, warrior, Indian agent, and writer in the Great Lakes region after the pattern of Frenchmen like Perrot and Lahontan. The greatest hero of the English side in the Seven Years' War, he traded on his popularity by publishing in England *A Concise Account of North America* (1765) and the romantic Noble Savagist play, *Ponteach, or the Savages of America: A Tragedy* (1766), about Pontiac, the leader of a native uprising following the Seven Years' War. Jonathan Carver was his subordinate at the fort at Michilimackinac, where he was commander in 1766–67. About this time Rogers was accused of corruption in the fur trade and of treasonable dealings with the French, and during the

Revolutionary War George Washington imprisoned him as a spy. He died in debt and disgrace.

Gabriel **Sagard**-Théodat: A lay brother in the Recollet order, he traveled to Canada on his mission to the Hurons in 1623–24 and returned to France immediately after. He published *Le grand voyage du pays des Hurons* (1632) and an expanded version, *Histoire du Canada* (1636), which includes material borrowed from other writers, much like Lescarbot's and LeClercq's histories.

John **Smith** (1580–1631): Explorer and colonial leader. He participated in the founding of Jamestown colony in 1607–9 and explored the rivers flowing into Chesapeake Bay in attempts to obtain food from the Indians. For more, including a list of his publications, see Chapter 2.

William **Strachey**: Secretary and historian of the early Virginia colony. He sailed for America in 1609 and was shipwrecked on Bermuda, where his party constructed two boats; the group reached Jamestown in 1610. This episode served as the basis for Shakespeare's *The Tempest*. Strachey returned to England in 1611 and wrote several tracts concerning the colony, as well as *The Historie of Travell into Virginia Britania*, which was not published until 1849.

Henri de **Tonti** (ca. 1650–1704): La Salle's most skilled lieutenant, he commanded the French posts on the Illinois River from their founding in 1679–80 until shortly before he died near Mobile in the new Louisiana colony. He traveled down the Mississippi in search of La Salle in 1686. When Joutel arrived at the Illinois post the next year and did not inform Tonti of his commander's death, Tonti set out to search again in 1689. The history of his writings is confusing. In 1697 there appeared at Paris a book titled *Dernières Découvertes dans l'Amérique Septentrionale de Monsieur de la Salle . . . par Chevalier de Tonti, Gouverneur de Fort St. Louis aux Illinois*. Tonti disavowed this work, however. Two short memoirs he did write were not published until long afterward. One can be found in Margry, 1:573–616, and the other in Kellogg, *Early Narratives of the Northwest*, 286–322.

Adriaen **Van der Donck** (1620–55): Dutch colonist and author of *A Description of the New Netherlands* ("Beschrijvinge van Nieuw Nederlant"), published in Dutch in 1655 and not translated into English until 1841. The text contains no exploration narrative but includes some good natural history, particularly of the beaver. He also wrote "A Remonstrance" or "Representation of New Netherlands," addressing what he saw as mismanagement of the colony, in 1649.

Roger **Williams** (ca. 1603–82): Is famous for many things and many texts beyond his ethnologically informative glossary of the Algonquian language, *A Key in to the Language of America* (1643). His beliefs in religious tolerance and the limits of church power made him a dangerous man in the eyes of the New England Puritan patriarchs, who forced him to flee Salem, Massachusetts, and set up a colony in exile in Rhode Island. There he became a friend and defender of the Narragansett Indians.

William **Wood**: Colonist in New England, 1629–33, and author of the promotional narrative *New Englands Prospect* (1634), which consists of descriptions of plants and animals and an ethnography of the Indians. The book was mocked by Thomas Morton, his contemporary rival in publishing promotional tracts about the young colony.

Notes

Preface

1. Jantz, "Images of America in the German Renaissance," 97–100, suggests that the name caught on because of a series of coincidences or homophonic puns. The explorer's name resembled native place names along the coast of South America explored around 1500: "Among the dozens of variants that could be mentioned are such striking ones as Amaracao, Maraca, Marica, Maracaibo" (99). In addition, there is a pun on a Greek word meaning " 'clear, pure, bright, dazzling land' or 'ever-young, ever-fair land' " (99). It is interesting that Olive Patricia Dickason adds an appendix to her book *The Myth of the Savage* discussing the possible native and European origins of the name Canada.

2. Bacqueville de La Potherie, *Histoire de l'Amérique Septentrionale*, 2:327–28; English version, Blair, *The Indian Tribes of the Upper Mississippi*, 2:113.

3. Nabokov and Snow, "Farmers of the Woodlands," 122.

4. Richard White, *The Middle Ground*, 196.

5. The influence of the Wild Man on the representation of the Savage has received a good deal of study. See Dickason, *The Myth of the Savage*; Bernheimer, *Wild Men in the Middle Ages*; and Dudley and Novak, *The Wild Man Within*.

Chapter One

1. The "Indian Books" are at the J. P. Morgan Library in New York City. For more on these, and on Thoreau's possible plans to use the notes to write a book about Indians, see Sayre, *Thoreau and the American Indians*, 101–22. Some Thoreau notebooks have been published in facsimile reproductions as *Canadian Notebooks* and *Thoreau's Fact Books*, edited by Kenneth W. Cameron.

2. Parkman, *France and England in North America*, 1:432.

3. Parkman, *Conspiracy of Pontiac*, 347.

4. Thoreau, *A Yankee in Canada*, 62.

5. Cecelia Tichi's article on the early American field in the influential recent survey of literary studies published by the Modern Language Association—Greenblatt and Gunn, *Redrawing the Boundaries*—reports the conclusion of prominent scholars that "New England was systematically privileged as *the* literature of this nation . . . its putative national scope is the result of its social construction by academic-publishing elites rooted in Boston" (215–16). The statement reflects recent work by Lawrence Buell, *New England Literary Culture from Revolution through Renaissance*, and Nina Baym, "Early Histories of American Literature: A Chapter in the Institution of New England." In spite of this critique of the privilege of New England, however, the article does not cite any books on southern or non-Anglo literature in the bibliography of recent work in the field of American literature before the Civil War. We have anticanonical criticism but little of a counter-canon to remedy the problem.

6. Axtell, *Beyond 1492*, 206.

7. See Josselyn, *Two Voyages to New England*, 32; McManis, *European Impressions of the New England Coast*, 37–40; and Thoreau, *Cape Cod*, 1016.

8. See Kupperman, *Settling with the Indians*, 19, 179.

9. See Seelye, *Prophetic Waters*, 350; Craven, *White, Red, and Black: The Seventeenth-Century Virginian*, 55–57.

10. See the entry for 1647 in Bradford, *Of Plymouth Plantation*.

11. Vaughan and Clark, *Puritans among the Indians*, 150.

12. "La chaine des postes" was the name for an official colonial project during the late seventeenth century. See Margry, *Découvertes et Etablissements*, vol. 5.

13. Purchas, *Hakluytus Posthumus, or Purchas His Pilgrimes*, 18:326.

14. Thoreau observed, after quoting Lahontan's passage through Chicago in 1688, that "the white man has but followed in the steps of the Indian. Where the Ind. made his portages, the white man makes his—or makes the stream more navigable. The New Englander goes to Wisconsin and Iowa by routes which the Indians discovered and used ages ago" (from "Indian Book" number 7 qtd. in Sayre, *Thoreau and the American Indians*, 114).

15. "The gridwork principle won out," according to Wayne Franklin in his *Discoverers, Explorers, Settlers*, plate 3. Franklin's book contains excellent discussions of Byrd's, Jefferson's, and other rectilinear schemes of surveying and settling.

16. There was also one text published in French in the seventeenth century by a Frenchman who emigrated to Virginia. Durand de Dauphiné was a Huguenot fleeing France after the revocation of the Edict of Nantes. His text

recounts no explorations and says very little about the Indians, concentrating on agriculture and the notorious heavy drinking of the Virginians. See *Un Français en Virginie*, ed. Chinard.

17. Much of the information in this paragraph is derived from Neal Salisbury's book *Manitou and Providence*. Salisbury suggests that the epidemic was the plague and that it was spread by the French explorers (101–3).

18. In ascribing the Pilgrims' choice of Cape Cod over the mouth of the Hudson to Dermer's advice, Salisbury is in a minority among historians. Bradford reports in both *Mourt's Relation* and *Of Plymouth Plantation* that bad weather and dangerous shoals caused them to turn back from an attempt to continue to the Hudson.

19. Craven, *White, Red, and Black*, 50.

20. Van der Donck, *A Description of the New Netherlands*, 93.

21. *Coureur de bois* means literally "forest runner" and is sometimes confounded with another French term for colonial fur traders, *voyageur*. The latter is used more often in reference to later periods, for colonists working as canoemen for a trader who held a license to buy beaver pelts, or for one of the English fur companies. *Coureurs de bois* is the better term for the explorer-fur traders of the seventeenth century such as Joliet and Perrot; it is sometimes reserved for traders who evaded the colony's monopoly concessions, although I do not use this restrictive meaning.

22. Richard White, *The Middle Ground*, 105–8.

23. Bowden and Ronda, *John Eliot's Indian Dialogues*, 23.

24. Vaughan and Clark, *Puritans among the Indians*, 150.

25. See Pearce, *Savagism and Civilization*, 27.

26. See Kupperman, *Settling with the Indians*, 161, 165.

27. Jennings, *The Invasion of America*, 57.

28. Roger Williams, *Complete Writings*, 6:2.

29. Atkinson, *Les relations de voyage du XVIIième siècle*, 4.

30. Hearne and Thompson and other English and Scottish fur company employees, including John Long and Alexander Henry, elder and younger, developed in the late eighteenth century a new style of exploration literature, one anchored in a capitalist context free of the concerns for, or tension with, religious and national authorities. For a fine analysis of this later mode, see Greenfield, *Narrating Discovery*.

31. I have integrated the two lists of four, which differ slightly, found on pp. 18 and 242 of *Regeneration Through Violence*.

32. Richter and Vaughan, *Crossing the Cultural Divide: Indians and New*

Englanders, 1605–1763, contains an exhaustive accounting of all reported captives and their fates. It reveals that the archetypal pattern was not so common as was generally believed.

33. For Axtell, this is true of virtually all of his writings; see Works Cited. Jennings, *The Invasion of America*, consists of an excellent general analysis in part 1, then turns to New England for an exhaustive exposé of misrepresentations of the Pequot War and King Philip's War by Puritans, especially John Winthrop. White's *The Middle Ground* is a fine study of relations between the French and the Algonquian Indians of the Great Lakes region in the seventeenth and eighteenth centuries. Salisbury, *Manitou and Providence*, is an ethnohistorical survey of southern New England. Trigger has written the definitive ethnohistory of the Hurons, *The Children of Aataentsic*.

34. There have been good studies written recently of the representations of the Indians in texts by Virginia colonists (Sheehan's *Savagism and Civility*, 1980), of those by all English explorers before 1640 (Kupperman's *Settling with the Indians*, 1980), and of those by French colonists (Jaenen's *Friend and Foe*, 1976, and Dickason's *The Myth of the Savage*, 1984), but no study of English *and* French colonists' representations of the Indians in the Atlantic coast and Great Lakes regions.

35. One of the best brief treatments of the problem is by David Murray in *Forked Tongues*, 1–4.

36. A long list of books and articles could be cited on anthropological theory and epistemology. See, for a start, the collections by Clifford and Marcus in *Writing Culture: The Poetics and Politics of Ethnography* and Basso and Selby in *Meaning in Anthropology*. As for Native North American literature before 1800, the search is extremely frustrating. Anthologies such as Mintz, *Native American Voices*, and Nabokov, *Native American Testimony*, and the material in the latest editions of the Norton and Heath anthologies of American literature, vol. 1, rely overwhelmingly on descriptions and quotations of Indians drawn from many of the missionary and explorer-ethnographer texts I analyze here (as in Calloway's and Armstrong's anthologies discussed in note 44 below) and on oral literature collected by anthropologists in the twentieth century. The best collection of writing by American Indians before 1800 is Peyer, *The Elders Wrote: An Anthology of Early Prose by North American Indians*. My own view is that readers in search of authenticity must be prepared to reconsider their definitions of literature and even writing and to study rock art, Midewiwin scrolls, and Mayan, Aztec, and Mixtec pictographs.

37. Hanke, *Aristotle and the American Indian: A Study of Race Prejudice in the Modern World*; Grafton, *New Worlds, Ancient Texts: The Power of Tradition and the Shock of Discovery*; Pagden, *The Fall of Natural Man: The American Indian and the Origins of Comparative Ethnology*.

38. Bacqueville de La Potherie and Charlevoix wrote with the larger aim of a history of New France, but their works still contain their own travel narratives and ethnographic sections. As a quick reference guide to help keep all these names straight, see the Biographical Dictionary at the back of this book.

39. Kolodny, *The Land Before Her*, 54.

40. Two books written about these "filles de roi" aggressively refute Lahontan's portrait of them. Réal Ouellet provides an excellent discussion of the controversy in his introduction (192–93). He calls the response "un véritable procès de diffamation" [a veritable trial for defamation] against Lahontan.

41. Lamothe-Cadillac, *Mémoire*, in Margry, 5:107; in English in Quaife, *The Western Country in the Seventeenth Century*, 45–46; Lawson, *A New Voyage to Carolina*, 194.

42. Onnontio is the Iroquois name for the French authorities, being a translation of the name of the former governor Montmagny. Corlar is the name for the English colonial leaders, having been carried over to the English from the name of an early Dutch trader, Van Curler (see Thwaites, ed., *New Voyages to North America*, 82, note 1).

43. See *The Ambiguous Iroquois Empire*, 183. The text of the "official" version is reprinted in Ouellet's edition of Lahontan, 1155–59, and a translation in O'Callaghan, *Documentary History of . . . New York*, 1:117–20.

44. Excerpts of the speech appear in Armstrong, *I Have Spoken: American History through the Voices of the Indians*, 7–8, and in Calloway, *The World Turned Upside Down: Indian Voices from Early America*, 118–20. Both give a brief summary of La Barre's speeches and of the political and military context.

Chapter Two

1. For these narratives, see Barbour, *The Jamestowne Voyages under the First Charter, 1606–1609*, or the introductory material to Arber's edition of Smith's *Works* and Strachey's *Historie of Travell into Virginia Britania*.

2. Knapp, *An Empire Nowhere*, 207.

3. See Miles's introduction to Champlain, *Voyages to New France, 1599–1603*, 8–10; also Bishop, *Champlain: The Life of Fortitude*, 14–24, 345–46.

4. Barbour, *The Three Worlds of Captain John Smith*, 313.

5. Champlain's maps and illustrations are analyzed in great detail by Gagnon in *Ces hommes dit sauvages*. As modern editions of Champlain, except for H. P. Biggar's massive six-volume edition of his complete works, do not include most of the maps, Gagnon's book is particularly useful.

6. Trigger, "Champlain Judged by His Indian Policy," 89.

7. This illustration is reproduced in VanDerBeets, *Held Captive by Indians*, 160.

8. See, for example, Bradford, *Of Plymouth Plantation*, end of 1625 entry.

9. Trigger, in his article "Champlain Judged by His Indian Policy: A Different View of Early Canadian History," argues that Champlain did not benefit from a benevolent attitude or a special talent for understanding the Indians, that he was ethnocentric and "A relatively unreflective and self-centered man" (89). I regard Trigger's piece as a salvo in a revisionist conflict over Champlain's reputation, one similar to that over John Smith, but of more recent tenure. I do not believe it conflicts with my thesis here that Champlain's greater success was due to the similarities between his leadership and that of his foes such as Tessoüat, for these similarities were not of Champlain's making.

10. The intersection of the Pocahontas legend and the Smith legend and the controversy over Smith's account is a topic beyond the scope of this chapter. Indeed, until recently it overshadowed everything for many of Smith's readers. Jeffrey Knapp addresses its implications within the sexual politics of English colonialism in *An Empire Nowhere*. J. A. Leo Lemay attempts an exhaustive review of the evidence in *Did Pocahontas Save Captain John Smith?* and concludes that she probably did. Helen Rountree, on the other hand, believes that the story is false (*Pocahontas's People*, 38).

11. Adams, *The Education of Henry Adams*, 222.

12. Lemay, *The American Dream of Captain John Smith*, 2. The first chapter of this book includes a survey of the reception of Smith's writings from a point of view sympathetic toward the captain.

13. The manipulation of reflected glory continues in the latter work, however, for Smith copied the accounts of others for his history of Bermuda (the Summer Isles) and of early English exploration of America. In this regard his *Generall Historie* resembles Lescarbot's *History of New France* and Thevet's *Singularités de la France antarctique*.

14. For more on the unusual style of Champlain's first work, see Bideaux, "*Des Sauvages*: Une singularité narrative."

15. Anthropologists and historians used to refer to a "Powhatan Confederacy," implying a political organization similar to the Iroquois', but more recent studies insist that Powhatan was a "paramount chief" (Rountree, *Pocahontas's People*, 10), and that the many tribes he ruled had not voluntarily banded together, as the Iroquois had.

16. "From the available ethnographic evidence, it appears that Powhatan saw an alliance with the English as a means of extending his power in the tidewater area while neutralizing the power of his western enemies" (Nash, "Image of the Indian in the Southern Colonial Mind," 211). "He then made what Smith understood as an offer . . . he would feed and protect them, and in exchange they would make him metal tools" (Rountree, *Pocahontas's People*, 38).

17. All references are to Barbour, *The Complete Works of Captain John Smith*. Where the episode is found in both the *Map of Virginia* and the *Generall Historie*, I will cite both pages, with the specific version quoted appearing first.

18. "Algoumequin" is a French variant of "Algonquin," but the tribe in question actually corresponds with a nation today called Ottawa, or more specifically the Kichespirini, as Trigger identifies it.

19. All page references and translations are from the Biggar edition, where the French and the translation are on the same page, and so I will cite the page number just once.

20. John Seelye, the only critic I have found to call attention to the similarities between Smith and Champlain, points out that both confronted natives of the Iroquois Confederacy: "In 1608, Smith encountered a war party of that 'nation' as they descended the Potomac, and in that same prophetic year Champlain made hostile contact with Iroquois as he explored the lake that bears his name, twin events that were tentative probes of imperial pincers, initial thrusts of epic ambitions" (*Prophetic Waters*, 84).

21. June Namias argues that Smith's hair grabbing and his dancer's posture in the two illustrations serve to feminize the chiefs (*White Captives*, 59).

22. This is another of the controversies that continue to occupy historians of the Jamestown colony. Hulme (*Colonial Encounters*, 142, 170) and Frederick Fausz (Sweet and Nash, eds., *Struggle and Survival in Colonial America*, 21–37) believe that Opechancanough was Don Luis, captive of the Spaniards, whereas Rountree (*Pocahontas's People*, 18) believes that he was not.

23. It is possible that before the introduction of firearms Native Americans did fight more "formal" battles between massed armies, with a design of victory by intimidation rather than total annihilation. By this theory it was the

threat of the gun, so effective here for Champlain and other Europeans (so long as the Native Americans did not have them), as well as its noise and the time required to reload it (once they did obtain them), that caused a shift to guerrilla-style tactics of stealth and surprise familiar from tales of "Indian atrocity" and from many ethnographic texts (see Axtell, *Beyond 1492*, 142, and Chapter 6 below).

24. Gagnon, *Ces hommes dits sauvages*, 58–59.

Chapter Three

1. Henry Bausum, for one, proposed John Smith and Peter Martyr as emblematic of traditions of the Ignoble and Noble Savage, respectively, in colonial American writing.

2. I will henceforth assume a distinction between the genres of travel narrative and exploration narrative. Travel narrative, and the growing body of critical studies about it, relies strongly on the narrator's preconceptions of the place traveled to and therefore on the earlier accounts of that place. Exploration narrative, on the other hand, supposes that the place has never before been visited by a member of the narrator's culture or audience. The distinction is complicated, however, by the degree to which ethnography is compiled from secondhand observations and prejudices and therefore resembles travel narrative more than exploration narrative.

3. For a good discussion of Hennepin's narrative and the controversies over its veracity, see Percy Adams, *Travelers and Travel Liars*, 47.

4. John Smith had done the same in his 1612 *Map of Virginia*. He commented: "In which Mappe observe this, that as far as you see the little Crosses on rivers, mountaines, or other places have beene discovered; the rest was had by information of the Savages, and are set downe, according to their instructions" (1:151).

5. This comment is in the "Listes et examen des auteurs que j'ai consultés . . ." of *Histoire de la Nouvelle France*, vol. 3, p. iv. This list is not included in Berthiaume's 1994 edition, *Journal d'un voyage*.

6. The relevant passage in Lamothe-Cadillac's text is in Margry, 5:125–26; and in English translation in Quaife, *The Western Country in the Seventeenth Century*, 73.

7. Sagean's account was first published in the *Mercure Galant* in 1711 and is available in Margry, 6:93–162. Bossu discusses it in the second-to-last letter

of his *Travels*, remarking (in the Feiler translation), "I do not know how reliable this report is" (212).

8. This group also included Job Hortop and Miles Philips, who were captured by the natives and later held by the Spanish colonists for more than twenty years. Their stories are among the most riveting in Hakluyt's *Principal Navigations* (Glasgow, 1904), 5:398–465. Philips mentions Ingram in his narrative (412). Two companions of Ingram's on the transcontinental trek had both died before the 1582 interview. Hakluyt did not include Ingram's relation in the 1598–1600 edition.

9. Hakluyt, *The Principal Navigations* (London, 1589), 2:560.

10. The titles in the table of contents do not always match the headings at the beginning of the chapters, and for the French I have used a combination of the two.

11. Sayre, *Thoreau and the American Indians*, 120.

12. Trigger, "Champlain Judged by His Indian Policy," 90.

13. Coetzee, "Idleness in South Africa," 120.

14. See the books cited in note 36 of Chapter 1.

15. Pratt, "Scratches on the Face of the Country," 127.

16. For Jean de Léry, see Léry, *History of a Voyage to the Land of Brazil*, trans. Whatley, 153.

17. The English translation was published in two volumes rather than three, with the *Mémoires* split between the two.

18. The translation renders these titles as "A short View of the Humors and Customs of the Indians," "The way of Worship, Used by the Savages," and "Belief of the Savages, and the Obstacles of their Conversion."

19. Pratt, "Scratches on the Face of the Country," 123, 122.

20. See the opening chapter to Fuller, *Summer on the Lakes*, and Kalm in the appendix to Bartram, *Observations on the Inhabitants*.

21. Kupperman, *Settling with the Indians*, 121.

22. Pratt, "Fieldwork in Common Places," 32.

23. Pratt makes the shift from coastal exploration to interior travels and narratives a key theme of her book *Imperial Eyes* and locates the shift in the eighteenth century. The process continued to the turn of the nineteenth century, when for Conrad the unknown interior of the dark continent is a figure for the unconscious of the mind.

24. See Grafton, *New Worlds, Ancient Texts*, 37–43.

25. See Lahontan, *Nouveaux voyages*, 1:189–95; English version, 1:145–49.

26. Richard White, *The Middle Ground*, 144.

27. See also the discussion of this scene by Pamela Regis, *Describing Early America*, 33–35.

28. Jaenen, *Friend and Foe*, 19.

29. The notion that the Native American societies encountered by the colonists were the degenerate remnants of an earlier civilization has an interesting history in itself. The notorious slanderer of American flora, fauna, and peoples, Cornelius de Pauw, was an adherent of this theory, which he used to support his belief that Europeans who migrated to America would degenerate there (see Gerbi, *The Dispute of the New World*, 53–60). With the discovery of the burial mounds in the Ohio valley in the late 1700s, the theory saw a revival among Anglo-American writers such as Thomas Jefferson, who sought a home-grown classicism to match Europe's.

30. Bouton, *Relation de la Martinique* (1640), cited by Atkinson, 122.

31. See, for example, Wood, *New Englands Prospect*, 73.

Chapter Four

1. Complicating the issue is the fact that in seventeenth-century English, "naked" did not mean completely without clothes. Roger Williams wrote of "a nakednesse" among the Indians "ordinary and constant, which although they have a Beasts skin, or an English mantle on, yet that covers ordinarily but their hinder parts and all the foreparts from top to toe . . . I say all else is open and naked" (*A Key in to the Language of America*, 110). See also Kupperman, *Settling with the Indians*, 39, and, for a discussion of English colonists' notions of clothing and status, 35.

2. Axtell, *The European and the Indian*, 59.

3. "Castor gras" is literally "greasy" or "fat" beaver, not "green" beaver.

4. From editor P. Tailhan's notes to Perrot, translated by Blair (*The Indian Tribes of the Upper Mississippi*, 1:264). Tailhan does not give the author or catalog number of the memoir.

5. For an analysis of the economics of the initial fur markets, see Delâge, *Bitter Feast*, 78–84.

6. Newman, *Company of Adventurers*, 61.

7. Dickason, *The Myth of the Savage*, 235

8. See Barbour, *Complete Works of Captain John Smith*, 1:165, and Le Moyne de Morgues, plate 25, in Lorant, *The New World*, 85.

9. Dickason, *The Myth of the Savage*, 78–79, cites several additional such passages.

10. Jefferson, *Notes on the State of Virginia*, 93. Jefferson was quoting the French naturalist Buffon and deriding the theory that the American land and its natives were less virile than in the Old World. For an exhaustive, majesterial survey of the controversy, see Gerbi, *The Dispute of the New World*.

11. Kupperman, *Settling with the Indians*, 37.

12. For a discussion of the issue, see Dickason, *The Myth of the Savage*, 44–45, 143–46. She comments that "basané" carries a connotation of the peasant classes, one of many efforts to compare the Indians with the lowest classes in Europe.

13. The two languages are similar, and anthropologists therefore regard the two peoples as more closely related to one another than to the Algonquian-speaking groups around them, but the Hurons or Wendats, allies of the French, were bitter enemies of the Iroquois and eventually were defeated by them and their English allies.

14. Laura Brown has analyzed how colonial trade commodities were associated with female vanity and ornament in misogynistic English satire of the Augustan Age: "Throughout the literary culture of this period, tortoise shell and ivory, the spices of Arabia, gems, gold, and silk are made to represent the primary objectives of mercantile capitalism, and these commodities in turn appear exclusively as the materials of the female toilet and wardrobe" (*Ends of Empire*, 114). That the beaver pelt, raw material for a luxury accessory worn predominantly by men, is not included in this list only adds to the force of Brown's argument.

15. I did not have access to the French original of this passage, as Margry included only about half of the text of the interrogations in his collection of documents. The text translated by R. T. Huntington for the *Iowa Review* 15 (1985) is unpublished and is preserved in the French Archives Nationales, Outre-Mer.

16. See Richard White, *The Middle Ground*, 119.

17. These quotations are from Margry's text of Joutel's journey in his *Découvertes et Etablissements*, 3:88–534. Margry collated Joutel's narrative, as edited by Michel (1713), with additional details drawn from other accounts of the epic journey. The passages do not appear in the Michel edition or its English translation, which says of Ruter and Grollet only that "They had, in that short Space of Time, so perfectly enur'd themselves to the Customs of the Natives,

that they were become meer Savages" (3:149). Therefore, I will translate these three quotations myself.

18. Díaz, *The Conquest of New Spain*, 60.

19. Reproduced in Dickason, *The Myth of the Savage*, 253.

20. John White's watercolors that deBry used for the engravings are reproduced in Paul Hulton's *America 1585: The Complete Drawings of John White* as well as in Lorant, *The New World*. Hulton, in his notes (17–18), explains that the five pictures of the Picts are probably based not on White's work, but on that of Jacques Le Moyne de Morgues, whose drawings and paintings, all but a couple of which are lost, served as the basis for deBry's *Florida*, published in 1591 the year after the Hariot/White *Virginia*. Hulton also believes that the "powncing" is tattooing, at least for the women (28).

21. The Pétun or tobacco nation was neighbor to the Hurons and lived on the Niagara Peninsula and northern shore of Lake Erie.

22. I have translated this passage from Tonti, *Dernières découvertes dans l'Amérique Septentrionale de M. de la Salle*, as quoted in Philippe Jacquin's introduction to his edition of Bossu's 1768 book, 31. However, Tonti disavowed this book when it appeared, so it may be a hoax inspired by the success of Hennepin's and LeClercq's relations of the first La Salle expedition. The reliable "Relation de Henri de Tonti" was first published by Pierre Margry in his collection of colonial documents (1:571–616) and was translated by Melville B. Anderson (Chicago, 1898).

23. I am grateful to Patricia Galloway for alerting me to the existence of this fascinating document.

24. Bossu, *Nouveaux voyages aux Indes Occidentales*, 191.

25. There is no direct translation of the second passage in the Feiler translation.

26. Native American languages show a tremendous diversity in number systems, with 2, 5, 8, 10, 20, and 40 each serving in different tongues as the base (which is 10 in our Arabic decimal system), and multiplication, addition, subtraction, and finger and toe tallies all contributing to the formation of words for numbers that linguists have recorded. See Michael Closs, "Native American Number Systems," in the collection he edited, *Native American Mathematics*.

27. From the 1768 *Nouveaux voyages aux Indes Occidentales*.

28. See Boone, "Introduction: Writing and Recording Knowledge."

29. Paul Williams, "Reading Wampum Belts as Living Symbols," 164.

30. In the judgment of editor Réal Ouellet, the first, second, and fourth Greek words should be ἄδηλον, μυθικὸν, and ζτορικὸν. I have also copied the Greek as it appears in the English edition.

31. Bossu, *Nouveaux voyages en Louisiane*, ed. Jacquin, 171. English translation is from Feiler, 190.

32. This trope, of writing communicating through touch rather than visual reading, resembles the "trope of the talking book" identified by Henry Louis Gates Jr. in early African slave narratives. See his article, "James Gronniosaw and the Trope of the Talking Book."

33. Lebeau may have been inspired by a similar anecdote in the *Relation of 1639* (*JR* 16:43–45) that tells of an Algonquin convert who requested a text of a litany from Quebec missionaries and revered the paper as a powerful charm. See Axtell, "The Power of Print in the Eastern Woodlands," 303.

34. For an excellent assessment of the ideological function of the image of the solemn, figurative, and formal Indian speaker, built largely on accounts of nineteenth-century treaty negotiations, see David Murray's *Forked Tongues*.

35. Sagard, *Histoire du Canada*, 2:325.

Chapter Five

1. See also 55–60. The bee is also part of the mythology of the Mormons, who nicknamed Utah "The Beehive State" to characterize their hardworking, communal society. A key difference from the beaver, however, is that the honey bee is believed to be a European introduction to the New World.

2. Gagnon, " 'Portrait du Castor,' " 201.

3. Newman, *Company of Adventurers*, 58.

4. The work in question is *Relation par lettres de l'Amérique Septentrionale (années 1709 et 1710)*, first published in Paris in 1904. As late as 1980, when a translation by Ivy Alice Dickson appeared, it was attributed to Father Antoine Silvy, S.J. However, Réal Ouellet, in his 1990 edition of Lahontan, reports that recent discoveries support an attribution to Intendent Antoine-Denis Raudot. Of the eighty-nine short letters that make up the text, the seventh concerns the beaver.

5. Josselyn, *New Englands Rarities Discovered*, 18.

6. Vaughan and Clark, *Puritans among the Indians*, 117.

7. Ælian, *On the Characteristics of Animals*, 2:51.

8. Nicolas, "Histoire naturelle des Indes Occidentales" (ca. 1675), folio

119, quoted in Gagnon, "Portrait du Castor," 205. Nicolas's manuscript is still unpublished and is conserved at the Bibiothèque Nationale, Paris. I am indebted to Gagnon's two articles and to Ouellet's notes for information on castoreum and the classical Roman view of the beaver.

9. See McKeon, *The Origins of the English Novel*, 47–55, 100–28.

10. In fact, such a dam would require fewer beavers or less time to construct. Enos Mills, the greatest beaver ethnographer of the twentieth century, reports measuring a dam in Montana 2,140 feet long, the work of a colony of beavers over many years. See Mills, *In Beaver World*, 79.

11. The engraving is reproduced in Dickason, *The Myth of the Savage*, 149, and Newman, *Company of Adventurers*, 54.

12. Jacquin, *Les Indiens blancs*, 110. The quotation is from Bougainville's memoir of the Seven Years' War.

13. See, for instance, Jennings, *The Invasion of America*, chapter 5.

14. Ouellet, in his edition of Lahontan, vol. 1, note 439, observes that this is probably a misprint for "terriers" as Charlevoix writes. In either spelling, it refers to the land (terre) dwelling as opposed to the usual pond lodge.

15. Bacqueville de La Potherie took a more gracious view of these burrows, calling them "maisons de la campagne" (Tyrrell, *Letters of La Potherie*, 342) [country houses (ibid., 236)].

16. Van der Donck had a different explanation: he attributed the abrasion on the back to an excess of labor rather than to laziness: "nearly all the inhabitants of the New Netherlands know that many skins are sold from which the outside wind hairs are worn off on the back, which are called wood-carriers' skins, because they carried wood for the construction of their houses; this is not done as the ancients relate, between the legs as upon a sled or wagon; but . . . the female places herself under the piece to be removed, which the male and the young ones support on her back to the place where it is used" (*A Description of the New Netherlands*, 116–17).

17. See Montesquieu, *De l'esprit des lois*, book 18, chapter 4; book 19, chapter 4.

18. Jacquin comments that a fur trader could make twice the wages of a laborer in Quebec (*Les Indiens blancs*, 127; see also 154–63).

19. See Calvin T. Martin, *Keepers of the Game*, 16.

20. Axtell, *The European and the Indian*, 260.

21. Pratt, *Imperial Eyes*, 33–34.

22. Tyrrell, *Letters of La Potherie*, 341; English edition, 234.

Chapter Six

1. Gagnon, *Ces hommes dits sauvages*, 50.

2. Axtell, *Beyond 1492*, 142; Dickason, *Canada's First Nations*, 151, my emphasis.

3. A possible middle position to the question of guerrilla versus field tactics in early America is proposed by Patrick Malone in *The Skulking Way of War*. Working with early New England sources, Malone cites the mystic massacre as the onset of a "total warfare" hitherto unknown even to the English, a large-scale conflict in which no prisoners were taken, no ethical, legal, or customary restrictions were applied, and the stated goal was genocide of the enemy. "Total warfare" was thus a new style more destructive than either native technique; it represents one more instance of colonists creating the very "savagery" for which they blamed the Indians.

4. To call Prussia a victor in the war pursued by Frederick the Great is perhaps inaccurate, for the war did not add any territory to the state. For a good summary of the end of the Seven Years' War, see Parkman, *Montcalm and Wolfe, France and England in North America*.

5. On the Iroquois Wars, see Dickason, *Canada's First Nations*, 149–56.

6. On the "denial of coevalness," see Fabian, *Time and the Other*.

7. Slotkin and Folsom, *So Dreadfull a Judgement*, 387.

8. Cecelia Tichi, in Greenblatt and Gunn, *Redrawing the Boundaries*, 214.

9. The most important of the Puritan captives' accounts from the period 1675–1725, including those of Rowlandson, Stockwell, Gyles, and Williams, as well as the brief relation by Cotton Mather of Hannah Swarton's captivity, are collected by Vaughan and Clark in *Puritans among the Indians*. In the discussion below I will cite page numbers from this text using the initials "VC."

10. See Richard White, *The Middle Ground*, 112–17, 180.

11. Margry, *Découvertes et Etablissements*, 3:460.

12. Ibid., 5:90; English version, Quaife, *The Western Country in the Seventeenth Century*, 23.

13. See Lahontan, *Nouveaux voyages*, 2:184; Charlevoix, *Journal d'un voyage*, 240.

14. On the outcome of the Sudbury fight, see Slotkin and Folsom, *So Dreadfull a Judgement*, 368–69.

15. Bossu, *Nouveaux voyages en Louisiane*, ed. Jacquin, 157.

16. Jennings, *The Invasion of America*, 169, cites the Indians' custom of

sparing women and children in war for later adoption as an instance of a genuine ethic of honor.

17. Bossu, *Nouveaux voyages en Louisiane*, ed. Jacquin, 75.

18. On the coup tale, see Wong, *Sending My Heart Back across the Years*.

19. Church, in Slotkin and Folsom, *So Dreadfull a Judgement*, 432–33.

20. Ibid., 442.

21. Bossu, *Nouveaux voyages en Louisiane*, ed. Jacquin, 134.

22. See Trigger, "Champlain Judged by His Indian Policy," 98.

23. Lamothe-Cadillac, in Margry, *Découvertes et Etablissements*, 5:94–95; English version, Quaife, *The Western Country in the Seventeenth Century*, 30.

24. Hennepin, *Description de la Louisiane*, 225; English version, *A Description of Louisiana*, 216. The following page references are also to these texts.

25. The syntax of this translation differs from the original. In a longer context: "We slept at the point of the lake of Tears, which we so called from the weeping and tears which this chief shed there all night long, or which were shed by one of his sons, whom he caused to weep when tired himself, in order to excite his warriors to compassion, and oblige them to kill us and pursue their enemies to avenge his son's death."

26. Cited by Tailhan in the notes to his edition of Perrot, *Mémoire sur les mœurs, coutumes, et relligion des sauvages de l'Amérique Septentrionale*, 183.

27. Bossu, *Nouveaux voyages en Louisiane*, ed. Jacquin, 164.

28. For descriptions of cannibalism and an analysis of its ritual significance and of Montaigne's essay, see Jaenen, *Friend and Foe*, 143–48, and de Certeau, *Heterologies*, 67–79.

Epilogue

1. Eunice Williams still attracts fascination today. See Demos, *The Unredeemed Captive*, and Medlicott, "Return to the Land of Light: A Plea to an Unredeemed Captive."

2. Margry, *Découvertes et Etablissements*, 1:139–40.

3. See *Historical Atlas of Canada*, plate 42. The events at Fort William Henry remain the subject of controversy. See Jennings, *Empire of Fortune*, 316–20, and Steele, *Betrayals: Fort William Henry and the "Massacre,"* both of which take exception to Parkman's account. Both sides in the debate depend on the accounts by explorer-ethnographers Louis-Antoine de Bougainville and Jonathan Carver.

4. Michel de Certeau also refers to the *sauvage* as "the return of what the economy of production had to repress in order to be founded as such" (*The Writing of History*, 228).

5. Four versions of the manuscript journal of Carver's travels, preserved in the British Museum, are quite different from the published account. John Parker, editor of *The Journals of Jonathan Carver and Related Documents* (31), suggests that the ghost editor responsible for the plagiarized passages was one Alexander Bicknell. One can only speculate that other exploration-ethnography texts may also have been embellished by such editors, much as engravers transposed features into the engravings for Champlain's and Smith's books.

Works Cited

I have attempted to provide citations in the text with a minimum of clutter and apparatus by using page references in parentheses wherever possible. These page numbers refer to the editions listed below. Generally these references are easy to follow because there is only one title per author, or I have given the title in the text, or other clues make it clear which work is referred to. With several exceptions, quotations from translations are followed by their own page references, and both texts are listed below. The exceptions include the following:

Bossu: For the 1768 *Nouveaux voyages aux Indes Occidentales*, page numbers refer to Jacquin's 1980 French edition, entitled *Nouveaux voyages en Louisiane*, which should be more readily available than the original. Feiler's translation is of the 1769 edition, which differs only slightly from the volume of 1768. Quotations from Bossu's second book appear only in the epilogue.

Cartier and Champlain: I have avoided confusion between many different editions of these explorers' books by using H. P. Biggar's editions of the complete works of each. These feature same-page translations, so I have cited the page numbers only once.

Jesuit Relations: I have cited the Thwaites edition, which has become standard for both francophone and anglophone scholars. As this has facing-page translations, the page references appear only once. I have used the initials *JR* for these citations.

Lafitau: Because Fenton and Moore's translation includes bracketed page numbers to the original French edition of 1724, I have cited these, and only once per quotation.

Lahontan: Réal Ouellet's *Œuvres complètes* and Reuben Thwaites's first American edition include bracketed page numbers to the first French and English editions of 1703, and I have used these.

LeClercq: All page references are to his first work, *Nouvelle relation de la Gaspesie*, and its translation.

Le Page du Pratz: The 1774 English translation is heavily abridged. Wherever possible, I use it, but I have sometimes been forced to furnish my own translations.

Lescarbot: Both sets of page numbers are from the Champlain Society edition, which includes the original French in the back, as do the Champlain Society editions of Dièreville, Denys, and Bacqueville de La Potherie.

Raudot/Silvy and Beverley are cited by the number of the letter or section in the text, rather than by page number.

Gabriel Sagard: All page numbers cited in parentheses are to his first work, *Le grand voyage du pays des Hurons*, and its translation.

John Smith: The Barbour edition is now the standard one, and I cite its page numbers.

I hope that this bibliography will be a useful reference to the literature of colonial New France. Therefore, a few first editions of primary works are included below even if this is not the edition cited; in other cases, the date of publication of the first edition is in parentheses. It will be important for some readers to know that certain works, such as those of Strachey, Radisson, and Perrot, were not published until hundreds of years after they were written. A few titles mentioned only for historical context, or well-known works referred to but not quoted, such as Melville's and Cooper's, have been omitted, and a few not quoted in the text are included for the sake of breadth.

Primary Sources

Adair, James. *The History of the American Indians, particularly those nations adjoining to the Mississippi, East and West Florida, Georgia, South and North Carolina, and Virginia. Containing an Account of their Origin, Language, Manners, Religious and Civil Customs, Laws, Form of Government, Punishments, Conduct in War and Domestic Life, their Habits, Diet, Agriculture, Manufactures, Diseases and Method of Cure, and other particulars, sufficient to render it a Complete Indian System.* 1775. Reprint. Ann Arbor: University Microfilms, 1966.

Ælian. *On the Characteristics of Animals.* 3 vols. Trans. A. F. Scholfield. Cambridge: Harvard University Press/Loeb Classical Library, 1958.

Anburey, Thomas. *Travels through the Interior of America.* 1789. Reprint. Boston: Houghton Mifflin, 1923.

Anon. *A Relation of Maryland; Together with A Map of the Country, The Conditions of Plantation, His Majesties Charter to the Lord Baltemore, translated into English.* 1635. Reprint. Ann Arbor: University Microfilms, 1966.

Anon. *State of the British and French Colonies in North America with respect to the Number of People, Forces, Forts, Indians, Trade, and other Advantages. . . .* 1755. Reprint. New York: Johnson Reprints, 1967.

Arber, Edward, ed. *Travels and Works of Captain John Smith, President of Virginia and Admiral of New England* (1608–31). 2 vols. Edinburgh: John Grant, 1910.

Armstrong, Virginia Irving, ed. *I Have Spoken: American History through the Voices of the Indians.* Chicago: Sage Books, 1971.

"B.," J. C. *Voyage au Canada, dans le nord de l'Amérique Septentrionale, fait depuis l'an 1751 à 1761.* Ed. Abbé H. R. Casgrain. Quebec, 1887. [English edition: *Travels in New France.* Ed. Sylvester K. Stevens, Donald H. Kent, and Emma Edith Woods. Harrisburg: Pennsylvania Historical Society, 1941.]

Bacqueville de La Potherie, Claude-Charles le Roi, Sieur de. *Histoire de l'Amérique Septentrionale.* 4 vols. Paris: J. L. Nion et F. Bidot, 1722. [See also Blair, Tyrrell]

Barbour, Philip, ed. *The Complete Works of Captain John Smith, 1580–1631.* 3 vols. Chapel Hill: Institute for Early American History and Culture/University of North Carolina Press, 1986.

———. *The Jamestowne Voyages under the First Charter, 1606–1609.* Hakluyt Soc. 2d ser., vols. 136–37. London: Hakluyt Society, 1969.

Bartram, John. *Observations on the Inhabitants, Climate, Soil, Rivers, Productions, Animals, and other matters worthy of Notice. Made by Mr. John Bartram, in his Travels from Pennsylvania to Onondago, Oswego, and the Lake Ontario, in Canada.* 1751. Reprint. Ann Arbor: University Microfilms, 1966 [includes Peter Kalm's letter about Niagara Falls].

Bernard, Jean-Frederic. *Receuil des voyages au nord.* 8 vols. Amsterdam: J.-F. Bernard, 1715–27.

———. *Relations de la Louisiane, et du fleuve Mississippi, ou l'on voit l'état de ce grand païs & les avantages qu'il peut produire . . .* 5 vols. Amsterdam: J.-F. Bernard, 1720.

Beverley, Robert. *The History and Present State of Virginia, in Four Parts. I. The History of the First Settlement in Virginia, and the Government thereof to the Present Time. II. The Natural Productions and Conveniences of the Country, Suited to Trade and Improvement. III. The Native Indians, Their Religion, Laws, and Customs, in War and in Peace. IV. The Present State of the Country, as to the Polity of the*

Government, and the Improvements of the Land. 1705. Reprint. Ed. Louis B. Wright. Chapel Hill: University of North Carolina Press, 1947.

Biggar, H. P., ed. *The Voyages of Jacques Cartier* (1534–42). Ottawa: F. A. Acland, 1924.

———, ed. *The Works of Samuel de Champlain.* 6 vols. Toronto: Champlain Society, 1922–36.

Black Hawk. *An Autobiography.* Ed. J. B. Patterson, trans. Antoine LeClair. 1833. Reprint. Ed. Donald Jackson. Urbana: University of Illinois Press, 1955.

Blair, Emma Helen, ed. and trans. *The Indian Tribes of the Upper Mississippi and Region of the Great Lakes as described by Nicolas Perrot, French commandant in the Northwest; Bacqueville de la Potherie, French royal commissioner to Canada; Morrell Marston, American army officer; and Thomas Forsyth, United States agent at Fort Armstrong.* 2 vols. Cleveland: Arthur H. Clark, 1911.

Bossu, Jean Bernard. *Nouveaux voyages dans l'Amérique Septentrionale, contenant, Une collection de Lettres écrites sur les lieux, par l'Auteur, à son ami, M. Douin, Chevalier, Capitaine dans les troupes du Roi, ci-devant son camarade dans le Nouveau Monde.* Amsterdam: Chez Changuion, 1777. [English edition: *New Travels in North America, 1770–1771.* Trans. Samuel Dorris Dickinson. Natchitoches, La.: Northwestern State University Press, 1982.]

———. *Nouveaux voyages aux Indes Occidentales; Contenant une Relation des différens Peuples qui habitent les environs du grand Fleuve Saint-Louis, appellé vulgairement le Mississipi; leur Religion; leur gouvernement; leurs mœurs; leurs guerres & leur commerce.* 1768. Reprint. *Nouveaux voyages en Louisiane.* Ed. Philippe Jacquin. Paris: Aubier Montaigne, 1980. [English edition: *Travels in the Interior of North America* (2d ed., 1769). Trans. Seymour Feiler. Norman: University of Oklahoma Press, 1962.]

Boucher, Pierre. *Histoire véritable et naturelle des mœurs et productions du pays de la Nouvelle France, vulgairement dite le Canada.* 1664. Reprint. Boucherville, Quebec: Societé Historique de Boucherville, 1964. [English edition: *Canada in the Seventeenth Century, from the French of Pierre Boucher.* Trans. Edward Louis Montizambert. Montreal: G. E. Desbarats, 1883.]

Bougainville, Louis-Antoine de. *Adventure in the Wilderness: The American Journals of Louis Antoine de Bougainville, 1756–1760.* Trans. Edward P. Hamilton. Norman: University of Oklahoma Press, 1964.

———. *Voyage autour du monde par le frégate du Roi La Boudeuse et la flûte L'Etoile.* 1771. Reprint. Paris: Gallimard/Folio, 1982. [English edition: *A Voyage round the World.* Trans. John Reinhold Forster. New York: Da Capo Press, 1967.]

Bowden, Henry W., and James P. Ronda, eds. *John Eliot's Indian Dialogues: A Study in Cultural Interaction (Indian Dialogues for Their Instruction in the Great Service of Christ,* 1671). Westport, Conn.: Greenwood Press, 1980.

Bradford, William. *Of Plymouth Plantation, 1620–1647.* Ed. Samuel Eliot Morison. New York: Alfred A. Knopf, 1966. [See also Winslow]

Brissot de Warville, Jacques Pierre. *Nouveau voyage dans les Etats-unis de l'Amérique Septentrionale, fait en 1788.* 3 vols. Paris: Buisson, 1791. [English edition: *New Travels in the United States.* Trans. Mara Soceanu Vamos and Durand Echeverria. Cambridge: Belknap/Harvard University Press, 1964.]

Byrd, William II. *The History of the Dividing Line betwixt Virginia and North Carolina* (1728) and *The Secret History of the Dividing Line betwixt Virginia and North Carolina.* New York: Dover, 1967.

Cabeza de Vaca, Alvar Nunez. *Travels in the Unknown Interior of North America.* 1542. Reprint. Trans. Cyclone Covey. Albuquerque: University of New Mexico Press, 1983.

Calloway, Colin G., ed. *The World Turned Upside Down: Indian Voices from Early America.* Boston: St. Martin's Press, 1994.

Cartier, Jacques. [See Biggar]

Carver, Jonathan. *The Journals of Jonathan Carver and Related Documents, 1766–1770.* Ed. John Parker. St. Paul: Minnesota Historical Society Press, 1976.

———. *Travels through the Interior Parts of North-America in the Years 1766, 1767, and 1768.* London: For the Author, 1778.

Cavelier, Jean. *The Journal of Jean Cavelier: The Account of a Survivor of LaSalle's Texas Expedition, 1684–88.* Trans. Jean Delanglez. Chicago: Institute of Jesuit History, 1938.

Champlain, Samuel de. *Voyages to New France, 1599–1603.* Ed. Edward Miles. N.p.: Oberon Press, 1971. [See also Biggar]

Charlevoix, Pierre François-Xavier de. *Journal d'un voyage fait par ordre du roi dans l'Amérique Septentrionale; où l'on trouvera la description Géographique, & l'Histoire Naturelle des Pays, que l'Auteur a parcourus, les Coûtumes, le Caractere, la Religion, les Mœurs, & les Traditions des Peuples, qui les habitent. Addressée à Madame la Duchesse de Lesdiguières* (3d vol. of *Histoire et description générale de la Nouvelle France,* 1744). 2 vols. Ed. Pierre Berthiaume. Montreal: Les Presses Universitaires de Montréal, 1994. [English edition: *Journal of a Voyage to North America.* 1761. Reprint. Ann Arbor: University Microfilms, 1966.]

Chateaubriand, François-Réné de. *Œuvres romanesques et voyages*. Vol. 1 of *Œuvres complètes*. Paris: Gallimard, Editions de la Pleaide, 1969.

——. *Travels in America*. 1827. Reprint. Trans. Richard Switzer. Lexington: University of Kentucky Press, 1969.

Child, Lydia Maria. *Hobomok* (1824) *and Other Writings on Indians*. Ed. Carolyn Karcher. New Brunswick: Rutgers University Press, 1986.

Church, Thomas [Benjamin Church]. *History of King Philip's War, commonly called the Great Indian War, of 1675 and 1676. Also of the French and Indian Wars at the Eastward, in 1689, 1690, 1692, 1696, and 1704*. 2d ed. Exeter, N.H.: J. & B. Williams, 1829.

Cohen, J. M., ed. and trans. *The Four Voyages of Christopher Columbus*. Harmondsworth, England: Penguin, 1969.

Colden, Cadwallader. *The History of the Five Indian Nations Depending on the Province of New York in America*. Pt. 1, 1727; Pt. 2, 1747. Reprint. Ithaca: Cornell University Press, 1964.

Coxe, Daniel. *A Description of the English Province of Carolana, By the Spaniards call'd Florida, And by the French La Louisiane*. 1722. Reprint. Gainesville: University Presses of Florida, Bicentennial Floridiana Facsimile Series, 1976.

Crèvecœur, J. Hector St. John de. *Letters from an American Farmer* (1782) *and Sketches of Eighteenth-Century America*. Ed. Albert Stone. Harmondsworth, England: Penguin, 1981.

Dampier, William. *A New Voyage round the World*. 1697. Reprint. New York: Dover, 1968.

Defoe, Daniel. *The Life and Strange Surprising Adventures of Robinson Crusoe, of York, Mariner: Who lived Eight and Twenty Years, all alone in an un-inhabited Island on the Coast of America, near the Mouth of the Great River of Oroonoque; Having been cast on Shore by Shipwreck, wherein all the Men perished but himself*. London: W. Taylor, 1719.

[Deliette]. "Memoir of De Gannes Concerning the Illinois Country." *Illinois Historical Collections 23: French Series, vol. 1*. Springfield: Illinois State Historical Society, 1934: 302–95. [See also Quaife]

Denton, Daniel. *A Brief Description of New York*. 1670. Reprint. New York: Columbia University Press for the Facsimile Text Society, 1937

Denys, Nicolas. *Histoire Naturelle Des Peuples, des Animaux, des Arbres & Plantes de l'Amérique Septentrionale, & de ses divers Climats. Avec une Description exacte de la Pesche des Moluës, tant sur le Grand-Banc qu'à la Coste; & de tout de qui s'y pratique de plus particulier, &c.* Paris: L. Billaine, 1672. [2d vol. of *Description geographique et historique des costes de l'Amérique Septentrionale.* English edition: *The Description and Natural History of the Coasts of North America (Acadia).* Ed. and trans. William F. Ganong. Toronto: Champlain Society, 1908. Reprint. New York: Greenwood Press, 1968.]

DePauw, Cornelius. *Recherches Philosophiques sur les Américains, ou mémoires intéressans pour servir à l'histoire de l'espèce humaine.* 1768. Reprint. 3 vols. Paris: Jean-François Bastien, l'an III de la République Française, [1793].

Díaz del Castillo, Bernal. *The Conquest of New Spain.* 1568. Reprint. Trans. J. M. Cohen. Baltimore: Penguin, 1963.

Diderot, Denis. *Supplément au voyage de Bougainville: Pensées philosophiques/lettre sur les aveugles.* Ed. Antoine Adam. Paris: Garnier-Flammarion, 1972.

Dièreville, N. de. *Relation du voyage du Port Royal de l'Acadie ou de la Nouvelle France, dans laquelle on voit un détail des divers mouvemens de la mer dans une traversée de long cours; la Description du Païs, les Occupations des François qui y sont établis, les manières des differents Nations Sauvages, leurs Superstitions, & leurs chasses; avec une dissertation exacte sur le Castor.* 1708. Trans. *Relation of the Voyage to Port Royal in Acadia or New France . . .* by Mrs. Clarence Webster. Toronto: Champlain Society, 1933.

Du Creux, François. *Historiae Canadensis ser Nouae Franciae.* Paris: Sebastien Cramoisy, 1664. [English edition: *History of Canada or New France in Ten Books in the Year of Our Lord 1656,* 2 vols. Ed. James B. Conacher, trans. Percy J. Robinson. Toronto: Champlain Society, 1951.]

Dumont de Montigny. *Mémoire historique sur la Louisiane contenant ce qui est arrivé de plus mémorable depuis l'année 1687 jusqu'à présent: avec l'établissment de la colonie françoise dans cette province de l'Amérique Septentrionale sous le direction de la Compagnie des Indes: le climat, la natur, & les productions de ce pays; l'origine et la religion des sauvages qui y habitent, leur mûrs et leurs coutumes, &.* Paris: C. J. B. Bauche, 1753. 2 vols. [Sometimes cataloged under Jean-Baptiste Le Mascrier.]

Durand de Dauphiné. *Voyages d'un François Exilé pour la Religion, avec une description de la Virgine & Marilan dans l'Amérique.* 1687. Reprint. *Un Français en Virginie.* Ed. Gilbert Chinard. Washington, D.C.: Institut Français de Washington, 1932.

Easton, John. "A Relacion of the Indyan Warr." 1675. Reprint. In *Narratives of the Indian Wars, 1675–1699,* ed. Charles H. Lincoln, 7–17. New York: Charles Scribner's Sons, 1913.

Eliot, John. *A Brief Narrative of the Progress of the Gospel among the Indians of New England.* Cambridge, Mass., 1670. [See also Bowden and Ronda]

Frost, John. *Pictorial History of Indian Wars and Captivities.* New York: N.p., 1873.

Garcilaso de la Vega, El Inca. *Royal Commentaries of the Incas and General History of Peru.* 1609. Reprint. Trans. Harold V. Livermore. Austin: University of Texas Press, 1966.

Gookin, Daniel. *Historical Collections of the Indians in New England. Of their several Nations, Numbers, Customs, Manners, Religion and Government, before the English planted there.* 1792. Reprint. New York: Arno Press, 1972.

Hakluyt, Richard. *The Principal Navigations, Voyages, and Discoveries of the English Nation.* 1589. Reprint. 2 vols. Cambridge: Cambridge University Press for the Hakluyt Society, 1965.

——. *The Principal Navigations, Voyages, Traffiques, and Discoveries of the English Nation.* 1598–1600. Reprint. 12 vols. Glasgow: MacLehose, 1904.

Hariot, Thomas. *A Briefe and True Report of the New Found Land of Virginia.* 1588. Reprint. London: Berhard Quaritch, 1893.

Hearne, Samuel. *Journal of a Voyage from Prince of Wales Fort in Hudson's Bay to the Northern Ocean, 1769, 1770, 1771, 1772.* Ed. Richard Glover. Toronto: Champlain Society, 1958.

Heckewelder, John. *An Account of the History, Manners, and Customs of the Indians Nations Who Once Inhabited Pennsylvania and the Neighboring States.* 1819. Reprint. New York: Arno Press and the New York Times, 1971.

Hennepin, Louis. *Description de la Louisiane, nouvellement découverte au Sud Ouest de la Nouvelle France par ordre du Roy, avec la carte du pays, les Mœurs & la Maniere de vivre des Sauvages.* Paris: Sebastien Huré, 1683. [English edition: *A Description of Louisiana.* Trans. John Gilmary Shea, 1880. Reprint. Ann Arbor: University Microfilms, 1966.]

——. *Nouvelle découverte d'un très grand pays situé dans l'Amérique entre le Nouveau Mexique et la mer glacial, Avec les Cartes, & les Figures necessaires, & de plus l'Histoire Naturelle et Morale, & les avantages qu'on en peut tirer par l'etablissement des Colonies Le Tout dedie à Sa Majesté Britannique Guillaume III.* Utrecht: Guillaume Broedelet, 1697. [English edition: *A New Discovery of a Vast Country in America . . .* London: For M. Bentley, J. Tonson, H. Bonwick, etc., 1698.]

Henry, Alexander. *Travels in Canada and the Indian Territories between the Years 1760 and 1776, by Alexander Henry, Fur Trader.* Ed. James Bain. Toronto: George N. Morang, 1901.

Hubbard, William. *A Narrative of the Troubles with the Indians in New-England, from the First Planting Thereof in the Year 1607. to this Present Year 1677: But Chiefly of the Late Troubles in the Last Two Years, 1675. and 1676; to which is added a Discourse about the Warre with the Pequods in the Year 1637.* Boston: John Foster, 1677.

Hunter, John Dunn. *Memoirs of a Captivity among the Indians of North America.* 1824. Reprint. Ed. Richard Drinnon. New York: Schocken Books, 1973.

Huntington, R. T. [See Talon]

James, Edwin. *Account of an Expedition from Pittsburgh to the Rocky Mountains in 1819–20.* 2 vols. Philadelphia: H. C. Carey and I. Lee, 1822.

Jefferson, Thomas. *Notes on the State of Virginia.* 1782. Reprint. In *The Portable Thomas Jefferson*, ed. Merrill D. Peterson, 23–232. Harmondsworth, England: Penguin, 1975.

Jemison, Mary. [See Seaver]

Jérémie, Nicolas. *Rélation du Détroit de la Baie de Hudson.* In *Receuil des Voyages au Nord*, ed. J.-F. Bernard, vol. 5. Amsterdam: J.-F. Bernard, 1720.

Jesuit Relations [See Thwaites]

Jewitt, John. *Narrative of the Adventures and Sufferings of John R. Jewitt, only survivor of the crew of the Ship Boston, During a Captivity of nearly 3 years among the Savages of Nootka Sound: with an account of the Manners, Mode of Living, and Religious Opinions of the Natives.* 1851. Reprint. Ed. Hilary Stewart. Vancouver: Douglas and McIntyre, 1987.

Johnson, Edward. *A History of New England. From the English planting in the Yeere 1628. untill the Yeere 1652. Declaring the form of their Government, Civill, Military, and Ecclesiastique. Their Wars with the Indians, their Troubles with the Gortonists, and other Heretiques. . . .* [a.k.a. "Johnson's Wonder Working Providence"]. Ed. J. Franklin Jameson. New York: Charles Scribner's Sons, 1910.

Johnson, Robert. "Nova Britannia." In vol. 1, *Tracts and Other Papers, Relating Principally to the Origin, Settlement, and Progress of the Colonies in North America, From the Discovery of The Country to the Year 1776.* Ed. Peter Force. Washington, D.C.: Peter Force, 1836–38.

Josselyn, John. *John Josselyn, Colonial Traveler: A Critical Edition of Two Voyages to New England.* 1674. Reprint. Ed. Paul J. Linholdt. Hanover, N.H.: University Press of New England, 1988.

——. *New Englands Rarities Discovered.* 1672. Reprint. Bedford, Mass.: Applewood Books, n.d.

Joutel, Henri. *Journal historique du dernier voyage qui fut M. de la Sale.* Ed. M. de

Michel. Paris: Estienne Robinot, 1713. [English edition: *Joutel's Journal of LaSalle's Last Voyage*. 1714. Reprint. Albany: Joseph McDonough, 1906.]

——. *Relation d'Henri Joutel. Voyage du M. de La Salle dans l'Amérique Septentrionale dans l'année 1685*. In Margry, *Découvertes et Etablissements*, 3:88–534. Paris: D. Jouaust, 1879–88.

Kalm, Peter. [See Bartram]

Kellogg, Louise P., ed. *Early Narratives of the Northwest*. New York: Charles Scribner's Sons, 1917.

La Condamine, Charles-Marie de. *Voyage sur l'Amazone*. 1766. Reprint. Ed. Hélène Minguet. Paris: François Maspero, 1981.

Lafitau, Joseph-François. *Mœurs des sauvages américains comparées aux mœurs des premiers temps*. Paris: Saugrain l'ainé et Charles Estienne Hochereau, 1724. [English edition: *Customs of the American Indians Compared with the Customs of Primitive Times*. Trans. and ed. William Fenton and Elizabeth Moore. Toronto: Champlain Society, 1974.]

Lahontan, Louis-Armand de Lom d'Arce, Baron de. *Nouveaux voyages de M. Le Baron de Lahontan, dans l'Amérique Septentrionale, qui contiennent une rélation des différens Peuples qui y habitent; la nature de leur Gouvernement; leur Commerce, leurs Coutumes, leur Religion; & leur manière de faire la Guerre. Tome Premier. / Memoires de l'Amérique Septentrionale, ou la suite des Voyages de M. le Baron de Lahontan. Qui contiennent la Description d'une grande étentuë de Païs de ce Continent, l'intérêt des François & des Anglois, leurs Commerces, leurs Navigations, les Mœurs & les Coutumes des Sauvages &c. Avec un petit Dictionnaire de la Langue du Païs. Le tout enrichi de Cartes & de Figures. Tome Second. / Suplément aux Voyages du Baron de Lahontan, Où l'on trouve des Dialogues curieux entre l'Auteur et un Sauvage de bon sens qui a voyagé. L'on y voit aussi plusieurs observations faites par le même Auteur dans ses Voyages en Portugal, en Espagne, en Hollande, & en Danemarck, &c. Tome Troisieme*. 3 vols. La Haye: Les Frères l'Honoré, 1703. [English edition: *New Voyages to North America*. 1703. Reprint. Ed. Reuben Gold Thwaites. Chicago: A. C. McClurg and Co., 1905.]

——. *Oeuvres complètes*. Ed. Réal Ouellet. Montreal: Les Presses de l'Université de Montréal, 1990.

Lamothe–Cadillac, Antoine. [See Quaife, Margry]

Laudonnière, Réné Goulainé de. *L'histoire notable de la Floride, situé es Indes Occidentales. Contenant les trois voyages faits en icelle par certains Capitaines et Pilotes françois, descrits par le capitaine Laudonnière, qui y a commané l'espace d'un an trois moys: à laquelle a esté adjousté un quatriesme voyage fait par le capitaine Gourgues*. Ed. M. Basanier, 1586. Reprint. Paris: P. Jannet, 1853. [English edition: *Three Voyages*. Trans. and ed. Charles E. Bennet. Gainesville: University Press of Florida, 1975.]

Lawson, John. *A New Voyage to Carolina, containing the exact description and Natural History of that Country, together with the present state thereof and a Journal of a Thousand Miles Travel'd thro; several Nations of Indians, Giving a particular Account of their Customs, Manners, etc.* 1709. Reprint. Ed. Hugh Talmadge Lefler. Chapel Hill: University of North Carolina Press, 1967.

Lebeau, Claude. *Avantures de Sr. C. Le Beau, avocat en Parlement, où voyage curieux et nouveau parmi les sauvages de l'Amérique Septentrionale.* 1738. Reprint. 2 vols. New York: Johnson Reprints, 1966.

LeClercq, Père Chrestien. *Nouvelle relation de la Gaspesie, qui contient les Mœurs et la Religion des Sauvages Gaspesiens Porte-Croix, adorateurs du Soliel & d'autres Peuples de l'Amérique Septentrionale, dite le Canada.* Paris: A. Auroy, 1691. [English edition: *New Relation of Gaspesia with the Customs and Religion of the Gaspesian Indians.* Ed. and trans. William F. Ganong, 1910. Reprint. New York: Greenwood Press, 1968.]

——. *Premier établissment de la Foy dans la Nouvelle France contenant la publication de l'Evangile, l'histoire des colonies françaises et les fameuses découvertes de la Salle.* 2 vols. Paris: A. Auroy, 1691. [English edition: *First Establishment of the Faith in New France.* Trans. J. G. Shea. New York: J. G. Shea, 1881.]

Lederer, John. *The Discoveries of John Lederer, In three several marches from Virginia to the west of Carolina, And other parts of the Continent: Begun in March 1669, and ended in September 1670. Together with A General Map of the whole Territory which he traversed.* Trans. Sir William Talbot, 1672. Reprint. Ed. William P. Cumming. Charlotteville: University of Virginia Press, 1958.

Le Page du Pratz, Antoine. *Histoire de la Louisiane, contenant la Découverte du ce vaste pays, sa Description géographique, un Voyage dans les Terres, l'Histoire Naturelle; les Mœurs, Coutûmes & Religion des Naturels, avec leurs Origines; deux Voyages dans le Nord du nouveau Mexique, dont un jusqu'à la Mer du Sud; ornée de deux Cartes & de 40 Planches en Taille douce.* 3 vols. Paris: De Bure, Veuve Delaguette, et Lambert, 1758. [English edition: *The History of Louisiana, or of the Wester Parts of Virginia and Carolina.* 1774. Reprint. Baton Rouge: Louisiana State University Press, 1983.]

Léry, Jean de. *Histoire d'un voyage faict en la terre du Brésil autrement dite Amerique. Le tout recueilli sur les lieux par Jean de Léry.* Geneva: Antoine Chuppin, 1578. [English edition: *History of a Voyage to the Land of Brazil.* Trans. Janet Whatley. Berkeley: University of California Press, 1992.]

Lesage, Alain. *Les Avantures de Monsieur Robert Chevalier, dit de Beauchêne, capi-*

taine de flibustiers dans la nouvelle France. 1732. Reprint. Lagrasse, France: Verdier, 1980.

Lescarbot, Marc. *Histoire de la Nouvelle France: Contenant les navigations & découvertes des François faites dans les golfe & grande rivière de Canada.* Paris: Jean Milot, 1609. [English edition: *The History of New France.* Trans. and ed. W. L. Grant, 1907–14. Reprint. New York: Greenwood Press, 1968.]

Long, John. *Voyages and Travels of an Indian Interpreter and Trader, describing The Manners and Customs of the North American Indians; with an Account of the Posts situated on the River Saint Laurence, Lake Ontario, etc. To which is added, A Vocabulary of The Chippeway Language. Names of Furs and Skins, in English and French. A List of Words in the Iroquois, Mohegan, Shawnee, and Esquimeaux Tongues, and a table, shewing The Analogy between the Algonkin and Chippeway Languages.* 1791. Reprint. Chicago: Lakeside Press, 1922.

Lorant, Stephen, ed. *The New World: The First Pictures of America.* New York: Duell, Sloan and Pearce, 1946 [Jacques Le Moyne de Morgues, John White, Thomas Hariot].

Loskiel, George Henry. *History of the Mission of the United Brethren among the North American Indians.* Trans. Christian Latrobe. London: The Brethren's Society for the Furtherance of the Gospel, 1794.

Margry, Pierre, ed. *Découvertes et Etablissements des François dans l'Ouest et le Sud de l'Amérique Septentrionale.* 6 vols. Paris: D. Jouaust, 1879–88.

Marshall, Joyce, ed. and trans. *Word from New France: The Selected Letters of Marie de l'Incarnation.* Toronto: Oxford University Press, 1967.

Mather, Increase. *A Brief History of the War with the Indians in New-England (From June 24, 1675, when Philip, alias Metacomet, the Principal Author and Beginner of the Warr, was Slain): Wherein the Grounds, Beginning, and Progress of the Warr, is Summarily Expressed; together with a Serious Exhortation to the Inhabitants of the Land.* Boston: John Forster, 1676.

Mintz, Steven, ed. *Native American Voices: A History and Anthology.* St. James, N.Y.: Brandywine Press, 1995.

Montaigne, Michel de. *Essais.* 1582. Reprint. 3 vols. Paris: Garnier, 1958. [English edition: *Essays.* Trans. J. M. Cohen. Harmondsworth, England: Penguin, 1958.]

Montesquieu, Charles-Louis de Secondat. *Lettres Persanes.* 1721. Reprint. Ed. Jean Starobinski. Paris: Gallimard, 1973.

———. *De l'esprit des lois.* 1748. Paris: Garnier-Flammarion, 1979.

Morton, Thomas. *New English Canaan or New Canaan. Containing an Abstract of*

New England. Composed in three Bookes (1637). Ed. Charles Francis Adams. Boston: Prince Society, 1883. Reprint. New York: Burt Franklin, 1967.

Nabokov, Peter, ed. *Native American Testimony: An Anthology of Indian and White Relations: First Encounter to Dispossession.* New York: Crowell, 1978.

O'Callaghan, E. B., ed. *The Documentary History of the State of New York.* 4 vols. Albany: Weed, Parsons, and Co., 1849–51.

Paine, Thomas. *The Age of Reason: Being an Investigation of True and Fabulous Theology.* Paris: Barrois/London: Eaton, 1794.

Penhallow, Samuel. *The History of the Wars of New-England, with the Eastern Indians. Or, a Narrative of their continued Perfidy and Cruelty. . . .* 1726. Reprint. Williamstown, Mass.: Corner House Press, 1973.

Perrot, Nicolas. *Mémoire sur les mœurs, coutumes, et relligion des sauvages de l'Amérique Septentrionale.* Ed. Père Tailhan. Leipzig and Paris: A. Franck, 1864. Reprint. New York: Johnson Reprints, 1968. [English translation in Blair, *Indian Tribes of the Upper Mississippi.*]

Peyer, Bernd, ed. *The Elders Wrote: An Anthology of Early Prose by North American Indians, 1768–1931.* Berlin: Reimer, 1982.

Prévost, Abbé de. *Le Philosophe Anglais, ou Histoire de Monsieur Clevelend, fils naturel de Cromwell.* 1731–39. Reprint. Vol. 2 of *Oeuvres de Prévost.* Ed. Jean Sgard. Grenoble: Presses Universitaires de Grenoble, 1978–86.

Purchas, Samuel. *Hakluytus Posthumus, or Purchas His Pilgrimes, Contayning a History of the World in Sea Voyages and Lande Travells by Englishmen and others.* 20 vols. 1625. Reprint. Glasgow: MacLehose, 1906.

Quaife, Milo, ed. *The Western Country in the Seventeenth Century: The Memoirs of Lamothe Cadillac and Pierre Liette.* Chicago: Lakeside Press, 1947.

Radisson, Pierre-Esprit. *Voyages of Peter Esprit Radisson, being an account of his Travels and Experience among the North American Indians from 1652 to 1684.* Ed. Gideon Scull. 1885. Reprint. New York: P. Smith, 1943.

Raudot, Antoine-Denis. *Relation par lettres de l'Amérique Septentrionale (années 1709 et 1710), editée et annotée par le. P. Camille de Rochemonteix de la Compagnie de Jesus.* Paris: Letouzey et Ané, 1904. [English edition: *Letters from North America.* Trans. Ivy Alice Dickson. Belleville, Ontario: Mika, 1980.]

Robin, Abbé de. *Nouveau Voyage dans l'Amérique Septentrionale.* Paris: 1783.

Rogers, Robert. *A Concise Account of North America: containing A Description of the several British Colonies on that Continent, including the Islands of Newfoundland, Cape Breton, &c. as to Their Situation, Extent, Climate, Soil, Produce, Rise, Government, Religion, Present Boundaries, and the Number of Inhabitants supposed to be in each. Also of The Interior, or Westerly Parts of the Country, upon the Rivers St. Laurence, the Mississipi, Christino, and the Great Lakes. To which is subjoined, An Account of the several Nations and Tribes of Indians residing in those Parts, as to their Customs, Manners, Government, Numbers, &c. Containing many Useful and Entertaining Facts, never before treated of.* 1765. Reprint. New York: Johnson Reprint, 1966.

———. *Ponteach, or the Savages of America: A Tragedy.* London: J. Millam, 1766.

Rousseau, Jean-Jacques. *Discours sur l'origine et les fondements de l'inégalité.* 1755. Reprint. Paris: Garnier-Flammarion, 1971.

———. *Essai sur l'origine des langues.* Bordeaux: Ducros, 1968. [English edition: *On the Origin of Language.* Trans. John H. Moran. Chicago: University of Chicago Press, 1966.]

———. *The Social Contract and Discourses.* Trans. G. D. H. Cole. London: Dent/Everyman's Library, 1973.

Sagard-Théodat, Gabriel. *Le grand voyage du pays des Hurons.* Paris: Denys Moreau, 1632. [English edition: *The Long Journey to the Country of the Hurons.* Trans. H. H. Langton. Toronto: Champlain Society, 1939.]

———. *Histoire du Canada.* 1636. Reprint. 3 vols. Paris: Tross, 1865.

Schoolcraft, Henry Rowe. *Algic Researches.* 1839. Westport, Conn.: Greenwood, 1974.

Seaver, James. *A Narrative of the Life of Mrs. Mary Jemison, Who was taken by the Indians, in the year 1755, when only about twelve years of age, and has continued to reside amongst them to the present time.* 1824. Reprint. Ed. June Namias. Norman: University of Oklahoma Press, 1992.

Silvy, Antoine. [See Raudot]

Slotkin, Richard, and James Folsom, eds. *So Dreadfull a Judgement: Puritan Responses to King Philip's War, 1676–1677.* Middletown, Conn.: Wesleyan University Press, 1978.

Smith, James. "An Account of the Remarkable Occurences in the Life and Travels of Col. James Smith (Now a Citizen of Bourbon County, Kentucky) During his Captivity with the Indians, in the years 1755, '56, '57, '58, & '59. In which the Customs, Manners, Traditions, Theological Sentiments, Mode of Warfare, Military Tactics, Discipline and Encampments, Treatment of prisoners, &c. are better explained, and more minutely related, than has been heretofore done, by any author on that subject." In *A Selection of Some of the Most Interesting Narratives of Outrages Committed by the Indians in their Wars with the White People,* ed. Archibald Loudon (1808), 119–251. Reprint. New York: Arno Press, 1971.

———. *A Treatise on the Mode and Manner of Indian War*. Paris, Ky.: Lyle, 1812.

Smith, John [See Barbour]

[Smith, William, and Thomas Hutchins.] *Historical Account of Bouquet's Expedition against the Ohio Indians, in 1764*. 1765. Reprint. Cincinnati: Robert Clarke, 1868.

Strachey, William. *The Historie of Travell into Virginia Britania*. 1849. Reprint. Ed. Louis B. Wright and Virginia Freund. London: Hackluyt Society, 1953.

Swift, Jonathan. *Gulliver's Travels*. World Classics Edition. Oxford: Oxford University Press, 1986.

Talon, Pierre, and Jean-Baptiste Talon. "Expedition to the Mississippi River by way of the Gulf of Mexico: An Account of the Interrogation of the two Canadians who are Soldiers in the Company of Feuguerolles and their Responses. Brest, February 14, 1698." Trans. R. T. Huntington. *Iowa Review* 15 (1985): 99–139.

Thevet, André. *André Thevet's North America: A Sixteenth-Century View*. Ed. Roger Schlesinger and Arthur Stabler. Kingston, Canada: McGill-Queen's University Press, 1986.

———. *Les singularités de la France antarctique*. 1557. Reprint. Ed. Frank Lestringant. Paris: Maspero/la Découverte, 1983.

Thompson, David. *The Narrative, 1784–1812*. Ed. Richard Glover. Toronto: Champlain Society, 1962.

Thwaites, Reuben Gold, ed. *The Jesuit Relations and Allied Documents: Travels and Explorations of the Jesuit Missionaries in New France, 1610–1791*. 73 vols. Cleveland: Burrows Brothers, 1896–1901. [See also Lahontan]

Tonti, Henri de. [?] *Dernières découvertes dans l'Amérique Septentrionale de M. de La Salle . . . par M. Chevalier de Tonti Gouverneur du fort St. Louis aux Islinois*. Paris: Jean Guignard, 1697.

———. *Relation of Henri de Tonti*. Trans. Melville B. Anderson. Chicago: Caxton Club, 1898. [For French original, see Margry]

Tyrrell, J. B., ed. and trans. *Letters of La Potherie* [*Histoire de l'Amérique Septentrionale*, vol. 1, Paris, 1753]. Reprint. In *Documents Relating to the Early History of Hudson Bay*. Toronto: Champlain Society, 1931.

VanDerBeets, Richard, ed. *Held Captive by Indians: Selected Narratives, 1642–1836*. Knoxville: University of Tennessee Press, 1973, 1994. [Includes Isaac Jogues's narrative]

Van der Donck, Adriaen. *A Description of the New Netherlands*. Trans. Jeremiah Johnson. Reprint. Ed. Thomas F. O'Donnell. Syracuse: Syracuse University Press, 1968.

Vaughan, Alden T., and Edward W. Clark, eds. *Puritans among the Indians: Accounts of Captivity and Redemption, 1676–1724.* Cambridge: Belknap Press of Harvard University Press, 1981. [Narratives of Gyles, C. Mather, Rowlandson, Swarton, Stockwell, and J. Williams]

Ward, Nathaniel. "On Women's Fashions." From *The Simple Cobbler of Aggawam, Willing to help 'mend his Native Country, Lamentably tattered both in the Upper-Leather and the Sole with all the honest stitches he can take* (1647). Reprint. In *Oxford Anthology of American Literature*, 20–25. New York: Oxford University Press, 1938.

Whitaker, Alexander. *Good Newes from Virginia.* 1613. Reprint. New York: Scholars Facsimiles and Reprints, 1936.

Williams, Roger. *Complete Writings.* 7 vols. New York: Russell and Russell, 1963.

——. *A Key in to the Language of America.* 1643. Reprint. Providence: Rhode Island and Providence Plantations Tercentenary Committee, 1936.

Winslow, Edward, and William Bradford. *A Relation of Journall of the beginning and proceedings of the English Plantation setled at Plimoth in New England, by certaine English Adventurers both Merchants and others. With their difficult passage, their safe arivall, their joyfull building of and comfortable planting themselves in the now well defended Towne of New Plimoth.* . . . 1622. Reprint. Ann Arbor: University Microfilms, 1966. [a.k.a. "Mourt's Relation"]

Winthrop, John. *A History of New England from 1630 to 1649.* Ed. James Savage. Boston: Little, Brown, 1853.

Wood, William. *New Englands Prospect. A true, lively, and experimentall description of that part of America commonly called New England: discovering the state of that Countrie, both as it stands to our new-come English planters; and to the old Native Inhabitants* (1634). Boston: Prince Society, 1865. Reprint. New York: Burt Franklin, 1967.

Secondary Sources

Adams, Henry. "Captain John Smith." *North American Review* 104 (1867): 1–30.

——. *The Education of Henry Adams.* Ed. Ernest Samuels. New York: Houghton Mifflin Riverside Edition, 1974.

——. *The Letters of Henry Adams.* 6 vols. Cambridge: Harvard University Press, 1982–88.

Adams, Percy. *Travelers and Travel Liars, 1660–1800*. Berkeley: University of California Press, 1962.

———. *Travel Literature and the Evolution of the Novel*. Lexington: University Press of Kentucky, 1983.

Anderson, Karen. *Chain Her by One Foot: The Subjugation of Native Women in Seventeenth-Century New France*. New York: Routledge, 1991.

Anzaldua, Gloria. *Borderlands: The New Mestiza*. San Francisco: Spinsters/Aunt Lute, 1987.

Arendt, Hannah. *On Revolution*. 1965. Reprint. Harmondsworth, England: Penguin, 1987.

Arens, W. *The Man-eating Myth: Anthropology and Anthropophagy*. Oxford: Oxford University Press, 1979.

Atkinson, Geoffroy. *The Extraordinary Voyage in French Literature before 1700*. New York: Burt Franklin, 1967.

———. *Les relations de voyages du XVIIième siècle et l'evolution des idées: Contribution à l'étude de la formation de l'esprit du XVIIIieme siècle*. New York: Burt Franklin, 1924.

Axtell, James. *Beyond 1492: Encounters in Colonial North America*. New York: Oxford University Press, 1992.

———. *The European and the Indian: Essays in the Ethnohistory of Colonial North America*. New York: Oxford University Press, 1981.

———. *The Invasion Within: The Contest of Cultures in Colonial North America*. New York: Oxford University Press, 1985.

———. "The Power of Print in the Eastern Woodlands." *William and Mary Quarterly* 44:2 (April 1987): 301–9.

Barbour, Philip. *The Three Worlds of Captain John Smith*. Boston: Houghton Mifflin, 1964.

Basso, Keith H., and Henry A. Selby, eds. *Meaning in Anthropology*. Albuquerque: University of New Mexico Press, 1976.

Bausum, Henry S. "Edenic Images of the Western World: A Reappraisal." *South Atlantic Quarterly* 67 (1968): 672–87.

Baym, Nina. "Early Histories of American Literature: A Chapter in the Institution of New England." *American Literary History* 1 (1989): 459–88.

Bercovitch, Sacvan. *The Puritan Origins of the American Self*. New Haven: Yale University Press, 1975.

Berkhofer, Robert. *The White Man's Indian: Images of the American Indian from Columbus to the Present*. New York: Alfred. A. Knopf, 1978.

Bernheimer, Richard. *Wild Men in the Middle Ages: A Study in Art, Sentiment, and Demonology.* Cambridge: Harvard University Press, 1952.

Berthiaume, Pierre. *L'Aventure américaine au XVIIIième siècle: Du voyage à l'écriture.* Ottawa: Les Presses de l'Université d'Ottawa, 1990.

Bideaux, Michel. "*Des Sauvages*: Une singularité narrative." *Etudes Françaises* 22 (1986): 36–45.

Bishop, Morris. *Champlain: The Life of Fortitude.* Toronto: McClellan and Stewart, 1963.

Boon, James A. *Other Tribes, Other Scribes.* New York: Cambridge University Press, 1982.

Boone, Elizabeth Hill. "Introduction: Writing and Recording Knowledge." In *Writing Without Words: Alternative Literacies in Mesoamerica and the Andes*, ed. Elizabeth Hill Boone and Walter D. Mignolo, 3–26. Durham: Duke University Press, 1994.

Boucher, Philip P. *Les Nouvelles Frances: France in America, 1500–1815.* Providence: John Carter Brown Library, 1989.

Broc, Numa. *La Géographie des philosophes: Géographie et voyageurs français au XVIIIième siècle.* Paris: Editions Orphys, n.d.

Brotherston, Gordon. "Towards a Grammatology of America: Lévi-Strauss, Derrida, and the Native New World Text." In *Europe and Its Others: Proceedings of the Essex Conference on the Sociology of Literature*, ed. Francis Barker et al., 2:61–77. Essex, England: Essex Conference, 1984.

Brown, Laura. *Ends of Empire: Women and Ideology in Early Eighteenth-Century English Literature.* Ithaca, N.Y.: Cornell University Press, 1993.

Brumble, David. *American Indian Autobiography.* Berkeley: University of California Press, 1988.

Buell, Lawrence. *New England Literary Culture from Revolution through Renaissance.* Cambridge: Cambridge University Press, 1986.

Chinard, Gilbert. *L'Amérique et le rêve exotique dans la littérature française au XVIIième et XVIIIième siècle.* Paris: Droz, 1934. [See also Durand de Dauphiné]

Clifford, James, and George Marcus, eds. *Writing Culture: The Poetics and Politics of Ethnography.* Berkeley: University of California Press, 1986.

Closs, Michael, ed. *Native American Mathematics.* Austin: University of Texas Press, 1986.

Coetzee, J. M. "Idleness in South Africa." In *The Violence of Representation: Literature and the History of Violence*, ed. Nancy Armstrong and Leonard Tennenhouse, 119–39. London: Routledge, 1989.

Craven, Wesley Frank. *White, Red, and Black: The Seventeenth-Century Virginian.* Charlottesville: The University Press of Virginia, 1971.

de Certeau, Michel. *Heterologies: Discourse on the Other.* Trans. Brian Massumi. Minneapolis: University of Minnesota Press, 1986.

——. *The Writing of History.* Trans. Tom Conley. New York: Columbia University Press, 1988.

——. "Writing vs. Time: History and Anthropology in the Works of Lafitau." Trans. James Hovde. *Yale French Studies* 59 (1980): 37–64.

deFrancis, John. *Visible Speech: The Diverse Oneness of Writing Systems.* Honolulu: University of Hawaii Press, 1989.

Delâge, Denys. *Bitter Feast: Amerindians and Europeans in Northeastern North America, 1600–1664.* Trans. Jane Brierley. Vancouver: University of British Columbia Press, 1993.

Demos, John. *The Unredeemed Captive: A Family Story from Early America.* New York: Alfred A. Knopf, 1994.

Derrida, Jacques. *Of Grammatology.* Trans. Gayatri Chakravorti Spivak. Baltimore: Johns Hopkins University Press, 1976.

——. *Writing and Difference.* Trans. Alan Bass. Chicago: University of Chicago Press, 1978.

Diamond, Stanley. *In Search of the Primitive: A Critique of Civilization.* New Brunswick, N.J.: Transaction Books, 1993.

Dickason, Olive Patricia. *Canada's First Nations: A History of Founding Peoples from Earliest Times.* Norman: University of Oklahoma Press, 1992.

——. *The Myth of the Savage and the Beginnings of French Colonialism in the Americas.* Edmonton: University of Alberta Press, 1984.

Doiron, Norman. "De l'epreuve de l'espace au lieu du texte: Le récit de voyage comme genre." In *Voyages: Récits et imaginaire,* ed. Bernard Beugnot, 15–31. Paris: Papers on Seventeenth-Century Literature, 1984.

——. "Voyage et Verité." In *Scritti sulla Nouvelle-France nel seicento,* ed. Alain Niderst, 11–26. Papers in Seventeenth-Century French. Paris: Nizet, 1984.

Duchet, Michèle. *Anthropologie et histoire au siècle des lumières: Buffon, Voltaire, Rousseau, Helvétius, Diderot.* Paris: François Maspero, 1971.

——. "Discours ethnologique et discours historique: Le texte de Lafitau." *Studies in Voltaire and the Eighteenth Century* 152 (1976): 607–23.

Dudley, Edward, and Maximilian Novak, eds. *The Wild Man Within: An Image in Western Thought from Renaissance to Romanticism.* Pittsburgh: University of Pittsburgh Press, 1973.

Euler, Robert. "Ethnohistory in the United States." *Ethnohistory* 19(3): 201–7.

Fabian, Johannes. *Time and the Other: How Anthropology Makes Its Object*. New York: Columbia University Press, 1983.

Fairchild, Hoxie. *The Noble Savage: A Study in Romantic Naturalism* (1928). New York: Russell and Russell, 1961.

Fenton, William. "J.-F. Lafitau: Precursor of Scientific Anthropology." *Southwestern Journal of Anthropology* 25 (1969): 173–87.

Fenton, William, and Elizabeth Moore. "Lafitau et la pensée ethnologique de son temps." *Etudes Littéraires* 10 (1977): 19–47.

Foucault, Michel. *The Order of Things: An Archeology of the Human Sciences*. Trans. unnamed. New York: Vintage, 1973.

Franklin, Wayne. *Discoverers, Explorers, Settlers: The Diligent Writers of Early America*. Chicago: University of Chicago Press, 1979.

Fuller (Ossoli), Margaret. *Summer on the Lakes in 1843*. Urbana: University of Illinois Press, 1991.

Gagnon, François-Marc. "Le Castor et ses 'signatures.'" In *Scritti sulla Nouvelle-France nel seicento*, ed. Alain Niderst, 255–64. Paris: Nizet, 1984.

——. *Ces hommes dits sauvages: L'histoire fascinante d'un préjugé que remonte aux premiers découvreurs du Canada*. Montreal: Libre Expression, 1984.

——. "'Portrait du Castor': Analogies et Representation." In *Voyages: Récits et imaginaire*, ed. Bernard Beugnot, 199–213. Paris: Papers on Seventeenth-Century Literature, 1984.

Gates, Henry Louis, Jr. "James Gronniosaw and the Trope of the Talking Book." In *African American Autobiography: A Collection of Critical Essays*, ed. William L. Andrews, 8–25. Englewood Cliffs, N.J.: Prentice-Hall, 1993.

Gerbi, Antonello. *The Dispute of the New World: The History of a Polemic, 1750–1900*. Trans. Jeremy Moyle. Pittsburgh: University of Pittsburgh Press, 1973.

Grafton, Anthony, with April Shelford and Nancy Siraisi. *New Worlds, Ancient Texts: The Power of Tradition and the Shock of Discovery*. Cambridge: Belknap/Harvard University Press, 1992.

Greenblatt, Stephen. *Marvelous Possessions: The Wonder of the New World*. Chicago: University of Chicago Press, 1991.

——. *Renaissance Self-Fashioning: From More to Shakespeare*. Chicago: University of Chicago Press, 1980.

Greenblatt, Stephen, and Giles Gunn, eds. *Redrawing the Boundaries: The Transformation of English and American Literary Studies*. New York: Modern Language Association, 1992.

Greenfield, Bruce. *Narrating Discovery: The Romantic Explorer in American Literature, 1790–1855*. New York: Columbia University Press, 1992.

Gura, Philip F. "John Who?: Captain John Smith and Early American Literature." *Early American Literature* 21:3 (1986): 260–67.

Hanke, Lewis. *Aristotle and the American Indian: A Study of Race Prejudice in the Modern World*. Bloomington: Indiana University Press, 1959.

Harris, R. Cole, ed. *From the Beginning to 1800*. Vol. 1 of *Historical Atlas of Canada/Atlas Historique du Canada*. Toronto: University of Toronto Press, 1989.

Hayes, Kevin J. *Captain John Smith: A Reference Guide*. Boston: G. K. Hall, 1991.

Hodgen, Margaret. *Early Anthropology in the Sixteenth and Seventeenth Centuries*. Philadelphia: University of Pennsylvania Press, 1964.

Hulme, Peter. *Colonial Encounters: Europe and the Native Caribbean, 1492–1797*. New York: Routledge, 1986.

Hulton, Paul. *America 1585: The Complete Drawings of John White*. Chapel Hill: University of North Carolina Press and British Museum Publications, 1984.

Innis, Harold A. *The Fur Trade in Canada*. New Haven: Yale University Press, 1930.

Jacquin, Philippe. *Les Indiens blancs: Français et Indiens en Amerique du Nord, XVIeme– XVIIIième*. Paris: Payot, 1987.

Jaenen, Cornelius. "France's America and Amerindians: Image and Reality." *History of European Ideas* 6 (1985): 405–20.

——. *Friend and Foe: Aspects of French-Indian Cultural Contact in the Sixteenth and Seventeenth Centuries*. Toronto: McClellan and Stewart, 1976.

——. "Les Sauvages Ameriquains: Persistence into the Eighteenth Century of Traditional French Concepts and Constructs for Comprehending Amerindians." *Ethnohistory* 29 (1982): 43–56.

Jantz, Harold. "Images of America in the German Renaissance." In *First Images of America: The Impact of the New World on the Old*, ed. Fredi Chiapelli, 1:91–106. Berkeley: University of California Press, 1976.

Jennings, Francis. *The Ambiguous Iroquois Empire: The Covenant Chain Confederation of Indian Tribes with English Colonies from Its Beginnings to the Lancaster Treaty of 1744*. New York: W. W. Norton, 1984.

——. "American Frontiers." In *America in 1492*, ed. Alvin Josephy, 339–67. New York: Vintage Books, 1993.

——. *Empire of Fortune: Crowns, Colonies, and Tribes in the Seven Years War in America*. New York: W. W. Norton, 1988.

——. *The Invasion of America: Indians, Colonialism, and the Cant of Conquest*. New York: W. W. Norton, 1976.

Josephy, Alvin M., ed. *America in 1492: The World of the Indian Peoples before the Arrival of Columbus*. New York: Vintage Books, 1993.

Knapp, Jeffrey. *An Empire Nowhere: England, America, and Literature from Utopia to The Tempest*. Berkeley: University of California Press, 1992.

Kolodny, Annette. *The Land Before Her: Fantasy and Experience of the American Frontiers, 1630–1860*. Chapel Hill: University of North Carolina Press, 1984.

Kropf, Lewis L. "Captain John Smith of Virginia." *Notes and Queries*, 7th ser. (1890).

Krupat, Arnold. *Ethnocriticism: Ethnography, History, Literature*. Berkeley: University of California Press, 1992.

Kupperman, Karen O. *Settling with the Indians: The Meeting of English and Indian Cultures in America, 1580–1640*. Totowa, N.J.: Rowan and Littlefield, 1980.

——, ed. *Captain John Smith: A Select Edition of His Writings*. Chapel Hill: University of North Carolina Press, 1988.

Leacock, Stephen, ed. *Lahontan's Voyages*. Ottawa: Graphic Publishing, 1932.

LeHuenen, Roland. "Le discours du découvreur." *Esprit Créateur* 30 (1990): 27–36.

Lemay, J. A. Leo. *The American Dream of Captain John Smith*. Charlottesville: University of Virginia Press, 1991.

——. *Did Pocahontas Save Captain John Smith?* Athens: University of Georgia Press, 1992.

Lestringant, Frank. "Champlain, Lescarbot, et la 'Conference' des histoires." In *Scritti Sulla Nouvelle-France nel seicento*, ed. Alain Niderst, 69–88. Papers on Seventeenth-Century Literature. Paris: Nizet, 1984.

Lévi-Strauss, Claude. *Tristes tropiques*. 1955. Reprint. Trans. John and Doreen Weightman. New York: Athaneum, 1984.

McKeon, Michael. *The Origins of the English Novel, 1600–1740*. Baltimore: Johns Hopkins University Press, 1987.

McManis, Douglas R. *European Impressions of the New England Coast, 1497–1620*. Chicago: University of Chicago Geographical Monographs, 1972.

Malone, Patrick. *The Skulking Way of War: Technology and Tactics among the New England Indians*. Lanham, Md.: Madison Books, 1991.

Martin, Calvin T. *Keepers of the Game: Indian-Animal Relationships and the Fur Trade*. Berkeley: University of California Press, 1978.

Martin, Horace T. *Castorologia, or the History and Traditions of the Canadian Beaver*. Montreal: Wm. Drysdale, 1892.

Marty, Martin E. *Pilgrims in Their Own Land: 500 Years of Religion in America*. New York: Penguin, 1984.

Medlicott, Alexander, Jr. "Return to the Land of Light: A Plea to an Unredeemed Captive." *New England Quarterly* 38 (1965): 202–16.

Métraux, Alfred. "Les precursors de l'ethnologie en France du XVIième au XVIIIième siècle." *Cahiers d'histoire mondiale* 7 (1963): 721–38.

Miller, Perry. *The New England Mind: The Seventeenth Century*. New York: Macmillan, 1939.

Mills, Enos A. *In Beaver World*. 1913. Reprint. Lincoln: University of Nebraska Press, 1990.

Momaday, N. Scott. *The Names: A Memoir*. Tucson: University of Arizona Press, 1987.

Morgan, Lewis Henry. *The American Beaver and His Works*. Philadelphia: J. B. Lippincott, 1868.

Morison, Samuel Eliot. *Samuel de Champlain: Father of New France*. Boston: Atlantic Monthly Press, 1972.

Murray, David. *Forked Tongues: Speech, Writing, and Representation in North American Indian Texts*. London: Pinter, 1991.

Nabokov, Peter, and Dean Snow. "Farmers of the Woodlands." In *America in 1492*, ed. Alvin Josephy, 339–67. New York: Vintage Books, 1993.

Namias, June. *White Captives: Gender and Ethnicity on the American Frontier*. Chapel Hill: University of North Carolina Press, 1993.

Nash, Gary B. "The Image of the Indian in the Southern Colonial Mind." *William and Mary Quarterly*, 3d ser., 29:2 (1972): 197–230.

——. *Red, White, and Black: The Peoples of Early America*. Englewood Cliffs, N.J.: Prentice-Hall, 1974.

Newman, Peter C. *Company of Adventurers*. Markham, Ontario: Penguin, 1985.

Ouellet, Réal. "La fin du voyage: Hasard et parodie chez Lahontan." *Etudes Françaises* 22 (1986): 87–96.

Pagden, Anthony. *The Fall of Natural Man: The American Indian and the Origins of Comparative Ethnology*. New York: Cambridge University Press, 1982.

Parkman, Francis. *France and England in North America*. 2 vols. New York: Library of America, 1983.

——. *The Oregon Trail* and *The Conspiracy of Pontiac*. New York: Library of America, 1991.

Pearce, Roy Harvey. *Savagism and Civilization: A Study of the Indian and the American Mind*. Baltimore: Johns Hopkins University Press, 1965.

——. "The Significances of the Captivity Narrative." *American Literature* 19 (1947): 1–20.

Pratt, Mary Louise. "Fieldwork in Common Places." In *Writing Culture: The Poetics and Politics of Ethnography*, ed. James Clifford and George Marcus, 27–50. Berkeley: University of California Press, 1986.

——. *Imperial Eyes: Travel Writing and Transculturation*. London: Routledge, 1992.

——. "Scratches on the Face of the Country, or What Mr. Barrow Saw in the Land of the Bushmen." *Critical Inquiry* 12 (Autumn 1985): 119–43.

Regis, Pamela. *Describing Early America: Bartram, Jefferson, Cr'evecoeur, and the Rhetoric of Natural History*. DeKalb: Northern Illinois University Press, 1992.

Richter, Daniel K. *The Ordeal of the Longhouse: The Peoples of the Iroquois League in the Era of European Colonization*. Chapel Hill: University of North Carolina Press, 1992.

Richter, Daniel K., and Alden T. Vaughan. *Crossing the Cultural Divide: Indians and New Englanders, 1605–1763*. Worcester, Mass.: American Antiquarian Society, 1980.

Roelens, Maurice. "L'Experience de l'espace américain dans les récits de voyage entre Lahontan et Charlevoix." *Studies in Voltaire and the Eighteenth Century* 155 (1976): 1861–95.

Rountree, Helen C. *Pocahontas's People: The Powhatan Indians of Virginia through Four Centuries*. Norman: University of Oklahoma Press, 1990.

Rue, Leonard Lee, III. *The World of the Beaver*. Philadelphia: Lippincott, 1964.

Said, Edward. *Orientalism*. Harmondsworth, England: Penguin, 1980.

Saldivar, Ramon. *Chicano Narrative: The Dialectics of Difference*. Madison: University of Wisconsin Press, 1990.

Salisbury, Neal. *Manitou and Providence: Indians, Europeans, and the Making of New England, 1500–1643*. New York: Oxford University Press, 1982.

Sayre, Robert F. *Thoreau and the American Indians*. Princeton: Princeton University Press, 1977.

Scarry, Elaine. *The Body in Pain: The Making and Unmaking of the World*. New York: Oxford University Press, 1985.

Schmitz, Neil. "Captive Utterance: Black Hawk and Indian Irony." *Arizona Quarterly* 48 (1992): 1–18.

Seelye, John. *Prophetic Waters: The River in Early American Life and Literature.* New York: Oxford University Press, 1977.

Sheehan, Bernard. *Savagism and Civility: Indians and Englishmen in Colonial Virginia.* Cambridge: Cambridge University Press, 1980.

Sioui, Georges. *Les Wendats: Une civilisation méconnue.* Sainte-Foy, Quebec: Les Presses de l'Université Laval, 1994.

Slotkin, Richard. *Regeneration Through Violence: The Mythology of the American Frontier, 1600–1860.* Middletown, Conn.: Wesleyan University Press, 1973.

Steele, Ian K. *Betrayals: Fort William Henry and the "Massacre."* New York: Oxford University Press, 1990.

Striker, Laura Polyani. "Captain John Smith's Hungary and Transylvania." In *Captain John Smith: His Life and Legend,* ed. Bradford Smith, 311–42. Philadelphia: Lippincott, 1953.

Thoreau, Henry David. *Cape Cod* in *Henry David Thoreau.* Ed. Robert F. Sayre. New York: Library of America, 1985.

——. *Journals of Henry D. Thoreau.* 14 vols. Ed. Bradford Torrey and Francis Allen. Boston: Houghton Mifflin, 1953.

——. *A Yankee in Canada, with Anti-Slavery and Reform Papers.* Boston: Houghton Mifflin, 1881.

Todorov, Tzvetan. *Nous et les autres.* Paris: Seuil, 1989. [English edition: *On Human Diversity: Nationalism, Racism, and Exoticism in French Thought.* Trans. Catharine Porter. Cambridge: Harvard University Press, 1993.]

Tompkins, Jane. *Sensational Designs: The Cultural Work of American Fiction, 1790–1860.* New York: Oxford University Press, 1985.

Torgovnik, Mariana. *Gone Primitive: Savage Intellects, Modern Lives.* Chicago: University of Chicago Press, 1990.

Trigger, Bruce G. "Champlain Judged by His Indian Policy: A Different View of Early Canadian History." *Anthropologica* 13 (1971): 85–114.

——. *The Children of Aataentsic: A History of the Huron People to 1660.* 2 vols. Montreal: McGill-Queen's University Press, 1976.

——. "The Indians and the Heroic Age of New France." Ottawa: Canadian Historical Association Booklets 30, 1977.

——. *Natives and Newcomers: Canada's 'Heroic Age' Reconsidered.* Kingston and Montreal: McGill-Queen's University Press, 1985.

Vizenor, Gerald. *The People Named the Chippewa*. Minneapolis: University of Minnesota Press, 1984.

Waddle, Robert S., Mary Christine Morkovsky, and Patricia Galloway, eds. *LaSalle, The Mississippi, and the Gulf*. Trans. Ann Linda Bell and Robert S. Weddle. College Station: Texas A & M University Press, 1987.

Warwick, Jack. "Récits de voyages en Nouvelle-France au XVIIième siècle." In *Scritti Sulla Nouvelle-France nel seicento*, ed. Alain Niderst, 283–305. Papers on Seventeenth-Century Literature. Paris: Nizet, 1984.

White, Hayden. "The Noble Savage Theme as Fetish." In *First Images of America: The Impact of the New World on the Old*, ed. Fredi Chiapelli, 1:121– 35. Berkeley: University of California Press, 1976.

White, Richard. *The Middle Ground: Indians, Empires, and Republics in the Great Lakes Region, 1650–1815*. Cambridge: Cambridge University Press, 1991.

Williams, Paul. "Reading Wampum Belts as Living Symbols." In *Indian Roots of American Democracy*, ed. José Barreiro, 60–65. Ithaca: Akwe:kon Press, 1992.

Winter, John F. "Les voyages de Lahontan et de Chateaubriand en Amérique." In *Les Récits de Voyages*, ed. Alain Niderst, 84–92. Paris: Nizet, 1986.

Wong, Hertha Dawn. *Sending My Heart Back across the Years: Tradition and Innovation in Native American Autobiography*. New York: Oxford University Press, 1992.

Index